ORTHODOX AND WESLEYAN

ECCLESIOLOGY

Orthodox and Wesleyan Ecclesiology

edited by

S T Kimbrough, Jr.

ST VLADIMIR'S SEMINARY PRESS
CRESTWOOD, NEW YORK 10707
2007

Library of Congress Cataloging-in-Publication Data

Orthodox and Wesleyan ecclesiology / edited by S T Kimbrough, Jr.
     p.   cm.
  Includes bibliographical references.
  ISBN 978–0–88141–268–0 (alk. paper)
     1. Church. 2. Orthodox Eastern Church—Doctrines—Congresses. 3. Methodist Church—
  Doctrines. 4. Wesley, John, 1703–1791. I. Kimbrough, S. T., 1936–

  BV600.3.073 2007
  262'.019—dc22

                                                                    2007039232

COPYRIGHT © 2007

ST VLADIMIR'S SEMINARY PRESS
575 Scarsdale Rd., Crestwood, NY 10707
1-800-204-2665
www.svspress.com

ISBN 978–0–88141–268–0

PRINTED IN THE UNITED STATES OF AMERICA

Contents

Abbreviations

ACCS	Ancient Christian Commentary on Scripture
ACW	Ancient Christian Writers. 1946–
Aphrahat, Dem.	*Aphraatis Sapientis Persae Demonstrationes*
CSCO	Corpus scriptorum christianorum orientalium. Edited by I.B. Chabot et al. Paris, 1903–
Ephrem, Res.	*Des heiligen Ephraem des Syrers Paschahymnen*
Ephrem, Virg.	*Des heiligen Ephraem des Syrers Hymnen de Virginitate,* Ephrem the Syrian
Eusebius, *HE*	Eusebius, *Eusebius Werke* (*The Ecclesiastical History*)
GCS	Die griechische christliche Schriftsteller der ersten [drei] Jahrhunderte
HR	*History of Religions*
JECS	*Journal of Early Christian Studies*
JLFA	*The Journal and Letters of Francis Asbury*
Loeb	*Loeb Classical Library*
MEA	*Methodist Experience in America: A Sourcebook, II*
NPNF	Nicene and Post-Nicene Fathers
NRSV	New Revised Standard Version
PG	Patrologia graeca [=Patrologiae cursus completes: Series graeca]. Edited by J.-P. Migne. 162 vols. Paris, 1857–1886

Philo, *Contempl. Life.*   Philo, *On the Contemplative Life*

PK   Papadopoulos-Kerameus Series

PL   Patrologia latina [=Patrologiae cursus completes: Series
                          latina]. Edited by J.-P. Migne. 217 vols. Paris, 1844–1864

PO   Patrologia Orientalis

SC   Sources chrétiennes. Paris, 1943–

Sozomen, *HE*   Sozomenus, *Kirchengeschichte* (*The Ecclesiastical History
                          of Sozomen*)

SVTQ   *St. Vladimir's Theological Quarterly*

Test. Dom.   *Testamentum Domini nostri Jesu Christi*

Theodoret, *HE*   Theodoret, *Kirchengeschichte* (*The Ecclesiastical History,
                          Dialogues and Letters*)

ZDMG   *Zeitschrift der deutschen morgenländischen Gesellschaft*

Contributors

THE REV. DR. JOHN BEHR, Dean of St. Vladimir's Orthodox Theological Seminary, Crestwood, New York, and Professor of Patristics

THE REV. DR. TED A. CAMPBELL, Associate Professor of Church History, Perkins School of Theology, Southern Methodist University, Dallas, Texas

THE REV. DR. JAMES H. CHARLESWORTH, George L. Collord Professor of New Testament Language and Literature, Editor and Director of the Dead Sea Scrolls Project, Princeton Theological Seminary

DR. TAMARA GRDZELIDZE, Executive Secretary, Faith and Order, World Council of Churches, Geneva, Switzerland

THE REV. J. SERGIUS HALVORSEN, priest of the Orthodox Church in America and Assistant Professor of Homiletics at Holy Apostles College and Seminary, Cromwell, Connecticut

THE REV. DR. RICHARD P. HEITZENRATER, William Kellon Quick Professor of Church History and Wesley Studies, The Divinity School, Duke University, Durham, North Carolina

THE REV. DR. JOHN JILLIONS, Assistant Professor of Theology, The Sheptytsky Institute of Eastern Christian Studies, Saint Paul University, Ottawa, Ontario, Canada

THE REV. DR. S T KIMBROUGH, JR., United Methodist scholar who has taught on the faculties of Princeton Theological Seminary, Princeton, New Jersey; New Brunswick Theological Seminary, New Brunswick, New Jersey; Illiricus Theological Faculty, Zagreb; Institut für Religionswissenschaft of the Kaiser Wilhelm University, Bonn, Germany; Wesley Theological Seminary, Washington, D.C.; the Theological School of Drew University, Madison, New Jersey

DR. DIMITAR POPMARINOV KIROV, Associate Professor, Orthodox Theological Faculty, University of Veliko Tarnovo, Bulgaria

DR. KATHLEEN MCVEY, Joseph Ross Stevenson Professor of Church History, Princeton Theological Seminary, Princeton, New Jersey

THE REV. SERGEI NIKOLAEV, E. Stanley Jones Professor of Evangelism, Ruediger and Gerlinde Minor Chair, Russia United Methodist Theological Seminary, Moscow, Russia

THE REV. DR. MICHAEL PLEKON, Associate at St. Gregory The Theologian Orthodox Church, Wappingers Falls, NY and a professor in the Department of Sociology/Anthropology and Program in Religion and Culture, Baruch College, City University of New York

THE REV. DR. RUSSELL E. RICHEY, Professor of Church History, Candler School of Theology, Emory University, Atlanta, Georgia

DR. ELIZABETH THEOKRITOFF, independent Orthodox scholar and translator, who has lectured at Holy Cross Orthodox Theological Seminary, Brookline, Massachusetts and the Institute for Orthodox Christian Studies in Cambridge, United Kingdom

THE REV. DR. GEOFFREY WAINWRIGHT, Cushman Professor of Theology at The Divinity School, Duke University, Durham, North Carolina

THE REV. DR. MAXINE WALKER, Professor of Literature and Director, Wesleyan Center for 21st Century Studies, Point Loma University, San Diego, California

THE REV. DR. FRANCES YOUNG, Professor Emeritus, formerly Edward Cadbury Professor of Theology in the University of Birmingham, United Kingdom

COMPANION VOLUMES

Orthodox & Wesleyan Spirituality (SVS Press 2002)

Orthodox & Wesleyan Scriptural Understanding and Practice (SVS Press 2005)

Introduction

The essays in this volume are presentations from the Fourth Consultation on Ortho-dox and Wesleyan Spirituality convened at St. Vladimir's Orthodox Theological Sem-inary, January 8–13, 2006, sponsored by the General Board of Global Ministries of The United Methodist Church and the faculty of St. Vladimir's Orthodox Theological Seminary, Crestwood, NY. The theme of the consultation was "One, Holy, Catholic, and Apostolic Church: Ecclesiology and the Gathered Community." Presentations to the consultation addressed not only ecclesiology in the theological sense, asking what the church fathers, the Wesleys, and contemporary Orthodox and Methodists mean when confessing faith in one, holy, catholic and apostolic Church, but also treated the place of the church, the local gathered community, and the "universal church," in a person's spiritual life, examining the exercise of obedience, discipline and authority in the community, the meaning of Tradition and traditions, the place and significance of holy people, and the Church's mission.

Part 1: Ecclesiology: Orthodox and Wesleyan Sources (Chapters 1–10)

In chapter 1, "Were Methodists Present at Constantinople 381?: Ecclesial Claims in the Light of the Four Notes of the Conciliar Creed," the Rev. Dr. Geoffrey Wainwright examines John Wesley's understanding of the four "notes" of the Church: one, holy, catholic, and apostolic. Wainwright explores the claims of both Roman Catholicism and Orthodoxy in turn, inquiring how they are the full expressions of the Church. He seeks to understand how John Wesley viewed the ecclesiology rooted in the Nicene-Constantinopolitan Creed and the location of the Church.

Wainwright carefully examines historic Methodism in the light of the primary and apostolic creeds of the Church, as well as contemporary statements of Roman Catholicism (e.g., *Lumen Gentium* and *Unitatis Redintegratio*) and Orthodoxy (e.g., the Russian Orthodox statement of 2000).

In conclusion, in the light of the openness of Methodist ecclesiology and its roots in catholicity and apostolicity, Wainwright encourages an exploration of ecumenical reintegration of unity. The heart of such exploration resides in the four "notes" of the Conciliar Creed outlined at the outset of the chapter—one, holy, catholic, and apos-tolic—and claimed by Roman Catholicism, Orthodoxy, and Methodism alike.

Chapter 2, "An Orthodox Reading of 1 Cor. 1:10–31: Any Room for Methodists?" by Very Rev. Dr. John Jillions examines the diversity of the "apostolic Christian commu-nity" expressed in 1 Corinthians 1. He is uninterested in justifying ecclesial diversity in the twenty-first century merely by citing the context Paul addresses at Corinth. Rather, he emphasizes Paul's primary instinct to include, not exclude, and draws an important example from early Jewish and Gentile Christianity, which lived side by side.

Fr. Jillions' keen analysis of the biblical texts raises the question—to what extent is the contemporary Church willing to rewrite its ecclesiology to include the spirit of the Pauline texts to "forbear, forgive, and include"? There is unquestionably a tension in the New Testament between unity and diversity. To what extent, however, the twenty-first-century church is willing to be modeled after the first-century Church in this regard remains to be seen.

Rev. Dr. Michael Plekon explores in chapter 3, "Return to the Sources in Twentieth-century Orthodox Ecclesiology: The Case of Nicolas Afanasiev," the ecclesiological research and interpretation of Fr. Afanasiev. Central to Plekon's discussion is Afanasiev's volume *The Church of the Holy Spirit* in which one discovers the author's pneumatological ecclesiology of the Church's primary expression being the eucharistic assembly. Central to this perspective is Afanasiev's now familiar statement: "The Church makes the Eucharist, and the Eucharist makes the Church." It is precisely the presence of the Holy Spirit, which sets the Church apart from other institutions, and the greatest gift of the Spirit to the Church is the gift of love.

In spite of the affirmative and negative criticism Afanasiev's views evoked, Plekon believes they are significant and more relevant today than during his lifetime. For example, Afanasiev studied the texts of the baptismal, ordination, and Eucharist liturgies as concelebrated by everyone, as indicated by the prayers in the plural. He was also a strong critic of legalism and clericalism, an aspect of his theological concern that often went unnoticed. Plekon believes Afanasiev's views have come of age and should be explored in contemporary theological scholarship and debate.

Chapter 4, "Return to the Sources in Twenty-first-century Methodist Ecclesiology: John Wesley's Ecclesiology in the Light of New Insights into the New Testament and Its Environment," is a unique study of John Wesley's views of the Church by the Rev. Dr. James H. Charlesworth done in the light of new insights from archeological and documentary evidence, and the New Testament, regarding Jesus' Judaism and his early followers. Charlesworth explores early sources known and unknown to John Wesley and reveals that "in many ways the movement within the Church of England John Wesley was attempting to shape was forged in the first century, within Judaism, and in some ways under the influence, direct or indirect, of Jewish rules for administration, as found, in certain ways, at Qumran."

Interestingly the views that emerge from Charlesworth's research into the New Testament period parallel Albert Outler's averment that "classical Wesleyan ecclesiology" is defined by unity, holiness, catholicity, and apostolicity.

Chapter 5 by the Rev. Sergei Nikolaev is entitled "Bulgakov and Florovsky: In Search of Ecclesiological Foundations." Sergius Bulgakov and Georges Florovsky were Russian Orthodox theologians forced to leave Russia during the first part of the twentieth century. In exile, both men addressed the problem of disunity within Christianity and became involved in the ecumenical movement. Nikolaev's study of the theology of these two men reveals their faithfulness to Orthodoxy and yet their distinctively differing views on the unity of the Church and the ecumenical role of Orthodoxy. Bulgakov maintained that the Church of Jesus Christ is a unity regardless of its schisms, whereas Florovsky asserted that the historic Orthodox Church equaled "the true Church." Bulgakov thought the divisions of the Church were overemphasized at the expense of the unity already present, while Florovsky claimed full Christian reunion could take place only with a "universal conversion to Orthodoxy." Nikolaev's exploration of the theology of both men renews the importance of their contributions to contemporary ecumenical dialogue.

In chapter 6, "The Unity of Revelation and the Unity of Tradition," Professor Kirov addresses a variety of issues related to the unity of God's revelation in the Old and New Testaments and in the Church. The cohesiveness of God's revelation in Scripture is expressed in and through the Incarnation, which is preserved in the tradition of the Church lived out in its experience as a eucharistic community. From an Orthodox perspective, Kirov maintains that revelation in tradition and Scripture is both a historical reality and a spiritual reality that is expressed in a relationship between God and human beings, and among human beings as part of the body of Christ. Hence he avers, "Only by entering the Church through repentance and baptism and practicing the eucharistic life is it possible to perceive the unity and fullness of salvation." The Church, as community, comprehends and shares God's revelation, which is by nature relational.

Kirov is careful to explain that there are many levels of tradition, even within the Church and that at times it is difficult to determine the Tradition behind the traditions. They may become multilayered with cultural influences and innovations and the Church may mistake "traditions" for Tradition, a true harbinger of God's revelation. Tradition is present within the traditions where they are consistent with doctrine and the experience of true faith.

In chapter 7, "Wesleyan Ecclesiology: Methodism as a Means of Grace," the Rev. Dr. Richard P. Heitzenrater examines John Wesley's view of the Church. Acknowledging that Wesley invested little time in the subject of ecclesiology, as he was not interested in setting up a separate church and was a committed priest of the Church of England, Heitzenrater underscores Wesley's acceptance of the views of the Church expressed in the Thirty-nine Articles of Religion. He shows how Wesley was able to hold in tension an understanding of the Church as the congregation of the faithful and as the fellowship of believers. The clear soteriological intent and focus of the Methodist movement made this tension sustainable and is no doubt one reason why the calling to a vocation of preaching, proclaiming the good news of the gospel, became an essential part of Wesleyan ecclesiology.

In Wesley's understanding of the Church, its members are to experience the presence of God. This transpires through the instituted means of grace (the Lord's Supper, fasting, prayer) and the prudential means of grace (works of mercy). All of the means of grace lead to the life of holiness and presence of God. In this way, Methodism was to be a means of reforming and renewing the Church.

The Rev. Dr. S T Kimbrough, Jr. addresses the subject "Wesleyan Ecclesiology: Charles Wesley's Understanding of the Nature of the Church" in chapter 8. While Charles often wrote thematically oriented books of hymns, such as, *Hymns on the Lord's Supper, Hymns on the Trinity, Hymns for the Nativity of our Lord,* and so forth, he never devoted a collection of hymns specifically to the theme of "the Church." Nevertheless, throughout his hymns and sacred poems he repeatedly commented on the nature of the Church and its activity. He addresses its apostolicity, catholicity, unity, and holiness, as Kimbrough shows throughout this chapter with numerous citations from his verse.

Charles Wesley understands the Church to be evangelical and sacramental, a community that proclaims the gospel and whose life is centered in the Eucharist and acts of mercy. The Eucharist is indispensable to the acts of mercy, since the central focus of Holy Communion is the experience of love, the love of God. This love is the impetus and matrix of acts of mercy. The Church is born by grace and sustained by love. One might say that the Church for Charles Wesley has a two-fold purpose: (1) evangelism, to share the good news of Jesus Christ, and (2) to live a life of personified love as a eucharistic community.

In chapter 9, "Understandings of Ecclesiology in United Methodism," the Rev. Dr. Russell E. Richey discusses the definition of United Methodism and its ecclesial sensibilities via four books: the Bible, *The United Methodist Hymnal* (1989), *The United Methodist Book of Discipline,* and *The Book of Worship.* The first two books shape the life of parishioners together, and the latter two provide the ritual paradigms from birth to death and weekly worship, with a central focus on hymns for singing, appointed Psalms, and Eucharist. Richey traces the evolution and development of all four books and speaks of them as being expressions in some measure of what he calls the "epistemological impulses" of Methodism: Scripture, experience, reason, and tradition.

The hymnal and *Discipline* "provided Methodists a Wesleyan grammar for the Christian life, a Wesleyan missional ecclesiology." The definitions of the Church and sacraments continue to this day to be those expressed in the Book of Common Prayer and the Articles of Religion and creeds of the Church of England. Richey shows how the hymnal and *Discipline,* which at first looked primarily inward toward distinctively Wesleyan identity, developed to the present day, and now "sustain the identity with a clearly catholic context." He is also careful to explain that there is not unanimity within Methodism when it comes to the sharing of the ecclesiological views expressed in its four primary documents. Nevertheless, the common foci in them remain the classic ecclesiological emphases expressed in the traditional creeds of the Church: oneness, holiness, catholicity, and apostolicity.

In chapter 10, "The Holiness of a Human Being: A Mark of Christian Spirituality," Dr. Tamara Grdzelidze studies one of the primary ecclesiological emphases of the creeds of the Church, namely holiness. The Church is a holy people. Addressing the questions In what sense is holiness a sign of human perfection? and How is holiness revealed in everyday life? the author takes her cues from both the Wesleyan and Orthodox traditions. Her Wesleyan sources are mainly John Wesley's sermon, "On Working Out Our Own Salvation" and Wesleyan hymns on the theme of "Christian holiness," and her Orthodox sources are two Georgian hagiographical texts from the eleventh century, *The Life of St. Euthymius the Athonite* and *The Life of St. George the Athonite.*

Dr. Grdzelidze emphasizes a synergistic approach to a life of holiness in which the *vita activa* and the *vita contemplativa* are inseparable, central foci of monastic life and, hence, of the lives of the Athonite monks she discusses. She makes clear that while

John Wesley sympathized with this synergistic posture, his expressions of the relationship of the two were quite different.

Part 2: Ecclesiology and Eschatology (Chapters 11–12)

In chapter 11, Rev. Dr. John Behr examines "The Eschatological Dimensions of the Church." He characterizes the eschatological tension of the Church with the familiar words "already-but-not-yet." However, he moves beyond the eucharistic ecclesiology of Nicholas Afanasiev and John Zizioulas and notes that Dumitru Staniloae recognizes the presence of the Church beyond the liturgical assembly. If one identifies the Church only via the eucharistic assembly, then one cannot see the Church elsewhere. Behr raises the question of how one may see the whole of the Christian life and of the Church "in terms of a perpetual baptismal/eucharistic/paschal participation in the mystery of Christ." Thus, a more balanced view of ecclesiology would emphasize the role and importance of baptism.

Behr notes that, from its earliest period, the Church is referred to primarily as the "Mother" or "Virgin Mother," in whose womb God's people are born anew to the body of Christ, "thus making the eschatological Lord present." He encourages further discussion of an ecclesiology that sees the ever-coming Christ in relation to baptism *and* Eucharist and to his Church, the Virgin Mother.

Chapter 12, "The 'Penultimate' Nature of the Church—the *Eschaton* Is Not Yet!" by the Rev. Dr. Frances Young extends the discussion of ecclesiology and eschatology. Exploring a paradigm of "now" and the "not yet," Dr. Young suggests that Orthodoxy and Methodism share a somewhat realistic and pragmatic view of the existence of the Church on earth, which she contrasts with the rather ideological ecclesiology found in Western Christianity and particularly in Roman Catholicism. While Dr. Young is clear that neither tradition—Orthodox nor Wesleyan—produced extended treatises on the subject of ecclesiology, she finds important Orthodox sources for her study in the *Apostolic Constitutions* and some letters of Basil of Caesarea (in which he appropriates metaphors about the Church from the *Apostolic Constitutions*, the *Catechetical Homilies* of Cyril of Jerusalem, and a few other sources). The primary Wesleyan sources are some of the sermons of John Wesley and the Articles of Religion of the Church of England.

Both Orthodox and Wesleyan traditions view the Church as a reality that has not yet been fully perfected and thus it is in process and not fully accomplished. Both traditions recognize "that the End is not yet, while celebrating the fulfillment of God's promise already in process and in anticipation of the *eschaton*, partially if not wholly, experienced in the life of the Church."

Part 3: Ecclesiology and Sacred Space (Chapter 13)

In chapter 13, "Methodist Ecclesiologies and Methodist Sacred Spaces," the Rev. Dr. Ted Campbell makes a journey through a variety of Methodist ecclesiological perspectives and the evolution of Methodist worship spaces. He speaks of "Methodist ecclesiologies" in the plural and views Methodists as having a "bipolar" understanding of the Church. This is a byproduct of their heritage within the Church of England and the tension created by moving from their "religious societies" to an organized "Church," a tension which is reflected in the Methodist attempt to hold fast to both the "instituted" means of grace (searching the Scriptures, Holy Communion, fasting, and Christian conference) and the "prudential" means of grace (observance of the General Rules, attendance at class and band meetings, and temperance, among others).

Methodist worship spaces also reflect a multi-layered ecclesiology, evolving from "cottage" and other informal worship spaces to camp-meeting gatherings in the nineteenth century to what Campbell calls "Methodist Gothic" architecture in the nineteenth and twentieth centuries. "The use of 'hybrid spaces,'" he claims, "uniquely reveals the ambiguity inherent in Methodist ecclesiologies." Nevertheless, the liturgical evolution of United Methodism with its inclusion by 1964 of the Nicene Creed in *The Methodist Hymnal*, reflects a move toward a more traditional Christian ecclesiology. This is certainly in concert with the deep commitment of John and Charles Wesley to historic Christian doctrine and liturgy.

Part 4: Ecclesiology and the Role of Women (Chapters 14–15)

Chapter 14 by Dr. Kathleen McVey bears the title "Ephrem the *kitharode* and Proponent of Women: Jacob of Serug's Portrait of a Fourth-century Churchman for the Sixth-century Viewer and Its Significance for the Twenty-first-century Ecumenist." At the center of McVey's discussion is a *mêmrâ* (metrical homily) attributed to Jacob of Serug (AD 449–521) on the subject of Ephrem the Syrian. Her analysis of Ephrem's role in endorsing women's choral singing is part of the common history shared by Orthodox and Methodists. Jacob's *mêmrâ* provides little biographical data regarding Ephrem, except for the fact that he established women's choirs and attributes to Ephrem the view that women and men are redeemed equally and have the right to sing in the Church's public liturgy.

McVey provides excellent exegesis and interpretation of Jacob's *mêmrâ*, as well as a perceptive survey of arguments for and against the right of women to sing in the public liturgy; she particularly notes the opposition in Latin and Greek sources. Jacob himself is a strong supporter of the ongoing role of Syrian Christian women as liturgical singers. While the Syrian Orthodox Miaphysite liturgical tradition of the sixth century placed a high emphasis on the role of women, the East Syrian/Nestorian tradition advocated the silence of women. McVey has provided a vital chapter in the study of the shared history of Christian communities as regards the role of women, which is essential to any discussion of ecclesiology.

In chapter 15, "We 'being many are one body': The Conciliarity of the Church as Exemplified in Lay Women," Dr. Elizabeth Theokritoff discusses further the role of women in the Church. She avers at the outset of the chapter that when one discusses the role of women in the Church, one immediately becomes aware of the clash of ecclesiologies. Her primary concern, however, is not whether women should become ordained but rather the recognition that God speaks as vibrantly through lay women as through clergy. Theokritoff lifts up the lives of a series of important women to illustrate this reality and how God may work through anyone. She first discusses Thecla, disciple and co-worker of the Apostle Paul and prototype of martyr, monastic, missionary, and preacher. Next, she addresses the life of Macrina, sister and mentor of Basil the Great and Gregory of Nyssa, who called her his "teacher." A discussion follows of Melania, the well-to-do widow from the upper echelons of Roman society, who at twenty-two years of age decided to devote the rest of her life to celibacy and became the monastic mentor of Evagrius of Pontus. The significant roles of three empresses—Pulcheria, Eirene, and Theodora—in convening three of the seven Ecumenical Councils, including the one that restored the veneration of icons, and their roles in defining the faith of the Church are also examined.

Conciliarity implies oneness, a unity of the Church that acknowledges that no one is saved alone. The members, men and women, bear one another's burdens. All are the temple of the Spirit.

Part 5: Ecclesiology: Word and Silence (Chapters 16–17)

Chapter 16, "Orthodox Ecclesiology from the Perspective of Preaching" is by Rev. Dr. J. Sergius Halvorsen, who is concerned with the questions: How is Orthodox ecclesiology shaped by preaching in its concrete context, and pastorally? What is the role of preaching in evoking a meaningful understanding of the Church on the part of its members? He responds to these and other questions through the lens of St. John Chrysostom's *Baptism Instructions*. Halvorsen finds these sermons, which address directly the sacramental transition from "non-believer" to "Christian," to be "benchmarks" for Orthodox ecclesiology. While not pleading for a "baptismal ecclesiology" per se, he notes that the concept of the "newly baptized" is an excellent introduction to Orthodox ecclesiology. At baptism one steps into the timeless reality of transformation in the Church.

Halvorsen explores a variety of metaphors used by St. John Chrysostom, which he finds pertinent to Orthodox ecclesiology. He does not see the eschatological paradigm of "already-and-not-yet" as useful in relating preaching effectively to Orthodox ecclesiology. Rather the new relationship in Christ and the Church has much more importance for the homiletical task, which is an ongoing clarion call to "the community of people who have been changed and empowered to act on God's behalf."

Taking her cue from Bishop Kallistos Ware's comment that "often poets are the best theologians of all and it would be good for the Church to pay them greater heed," in chapter 17, Dr. Maxine Walker addresses the subject, "The 'Sounds of Silence' in the Gathered Community." Her focus is on what the poet T. S. Eliot might have to say to the Church today. Poignant questions are posed for the subject of ecclesiology. "How will the gathered community speak that which cannot be spoken? What is the unifying C/center? How is Tradition now?" Walker utilizes Eliot's poem "Little Gidding" as a means of exploring the inner silence that is at the heart of gathered community. She inquires what articulates Tradition when, for example, the silence of the mystery of the Eucharist is central to its meaning. Is it possible, as Eliot says in one of the *Four Quartets,* "Dry Salvages," "we had the experience but missed the meaning"?

Walker leaves it to those who wish to do so to apply her analysis to the subject of ecclesiology, which is perhaps what the poet would do. One paragraph stands out in this regard, which is perhaps one of the most fitting conclusions to this volume, for it raises the question of how Divine Love intersects the temporal. If this does not transpire, there is no ecclesiology. Walker writes:

> In every church, we stand in a graveyard, a place where lifetimes were part of the "pattern," the pattern of a lifetime of moments. In every church service, we are standing in the place where the silent dead speak. They speak of the intense moment when Divine Love bisects the temporal. "Love is most nearly itself / when here and now cease to matter" (Eliot's "East Coker" 129). The significance of this paradox is that with its wisdom that moves deeper than knowledge, we can "feel" winds move the vast waters to a place that is unfamiliar, still, and still moving. Now time can be redeemed. The Incarnation and Christ's presence in the Eucharist is the turning point of the world, the true axis of all paradoxes.

The contributors to this volume speak from their own lived tradition, permeated with their personal experience within ecumenical dialogue. Therefore, as they explore the question of what it means to be "Church," they each do so from the roots of their own faith communities, while stretching to discover their communities' boundaries and borders. In so doing, some may not reflect the official positions of their respective churches (or St. Vladimir's Seminary Press). Nevertheless, in bearing this responsibility, necessitated by honest exploration, they also sound a clarion to both Orthodox and Wesleyan churches, after centuries of discord and division, to reconsider: What does it mean to be the body of Christ? And, for their courage and enduring love in this process, I am grateful.

—*S T Kimbrough, Jr.,*
   Editor

PART 1

Ecclesiology:
Orthodox and Wesleyan Sources

1

Were Methodists Present at Constantinople 381? Ecclesial Claims in the Light of the Four Notes of the Conciliar Creed

Geoffrey Wainwright

Several times I have accompanied parties of Methodist pilgrims to biblical and patristic sites in the Near East in order to provide scriptural, historical, and theological background to the events that took place there in ancient times. At Nicea, Constantine's palace lies under the lake, but in the ruins of the Wisdom Church I wove together the themes of the First and the Seventh Ecumenical Councils held in those respective locations. At Ephesus, the Mary Church was the place to expound the significance of the Third Ecumenical Council for the doctrine of the Incarnation and to invoke the metaphysical words of Charles Wesley's couplet:

> Being's source begins to be,
> And God himself is born—

as well as his tender picture of the Theotokos:

> Who gave all things to be,
> What a wonder to see
> Him born of His creature, and nursed on her knee.

In 1990 our party visited Justinian's Eirene Church in Istanbul, the location of the Fifth Ecumenical Council held in 553; but in the absence of Constantine's church, which had housed the Second Ecumenical Council in 381, I spoke about that Second Council rather than the Fifth. The Eirene Church is now a Turkish state museum, and religious manifestations are prohibited; but in my academic address I took the opportunity to have the audience rehearse the third article of the Nicene-Constantinopolitan Creed with me, line by line (without the "filioque," naturally).

The Creed's placement of ecclesiology between pneumatology ("the life-giving Holy Spirit") and eschatology ("the life of the world to come") is significant for a just understanding of the *notae ecclesiae*. Stretched between its origin at Pentecost and its consummation in the final kingdom, the Church is indwelt, sustained, and transformed by the Spirit, who is the "firstfruits" (Rom. 8:23), the "earnest" and the "seal" (2 Cor. 1:22; 5:5; Eph. 1:13–14; 4:30) of full redemption. This dynamic perspective allows for degrees and growth in the Church's embodiment of its four characteristics—its unity, holiness, catholicity, and apostolicity. Such a systematic framework will accommodate my exposition of John Wesley's understanding of the Church, of historic Methodism's course and ecclesial claims, and of contemporary Methodism's place and prospects on the ecumenical scene.

In the first and longest section, intended as informative for our Orthodox partners in this conversation, I shall examine how John Wesley understood the ecclesiology embedded in the Nicene-Constantinopolitan Creed and try to discern where he identified the Church so described.[1] Next I shall sketch how historic Methodism may have claims to meet the creedal criteria of ecclesiality, whether as Wesley understood them or perhaps in some modified sense. Third, I will look at how Methodist ecclesiality might be configured in an ecumenical search for the reintegration of unity. As we progress, I will compare the Wesleyan and Methodist interpretations of the Church and its "notes" with those both of Orthodoxy and of Roman Catholicism, since those are the places in which, in their respective yet so similar ways, the greatest historical and theological challenges lie.

1. The Church according to John Wesley

The earliest of the pieces in the Wesleyan dossier proper is the expansion upon the Nicene-Constantinopolitan Creed wherein John Wesley set out the faith of "a true Protestant" in his open *Letter to a Roman Catholic* of 1749.[2] He begins by declaring belief in the "one God" as "Father of all things" and in a "higher sense, the Father of his only Son, whom he hath begotten from all eternity." Next, "Jesus of Nazareth" is confessed as "the Saviour of the world," being "the proper, natural Son of God, God of God, very God of very God," the "Lord of all things," having been "made man, joining the human nature with the divine in one person, being conceived by the singular operation of the Holy Ghost and born of the Blessed Virgin Mary, who, as well after as before she brought him forth, continued a pure and unspotted virgin." After rehearsing the passion, death, resurrection, ascension, heavenly session, and expected return of Christ in judgment, Wesley develops the third article of the Creed in four paragraphs thus:

> I believe the infinite and eternal Spirit of God, equal with the Father and the Son, to be not only perfectly holy in himself, but the immediate cause of all holiness in us: enlightening our understandings, rectifying our wills and affections, renewing our natures, uniting our persons to Christ, assuring us of the adoption of sons, leading us in our actions, purifying and sanctifying our souls and bodies to a full and eternal enjoyment of God.

> I believe that Christ and his Apostles gathered unto himself a church to which he has continually added such as shall be saved; that this catholic (that is, universal) Church, extending to all nations and all ages, is holy in all its members, who have fellowship with God the Father, Son and Holy Ghost; that they have fellowship with the holy angels who constantly minister to these heirs of salvation, and with all the living

members of Christ on earth, as well as all who are departed [this life] in his faith and fear.

I believe God forgives all the sins of them that truly repent and unfeignedly believe his holy gospel; and that, at the last day, all men shall rise again, every one with his own body.

I believe that, as the unjust shall after the resurrection be tormented in hell for ever, so the just shall enjoy happiness in the presence of God to all eternity.

Now listen to the summary passage by which Fr. Boris Bobrinskoy introduces the chapter on "Trinitarian Theology in the Fathers and in the Councils" in his book *The Mystery of the Trinity*:

As much as the New Testament, the patristic writings reflect the fundamental profession of faith of the Church in Jesus Christ, dead and risen. It is from the core of a christological approach that the trinitarian vision of the Apostolic Fathers and their successors unfolds. Likewise, at the origin of the pneumatology of early Christianity is the pentecostal advent of the Spirit and His permanent dwelling in the Church. According to the manifold experience of the Spirit in the early Church, the Spirit is the giver of the new life, the author of the transformation of the heart, of holiness, of faithfulness to Christ; He is also the Spirit of the prophetic and charismatic gifts (see Acts and 1 Corinthians), in the context of an eschatological expectation, of the inauguration of the messianic times, in the sacramental "today" of the Church. Thus, more than a reflection *about* the Spirit, the Fathers share with us an expression of an experience *of* the Spirit in the Church. . . . The Church is the place of the Spirit.[3]

There is striking similarity between Bobrinskoy's and Wesley's descriptions of the soteriological functions of the Holy Spirit (both, of course, grounded in the redemptive work of Christ): Bobrinskoy's Holy Spirit as "the giver of the new life, the author of the transformation of the heart, of holiness, of faithfulness to Christ" is easily matched with Wesley's Holy Spirit as the "cause of all holiness in us: enlightening our understandings, rectifying our wills and affections, renewing our natures, uniting our persons to Christ, assuring us of the adoption of sons, leading us in our actions, purifying and sanctifying our souls and bodies to a full and eternal enjoyment of God." With little effort, resemblances can also be demonstrated between Wesley's and Bobrinskoy's pneumatology in the ecclesiological dimension, and perhaps even the eschatological.

No one would suspect Boris Bobrinskoy—or any other Orthodox or Catholic theologian—of placing the individual before the Church. Yet that is what Protestants are sometimes accused of. Some plausibility is lent to the charge by the Protestant habit of treating the dogmatic topics of justification and sanctification before treating Church and sacraments. But John Wesley—at least in the passage in question—cannot be convicted of individualism. That "us" and "our" are not mere collectives but bear a genuinely corporate character is shown by the immediacy of Wesley's reference to the Church, which Christ (and his apostles) first "gathered," and to which Christ "has continually added."

Let us then begin to examine Wesley's ecclesiology on the basis of his exposition of the Nicene-Constantinopolitan Creed. We shall have to come to the delicate matter of his concrete identification of the earthly Church, but we may first note some matters that are, in principle, not controversial among Methodists, Catholics and Orthodox. First is Wesley's assertion of the fellowship that exists with "the holy angels" and with "all who are departed [this life] in his faith and fear." This fellowship—epitomized in the Sanctus of the eucharistic liturgy—is primarily doxological. A text from the Wesley brothers' *Hymns on the Lord's Supper*, expresses and enacts it thus (no. 96):

> Happy the souls to Jesus join'd,
> And saved by grace alone;
> Walking in all Thy ways we find
> Our heaven on earth begun.
>
> The church triumphant in Thy love,
> Their mighty joys we know;
> They sing the Lamb in hymns above,
> And we in hymns below.
>
> Thee in thy glorious realm they praise,
> And bow before Thy throne;
> We in the kingdom of Thy grace,
> The kingdoms are but one.[4]

Another hymn by Charles Wesley links the Church militant and the Church triumphant in this way:

> Come, let us join our friends above
> That have obtained the prize,
> And on the eagle wings of love
> To joys celestial rise:
> Let all the saints terrestrial sing
> With those to glory gone;
> For all the servants of our King,
> In earth and heaven are one.
>
> One family we dwell in Him,
> One Church, above, beneath,
> Though now divided by the stream,
> The narrow stream of death. . . .[5]

The kingdoms of grace and of glory form a single realm; the saints terrestrial and the saints celestial constitute a single family. Yet an eschatological tension still obtains: for all the joys that are therein "tasted," the sacramental Supper of the Lord remains but "a pledge of heaven" (as section III of the *Hymns on the Lord's Supper* puts it).

We edge towards the problematic when we look at John Wesley's understanding of the four "notes" of the Church: one, holy, catholic, and apostolic. To the brief statements in his irenic *Letter to a Roman Catholic* must be added Wesley's exposition of the *notae ecclesiae* in what is chronologically the second piece in our Wesleyan dossier on the Creed, namely his epistolary refutation of the tract *A Caveat against the Methodists,* attributed to the Roman Catholic bishop Richard Challoner (1761). Eschewing for the moment Wesley's criticisms of the Church of Rome, we will concentrate on what he claims not only for "the Methodists," but also for the Church of England and the Reformed or Protestant churches generally. Other writings of Wesley may be invoked where he deals with one or other of the four notes in particular.

Challoner has claimed for the Roman Catholic Church alone the "prophecies" that the Old Testament makes "relating to the Church" and the "glorious promises" that the New Testament makes to the Church and the "glorious characters" (he has in mind the "notes") that the New Testament attributes to it. Wesley's assertions in the face of Challoner's claims are these:

> It is true, "all these promises, prophecies, and characters [contained in the Old and New Testaments] point out a society founded by Christ himself, and by his commission propagated throughout the world, which should flourish till time should end." And such is the Catholic Church, that is the *whole body* of men endued with faith, working by love, dispersed over the whole earth, in Europe, Asia, Africa, and America. And this Church is "ever one"; in all ages and nations it is the one body of Christ; it is "ever holy," for no unholy man can possibly be a member of it. It is "ever orthodox"; so is every holy man, in all things necessary to salvation; "secured against error," in things essential, "by the perpetual presence of Christ"; and "ever directed by the Spirit of truth," in the truth that is after godliness. This Church has "a perpetual succession of pastors and teachers, divinely appointed and divinely assisted." And there has never been wanting, in the Reformed churches, such a succession of pastors and teachers, men both divinely appointed and divinely assisted; for they convert sinners to God, a work none can do unless God himself doth appoint them thereto and assist them therein; therefore *every part* of this character is "applicable" to them. Their teachers are the proper successors of those who have delivered down, through all generations, the faith once delivered to the saints; and their members have true, spiritual communion with the *one, holy* society of true *believers.* Consequently, although they are not the *whole* "people of God," yet they are an undeniable *part* of his people.[6]

Regarding the four notes, let us take catholicity first. Wesley may at first sight make too easy an equivalence between "catholic" and "universal." There is, of course, no fundamental difficulty with Wesley's speaking of the Church "extending to all nations and all ages"; but we might look for more of what the Orthodox theologian Nikos Nissiotis called "the qualitative meaning of catholicity."[7] In the mid-fourth century, St. Cyril of Jerusalem fuses "quantitative" and "qualitative" elements when he expounds to the catechumens the meaning of "catholic" in the creed: "The Church is called catholic because it is spread throughout the world, from end to end of the earth; also because it teaches universally and completely all the doctrines which man should know concerning things visible and invisible, heavenly and earthly; and also because it subjects to right worship all mankind, rulers and ruled, lettered and unlettered; further because it treats and heals universally every sort of sin committed by soul and body, and possesses in itself every conceivable virtue, whether in deeds, words, or in spiritual gifts of every kind" (*Catechetical Lecture XVIII*). Such might (I suppose) constitute a good checklist for all claimants to ecclesiality. And some, at least, of these qualitative features are not lacking in Wesley's notion of catholicity: to churchliness belong the truths that are necessary to salvation and that make for godliness.

What, then, of holiness? Perhaps Wesley's fullest exposition of this ecclesial note in connection with its creedal occurrence is found in the third and last of the most significant pieces in our Wesleyan dossier, namely his late sermon "Of the Church" (1785):

> How many wonderful reasons have been found out for giving it [the Church] this appellation! One learned man informs us, "The Church is called holy because Christ the head of it is holy." Another eminent author affirms, "It is so called because all its ordinances are designed to promote holiness"; and yet another, "Because our Lord *intended* that all the members of the Church should be holy." Nay, the shortest and the plainest reason that can be given, and the only true one, is: the Church is called "holy" because it is holy; because every member thereof is holy, though in different degrees, as he that called them is holy.... It follows that not only no common swearer, no sabbath-breaker, no drunkard, no whoremonger, no thief, no liar, none that lives in any outward sin; but none that is under the power of anger or pride, no lover of the world—in a word, none that is dead to God—can be a member of his Church.[8]

Albert Outler, scholarly editor of Wesley's Sermons, comments that here "Wesley echoes what might be called Montanist views" or, in another place, that "Wesley is closer to the Donatists and Anabaptists than to most of his fellow Anglicans."[9] Wesley commits, according to Outler, "a drastic oversimplification of a complex question about the holiness of the Church." No doubt this is true, but some nuances may be noted. In this very passage, Wesley allows "different degrees" of holiness among the members of the Church. In the *Letter to a Roman Catholic*, Wesley declares his belief that "God forgives all the sins of them that truly repent and unfeignedly believe his holy gospel"—and there is no cause to think that he excluded penitent back-sliders from God's mercy. Wesley was well aware of the reality, as well as the problematic character, of "sin in believers" (Sermon 13 is titled "On Sin in Believers"). Moreover, one must consider the limited definition that Wesley gives of sin, at least in his defense of the possibility of "Christian perfection": the positive state of "perfect love" towards God and man would be spoiled only by "the voluntary transgression of a known law."[10] As a final nuance, one may note Wesley's comment on Matthew 22:14: "Many hear [the Gospel], few believe. Yea, many are members of the visible but few of *the invisible Church.*"[11] Orthodox theologians will hear an echo of Augustine but should not yet dismiss Wesley as an "invisibilist"—a matter we shall revisit. Meanwhile, I merely suggest that Wesley's dynamic view of sanctification—a "pressing onward to the goal of perfection" (cf. Phil. 3:12–16)—might have value not only for the individual believer but also for the Church in its corporate character in this time between the times. The notion of pressing on to perfection may indeed have implications for the way in which ecclesial unity, too, is conceived and practiced, for there is surely a dynamic dimension to our Lord's prayer that his followers might be "perfected into one (*hina ôsin teteleiômenoi eis hen*)" (John 17:23).

Regarding unity, Wesley clearly implies the unicity of the Church in the comprehensive sense when, in his exposition of the Creed, he writes: "Christ and his Apostles gathered unto himself a Church to which he has continually added such as shall be saved." This one Church is characterized within itself and in relation to God by the sevenfold unity that, in his sermon "Of the Church," Wesley delineates on the apostolic basis of Ephesians 4:

> The catholic or universal Church is all the persons in the universe whom God hath so called out of the world . . . as to be "one body," united by "one Spirit," having "one faith, one hope, one baptism, one God and Father of all, who is above all, and through all, and in them all." . . . A [geographically] particular church may consist of any number of members, whether two or three, or two or three millions. But still, whether it be larger or smaller, the same idea is to be preserved. They are one body, and have one Spirit, one Lord, one hope, one faith, one baptism, one God and Father of all.[12]

How, more precisely, is this one body "one"? While some constitutive features of the Church are not apparent to physical sight, there is nothing programmatically "invisibilist" about Wesley's ecclesiology. In the sermon "Of the Church," Wesley speaks of "a congregation or body of people united together in the service of God" or "who assemble themselves together to worship God the Father and his Son Jesus Christ"; and he takes Scripture in the "plain, literal sense" to refer by "the one baptism" to "the outward sign our one Lord has been pleased to appoint of all that inward and spiritual grace which he is continually bestowing upon his Church" and "a precious means whereby this faith and this hope are given to those that diligently seek him." Wesley knows that "every follower of Christ is obliged, by the very nature of the Christian institution, to be a member of some particular congregation"; yet, in the sermon "Catholic Spirit" (1750), this is tempered by the recognition, in an historical situation of *dis*-unity, that "a difference in opinions or modes of worship may prevent an entire external union."[13] Wesley's argument and plea that such differences need not "prevent our union in affection" is not grounded in "speculative latitudinarianism," such as would neglect "the first elements of the Gospel of Christ" or undercut "the main branches of Christian doctrine"; tolerable differences of "opinion" concern debatable *theologoumena*, not basic dogma. Nor is Wesley's argument and plea grounded in "practical latitudinariansm": "The man of a truly catholic spirit" is convinced that his congregation's "manner of worshiping God is both scriptural and rational," and "there he partakes of all the ordinances of God. There he receives the Supper of the Lord. There he pours out his soul in public prayer, and joins in public praise and thanksgiving. There he rejoices to hear the word of reconciliation, the Gospel of the grace of God." At its best, the modern ecumenical movement, under the presumed inspiration of the Holy Spirit, seeks precisely to restore those conditions of faith and order in which an increasing "union in affection" may find embodiment in a full, visible unity such as Wesley could not contemplate in his time.

Regarding the fourth note, apostolicity: In his *Letter to a Roman Catholic*, Wesley begins the ecclesiological section of his exposition of the Creed with an affirmation of the Church's apostolic foundation. In his rebuttal of Challoner, Wesley claims that the "perpetual succession of pastors and teachers" promised to the Church "has never been wanting in the Reformed Churches." Evidence of their divine appointment and assistance is found in the fact that "they convert sinners to God." They thus prove "the proper successors of those who have delivered down, through all generations, the faith once delivered to the saints." It will be remembered that when Irenaeus or even Tertullian first invoked episcopal succession, the point was to assert, over against Gnostic distortions and outright heresies, the integrity of the apostolic faith such as it was maintained in churches founded by the apostles themselves and in churches which had, in turn, been founded from those churches. The primary function of the successive bishops was preaching and teaching the gospel, and this function was the interest of St. Hegesippus and St. Epiphanius in drawing up their lists of those who had held the office in key places.

Where, concretely, does Wesley locate the Church? His sermon "Of the Church" includes a differentiated discussion of Article 19 of the Anglican Articles of Religion: "The visible Church of Christ is a congregation of faithful men, in which the pure Word of God is preached, and the sacraments be duly administered . . . ." This is supposed by Wesley to refer to both "the universal Church" and "the several [geographically] particular churches of which it is composed." He takes the definition to intend "a congregation of believers" in the sense of "men endued with 'living faith' " (Articles 12 and 29 use the phrase "lively faith"). As the Anglican Article 19 proceeds, it appears that "those congregations in which the pure Word of God (a strong expression) is not preached are no parts either of the Church of England or the Church catholic. As neither are those in which the sacraments are not duly administered." To this Wesley himself adds this commentary:

> I will not dare to defend the accuracy of this definition. I dare not exclude from the Church catholic all those congregations in which any unscriptural doctrines which cannot be affirmed to be "the pure Word of God" are sometimes, yea, frequently preached. Neither all those congregations in which the sacraments are not "duly administered". Certainly if these things are so, the Church of Rome is not so much as a part of the catholic Church; seeing therein neither is "the pure Word of God" preached nor the sacraments "duly administered". Whoever they are that have "one Spirit, one hope, one Lord, one faith, one God and Father of all", I can easily bear with their holding wrong opinions, yea, and superstitious modes of worship. Nor would I on these accounts scruple still to include them within the pale of the catholic Church. Neither would I have any objection to receive them, if they desired it, as members of the Church of England.[14]

While Wesley seems at first to contemplate the possibility of "the Church of Rome" as at least "a part of the catholic Church," the argument shifts towards recognizing individuals as, in this and perhaps other cases, Christians *despite* their particular ecclesiastical allegiance. We shall return to Wesley's evaluation of "the Church of Rome," but meanwhile we revert to our principal question: where is "the Church" positively located?

The crux of the matter for Wesley is "living faith," by which he means a faith active in love toward God and neighbor. The preaching of the Word and the administration of the sacraments nourishes such a community and its members—that is clear from the second half of the sermon "Of the Church," in which Wesley goes on to expound Ephesians 4:1–3: "Walk worthy of the vocation wherewith we are called"; also from the latter part of the *Letter to a Roman Catholic*, where Wesley, after displaying the "belief" of "a true Protestant," asserts that unless he "practice accordingly, all his faith will not save him," and invites the Catholic to share that practice on the basis of a largely common faith; and from paragraphs 14–18 in the sermon "Catholic Spirit," in which Wesley develops a favorite text, Galatians 5:6: "Is thy faith *energoumenê di' agapês*, filled with the energy of love?" The subservience of preaching and sacraments to Christian faith and life does not entail a "Donatist" view of the ministry, for, as Wesley declares in the sermon "On Attending the Church Service" (1787), God "does not, will not, suffer his grace to be intercepted, though the minister will not receive it himself. . . . We know by our own happy experience, and by the experience of thousands, that the word of the Lord is not bound, though uttered by an unholy minister; and the sacraments are not dry breasts, whether he that administers be holy or unholy."[15] From his own perspective as an ordained minister of the Church of England, Wesley held that the only reasons that could justify his "separation" from that institution would be: its imposition of acts that Scripture forbids or its omission of acts that Scripture commands; its denial of liberty to evangelize; its requirement of false doctrine.[16] Wesley did not judge that things had come to such a pass, either for laypeople or for ministers. Indeed, he all along insisted that members of the Methodist Societies—who in their great majority belonged to the Church of England—should stay within the Established Church, attending all its ordinances, in order to "leaven the whole."[17] In his "Reasons Against a Separation from the Church of England" (1758), he declared that God's chief design in "raising up" the Methodists and "sending out" their preachers was to "quicken our brethren," "the lost sheep of the Church of England"; and this he stood by to the end.[18] Historically, there is a resemblance between the Methodist societies and the "*ecclesiolae in Ecclesia*" of the Pietist groups within the German Protestant Churches. Wesley insisted that the purpose of the Methodist societies (with their "classes" and "bands") was not only to further their members' own growth in that "holiness without which no one shall see the Lord" (Heb. 12:14) but also to "spread scriptural holiness over the land."[19]

I promised to return to John Wesley's evaluation of the Roman Catholic Church in his day, especially in relation to the *notae ecclesiae*; and I do this now, as a transition towards a reading of Methodist history in the light of the creedal "notes." My contemporary purpose is to help Methodists extract the beam from our own eye, so that we may be able, with critical self-examination and the aid of all our serious ecumenical partners, to catch and follow a vision of the Church such as we, and they, in the Nicene-Constantinopolitan Creed confess it to be.

Against Challoner, Wesley asserts that "the Church of Rome, in its present form, was not 'founded by Christ himself.' All the doctrines and practices wherein she differs from us were not instituted by Christ; they were unknown to the ancient Church of Christ; they are unscriptural *novel* corruptions." Moreover, Wesley denies "that the Roman bishops came down by *uninterrupted* succession from the apostles": "I never could see it proved, and I am persuaded I never shall. But unless this is proved, your own pastors, on *your* principles, are no pastors at all." Again, "if God had sent them [your pastors and teachers], he would confirm the word of his messengers. But he does not; they convert no sinners to God." Whether in terms of antiquity, continuity or fruitfulness, so much for the "apostolicity" of the Church of Rome!

What of its "universality"? "Neither is *that* Church 'propagated throughout the world.' " The "Asiatic, the African, and the Muscovite Churches (to name no more) never were contained in it." Rome can at most be "a part," not "the whole."

Well, "unity" then? "It is not in unity with itself: it is to this day torn with numberless divisions." Historically, such divisiveness gives the lie to the Church of Rome's being "secured against error, either by Christ or his Spirit: witness Pope against Pope, Council against Council, contradicting, anathematizing each other—the instances are too numerous to be recited."

It is with "holiness," however, that Wesley's argument is clinched: "Look at the Romanists in London or Dublin. Are these the 'Holy,' the only 'Holy Church? Just such holiness is in the bottomless pit." In sum, "whatever may be the case of some particular souls, it must be said, if your own marks be true, the Roman Catholics, in general, are not 'the people of God.' "20

Lest others think they stood while Rome fell, let us examine another of Wesley's texts from twenty years later: "The General Spread of the Gospel" (1783).21 No doubt on the basis of travelers' tales, and somewhat after the manner of Diogenes looking for one just man, Wesley conducted a literary tour of the globe in search of holiness.22 He begins: "In what a condition is the world at present! How does darkness, intellectual darkness, ignorance, with vice and misery attendant upon it, cover the face of the earth!" Not only among "the heathen" and "the Mahometans" but also among "the Christians in the Turkish dominions," whether in the Peloponnese (where "the best of them" live) or "scattered up and down in Asia." These last are "a proverb of reproach to the Turks themselves, not only for their deplorable ignorance, but for their total, stupid, barbarous irreligion." No better fare "the southern Christians, those in Abyssinia," or "the northern churches, under the jurisdiction of the Patriarch of Moscow." As to "the Western churches":

> They have abundantly more knowledge; they have more scriptural and more rational modes of worship. Yet two-thirds of them are still involved in the corruptions of the Church of Rome; and most of these are entirely unacquainted with either the theory or practice of religion. And as to those who are called Protestants or Reformed, what acquaintance with it have they? Put Papists and Protestants, French and English together, the bulk of one and of the other nation; and what manner of Christians are they? Are they "holy, as he that hath called them is holy" [1 Pt. 1:15]? Are they filled with "righteousness, and peace, and joy in the Holy Ghost" [Rom. 14:17]? Is there "that mind in them which was also in Christ Jesus" [Phil. 2:5]? And do they "walk as Christ also walked" [1 John 2:6]? Nay, they are as far from it as hell is from heaven.

The good news is that the judgment is followed by the promise, for the scriptural text on which Wesley bases his sermon is Isaiah 11:9: "The earth shall be full of the knowledge of the Lord, as the waters cover the sea." In the rest of the sermon, Wesley goes on to recount—in what might be thought a self-congratulatory way, were everything not ascribed to grace—"what God has already done" through the Methodist movement, intending this as encouragement to work and pray for the universal coming of God's kingdom. With that, we may move to consider, at least in an indicative way, subsequent Methodist history in light of the four notes of the Church.

2. Historic Methodism measured by the creedal criteria

Describing and envisioning "The General Spread of the Gospel," Wesley, in 1783, recounted the rise of Methodism in this way:

> Between fifty and sixty years ago God raised up a few young men in the University of Oxford, to testify those grand truths which were then little attended to:
>
> That without holiness no man shall see the Lord [cf. Heb. 12:24];
>
> That this holiness is the work of God, who worketh in us both to will and to do [cf. Phil. 2:13];
>
> That he doth it of his own good pleasure, merely for the merits of Christ;
>
> That this holiness is the mind that was in Christ [cf. Phil. 2:5], enabling us to walk as Christ also walked [cf. 1 John 2:6];
>
> That no man can thus be sanctified till he is justified; and
>
> That we are justified by faith alone.
>
> These great truths they declared on all occasions in private and in public; having no design but to promote the glory of God, and no desire but to save souls from death.[23]

The "little leaven spread wider and wider": "More and more saw the truth as it is in Jesus, and received it in the love thereof. More and more 'found redemption through the blood of Jesus, even the forgiveness of sins' [cf. Col. 1:14]. They were born again of his Spirit, and filled with 'righteousness, and peace, and joy in the Holy Ghost' [cf. Rom. 14:17]." The movement extended through Britain and Ireland and "a few years after, into New York, Pennsylvania, and many other provinces in America, even as high as Newfoundland and Nova Scotia." And this was but the dawn. Would not the work of God spread "first through the remaining provinces, then through the isles of North America?" And at the same time, "from England to Holland," from there "to the Protestants in France, to those in Germany, and those in Switzerland. Then to Sweden, Denmark, Russia, and all the other Protestant nations in Europe." Next to "countries where Romanists and Protestants live intermixed and familiarly converse with each other." Then to "those countries that are merely popish, as Italy, Spain, Portugal." And gradually "to all that finally name the name of Christ in the various provinces of Turkey, in Abyssinia, yea, and in the remotest parts, not only of Europe, but of Asia, Africa, and America." With the increase of holiness, "the grand stumbling-block being thus happily removed out of the way, namely the lives of the Christians," then "the Mahometans will look upon them with other eyes, and begin to give attention to their words," as will happen also among "the heathen nations." Next will come "those more distant nations with whom the Christians trade": "The God of love will prepare his messengers and make a way . . . into the deepest recesses of America, and into the interior parts of Africa, yea, into the heart of China and Japan, with the countries adjoining to them." And even to those nations that "have no intercourse either by trade or any other means with Christians of any kind, such [as] the inhabitants of the numerous islands in the South Sea," God will raise up and send preachers.

Wesley's vision culminates in the grand peroration to his sermon on "The General Spread of the Gospel":

> We have strong reason to hope that the work [God] hath begun he will carry on unto the day of his Lord Jesus [cf. 1 Cor. 5:5; 2 Cor. 1:14]; that he will never intermit this blessed work of his Spirit until he has fulfilled all his promises; until he hath put a period to sin and misery, and infirmity, and death; and re-established universal holiness and happiness, and caused all the inhabitants of the earth to sing together, "Hallelujah! The Lord God omnipotent reigneth!" [cf. Rev. 19:6]. "Blessing, and glory, and wisdom, and honour, and power, and might be unto our God for ever and ever!" [Rev. 7:12].[24]

With hindsight we can of course say that things did not quite work out that way in the intervening period of history (although the eschatological hope remains integral to the Christian faith, whatever may be the modes of its realization). Nevertheless, Wesley's sermon adumbrated certain features of "mission history" during the following century and a half; and in that history, Methodism played a role that is no less honorable than that of other evangelically motivated bodies in Protestantism and indeed Catholicism.[25] Bearing in mind the "eschatological reserve" that should qualify all such claims, the role of Methodism in evangelism at home and mission abroad should be part of the evidence when Methodist claims to *apostolicity* are being evaluated. Thus Nikos Nissiotis, when discussing the validity of ministerial orders in other churches, argued that one should not begin from a confessionally antagonistic position but should rather take into account the "total reality" of that other church, including its "missionary activity" and its "present charismatic life."[26] In the other direction, Methodists should be open to learn from churches that deliberately root their transmission of the gospel in a tradition of faith and practice that reaches back to the apostolic age itself.

Mention of the "charismatic life" points to another note of the Church. It will be remembered that St. Cyril of Jerusalem included "spiritual gifts of every kind" in his definition of *catholicity*. Historically, Methodism has preached, taught, and practiced a strong pneumatology. It has been keen to discern and encourage the varied gifts of the Spirit among laypeople, both men and women, within the general life of the Church. These gifts have sometimes been channeled into such pastoral functions as "class leader," such diaconal functions as "poor stewards," such educational functions as "Sunday School teacher," such priestly functions as the conduct of "prayer meetings" where the Lord is addressed extemporaneously. On the more formal liturgical side, Methodism has rejoiced in the hymns of Charles Wesley with their manifold doctrinal, soteriological, ecclesiological, sacramental, and experiential dimensions.[27] Methodism should be open to seeing these acoustical icons complemented by the visual ones possessed by other churches. In the words of Pope John Paul II in his 1995 encyclical *Ut Unum Sint*, ecumenical dialogue properly involves not only an "exchange of ideas" but an "exchange of gifts" (28). Catholicity can be enriched because God is generous in his giving. God's gifts have only to be recognized.

The fundamental and all-embracing divine gift is that of *holiness*. Perhaps Wesley's favorite description of his own calling and that of Methodism was to "spread scriptural holiness." He and his helpers preached "entire sanctification" or "Christian perfection" understood as the single-hearted love of God and neighbor. The twin vehicles and expressions of such love were "works of piety" (prayer, fasting, searching the Scriptures, partaking of the Lord's Supper as "means of grace") and "works of mercy" ("doing good unto all men, to their souls and to their bodies"): "God works [in you]; therefore you *can* work. God works [in you]; therefore you *must* work."[28] Wesley looked for personal, communal, and social holiness. It is for others to judge how well Methodism has followed Wesley in the way of "social holiness" that he led through prison visiting and agitating for reform, through setting up dispensaries for the sick, combating addictions, and establishing schools for children.[29] If individual Methodists have embodied holiness, it speaks well for the ecclesial communities in which their lives have been nourished. It may even be that other churches will come to recognize the Wesley brothers in their calendars and litanies of saints: *Sancti Ioannes et Carole, orate pro nobis*. For their part, Methodists would benefit from a more intense engagement with the "communion of the saints" from every time and place.

The attribution of holiness to the Church is a delicate matter. We have heard John Wesley say "no unholy man can possibly be a member of it." Yet, in adapting the Book of Common Prayer for *The Sunday Service of the Methodists*, he did not remove either the "general confession" (that is, of sin) from Morning Prayer or the summons from the Order for the Lord's Supper: "Ye that do truly and earnestly *repent of your sins* and are in love and charity with your neighbours, and intend to lead a new life, following the commandments of God, and walking from henceforth in his holy ways: Draw near with faith, and take this holy sacrament to your comfort; and make your humble confession to Almighty God, meekly kneeling upon your knees." The Bishops' Council of the Russian Orthodox Church, in its statement *Basic Principles of the Attitude of the Russian Orthodox Church toward the Other Christian Confessions* (August 14, 2000), declares that "any sin distances a person from the Church to a greater or lesser degree, but it does not cut him off from her altogether" (1.10); and the Orthodox churches administer the sacrament of penance to the baptized who confess their sins. For individual Christians, it appears that Wesleyans and Orthodox view holiness as a vocation that may only be imperfectly realized at any given stage in the course of a life ("every member [of the Church] is holy, though in different degrees, as he that called them is holy," said Wesley); and certainly holiness admits of growth, as the Christian "presses on to perfection." But do the sins of individuals affect the holiness of the Church as such? The Orthodox traditionally deny this, on the grounds that the Church is precisely the sacramental *source* of holiness; and it seems that Wesley also should maintain the utter holiness of the Church, though perhaps more typically on the grounds of its *composition* by the sanctified. But both Orthodox and Wesleyans admit the personal and *institutional* failings of ordained and lay members of their communities, individually and corporately: one should "not ignore," says the Russian statement of 2000, "the tragic shortcomings and failures which marked the history of the Church" (1.19).[30]

The Roman Catholic Church may have provided a conceptual and practical framework for an appropriate treatment of this delicate question when the Second Vatican Council portrays the pilgrim Church, "embracing sinners in her midst," as "at once holy and always in need of purification, ceaselessly pursuing the path of penitence and renewal" (*Lumen Gentium*, 8). Nikos Nissiotis, an Orthodox observer at Vatican II, speaks of the "dialectic" in which penitence is the only possible basis for sinful humanity's response to the perfect action of God and the Spirit-empowered effort to enter into communion with the fullness of the Triune God. For Orthodoxy, according to Nissiotis, the Church "is both: she is the infallible Church, which does not do penance, because 'she is without spot or wrinkle' (Eph. 5:27); at the same time, she embraces all sinners who must never cease to do penance."[31]

The recognition of sinfulness brings us to the most neuralgic point in the consideration of the *notae ecclesiae*: the first and last attribute of *unity*—in relation to the historic divisions among Christians and their communities. The Russian statement of August 2000 affirms that "the Orthodox Church is the true Church in which the Holy Tradition and the fullness of God's saving grace are preserved intact" (1.18). A Methodist may perhaps be forgiven for remarking on the irony of the temporal coincidence of this statement with the *Dominus Iesus* declaration from the Roman Congregation for the Doctrine of the Faith, which reaffirmed the teaching of Vatican II that it is "in the Catholic Church, governed by the successor of Peter and by the bishops in communion with him," that "the sole Church of Christ, which in the Creed we profess to be one, holy, catholic and apostolic"—"subsists" (*Lumen Gentium*, 8). Before we Methodists spoil our ecumenical manners by smirking at these mutually exclusive claims, however, we need to hear how our own historical emergence strikes the Orthodox. Again, the Russian statement of 2000 reads: "In the second millennium, the separation of the Roman Church [from the (one Orthodox) Church] was followed by internal divisions in Western Christianity, brought about by the Reformation, which resulted in the continual formation of different Christian denominations outside of communion with the Roman see" (1:13). While the great churches of East and West read differently the causes and consequences of the break between them in 1054, the Russian Orthodox reading of the subsequent Western history closely resembles the thesis of the seventeenth-century French Catholic bishop Jacques-Bénigne Bossuet in his *Histoire des variations des églises protestantes* (1688).

The threat of "separation" from the Church of England haunted John Wesley from the first Methodist Conference in 1744 onwards.[32] We have seen him resisting pressures from Methodist preachers and people; but in 1784 he apparently ignored the advice of his brother Charles that "ordination means separation" when he took it upon himself to ordain Coke, Whatcoat and Vasey for ministerial service in North America. In mitigation, John Wesley could invoke the political independence of the United States from the British crown (and thereby the ecclesiastical independence of American Anglicans/Methodists from the Church of England) as well as the earlier failure of the Bishop of London to provide sufficient pastors for the American colonies belonging to his diocese. The fact remains, however, that from the 1790s onward,

Methodism on both sides of the Atlantic showed a marked tendency to internal fissi-parity. Although these separations—both from Anglicanism and within Method-ism—rarely if ever involved grave doctrinal differences, note should be taken, *mutatis mutandis*, of what the Russian Orthodox statement says with regard to schisms: "Divi-sions and differences cannot all be reduced to various non-theological factors" (2.8), and "a division, even if it happens for non-doctrinal reasons, is a violation of Ortho-dox teaching on the nature of the Church and leads ultimately to distortions in the faith" (1.14).

On the positive side, it can be said in Methodism's favor that several of the nine-teenth-century schisms (though admittedly not all of them) were healed in the course of the twentieth century. In Britain, reunions in 1907 and 1932 brought the New Con-nexion, the United Methodist Free Churches and the Primitive Methodists together with the preponderant Wesleyan Methodists in the Methodist Church of Great Britain. In the United States, the Methodist Episcopal Church, the Methodist Episco-pal Church (South), and the Methodist Protestant Church in 1939 joined to form "The Methodist Church," while a further merger involving the Germanic "Evangelical United Brethren" constituted "The United Methodist Church" in 1968. Arising from the Oecumenical Methodist Conferences that had met at ten-yearly intervals since 1881, the World Methodist Council, for its part, took its present shape in 1951 as "an association of the churches in the Methodist tradition throughout the world." Its con-stitutional purpose is "to serve [these churches] and to give unity to their witness and enterprise," without "seeking to legislate for them or to invade their autonomy." In a statement of "Wesleyan Essentials of Christian Faith" adopted by the Council in 1996, the "people called Methodists," deriving in the first place from "the work of John and Charles Wesley in eighteenth-century England, which quickly spread to every corner of the world," are said to "form a family of churches" which "claim and cherish our true place in the one holy, catholic and apostolic Church"; and the first three items in the enumeration of "our beliefs" state that "Methodists affirm the Holy Scriptures of the Old and New Testaments as the primary rule of faith and practice and the center of theological reflection; profess the ancient ecumenical creeds, the Apostles' and Nicene Creeds; seek to confess, to interpret and to live the apostolic faith, the faith once delivered to the saints." On the broader scene, Methodist individuals have been among the pioneers of the modern ecumenical movement, beginning with the Amer-ican layman John R. Mott (1865–1955), and Methodist churches have almost invariably been the first to join "councils of churches" at the local, national, regional, and global levels. Methodists have surrendered their particular ecclesiastical identity in order to constitute, with other Protestant traditions, "united churches" of one kind or another (so in Canada, South India, North India, Zambia, Australia, Belgium). Claiming itself to be "part of the Church universal," the United Methodist Church constitutionally "believes that the Lord of the Church is calling Christians everywhere to strive toward unity, and therefore it will seek, and work for, unity at all levels of church life."

With that we come to the current state of ecumenism, and particularly to Methodist claims of ecclesiality in relation (for present purposes) to those two bodies which make the strongest exclusive claims to be "the Church," namely the Roman Catholic and the Orthodox.

3. Methodist ecclesiality and the ecumenical reintegration of unity

At first blush, the Orthodox churches make the most massive claims for their own exclusive status as Church. With unabashed boldness, the opening paragraph of the Russian statement of 2000 explicitly equates the Orthodox Church with the one, holy, catholic and apostolic Church and implicitly defines the four creedal attributes:

> The Orthodox Church is the true Church of Christ established by our Lord and Saviour Himself, the Church confirmed and sustained by the Holy Spirit, the Church about which the Saviour Himself has said: "I will build my church; and the gates of hell shall not prevail against it" (Matt. 16:18). She is the One, Holy, Catholic and Apostolic Church, the keeper and provider of the Holy Sacraments throughout the world, "the pillar and ground of the truth" (1 Tim. 3:15). She bears full responsibility for the proclamation of the truth of Christ's Gospel, as well as full power to witness to "the faith which was once delivered unto the saints" (Jude 3).

For all its emphasis on the indivisible unity of this one self-identified Church, however, the statement later recognizes that "communities which have fallen away from Orthodoxy have never been viewed as fully deprived of the grace of God. Any break from communion with the Church inevitably leads to an erosion of her grace-filled life, but not always to its complete loss in these separated communities," and "there remains a certain incomplete fellowship which serves as the pledge of a return to unity in the Church, to catholic fullness and oneness" (1.15). In this situation, "the ecclesial status of those who have separated themselves from the Church does not lend itself to simple definition," for "in a divided Christendom, there are still certain characteristics which make it one: the Word of God, faith in Christ as God and Saviour come in the flesh (1 John 1:1–2; 4: 2, 9), and sincere devotion" (1.16). The fact that persons "returning" to Orthodoxy are received according to a variety of rites (baptism, chrismation, repentance) is said to show that "the Orthodox Church relates to the different non-Orthodox confessions in different ways": "The criterion is the degree to which the faith and order of the Church, as well as the norms of Christian spiritual life, are preserved in a particular confession" (1.17). Nevertheless, no precise grades are awarded: "By establishing various rites of reception, the Orthodox Church does not assess the extent to which grace-filled life has been preserved intact or distorted in a non-Orthodox confession, considering this to be a mystery of God's providence and judgment" (ibid.). Despite this reverent agnosticism, could there be just a hint—with the language of "incomplete fellowship" and "certain characteristics" held in common, of "degrees" in the preservation of faith and order, in the maintenance and practice of the grace-filled life—toward a slightly more differentiated notion of ecclesial unity than first apparent in the Russian statement?[33]

Such nuance can certainly be detected in Roman Catholicism from the Second Vatican Council onward. The switch in the Dogmatic Constitution on the Church from the draft "*est*" to the final "*subsistit in*" re-described the relation between "the one and only Church of Christ" and "the Catholic Church governed by the successor of Peter and the bishops in communion with him" from one of simple identity to one which, while allowing no lack in the ecclesial status of the Roman Catholic Church, nevertheless could accommodate in an ecclesiologically significant way the "many elements of sanctification and truth that are found outside its institutional structures (*extra eius compaginem*), and which, as gifts proper to the Church of Christ, impel towards catholic unity" (*Lumen Gentium*, 8). The conciliar Decree on Ecumenism specifies such "good things (*bona*)" that "can exist outside the visible limits of the Catholic Church (*extra visibilia ecclesiae catholicae saepta*)": "the written Word of God; the life of grace; faith, hope and charity, with the other interior gifts of the Holy Spirit, as well as visible elements" (*Unitatis Redintegratio*, 3). Not only are "separated brethren" who "believe in Christ and have been validly baptized" thereby "put in a certain, albeit imperfect, communion with the Catholic Church (*in quadam cum ecclesia catholica communione, etsi non perfecta*)" but their liturgical actions—"variably according to the condition of each church or community"—"can without doubt effectively engender a life of grace and aptly give access to the communion of salvation" (ibid.). Thus, since "the Spirit of Christ has not refrained from using them as means of salvation which derive their efficacy from the fullness of grace and truth entrusted to the Catholic Church," it follows that "the separated churches and communities, though we believe them to suffer from certain defects, are by no means deprived of meaning and importance in the mystery of salvation (*nequaquam in mysterio salutis significatione et pondere exutae sunt*)" (ibid.). Pope John Paul II, in his 1995 encyclical *Ut Unum Sint*, appeared to take things yet further by declaring that "insofar as" the aforementioned elements of sanctification and truth "are present in other Christian communities, the one Church of Christ *is effectively present in them*" (11; emphasis added). All of these statements put a more generous and more dynamic complexion on the understanding of unity. While Roman Catholics "believe that the unity of the one and only Church subsists in the Catholic Church as something she can never lose," they "hope that it will continue to increase (*crescere*) until the end of time" (*Unitatis Redintegratio*, 4). Correspondingly, the work of the Holy Spirit among the presently separated brethren could bring to "a more perfect realization" the mystery of Christ and the Church, whereas the existence of divisions "renders it more difficult for the Catholic Church itself to express all aspects of the fullness of catholicity in actual life" (ibid.).

Where might Methodists fit into all this? To take the church to which I belong, the Methodist Church of Great Britain: "The Methodist Church," according to its constitution, "claims and cherishes its place in the Holy Catholic Church." Doctrinally, it "rejoices in the inheritance of the Apostolic Faith and loyally accepts the fundamental principles of the Protestant Reformation. . . . The Doctrines of the Evangelical Faith which Methodism has held from the beginning and still holds are based upon the Divine revelation recorded in the Holy Scriptures." Moreover, the Methodist Church "recognizes two sacraments, namely Baptism and the Lord's Supper, as of Divine Appointment and of perpetual obligation, of which it is the privilege and duty of members of the Methodist Church to avail themselves"; and "the Ministers of the Methodist Church are set apart by ordination to the Ministry of the Word and Sacraments." So far, so good, perhaps; but there are grounds for hesitation. Might Methodism be claiming, on the one hand, too much for itself; or, on the other hand, too little?

On the first front, we may recall the famous essay written by the unquestionably Methodist Albert Outler under the title "Do Methodists Have a Doctrine of the Church?":

> [Methodism] has never developed—on its own and for itself—the full panoply of bell, book, and candle that goes with being a "proper" church properly understood. This makes us *une église manquée*, theoretically and actually. . . . One of our difficulties, I suggest, is that Methodism's unique ecclesiological pattern was really designed to function best *within* an encompassing environment of *catholicity*. . . . We need a catholic church within which to function as a proper evangelical order of witness and worship, discipline and nurture.[34]

In the other direction, a recent statement adopted by the British Methodist Conference floats the idea of "a less tightly drawn criterion [of ecclesiality]: wherever people join together to respond to Christ as Lord, there is the Church." And the historically and theologically rather loose remark is added that "Methodists have generally been reluctant to unchurch any body of professedly Christian believers, even where they may lack certain elements—for example, the celebration of the two gospel sacraments—which Methodists consider normative for the Church."[35] On the one hand, then, Methodism may be deficient in ecclesiality, at least as far as a supporting context is concerned; on the other hand, ecclesiality may be so loosely defined that any claim to belong to "the Church catholic" is reduced in value.

What might be the way through? Some Methodists, and I am among them, look for an integration, or reintegration, into the classic Christian Tradition via the gift of an episcopacy persuasively rooted in the historic succession that could bring into focus both the continuity of the Church and its authoritative teaching—two aspects of apostolicity. The unresolved millennial split between Eastern and Western Christendom confronts us with a dilemma. Some Orthodox ecumenists consider that the first move must be for the West to set its own house in order. Certainly the World Methodist Council and its member churches have been in uninterrupted dialogue with the Roman Catholic Church since the Second Vatican Council.

In its Singapore Report of 1991 on *The Apostolic Tradition*, the Joint Commission for Dialogue between the World Methodist Council and the Roman Catholic Church said this about the confession and location of the Church:

> Catholic and Methodist formularies differ over the concrete location of the Church which they both confess. While Wesley and the early Methodists could recognize the presence of Christian faith in the lives of individual Roman Catholics, it is only more recently that Methodists have become more willing to recognize the Roman Catholic Church as an institution for the divine good of its members. For its part, the Roman Catholic Church since Vatican II certainly includes Methodists among those who, by baptism and faith in Christ, enjoy "a certain though imperfect communion with the Catholic Church"; and it envisages Methodism among those ecclesial communities which are "not devoid of meaning and importance in the mystery of salvation." (100)

The Commission recognized John Wesley's intention—amid a "fresh and extraordinary outpouring of the gift of the Spirit who never ceases to enliven and unify the Church"—to "maintain unity of faith with the Church of all ages" (93); and the report then went on:

> As we continue to consider remaining differences over the sacramental nature of ordination and the form of succession and oversight, we rejoice in the work of the Spirit who has already brought us this far together, recognizing that the ecumenical movement of which we are part is itself a grace of the Holy Spirit for the unity of Christians. When the time comes that Methodists and Catholics declare their readiness for that "full communion in faith, mission and sacramental life" towards which they are working ("Towards a Statement on the Church," 20), the mutual recognition of ministry will be achieved not only by their having reached doctrinal consensus but it will also depend upon a fresh creative act of reconciliation which acknowledges the manifold yet unified activity of the Holy Spirit throughout the ages. It will involve a joint act of obedience to the sovereign Word of God. (94)

Nothing further is said about the "fresh creative act of reconciliation," but what is "mutual" and "joint" need nevertheless not be symmetrical.

Certainly, doctrine is of fundamental importance in ecumenical dialogue, as Pope John Paul II recognized throughout his encyclical *Ut Unum Sint*. Christian and churchly unity can only be unity in the truth of the gospel. Both the Russian and the Roman texts of 2000 rightly reject the relativism that characterizes contemporary culture, theoretically and practically, philosophically and ethically—what Pope Benedict XVI has labeled "the dictatorship of relativism."

With the matter of ecclesial unity in the evangelical truth I come explicitly to the playful and provocative question by which I entitled this essay, and which has been its implicit concern all along: Were Methodists present at Constantinople 381?

Envoi

Were Methodists present at Constantinople 381? Give or take a "filioque," we profess the same faith the conciliar bishops taught. But the Church—confessed as "one, holy, catholic, and apostolic"—has had its ups and downs in the course of its pilgrimage toward the heavenly city and the definitive kingdom, where it will doubtless be perfected in all its characteristics. Some might say that Methodists left the track in 1054, or in 1534, or in 1784. Put another way, however, it might be that Methodists in their particular identity joined the journey only in the eighteenth century. In any of those cases, we need the help of those who self-consciously claim to have stayed the course from the beginning. It would be to our benefit if, in addition to the dialogue with Roman Catholicism, we could pick up again the preliminary conversations between the World Methodist Council and the Ecumenical Patriarchate that began in the early 1990s—but have since stalled—with a view to an eventual dialogue with Pan-Orthodoxy.[36] Meanwhile, we enjoy in their own right this series of colloquia—from St. Vladimir's Orthodox Theological Seminary in 1999 through Bristol in 2000 and Crete in 2002 to St. Vladimir's again now in 2006—under the generous auspices of the Orthodox theological seminary and the General Board of Global Ministries of the United Methodist Church.[37] We are grateful.

Endnotes

[1]Why the concentrated attention on John Wesley? In a study presented in the course of preliminary conversations between the World Methodist Council and the Ecumenical Patriarchate, I painted John Wesley as the nearest particular Methodist equivalent to a "Church Father." John Wesley is "our spiritual progenitor," "our senior evangelist," "our doctrinal and moral teacher," and "our liturgist and [with his brother Charles] our hymnographer." See Geoffrey Wainwright, *Methodists in Dialogue* (Nashville: Abingdon Press, 1995), pp. 161–178 ("Tradition and the Spirit of Faith: Methodists Address the Orthodox").

[2]This Letter gained ecumenical attention through its inclusion in the anthology edited by Albert C. Outler, *John Wesley* (New York: Oxford University Press, 1964, pp. 492–499) and the monographic edition by Michael Hurley, *John Wesley's Letter to a Roman Catholic* (London-Dublin-Melbourne: Geoffrey Chapman; Nashville-New York: Abingdon Press, 1968).

[3]Boris Bobrinskoy, *The Mystery of the Trinity: Trinitarian Experience and Vision in the Biblical and Patristic Tradition* (Crestwood, NY: St. Vladimir's Seminary Press, 1999), p. 198; cf. *Mystère de la Trinité: Cours de théologie Orthodoxe* (Paris: Éditions du Cerf, 1986), p. 200.

[4]George Osborn (ed.), *The Poetical Works of John and Charles Wesley*, 13 vols. (London: Wesleyan-Methodist Conference Office, 1868–1872), 3:286. The *Hymns on the Lord's Supper* (1745), comprising 166 texts, have attracted ecumenical attention since the mid-twentieth century.

[5]Osborn, *The Poetical Works*, 6:215.

[6]From Wesley's *Journal* for February 19, 1761; see *The Works of John Wesley* (Bicentennial Edition), vol. 21, ed. by W. R. Ward and R. P. Heitzenrater (Nashville: Abingdon Press, 1992), pp. 303–308.

[7]Nikos A. Nissiotis, *Die Theologie der Ostkirche im ökumenischen Dialog: Kirche und Welt in orthodoxer Sicht* (Stuttgart: Evangelisches Verlagswerk, 1968), pp. 86–104 ("Die qualitative Bedeutung der Katholizität"). Nissiotis grounds the catholicity of the Church in the full range of the triune God's work of creation, redemption, and consummation.

[8]Sermon 74, "Of the Church" (1785); see *The Works of John Wesley* (Bicentennial Edition), vol. 3, ed. by A. C. Outler (Nashville: Abingdon Press, 1986), pp. 45–57. In his refutation of Challoner, Wesley said succinctly "no unholy man can possibly be a member of [the Church]"; and in his *Letter to a Roman Catholic* he wrote "I disclaim all common swearers, Sabbath-breakers, drunkards, all whoremonger, liars, cheats, extortioners – in a word, all that live in open sin. These are no Protestants; they are no Christians at all. Give them their own name: they are open heathens. They are the curse of the nation, the bane of society, the shame of mankind, the scum of the earth."

[9]See Outler, *John Wesley*, p. 316; and *Works*, 3:55, respectively.

[10]Lutherans and Calvinists find this a superficial definition of sin. The Lutheran-Roman Catholic "Joint Declaration on the Doctrine of Justification" of 1999 shows Catholics distinguishing between "concupiscence" (a remaining "inclination which comes from sin and presses towards sin") and "sin properly so called" (paragraph 30), so that they may be more sympathetic to Wesley's notion and advocacy of "Christian perfection" or "perfect holiness" or "entire sanctification."

[11]*Explanatory Notes upon the New Testament*, ad loc.; cf. *Works*, 3:56, n. 56.

[12]*Works*, 3:48–51.

[13]Sermon 39, "Catholic Spirit" (1750); see *Works*, vol. 2, ed. by A. C. Outler (Nashville: Abingdon Press, 1985), pp. 79–95.

[14]*Works*, 3:52.

[15]Sermon 104, "On Attending the Church Service" (1787); see *Works*, 3:464–478, here 477.

[16]See Sermon 75, "On Schism" (1786), in *Works*, 3:58–69; cf. Geoffrey Wainwright, "Schisms, Heresies and the Gospel: Wesleyan Reflections on Evangelical Truth and Ecclesial Unity," in K. Tanner and C. A. Hall (eds.), *Ancient & Postmodern Christianity: Paleo-Orthodoxy in the 21st Century: Essays in Honor of Thomas C. Oden* (Downers Grove: InterVarsity Press, 2002), pp. 183–198.

[17]To "leaven the whole" was a favorite phrase of Wesley's in this connection. He used it already at the first Methodist Conference in 1744; see Outler, *John Wesley*, p. 143.

[18]*Works* (Bicentennial Edition), vol. 9, ed. by R. E. Davies (Nashville: Abingdon Press, 1989), pp. 332–341; cf. pp. 567–580.

[19]For "The Nature, Design, and General Rules of the United Societies," see *Works*, 9:67–73. "To spread scriptural holiness over the land" is a phrase found in the so-called "Large Minutes," a cumulative collec-

tion from the "several conversations" held at Methodist Conferences between 1744 and 1789.

[20] *Works*, 21:303–308.

[21]Sermon 63, "The General Spread of the Gospel" (1783); see *Works*, 2:485–499.

[22]Bibliographical candidates are John Covel, *Some Accounts of the Present Greek Church* (Cambridge 1722) and certainly Thomas Salmon, *Modern History; or, the Present State of all Nations* (3rd edn, 3 vols., London 1744–46), which was a major source for part one of Wesley's treatise *The Doctrine of Original Sin* (1757).

[23] *Works*, 2:490–91.

[24] *Works*, 2:499.

[25]For a classic account see volumes 4 through 7 of Kenneth Scott Latourette's *History of the Expansion of Christianity* (New York: Harper, 1937–1945). After suffering denigration from a generation or two of "post-colonial" historians, the modern missionary movement is now regaining some admirers.

[26]Nissiotis, *Die Theologie der Ostkirche im ökumenischen Dialog*, p. 14.

[27]In the 1780 *Collection of Hymns for the Use of the People Called Methodists*, which long formed the backbone of official hymnody in both British and American Methodism, the soteriological and experiential dimensions dominate; but Methodists also inherit from the Wesleys hymns for the great festivals and for the Lord's Supper.

[28]See Sermon 85, "On Working Out Our Own Salvation" (1785), in *Works*, 3:199–209.

[29]According to the Lima text of Faith and Order, "service to the sick and needy" is one of the multiple strands by which the *apostolicity* of the Church is continued and maintained (*Baptism, Eucharist and Ministry*: "Ministry," 34).

[30]The Muscovite text can be found, in English, at http://www.mospat.ru/chapters/e_principles/

[31]Nissiotis, *Die Theologie der Ostkirche im ökumenischen Dialog*, pp. 102, 104.

[32]For the question at the 1744 Conference, see Outler, *John Wesley*, pp. 142–43.

[33]See, for instance, John Behr, "The Trinitarian Being of the Church," in *St. Vladimir's Theological Quarterly* 48 (2004): 67–88.

[34]A. C. Outler, "Do Methodists Have a Doctrine of the Church?" in Dow Kirkpatrick (ed.), *The Doctrine of the Church* (Nashville: Abingdon Press, 1964), pp. 11–28; here pp. 25, 26–27.

[35]*Called to Love and Praise: A Methodist Conference Statement on the Church* (Peterborough: Methodist Publishing House, 1999), here p. 22.

[36]See the introductory brochure, *Orthodox and Methodists* (Lake Junaluska, North Carolina: World Methodist Council, n.d [1996]).

[37]See the two volumes edited by S T Kimbrough, Jr., *Orthodox and Wesleyan Spirituality* (Crestwood, NY: St. Vladimir's Seminary Press, 2000), and *Orthodox and Wesleyan Scriptural Understanding and Practice* (Crestwood, NY: St. Vladimir's Seminary Press, 2005).

2

An Orthodox Reading of 1 Cor. 1:10–31: Any Room for Methodists?

John A. Jillions

1 Cor. 1:10–31:

Now I appeal to you, brothers and sisters, by the name of our Lord Jesus Christ, that all of you be in agreement and that there be no divisions among you, but that you be united in the same mind and the same purpose. For it has been reported to me by Chloe's people that there are quarrels among you, my brothers and sisters. What I mean is that each of you says, "I belong to Paul," or "I belong to Apollos," or "I belong to Cephas," or "I belong to Christ." Has Christ been divided? Was Paul crucified for you? Or were you baptized in the name of Paul? I thank God that I baptized none of you except Crispus and Gaius, so that no one can say that you were baptized in my name. (I did baptize also the household of Stephanas; beyond that, I do not know whether I baptized anyone else.) For Christ did not send me to baptize but to proclaim the gospel, and not with eloquent wisdom, so that the cross of Christ might not be emptied of its power. For the message about the cross is foolishness to those who are perishing, but to us who are being saved it is the power of God. For it is written, "I will destroy the wisdom of the wise, and the discernment of the discerning I will thwart." Where is the one who is wise? Where is the scribe? Where is the debater of this age? Has not God made foolish the wisdom of the world? For since, in the wisdom of God, the world did not know God through wisdom, God decided, through the foolishness of our proclamation, to save those who believe. For Jews demand signs and Greeks desire wisdom, but we proclaim Christ crucified, a stumbling block to Jews and foolishness to Gentiles, but to those who are the called, both Jews and Greeks, Christ the power of God and the wisdom of God. For God's foolishness is wiser than human wisdom, and God's weakness is stronger than human strength. Consider your own call, brothers and sisters: not many of you were wise by human standards, not many were powerful, not many were of noble birth. But God chose what is foolish in the world to shame the wise; God chose what is weak in the world to shame the strong; God chose what is low and despised in the world, things that are not, to reduce to nothing things that are, so that no one might boast in the presence of God. He is the source of your life in Christ Jesus, who became for us wisdom from God, and righteousness and sanctification and redemption, in order that, as it is written, "Let the one who boasts, boast in the Lord." (NRSV)

Introduction: Are Methodists in the Church?

I would like to take a tiny slice of apostolic church life as revealed in 1 Cor. 1:10–31 and examine it in dialogue with the questions being raised today about ecclesiology. This is not a full exegetical study, and I will focus on just a few points that might be relevant to our discussion. Then I would like to look at one strand of modern Orthodox thinking that picks up on the ecclesiology of the apostolic church. In the 1940s, during the Holocaust, Fr. Lev Gillet wrestled with the question of how Jews could be reintegrated into Christian thinking on the Church, after almost two millennia of exclusion. His *Communion in the Messiah* (1942) looks behind the anti-Jewish polemics and canons of the patristic age to the earliest period of the Church's life when Jewish and Gentile Christianity lived side-by-side. I believe his methodology is absolutely germane to our own discussion on how today's Methodists may have a place in an Orthodox understanding of the Church. But first I will need to put the discussion in context with an extended introduction.

This paper is mainly addressed to the Orthodox, since we are the ones who have trouble figuring out how to include anyone but ourselves in the Church—unless, of course, the Methodists would consider converting to Orthodoxy.

There are many Orthodox who believe that Methodists are not part of the Church and therefore are not properly Christian at all, whatever they themselves may think. For these Orthodox, there is only one true Church, and the only acceptable dialogue would be aimed at getting Methodists to abandon their false ways and to be chrismated (or, more likely, baptized) Orthodox. Any other kind of dialogue is just a "strange spiritual polygamy," as one priest in Canada recently wrote, "where Christ has many brides, many churches."

> The Orthodox have never entertained this idea, and Orthodox people who subscribe to it today have either picked it up outside the Church, or have made a purposeful search for any biblical or patristic quotes they can find to back up their innovative ideas. This should not be a surprise, since this is the way in which virtually every heresy has emerged in the history of the Church.

> As Orthodox who yearn to share the unique treasures of Christ's Church with the world, it is not honest—with ourselves or with the heterodox we claim to love—to speak as some do, of "deeper communion between churches," for this blurs the fact that inter-Christian dialogues are dialogues between the Church and those who have left Her, in the hope of calling all back to Her.[1]

For the proponents of this Orthodox ecclesiology, the Methodist, no less than the atheist, is an unbeliever with whom the Orthodox should avoid partnerships, collaboration and dialogue. This writer applies to all outsiders indiscriminately Paul's words in 2 Cor. 6:14–15:

> Do not be mismated with unbelievers. For what partnership have righteousness and iniquity? Or what fellowship has light with darkness? What accord has Christ with Be'lial? Or what has a believer in common with an unbeliever? (RSV)

This is an extreme view, but it is far from rare, especially among clergy. Yet even those who like and find many features of Methodist life attractive are not sure how to include them theologically in the Church. The best that can be done usually is to say that parts of Methodism "look like" us Orthodox, and that is good. The more Methodists look like us, the more we can say that there is something of the Church in them. And this is why we can collaborate with them at meetings like this. In fact, this is the official policy of the Orthodox Church in America (OCA):

> The possibility of positive collaboration with non-Orthodox Christians is founded in the indisputable fact that, despite all the differences which do exist between the Orthodox Church and other Christian confessions, the non-Orthodox Christians have preserved some doctrines and practices which are compatible with those of the Orthodox Christian Tradition.[2]

This is meant to be positive, and in contrast to the earlier extreme view it is. But even here it is clear that Methodists are not in the Church until you take all their good potential and activate it properly in Orthodoxy. This is the logical conclusion of today's standard Orthodox position.

There is some good-willed confusion about this among the Orthodox, and some say we don't proselytize people like Methodists who already have a Christian base and are "churched." Here is an excerpt from a recent *Boston Globe* interview with Bishop Nikon (Liolin), the new OCA bishop of New England.

> **Q:** Why should [people] consider being an Orthodox Christian?
>
> **A:** We want to begin with a relationship with God, a relationship with Christ. When I'm talking about outreach, I'm not talking about trying to reach people that are churched. Many people in the United States attend churches; however, there are more unchurched in the United States than there are churched. So we're trying to reach people that really have no relationship with God, do not have any faith. The Orthodox do not proselytize those who already have a Christian base.
>
> Yes, there was a separation between the east and the west churches. However, there are continually dialogues to see how we can come closer. A few years ago, it was an Orthodox priest who was president of the World Council of Churches.[3]

Does this imply that Methodists are in the Church or not? Or are we just exercising a kind of missionary triage system, leaving them up to God while we look for the truly spiritually homeless? Some Orthodox can live with this untidiness. But church policy still harbors the desire that they would become "completed" Methodists by joining the Orthodox Church. So, for example, the Antiochian Orthodox Christian Archdiocese of North America has on its website a useful feature called "Ask an X." Methodists can email an ex-Methodist who became Orthodox and get a personal account of what it's like to join.

> Ask an "X" about Orthodoxy: Here's where you can direct questions about Orthodoxy to people who came to the Church from other backgrounds: "ex" Catholics, "ex" Baptists, and so forth. They will understand where you're coming from, because they've been there.

They list about twenty ex-somethings to fit a variety of seeker backgrounds. Whatever church you belong to, however God has acted in your life up to now, the true trajectory of every Christian's life is ultimately toward the unknown Orthodox homeland. Anything less is not quite right because it is not the fullness of the Church. Don't get me wrong. There are lots of seekers who are looking for something more than what they have now, and Orthodox Christianity may be exactly what they need. "Ask an X" may be a lifeline for them. But do we Orthodox need to deny that Methodists and others are members of Christ's Church?

This is official policy for Orthodox participants in the ecumenical movement. Those who represent the Church, who form close bonds of friendship with representatives of other churches, who believe in dialogue and learning from each other, still have to fall back on this position and keep asserting (at least to their Orthodox constituents) that their ultimate purpose is to witness Orthodoxy to others. Logically, this is the best that can be done given an ecclesiology that depends on sharing communion with a bishop who confesses the faith of the one, holy, catholic and apostolic Church, which is the Orthodox Church. There can be no invisible Church. The Church must have an address, as I was once told. And so, according to this position, to be in the Church means sharing the same address.

> Genuine Christian unity is possible only where men [sic] are one in Christ and the Holy Spirit, fully united in the truth, love and holiness of God. This unity is possible only in the one Church which Christ founded, against which "the gates of hell shall not prevail" (Matt. 16:18). This unity is possible only in that Church which has preserved whole and unchanged the teachings of Christ and His apostles, prophets, martyrs and saints. This unity is possible only in that Church which continues to proclaim the revelation of God in its fullness, not only in its doctrines and morals, but also in the whole order of spiritual, sacramental and hierarchal church life as established in the apostolic Christian community.[4]

Significantly, these passages are quoted by a Canadian Orthodox nun *refuting* the hard-line stance I gave at the start of this paper.[5] She was making the point that but for ecumenical dialogue she would never have become Orthodox, since she first encountered orthodoxy while still an Anglican through the Fellowship of St. Alban and St. Sergius. Even the late Fr. John Meyendorff, who participated so actively in the ecumenical movement on many levels, when speaking of the non-Orthodox whom he liked and worked with once said, "Right people, wrong church" (of the Orthodox he added, "Right church, wrong people").

At this point some Methodists may be wondering whether they even want a room in the Orthodox heavenly mansion.

There are two problems with the current policy. The first is that it does not adequately encompass the positive experience of those Orthodox who meet, eat with and worship with other Christians, including Methodists. Everywhere we turn we see Christians of deep faith bringing forth the fruit of the Holy Spirit, making a difference in this world in the name of Christ. How do we include that experience in our understanding of Church? How do we account for the formation in Christ that these people have received in other churches? Our current official ecclesiology is too stingy on this point. The Apostle Peter was led to question his Jewish-Christian ecclesiology when confronted with a live Gentile, Cornelius, who experienced the Holy Spirit in exactly the same way he had. He and the apostles were willing to re-write their ecclesiology to include the Gentiles based on this experience. Could Orthodox to do the same with Methodists?

This is where my topic comes in, because the second problem with the current official position is that it does not reflect the diversity of the "apostolic Christian community." Indeed, one of the main findings of New Testament studies in the last thirty years has been just how diverse the life of the first century Church could be. Paul's Corinth is a prime example.

Factions in Corinth

Although there is disagreement over whether the problem in Corinth was mere quarrelling between cliques or pitched battles between well-established parties, most agree that there was some serious trouble in Corinth, even more than is reflected in the names attached to the factions in 1 Cor. 1:12: Apollos, Cephas, Paul and Christ. There was friction over thinking on marriage, celibacy, the nature of Christian community life, food offered to idols, freedom and ascetic life, how to relate to the surrounding community, resurrection, baptism, Eucharist, spiritual gifts, speaking in tongues. One of the dominant tendencies in Corinth was to think of themselves, whatever faction, as wiser than anyone else, unique and special. This was as true of the Corinthian community as a whole as it was for these individual factions, so Paul needs to begin his letter with a reminder that there were others around the world who also called on Christ.

> 1:2 To the church of God that is in Corinth, to those who are sanctified in Christ Jesus, called to be saints, together with *all* those who in *every* place call on the name of our Lord Jesus Christ, both *their* Lord and ours . . .

Paul has given us the names associated with various factions, but what was their particular content? He does not say, nor does he seem to care. He dismisses them and immediately moves on to remind the Corinthians of their baptism and earliest commitment to the undivided Christ. As far as he is concerned, these factions deal in distracting and inconsequential side issues. The Corinthians had lost all sense of perspective and magnified the importance of their own nuances. Their differences do not touch on the essence of the faith so he does not even waste time grappling with their content. He is much more concerned about factions as such, and that they had coalesced around these names, with boastful attachment to particular teachers (1 Cor. 3:21–23), so that the Corinthians are "puffed up in favor of one against another" (1 Cor. 4:6–8). By refusing to address the content of these factions, Paul tells the Corinthians that they have drawn the circle of "ins" and "outs" much too tightly.

While Paul does not focus on the content of the Corinthian factions, it is useful for us to consider it, even superficially, in order to have a picture of the level of diversity in thought that Paul accepts so easily within the one Church.

(1) The teaching and methods of the Alexandrian **Apollos** (cf. Acts 18:24–19:1) may have suited the philosophically and rhetorically inclined, offering an approach to Christian life through the intellect. This outlook may have been especially attractive to those who were familiar with the writings of Philo, St. Paul's Alexandrian contemporary who sought to produce a synthesis of Greek philosophy and Jewish revelation.

(2) It is possible that **Cephas** visited Corinth, but more likely his name was attached to a faction that preferred to understand Christianity through a less philosophical reading of the Scriptures and Jewish law, and continued to shape their Christian life on close observance of at least some aspects of the law.

(3) Although the content of this group is the most debated, followers of "**Christ**" may have been especially attracted by an emphasis on individual spirituality, prayer, ascetic life, and may have considered themselves to be the only true followers of Christ in Corinth.

(4) The faction that used **Paul's** name may have been a "freedom" party, emphasizing Christian liberty in matters of thought and behavior. Or perhaps they were insisting that Paul alone was the true teacher of the faith.

Even if these characterizations are not entirely accurate we can see that Corinth had spawned a range of Christian interpretations and emphases which St. Paul considered permissible within the one Church.

Corinthian certainties

I would like to focus now on the two passages Paul quoted from the Old Testament, because these shed particular light on Paul's attitude toward the Corinthian certainties.

> **1:19** γέγραπται γάρ· ἀπολῶ τὴν σοφίαν τῶν σοφῶν, καὶ τὴν σύνεσιν τῶν συνετῶν ἀθετήσω.

> For it is written, "I will destroy the wisdom of the wise, and the discernment of the discerning I will thwart." (NRSV)

Compare this to the text of Isaiah from which it is taken.

> διὰ τοῦτο ἰδοὺ ἐγὼ προσθήσω τοῦ μεταθεῖναι τὸν λαὸν τοῦτον καὶ μεταθήσω αὐτοὺς καὶ ἀπολῶ τὴν σοφίαν τῶν σοφῶν καὶ τὴν σύνεσιν τῶν συνετῶν κρύψω. (Isa. 29:14, LXX)

> so I will again do amazing things with this people, shocking and amazing. The wisdom of their wise shall perish, and the discernment of the discerning shall be hidden. (NRSV)

Notice how Paul substitutes ἀθετήσω for κρύψω. Does this reflect use of a different text, a mistaken recollection of the passage, or a deliberate adaptation? All have been suggested, but in any case, the Isaiah passage is more forceful in Paul's hands. Ἀθετέω can be variously translated as frustrate, thwart, annul, declare invalid, reject, refuse, ignore; make invalid, set aside; break. Paul applies this to the wise certainties of the Corinthian factions. Could it also be applied to later ecclesiological certainties?

The context of the quotation in Isaiah makes Paul's words an even more stinging rebuke to the wise.

> **Isa. 29:9–16** Stupefy yourselves and be in a stupor, blind yourselves and be blind! Be drunk, but not from wine; stagger, but not from strong drink! For the LORD has poured out upon you a spirit of deep sleep; he has closed your eyes, you prophets, and covered your heads, you seers. The vision of all this has become for you like the words of a sealed document. If it is given to those who can read, with the command, "Read this," they say, "We cannot, for it is sealed." And if it is given to those who cannot read, saying, "Read this," they say, "We cannot read." The Lord said: Because these people draw near with their mouths and honor me with their lips, while their hearts are far from me, and their worship of me is a human commandment learned by rote; **so I will again do amazing things with this people, shocking and amazing. The wisdom of their wise shall perish, and the discernment of the discerning shall be hidden.** Ha! You who hide a plan too deep for the LORD, whose deeds are in the dark, and who say, "Who sees us? Who knows us?" You turn things upside down! Shall the potter be regarded as the clay? Shall the thing made say of its maker, "He did not make me"; or the thing formed say of the one who formed it, "He has no understanding"? (NRSV)

Paul rebukes the Corinthians because they have become so attached to their point-of-view that they have lost sight of the low, despised, crucified Christ.

> **1:27–29** But God chose what is foolish in the world to shame the wise; God chose what is weak in the world to shame the strong; God chose what is low and despised in the world, things that are not, to reduce to nothing things that are, so that no one might boast in the presence of God.

I wonder if the presence in this world of so many faithful Christians who are outside our Orthodox boundaries, whose very existence as Church we deny, is not God's way of shaming the "wisdom" and "boasting" of the Orthodox.

The worst accusation that can be made against an Orthodox ecumenist these days is that he or she is a relativist. But Paul was also a relativist when it came to anything besides Christ. "I decided to know nothing among you except Jesus Christ and him crucified" (1 Cor. 2:2). All other wisdom is secondary, including the certainties touted by the Corinthians. He emphasizes this again in the last verse of this chapter, with another citation.

> **1:30–31** He is the source of your life in Christ Jesus, who became for us wisdom from God, and righteousness and sanctification and redemption, **1:31** in order that, as it is written, **"Let the one who boasts, boast in the Lord"** (ἵνα καθὼς γέγραπται· ὁ καυχώμενος ἐν κυρίῳ καυχάσθω).

This citation comes from Jeremiah 9:24 (9:23 LXX), and is a favorite of Paul. He uses it again in 2 Cor. 10:17 (although as Jerome Murphy-O'Connor points out it is a truncated citation, *NJBC* 49:16). Philo also cites the passage to emphasize the single-minded Jewish focus: "Let God alone be thy boast and thy chief glory" (*Special Laws*, 1.311).

9:22–23 Τάδε λέγει κύριος· Μὴ καυχάσθω ὁ σοφὸς ἐν τῇ σοφίᾳ αὐτοῦ, καὶ μὴ καυχάσθω ὁ ἰσχυρὸς ἐν τῇ ἰσχύι αὐτοῦ, καὶ μὴ καυχάσθω ὁ πλούσιος ἐν τῷ πλούτῳ αὐτοῦ, ἀλλ' ἢ ἐν τούτῳ καυχάσθω ὁ καυχώμενος, συνίειν καὶ γινώσκειν ὅτι ἐγὼ εἰμὶ κύριος ποιῶν ἔλεος καὶ κρίμα καὶ δικαιοσύνην ἐπὶ τῆς γῆς, ὅτι ἐν τούτοις τὸ θέλημά μου, λέγει κύριος.

9:23–24 Thus says the LORD: Do not let the wise boast in their wisdom, do not let the mighty boast in their might, do not let the wealthy boast in their wealth; **but let those who boast, boast in this, that they understand and know me, that I am the LORD;** I act with steadfast love, justice, and righteousness in the earth, for in these things I delight, says the LORD.

Paul could also be thinking of Psalm 5 (used during the entrance prayers of the Liturgy of St. John Chrysostom).

5:12 καὶ εὐφρανθήτωσαν πάντες οἱ ἐλπίζοντες ἐπὶ σέ· εἰς αἰῶνα ἀγαλλιάσονται, καὶ κατασκηνώσεις ἐν αὐτοῖς, καὶ καυχήσονται ἐν σοὶ πάντες οἱ ἀγαπῶντες τὸ ὀνομά σου.

But let all who hope in Thee rejoice, let them ever sing for joy; and do Thou dwell in them, that all those who love thy name may boast in thee.

Notice the emphasis on *all*: "*all* who hope in Thee," "*all* those who love thy name." This may or may not be Paul's source, but it certainly fits well with his message to the Corinthians that there is a wider body of Christians than just themselves (see again 1 Cor. 1:2; similarly, compare 2 Tim. 4:8, read in the Orthodox Church on the Sunday before Epiphany—"Henceforth there is laid up for me the crown of righteousness, which the Lord, the righteous judge, will award to me on that Day, and not only to me but also to *all* who have loved his appearing [ἐπιφάνειαν]").

The Fathers on factions

There are a few patristic commentaries on this passage that are helpful to our discussion. All of these are found in Gerald Bray's volume on *1–2 Corinthians*[6] in the *Ancient Christian Commentary on Scripture* (ACCS) series edited by Thomas C. Oden.

1:10a Origen says that "the visible church is a mixed body consisting of both righteous and unrighteous people." Nevertheless, one can be sure not to be in schism if he or she: 1) agrees with right doctrine and the Church's teaching on Father, Son and Holy Spirit, on the dispensation concerning us, the resurrection and judgment and 2) follows the rules of the Church.[7]

1:10b John Chrysostom looks for a deeper unity than formal agreement on words since "it is possible to be united in faith without being united in love."[8]

1:12 Clement of Rome in writing to a later generation of troublesome Corinthians minimizes the fault of the earlier division because he sees this as a mark of devotion to the apostles. "... [Even] then you were given to factions. But that factiousness involved you in less guilt, because then you were partisans of highly reputed apostles and those commended by them."[9]

This reminds me of a Baptist woman I once met in Rahway, New Jersey, where I served a parish for seven years. During a conversation after an ecumenical Thanksgiving Day service, someone was lamenting the number of churches that the little town of Rahway had spawned over the years. She disagreed. "Oh no, honey, more churches is a sign of zeal!"

John Chrysostom did not see these factions as a sign of zeal. On the contrary, he says that the coalescing of factions around a name is the great sin of Corinth. Indeed, even Christ is made out to be head of a faction and not of the whole Church.

> The quarrelling at Corinth was not over trivial matters but over something fundamental. Even those who said they were of Christ were at fault, because they were implicitly denying this to others and making Christ the head of a faction rather than the whole church.[10]

1.14 Ambrosiaster takes a similar line and sees the Corinthians as arrogant exclusivists who thought they were better than other Christians elsewhere. "These Corinthians were like the Novatianists and the Donatists of today, who claim baptism for themselves and do not recognize anybody else's."[11]

Unity and diversity in Corinth

Paul consistently pleads for unity, beginning with the first verse of our text today.

> **1:10** I appeal to you brethren, by the name of Lord Jesus Christ, that all of you agree and that there be no dissensions among you, but that you be united in the same mind and the same judgment.

He repeatedly exhorts congregations to agree with one another (τὸ αὐτὸ φρονεῖτε, lit. "to mind the same thing," Rom. 15:5, 2 Cor. 13:11, Phil. 4:2). But this does not mean, as Jerome Murphy-O'Connor asserts, that Paul "is sensitive to *any* lack of unity" (*NJBC* 49:13, editorial emphasis). While Paul's rhetoric calls for unity, what he means is unity around the central message of the gospel, and in practice he is tolerant of quite a bit of diversity. In fact, Paul "is able to distinguish between essential matters and matters of indifference (*adiaphora*) on which equally committed Christians might agree to differ."[12] Nor were the legitimate differences merely social and cultural. As Ben Witherington rightly points out, Paul's emphasis on coming to the "same mind" indicates "the problems are, therefore, intellectual in part and a matter of different viewpoints as well as diverse social conditions and lifestyles."[13] One could have a different theological outlook while still being recognized as part of the same community. As James Dunn says, "*There were Gnostics within the church at Corinth, and Paul did not denounce them as non-Christian, sham believers*. He rebuked them for their pride and lack of love, but he nonetheless recognized them to be members of the body of Christ."[14]

But there were more limits than Dunn admits, and Paul did not advocate this degree of tolerance everywhere. In Galatia rigid insistence that Jewish circumcision, ritual observances, and liturgical calendar were required of Christians was for Paul an unacceptable rewriting of the gospel because it denied the heart of the gospel message (Gal. 2:16, 3:24–25, 5:1, 6:12–15); likewise, at Colossae Paul could not include as legitimate diversity those who insisted that everyone had to follow prescribed ascetic and liturgical practices based on alleged mystical experiences (Col. 1:16–23). Thus, while accepting the presence of diverse practices and emphases within the churches, St. Paul consistently resisted attempts to (1) make absolute any one of these and (2) to increase the requirements for Christian life beyond what was originally preached.

Paul's main instinct appears to be inclusive rather than exclusive. It is true that alongside the many passages exhorting communities to work for the unity of the body, we also find a number of important texts that exhort communities to avoid, shun or cut off those who create dissensions "in opposition to the doctrine which you have been taught" (Rom. 16:17; see also 1 Cor. 5:1–13, 16:21; Gal. 1:9; 2 Tim. 2:16, 3:5; Titus 1:10–13, 3:9–11). In 1 Cor. 5:1ff, for example, Paul refuses to judge the outside world, but does insist on caring for the health of the *Church* (5:10). He demands in the sternest terms that they not associate with immoral Christians, and asserts his complete authority to judge them in this matter:

> 5:11–13 But rather I wrote to you not to associate with any one who bears the name of brother if he is immoral or greedy, or is an idolater, reviler, drunkard or robber—not even to eat with such a one. For what have I to do with judging outsiders? Is it not those inside the church whom we are to judge? God judges those outside. "Drive out the wicked person from among you" (Cf. Deut. 17:7).

While serious discipline of this kind is sometimes necessary to preserve the Church's health, Paul is loath to use it. His desire is to forbear, forgive, and include. And as for membership in the Church, he consistently resists attempts to raise the barriers and make it hard to join. He looks instead for ways to bring and keep people in, to look for the minimal step to which he can say "yes," even if that means working initially with a messy mixture of interpretations within the one Church. In the end, his criterion for inclusion and for exclusion is the same: "love for the Lord." "If anyone has no love for the Lord, let him be *anathema*" (1 Cor. 16:22a).

Unity and diversity in the New Testament

The range of acceptable differences in Corinth is reflective of an even wider range throughout the Church in the first century. As James Dunn writes at the end of his seminal *Unity and Diversity in the New Testament* (1977): "We must conclude . . . that *there was no single normative form of Christianity in the first century.*[15] Yet, there is an equally clear unifying factor: the person of Christ. Dunn shows "the surprising extent to which the different unifying factors in first-century Christianity focus again and again on Christ, on the unity between Jesus the man and Jesus the exalted one."[16]

This applies especially to ecclesiology. Veselin Kesich, my own New Testament teacher at St. Vladmir's Orthodox Theological Seminary, says that for the early Church's ecclesiology "the unifying center is the person of Christ."[17] He cautions against the temptation to iron out the texture of differences from this early period.

"Those who attempt to harmonize these elements usually minimize or neglect the complexity of the data and thus impoverish the message of the Gospel."[18] Raymond Brown also insists "a frank study of the New Testament ecclesiologies should convince every Christian community that it is neglecting part of the New Testament witness."[19]

> I contend that in a divided Christianity, instead of reading the Bible to assure ourselves that we are right, we would do better to read it to discover where we have not been listening.[20]

Brown is sensitive to the possibility that the very existence of such diversity in the New Testament church will help justify the continuing existence of divisions within the Church of today. Instead, we should see that substantial diversity was possible in the early church while being bound together by faith in Christ. This should re-invigorate efforts to unite today on the same basis.

> New Testament diversity cannot be used to justify Christian division today. We modern Christians have broken koinonia with each other; for explicitly or implicitly, we have excommunicated each other and/or stated that other churches are disloyal to the will of Christ on major issues. Such a divided situation does not have New Testament approbation.[21]

He contends that the differences in these first-century churches emerged as responses to challenges that each church faced as questions of survival. A persecuted church under attack from its Jewish neighbors, a Johannine community for example, necessarily takes on an "us versus them" mentality that shapes the theological outlook as well. But each such decision also resulted in some loss of catholicity for that church, at that locale, at that time, since not all paths can be followed at once. Every time such a choice is made there is a narrowing of the catholicity of the Church.

> For every theological insight one pays a price. The more brilliant the insight, the more likely that other aspects of truth will be put into the shade, often to be overlooked or forgotten. A balanced religious group, sufficiently confident of its great insights, is not afraid peacefully to look back in order to reclaim what was lost by the very fact that it urged those insights so strongly. But where polemic had been the midwife bringing to birth a community's identifying insights, the possibility of reaching back to regain some of the lost heritage is significantly diminished.[22]

Lev Gillet: *Communion in the Messiah*

Brown's hope that we could "reclaim what was lost" from the tradition is exactly Fr. Lev Gillet's approach to reconsidering the role of Judaism within the providence of God today. Herein we have some hope for recovering an ecclesiology that could move Orthodox and Methodists closer together as well. Fr. Lev, who wrote most often under the pseudonym "A Monk of the Eastern Church," died in 1980 and is best known for works on prayer, spiritual life, and the church year. His important but neglected book *Communion in the Messiah: Studies in the Relationship between Judaism and*

Christianity[23] looks back to the earliest period of the Church, when Jewish and Gentile Christianity were able to live side by side. He offers, it seems to me, a way to get past present stalemates, go back to the tradition and unearth a wider Orthodox ecclesiology than we generally have today, one that could indeed include the Methodists.

Fr. Lev's main idea is that sympathetic dialogue must be substituted for "one-sided mission to the Jews." He rejects supersessionism and sees that Judaism continues to have a role in God's plan. He accepts the divinely blessed existence of Judaism alongside Christianity. More controversially, he would also like to see a resurgence of a genuinely Jewish form of Christianity. Christians must not give up mission, but should engage in dialogue and see mission as a two-way street: the Jews have a God-given mission to the Church.

This is a hard sell in the Orthodox world. Indeed, blanket warnings about Jews were a commonplace in the Byzantine tradition. A number of canons explicitly forbid any familiarity with Jews.

> Let no one in the priestly order nor any layman eat the unleavened bread of the Jews, nor have any familiar conversation with them, nor summon them in illness, nor receive medicines from them, nor bathe with them; but if anyone shall take in hand to do so, if he is a cleric, let him be deposed, but if a layman let him be cut off (*Trullo,* 11).

> If any clergyman or layman shall enter into a synagogue of the Jews or heretics to pray, let the former be deposed and let the latter be excommunicated (*Apostolic Canons,* 64).[24]

Fr. Lev wants to go back to an earlier tradition when Jewish Christianity was the model of church life. Later hostility toward Judaism and Jewish forms of Christian life were sad deformations that forgot the love that Jesus and the earliest disciples shared for the synagogue and Temple. The Jerusalem Council (Acts 15) represented the generosity of Jewish Christians—then the majority—toward the new Gentile converts and was "a defeat of the Judaizing extremists."[25] "It promulgated on the whole, the freedom from Jewish customs which Paul claimed for the Gentiles. It consecrated the existence with equal rights of the Gentile Church."[26] But this generosity was not reciprocated when circumstances changed and Jewish Christians became the minority.

> When the numerical proportion of the believers was altered and Judaeo-Christianity reduced to a nucleus, this nucleus was practically swallowed up by the Gentile Christian environment. The Church of the Gentiles, forgetting the broad-minded and large-hearted attitude of the ancient Church of Jerusalem towards the Greeks, disdained the Jewish Christians, supplanted them, and finally treated them as strangers and prohibited their old customs. The Gentile Christians proved to be narrower than the circumcised Christians.[27]

Fr. Lev would like to see room made for Jewish Christianity once again, but says this should not be confused with adding members to existing "Gentile Churches." While this may be the only practical solution for the time being for those who wish to become Christian, he does not think this is "either normal or desirable." He advocates the restoration of an authentic Jewish Christianity "inside the Church universal" as the only true solution. What he means by "Church universal" becomes clearer as he explains his proposal.

He sees two possibilities for Jewish Christianity: "unsynagogued" and "synagogued."

> "Un-synagogued" Jewish Christianity means a Jewish Christianity which has broken its ties with the synagogue. Such a Jewish Christian group might exist under two forms. It could be a special and autonomous branch of one of the present Christian Churches, e.g., of the Eastern Orthodox Church, or of the Roman Catholic Church, or of the Episcopal Churches in communion with Canterbury. The condition of this branch, having its own ritual, discipline, and theological tradition, would offer some analogies with the position of the Eastern Uniat Churches in the Church of Rome. Or the Jewish Christian group could become an independent Christian Church, like the Moravian and Waldensian Churches.[28]

"Synagogued" Jewish Christianity refers to a community that "keeps, as far as possible, its ties with the Synagogue." These are "Jews who accept faith in Christ but do not wish to secede from the synagogue."[29]

This he admits is more complex than the "unsynagogued" solution. Some will be satisfied to keep their faith in Christ as a matter of the heart. Others will want to supplement their synagogue life with some attachment as well to a Christian church. He notes that Quakerism, "by its silent worship, absence of ritual, undogmatic frame of mind, makes this koinonia particularly easy, and may play a great part in building bridges between Judaism and Christianity."[30] Still others will continue their synagogue life while adding their own home gatherings, as in the apostolic church. "The transformation of Jewish rites into sacraments, as it was achieved by Jesus and his disciples, might perhaps be attempted again in circumstances not dissimilar from the present ones."[31]

What freedom he grants to these new Jewish Christian communities, what breadth he gives the Church! Clearly, Fr. Lev does not equate "the Church universal" with the Orthodox Church. These ideas take Fr. Lev far out into the deep, a great distance from the shores of cautious Orthodox ecclesiology.

Making room for the Methodists

Whenever anyone has "love for the Lord," how could he or she *not* be in the Church of Christ? Can we accept that, regardless of past history, God has a continuing purpose for both Orthodox and Methodists and that he works through both? Maybe we cannot unite our congregations. Jesus after all said it is best not to mix old and new wine, but to let them stay in their own wineskins "and so both are preserved" (Matt. 9:17). Could we apply this today? Orthodox and Methodists, different casks of wine, but agreeing that we belong in the same wine cellar?

Endnotes

[1]Priest Geoffrey Korz, *The First Urban Christians: The Social World of the Apostle Paul.* 2nd ed. (New Haven/London: Yale University Press, 2003), 12.

[2]*Encyclical Letter of the Holy Synod of Bishops of the Orthodox Church in America on Christian Unity and Ecumenism,* 1973.

[3]Rich Barlow, interview with Bishop Nikon (Liolin), *Boston Globe,* 12/31/05.

[4]*Encyclical,* 1973.

[5]Mother Sophia (Zion), "On 'Walling Off'," *Canadian Orthodox Messenger,* New Series 16:4 (Autumn 2005): 19–20.

[6]Gerald Bray, ed., 1–2 Corinthians in the series *Ancient Christian Commentary on Scripture,* Vol. VII (Chicago/London: Fitzroy Deaborn, 1999); henceforth cited as ACCS followed by the page number.

[7]*Epistle to the Corinthians* 1:4, ACCS, 9.

[8]*Homilies on the Epistles of Paul to the Corinthians* 3:2, ACCS, 9.

[9]*Epistle to the Corinthians* 47:3–4, ACCS, 9.

[10]Homilies on the Epistles of Paul to the Corinthians 3:5, ACCS, 10.

[11]Corpus Scriptorum Ecclesiasticorum Latinorum 81.11–12, ACCS, 11.

[12]Ben Witherington, *Conflict and Community in Corinth: A Socio-Rhetorical Commentary on 1 and 2 Corinthians* (Grand Rapids: W. B. Eerdmans, 1994), 97.

[13]Ibid., 96.

[14]James Dunn, *Unity and Diversity in the New Testament: An Inquiry into the Character of Earliest Christianity* (London: SCM Press, 1977), 179; Dunn's editorial emphasis.

[15]Dunn, 373; his editorial emphasis.

[16]Ibid.

[17]*St. Vladimir's Theological Quarterly* 19:2(1975): 110; henceforth cited as *SVTQ.*

[18]Ibid.

[19]Raymond Brown, *The Churches the Apostles Left Behind* (Mahwah, NJ: Paulist Press, 1984), 149.

[20]Ibid., 150.

[21]Ibid., 147–148.

[22]Ibid., 117.

[23]Lev Gillet, *Communion in the Messiah: Studies in the Relationship between Judaism and Christianity* (London: Lutterworth, 1942).

[24]Adapted from H. R. Percival, *The Seven Ecumenical Councils* (Nicene and Post-Nicene Fathers, Vol XIV), Grand Rapids: William B. Eerdmans, 1977 [1899].

[25]Gillet, 9.

[26]Ibid.

[27]Ibid.

[28]Ibid., 207.

[29]Ibid.

[30]Ibid., 208.

[31]Ibid.

3

Return to the Sources in Twentieth-century Orthodox Ecclesiology: The Case of Nicolas Afanasiev

Michael Plekon

In some ways Fr. Nicholas was a man of one idea, or, it may be better to say, *one vision*. It is this vision that he described and communicated in what appeared sometimes as "dry" and technical discussions. A careful reader, however, never failed to detect behind this appearance a hidden fire, a truly consuming love for the Church. For it was the Church that stood at the center of that vision, and Fr. Afanasiev, when his message is understood and deciphered, will remain for future generations a genuine renovator of ecclesiology.[1]

Memories and memoirs can be most revealing as well as obscuring. The recently published selections from Fr. Alexander Schmemann's journals attest to this.[2] The quotation above however comes from one of the typically succinct obituaries Fr. Schmemann was accustomed to writing and in many ways summarizes not only who Fr. Nicolas Afanasiev (1893–1966) was but also his key contribution.[3] It is telling that another vignette of Fr. Afanasiev in the often acerbic but usually accurate memoirs of Fr. Basil Zenkovsky both confirms the Schmemann view while adding something that perhaps obscures or even misunderstands the man. Zenkovsky several times notes Afanasiev's reticent personality, his characteristic diffidence, while at the same time observing the force with which Fr. Afanasiev expressed his convictions.

If there is something of an enigma here, it is not so much about Afanasiev as a person but about the history of his work in ecclesiology. Almost from the start of his academic career, he was interested in the ways in which the canons were related to the actual structure and life of the Church. He studied in Belgrade with historian A. P. Dobroklonsky and was shaped in his own work by his teacher's rigorous historiographic research methods. He was both student and later colleague of the philosopher and psychologist Fr. Basil Zenkovsky in Belgrade and at the same time active in the Brotherhood of St. Seraphim there with later colleagues Fr. Cyprian Kern and Bishop Cassian (Bezobrazov). Eventually he was invited to teach canon law at St. Sergius Theological Institute in Paris by its dean, Fr. Sergius Bulgakov, who would also come to have a strong influence on him. From Bulgakov, Afanasiev acquired a sense for the centrality of the Eucharist as well as a thorough return to the sources in understanding the Church and its relationship to the world. These very same influences would later be recognized and appreciated by the great liturgical theologian Fr. Alexander Schmemann, himself a student of Bulgakov, as well as colleague and protégé of Afanasiev.

From 1930 until 1940 Afanasiev taught at St. Sergius Theological Institute in Paris. He contributed a brilliant essay on whether the canons are changeable or not (they are) in the anthology *Zhivoe predanie* (*Living Tradition*).[4] His participation in this manifesto of progressive Orthodoxy, shaped by the Moscow Council of 1917–18, revealed his stance among those reaching out to the churches and cultures of the West under the expansive leadership of Metropolitan Evlogy (Georgievsky). He was among the majority who defended Fr. Sergius Bulgakov from charges of heresy brought by members of the Karlovtsy Synod (the later Russian Orthodox Church Outside Russia), Patriarch Sergius of Moscow and the later eminent theologian Vladimir Lossky. On January 8, 1940, he was taken around the altar in procession in the Orthodox ordination rite by Frs. Bulgakov and Kern and made a priest by Metropolitan Evlogy. From 1941 until 1947, throughout WWII, he served as the pastor of an Orthodox parish in Tunisia at the request of Archbishop Vladimir of Nice. His wife noted in her memoir his dedication to his people, his love for the liturgical services and his efforts to continue work on what would become *The Church of the Holy Spirit* even without reference resources. He took care of all the people in his community whether they were Orthodox or Catholic, Muslim or nonbelievers. Upon his return to St. Sergius, he completed the first version of *The Church of the Holy Spirit* and defended it for the doctorate in 1948. As Marianne Afanasiev describes it, a full teaching load, his official positions as treasurer of St. Sergius and canon law advisor to the bishop and diocese, and a prominent position in ecclesiology and ecumenical work consumed the last two decades of his life.

It is remarkable that throughout these busy years he managed to publish numerous articles, many of which formed the body of such books as *The Church of the Holy Spirit*, *The Lord's Supper* and the never-completed companion volume to the first, *The Limits of the Church*.[5] The unpublished outlines and notes for his courses contain further studies. At the recommendation of Patriarch Athenagoras I, Afanasiev was appointed an official ecumenical observer at Vatican II, where his ecclesiological work left its imprint particularly in *Lumen gentium*, the dogmatic constitution on the Church.[6] Both a strong proponent of ecumenical activity as well as critic of certain of its outcomes, he witnessed the formal suspension of the anathemas of the eleventh century by Patriarch Athenagoras I and Pope Paul VI. After a few weeks' illness, he died on December 4, 1966.

It is not as if Fr. Afanasiev's works were simply forgotten after his death. *The Church of the Holy Spirit*, which he had been revising, was posthumously published in 1971.[7] Perhaps his legacy lived and was most dramatically effective in the work of Frs. Alexander Schmemann and John Meyendorff. Schmemann turned minds around to the *prima theologia*, a "liturgical theology" which did not dwell only on the details of liturgical history and the rites but sought to encompass all of ecclesial life, with the liturgy as the source of both faith and practice. Schmemann's effort to restore as well as reform the liturgical life of the Orthodox Church was massive in impact. Not only did the language of the people return, rather than Slavonic or ancient Greek, but the prayers were said aloud, especially the *anaphora,* the eucharistic prayer. This was not just didactic but so that the entire assembly could pray or better, as Afanasiev repeatedly stressed, could concelebrate the liturgy with the president as the baptized, priestly, prophetic, and royal people of God. Further, Schmemann and Meyendorff fought for the "local church": so crucial for Afanasiev in his efforts to gain autocephaly for his own church body in America, with the ultimate goal a united, truly local church in America. Afanasiev is often criticized for having no place for mission or outreach in his ecclesiological view; yet this alleged deficiency is best countered by attention not only to what he actually wrote but also to the engagement with culture and society of Afanasiev's own "local church," the exarchate of Paris and the Orthodox Church in America, shaped by those he helped form, Frs. Schmemann and Meyendorff.

If all of Fr. Afanasiev's ecclesiological research and interpretation could be summed up, it would be the line that has now become familiar: "*The Church makes the Eucharist, the Eucharist makes the Church.*" Now, years after Vatican II's dogmatic constitution on the Church, *Lumen gentium,* in which Afanasiev's vision was expressed (credited to him in the Conciliar *Acta*) we take for granted the eucharistic nature of the Church and the ecclesial nature of the Eucharist, but previously both the Eastern and Western churches saw things otherwise.[8] More often, the Church was the canons, the hierarchical structure, the formal ecclesiastical organization, and the historical and social institution. More often, it was the question of who was in charge, and who could do or not do this action. It was a matter of rules, protocols, rubrics, and these in turn dependent upon the status of hierarch, cleric, or layperson in a complex internal social structure. The "return-to-the-sources" on the part of so many scholars who were Afanasiev's contemporaries was both to the "mind" and the practice of the Church of the Fathers. The reform here was both restoration of tradition, and since that tradition was living, an authentic renewal as well. The way forward was back—to the Scriptures, the liturgy, and its texts, to the lived experience of the Church as a community that prayed and served God and the neighbor.

As both the *Church of the Holy Spirit* and *The Lord's Supper* make clear, individualism was the dominant strain in eucharistic celebration as well as piety. This piety made reception of Holy Communion a rare event, preceded by extreme ascetic practices of "preparation," *govenie,* in the Russian idiom. If one could freeze-frame the year of, say 1950, on any given Sunday morning at the principal Liturgy there would be few if any communicants in Orthodox and Roman Catholic churches and very likely no eucharistic celebration in other communions such as the Anglican, Lutheran, and Reformed. The eucharistic nature of the Church and the churchly nature of the Eucharist were by no means dominant in the ecclesial consciousness, nor had they been for years.

Afanasiev was not alone in his efforts to "return to the sources" of the Church's life. In this he accompanied that ecumenical *ressourcement* group of scholars whose work later shaped much of the thinking of Vatican II. These included Jean Daniélou, Yves Congar, Oscar Cullman, Gregory Dix, Bernard Botte, I.-M. Dallmais, M. D. Chenu and Henri de Lubac, among others. The photographs of participants in the

first liturgical weeks at St. Sergius Institute (started by Fr. Afanasiev and Fr. Kern) testify to the ecumenical character of both the "return to the sources" and the efforts in
liturgical renewal. Later, there was the citation of his name by these and other such
graduates as Frs. Schmemann and John Meyendorff. Theologians such as Aidan
Kavanagh, J. M.-R. Tillard, Bishop Hilarion Alfeyev, and Boris Bobrinskoy recognize
the importance of his contributions.[9] Though aimed at different issues, Paul Bradshaw's work also confirms the eucharistic shape of ecclesiology.[10] Even his critics indicate a debt to his pioneer work in returning to the ecclesiology of the ancient
Church.[11] Relatively few critics outrightly dismiss Afanasiev's framework.[12]

But criticism as well as limitation there must always be. Fr. Afanasiev's work is
now over a half-century old. It began in articles even further back, in the 1930s, but
the ecclesiological focus crystallized in the late 1940s. Cut off from research libraries
and colleagues by his pastoral care of the Orthodox parish in Tunisia during WWII,
Afanasiev only completed a first draft of *The Church of the Holy Spirit* in 1948, defending it for his doctoral degree that year. He had published many of the chapters as journal articles and he continued this for the second companion volume, *The Limits of the
Church*. But *The Church of the Holy Spirit* was only published posthumously, first in
Russian in 1971 and in French translation in 1975.

Thus it is necessary to locate the eucharistic ecclesiology of *The Church of the Holy
Spirit* within the scholarly context of its time, admitting that research has progressed,
that other studies would have to be consulted, and, perhaps, even some perspectives
modified. Perhaps his interpretation of St. Cyprian's "universal ecclesiology" is
skewed, taking what Cyprian judged to be a description of the local church in
Carthage for the Church worldwide. Possibly criticism stems from uneasiness with
many of Afanasiev's conclusions, reading, for example, anti-clericalism into his critique of the emergence of a clerical caste. I wonder whether or not the assumptions of
some Western, Roman Catholic critics originate in the decentralized, localized ecclesiology Afanasiev sketches; an ecclesiology still evident in the Eastern churches and
continually baffling, if not problematic, to some Western observers. I would echo the
criticism that Fr. John Meyendorff directed at Afanasiev's critical response to the
important reforming Moscow Council of 1917–18.[13] Afanasiev was critical of the
Council's use of the representation of the lower clergy and laity by delegates. He also
objected to the deliberative role these delegates took in that council. Here and elsewhere he seems to draw a definitive line around the particular ministries of bishops,
clergy, and laity, lines that have been blurred virtually on a regular basis through
church history.

Yet despite these and other criticisms, Afanasiev's ecclesiological study is still significant and perhaps even more relevant than when he was writing a half century ago.
The appearance of *The Church of the Holy Spirit* in translation will allow both further
analysis and criticism as well as assimilation of its conclusions. There is, for example,
at present among the Orthodox (members of the episcopate in particular) significant
ecclesiastical opposition to the essential conciliar or sobornal nature of the Church's
liturgy and structure. But when faced with the empirical history of the Church, it is
hard to imagine scholarly refutation of its conciliar nature, East or West. Thus while
the restorations and reforms of the Moscow Council of 1917–18 were implemented in

only a few local churches, it is still difficult to dismiss the council's appeals to the liturgy, the Scriptures, patristic writings, and the structure and actions of many earlier general and local councils.

Likewise it is difficult to refute the eucharistic shape of the Church that Afanasiev points to in so many sources: Pauline letters; the Gospels; the writings of Ignatius of Antioch as well as Cyprian of Carthage, whom he views as a proponent of a "universal ecclesiology"; also John Chrysostom, Augustine, the *Didaché*, and Justin Martyr. And then there are both the ancient and present texts of the eucharistic liturgies themselves.

Most often the only work of Fr. Afanasiev's that is referred to is his essay, "The Church that Presides in Love," on the question of the primacy of the See of Peter in the churches.[14] There he briefly develops the work that he unfolds in much greater depth in *The Church of the Holy Spirit*. It is a meticulous examination of the early Church's eucharistic ecclesiology. Though often faulted for focusing solely on the Eucharist, the study begins in fact with what happens in *baptism and chrismation*, namely the consecration of each member of the Church as priest, prophet, and king. Contrary to later theology that would divide the Church into clergy and laity on the basis of consecration for ministry, Afanasiev examines the texts of the baptismal liturgy as well as those of ordination and the Eucharist itself to show that all Christians are consecrated to priestly ministry. All the people of God, not just the bishops, presbyters and deacons, celebrate the Eucharist. More precisely, all concelebrate Eucharist, as the prayers in the plural indicate. Likewise the same prayers of ordination as well as the testimonies of such fathers as Ignatius of Antioch and Irenaeus of Lyons are scrutinized in the emergence of the office of bishop from that of first presbyter. If the Eucharist cannot be celebrated unless done so by the presidents and the rest of the assembly, it follows that the calling and setting apart of the presidents must be for service. All were consecrated in baptism and chrismation for service to God in the Eucharist. All are also consecrated thereby to further service in the Church and the world, the service depending on one's place (*topos*) or position in the assembly.

Central to the life of the early church for Afanasiev was the *constant presence and work of the Holy Spirit:* "Where the Spirit is, there is the Church and all grace." Historian that he was, he consistently faulted theologians for neglecting the divine nature and activity of the Church. Nevertheless he also faulted those who would over spiritualize the Church's structures and activities, seeing such as near-Nestorian tendencies. Afanasiev further stresses the communal nature of the Church: it is not just the sum of its members. Rather, like Emile Durkheim, he recognized that as a collectivity it had a social reality *sui generis.* In the Church, no one ever spoke or acted alone but "always and everywhere together" with the others, the *epi to auto* of Acts that punctuates his writings. Fundamental to his vision is *the royal priesthood of all the baptized.* Fr. Michel Evdokimov personally related many Sunday dinners in which Fr. Afanasiev and his own father, the lay theologian Paul Evdokimov, both on the St. Sergius faculty, would discuss their work. One finds the vision of the priesthood of all the baptized prominent in Evdokimov's writings as a result. One could easily characterize Afanasiev's view of ecclesiology as pneumatological, for while seeing the Church's primary expression as the eucharistic assembly, what distinguishes the Church from all other institutions is the presence and the gifts of the Spirit. The paramount gift of the Spirit for Afanasiev, as one can read in the last chapter of *The Church of the Holy Spirit*, was the "authority of love" (*vlast' lyubvi*). The Spirit's love ruled the early church, not laws, clerical elites or political figures. However, this graced sense of consecrated membership and eucharistic community did not endure very long on its own. In the chapters that unfold here Afanasiev carefully tracks the emergence of dominance of law and of a clerical caste in the Church. Here too one might emphasize that for Afanasiev the elements (*panta*) of the Church that were not formed within the purview of love, even if they endured for centuries, would never be properly "of" the Church nor affect its true life as one connected to the kingdom of love.[15]

The other somewhat controversial emphasis of Afanasiev is his insistence that the structure of the Church is, above all, local: the immediate community that celebrates the Eucharist and extends itself in ministry to the world. The *"local church"* was not some isolated, atomic unit over against the universal "Church of God in Christ." The only church known in the early centuries was the "local church" of this household or this city. That the "local church" possessed all the fullness of the Church was without question. However, contrary to his critics, Afanasiev is almost obsessive in his insistence that the local church is *only the Church in communion with*, along with, all the other churches. In formulaic terms, $1+1+1=1$. The aggregation of many local churches does not constitute a church greater than any one of them. This said, it is impossible to fault Afanasiev for a reduction of the Church to its smallest local expression. The "parish" of our time may indeed be the "local church" in the sense that the early Christians understood it, yet one cannot simply equate today's parish with the "local church" of which Afanasiev speaks and pit it against say the deanery, diocese, national church or the Church catholic and ecumenical (*oikumene*).

Afanasiev's examination of the early church in *The Church of the Holy Spirit* as well as his careful application of this to the church of his time remains relevant for us today, almost over a half century after he completed the first draft of it. Both the Eastern and Western churches face the challenges of external indifference as well as internal ones of extremism and despair. Fr. Afanasiev's analysis and in particular his critique of the emergence of legalism and clericalism in the Church is distinctive, a voice not heard in Protestant, Catholic, and Orthodox theological scholarship and debate. His vision is rooted in the bread and cup on the holy table and in the Spirit-driven community gathered round it.[16] He ended the introduction to this work much as his colleague and teacher Fr. Sergius Bulgakov ended many of his books, with the Church's eschatological cry, the name of the One who was to come and always is coming: the name of the Lord Jesus Christ. For this reason, his voice deserves to be heard.

Endnotes

[1]Alexander Schmemann, "In memoriam—Fr. Nicolas Afanasiev," *St. Vladimir's Theological Quarterly* 10.. 4 (1966): 209. The imprint of Fr. Afanasiev's writing and teaching can be found throughout the work of Fr. Schmemann and for that matter, Fr. John Meyendorff. See for example, *The Eucharist: Sacrament of the Kingdom*, trans. Paul Kachur, (Crestwood, NY: St. Vladimir's Seminary Press, 1988) one of the rare times that Afanasiev is credited explicitly on 14, 17, 19. Also see 242–244.

[2] *The Journals of Father Alexander Schmemann 1973–1983*, ed. and trans. Juliana Schmemann (Crestwood, NY: St. Vladimir's Seminary Press, 2000).

[3] Biographical sketches of Fr. Afanasiev by his wife, Marianne, are the source for the following: "La genèse de L'Église du Saint-Esprit," in both *Tserkov Dukha Sviatogo* (Paris: YMCA Press, 1971) and *L'Église du Saint-Esprit*, trans. Marianne Drobot (Paris: Éditions du Cerf, 1975) and "Nicolas Afanasieff—essai de biographie," *Contacts* 66.2 (1969): 99–111. Andrei Platonov maintains substantial online collection of materials on Fr. Afanasiev: http://www.golubinski.ru/academia/afanasieffnew.htm (last accessed August, 2005). Also see my *Living Icons: Persons of Faith in the Eastern Church* (University of Notre Dame Press, 2002, 2004), 149–177.

[4] "The Church's Canons: Changeable or Unchangeable," in *Tradition Alive: On the Church and the Christian Life in Our Time, Readings from the Eastern Church*, ed. by Michael Plekon (Lanham, MD: Sheed & Ward/Rowman & Littlefield, 2003), 31–46.

[5] See Marianne Afanasiev's discussion in *L'Église du Saint-Esprit*, 20–21 as well as the notes to Nicolas Afanasieff, "L'Église de Dieu dans le Christ," *La pensée orthodoxe* 13.2 (1968): 1–38.

[6] See Aidan Nichols, O.P., *Theology in the Russian Diaspora: Church, Fathers, Eucharist in Nikolai Afanas'ev, 1893–1966* (Cambridge: Cambridge University Press, 1989), 253, 270. The reference is to *Acta Synodalia Sacrosancti Concilii Oecumenici Vaticani Secundi* (Vatican City, 1971), vol. I, pt. 4, 87, note 2; vol. II, pt. 1, 251, note 27; vol. III, pt. 1, 254.

[7] *Tserkov Dukha Sviatogo*, Paris: YMCA Press, 1971; *L'Église du Saint-Esprit*, trans. Marianne Drobot, Paris: Cerf, 1975; *The Church of the Holy Spirit*, trans. Vitaly Permiakov, ed. Michael Plekon, Foreword by Rowan Williams, University of Notre Dame Press, 2007.

[8] See for example *The Catechism of The Catholic Church*, (New York: Doubleday/ Image, 1995), paragraphs 1118, 1166–67, 1343, 1396, 1407, 2177.

[9] See Aidan Kavanagh, *On Liturgical Theology* (Collegeville, MN: Pueblo/Liturgical Press, 1984); J. M.-R. Tillard, *Church of Churches; Flesh of the Church, Flesh of Christ*, (Collegeville, MN: Michael Glazier/Pueblo/Liturgical Press, 1992, 2001); Hilarion Alfayev, "Orthodox Theology on the Threshold of the 21st century"; and Boris Bobrinskoy, "The Holy Spirit in 20th-century Russian Theology," *The Ecumenical Review* 52 (July 2000).

[10] Paul F. Bradshaw, *Eucharistic Origins* (New York: Oxford University Press, 2004).

[11] Over the years critics have included Metropolitan John (Zizioulas), Bishop Kallistos (Ware), Aidan Nichols, Peter Plank, T. Camelot, Paul McPartlan, and John Erickson. See among these Joseph G. Aryankalayil, *Local Church and Church Universal: Towards a Convergence between East and West: A Study on the Theology of the Local Church according to N. Afanasiev and J. M.-R. Tillard with Special Reference to Some of the Contemporary Catholic and Orthodox Theologians* (Fribourg, 2004).

[12] An exception appears to be Lucian Turcescu, *Dimitru Staniloe: Tradition and Modernity in Theology*, (Iasi/ Oxford: Center for Romanian Studies, 2002,) especially "Eucharistic Ecclesiology or Open Sobornicity," 83–103.

[13] John Meyendorff, "Hierarchy and Laity in the Orthodox Church," *Vestnik RSKhD [Messenger of Russian Student Christian Movement]* 39 (Paris, 1955): 36–45, Also see Hyacinthe Destivelle, *Le concile de Moscou (1917–1918)*, Paris: Cerf, 2006, 264–270, 273–275.

[14] *The Primacy of Peter*, ed. John Meyendorff, (Crestwood, NY: St. Vladimir's Seminary Press, 1992), 91–143.

[15] I am indebted to my colleague Fr. Alexis Vinogradov for this insight.

[16] Also see Fr. Afanasiev's very bold application of his ecclesiological perspective to the issues of restoring unity among the churches in his essays, "*Una sancta*" and "The Eucharist: The Principal Link between the Catholics and the Orthodox," in *Tradition Alive: On the Church and the Christian Life in Our Time-Readings from the Eastern Church*, ed. Michael Plekon, (Lanham, MD: Sheed & Ward/Rowman & Littlefield, 2003), 3–30, 47–49.

4

Return to the Sources in Twenty-first-century Methodist Ecclesiology: John Wesley's Ecclesiology in Light of New Insights into the New Testament and Its Environment

James H. Charlesworth

Purpose. In this essay I will explore the ecclesiology of John Wesley (1703–1791) in light of new insights into the origins of Christianity when it was definitively a Jewish movement. It should become clear that an ecclesiology for the new millennium might be offered by examining Wesley's ideas in terms of new insights obtained from challenging discoveries from Second Temple Judaism, the Judaism of Jesus and his earliest followers. These new discoveries generate three areas of research. First, the Dead Sea Scrolls are full of ideas precursory to Wesley's theology and ecclesiology. Second, the ecclesiological dimensions of the Palestinian Jesus Movement (a technical term for what earlier New Testament experts called "the early church") need to be reexamined in light of archaeology and documentary evidence. Third, the New Testament preserves documents that took shape in the first Christian century and need to be explored with the new perspectives that have replaced the once dominant Bultmannian School.[1]

In this venture I need a guide or rudder to help me explore Wesley's ecclesiology, through the rapids of both the first century BCE and first century CE. We shall explore some early Jewish texts that Wesley could not have known. The guide and rudder I have chosen is William J. Abraham's *Wesley for Armchair Theologians*.[2]

Why have I chosen this text? It is partially because the author is the Albert Cook Outler Professor of Wesley Studies and University Distinguished Teaching Professor at Perkins School of Theology, Southern Methodist University. Abraham's presentation of Wesley's thought is rigorous and sometimes critical. It is refreshing to read a theologian who has mastered Wesley's theology and who does not make him into an idol, as I fear is too often the case among Methodists. Abraham reveals a special integrity, as when he states that Wesley's position on perfection and certainty is "difficult to swallow."[3]

Abraham also places an emphasis on Wesley's love for and dependence on pre-fourth-century Christian theology and Christology. That dimension helps us as we convene another symposium between Orthodox and Methodist scholars. Again, I wish to express my indebtedness to the Holy Council of Saint Catherine's Monastery and to His Eminence Archbishop Damianos with whom I have worshiped many times over the past thirty years, and to them I dedicate these reflections.[4]

Perspective. The perspective I bring to a study of Wesley's ecclesiology is that of a specialist in Early Judaism, the historical Jesus, the Gospel of John, and the origins of Christianity. Additionally, I have chosen Charles Wesley's hymn "Lo the church with gradual light" as a means of organizing this chapter. Charles Wesley (1707–1788)[5] wrote over 9,000 hymns and sacred poems, and many of them help us understand the meaning of "the Church" for the Wesleys.

The ecclesiology of John Wesley

In his sermon "Of the Church," John Wesley exclaims, "Here, then, is a clear unexceptionable answer to that question, 'What is the Church?' "[6] It is not clear whether his words "Here, then," are intended to refer to what he has just written or what is to follow. In either case there is no clear, "unexceptionable answer" to the question, "What is the Church?" Wesley is satisfied merely to state that the catholic or universal Church constitutes "all the persons in the universe whom God hath so called out of the world," and who share "one body," and "one Spirit," and "one faith, one hope, one baptism; one God and Father of all, who is above all, and through all, and in them all."[7]

These words scarcely clarify what one means systematically by "the Church." Following A. C. Outler, Richard P. Heitzenrater, thus, is correct to point out that John Wesley did not develop a systematic doctrine of the Church.[8] Does that mean, as W. J. Abraham reports, "Wesley's doctrine of the church is inherently unstable"?[9] I shall attempt to show what has led me to conclude that while John Wesley may not have been systematic, he was coherent in his ecclesiology.

This seems evident not only from Wesley's words but also from the fact that he did not write tomes on the dogma of the church or a systematic theology. He wrote journals, sermons, and letters. I find this non-systematic dimension of Wesley's thought appealing, since many leading minds today, and all the phenomenologists,[10] point out that a system is possible only when aspects of what you are describing are ignored, and that ignoring something is based on analysis at least one step removed from that aspect of life being focused on. I also contend that the sometimes random and contradictory statements by Wesley are attractive as they are closer to the experience of real life than analyses, let alone systematization, would allow. Wesley's non-systematic, but coherent, reflections on ecclesiology free Wesley scholars and Methodists from being bound to some rigid eighteenth-century definition of the Church. We Methodists are free to explore the meaning of the Church in a new millennium filled with new challenges, such as those from Muslim extremists. Thus we are not chained to a concrete concept that might sink the ship of the Church.

John Wesley depended on the definition of the Church supplied by the Anglican Church. He admits his thoughts are "exactly agreeable to the nineteenth Article of our Church, the Church of England":[11] *"The visible Church of Christ is a congregation of faithful men, in which the pure word of God is preached, and the sacraments be duly administered."*[12] What is the meaning of "faithful men"? The Latin equivalent *coetus credentium* means "a congregation (or meeting) of believers."[13]

In order to comprehend Wesley's concept of the Church we should not, as with most theologians, focus on what he wrote or said. We should concentrate on what he did. Wesley's genius expressed itself in his actions. Wesley may have been a folk theologian who did not produce a masterpiece about the Church, as did Origen,[14] Augustine,[15] Chrysostom,[16] Thomas, Calvin,[17] and Barth. That is primarily because Wesley was focused on preaching, action, and organization. He was one of the greatest organizers in the history of religion. And he developed a method for the Church to survive during the time of the American Revolution. This was a time in human history when logic and reason were replacing revelation as the means to obtain knowledge. It was also a period in which many intellectuals were becoming deists and even atheists. Comprehending the context of his life and thought is, of course, fundamental to understanding the journals, sermons, and letters he wrote. As we venture ahead into a new millennium, we should keep in mind that Wesley's thought was significantly shaped by the exceptional political, intellectual, and spiritual revolutions of his time.

In 1744 John Wesley stated the inference "that God is now visiting his people" could not be denied.[18] One year later, in *Poor Richard's Almanac*, Benjamin Franklin published "To God we owe fear and love; to our neighbors justice and character; to ourselves prudence and sobriety."[19] Wesley and Franklin would have agreed in a century that saw the emergence of Methodism and the birth of America.

Wesley saw the Church as a Tutor. Its task was to nurture believers in their own search for holiness and spiritual growth. With Charles Wesley, John Wesley sought to develop a movement that helped its members experience God's love and feel justification, regeneration, and sanctification.

A doctrine of ecclesiology can be developed from the top down or from the bottom up. If you begin with God and work downward, you might be in danger of minimizing the importance of the average person. If you begin at the bottom and construct ecclesiology from the bottom to the top, there is the danger of being anthropocentric, minimizing the sin that defines all humans, and never reaching beyond human frailty. The latter can be overcome by stressing the goodness of grace, the presence of the Holy Spirit, and the continuing desire of the Creator to reach and be present with his creature, the human.

John Wesley conceived a doctrine of the Church from the bottom up.[20] He stressed pneumatology over ecclesiology and thereby resisted the need to define "the Church." As W. J. Abraham states, "Wesley started from the bottom and developed a vision of the church as a body of believers whose faith unites them to Christ, who in turn unites them to every other believer. Here the primacy of honor is given to pneumatology."[21]

Meditating on this insight helps me realize why I feel at home within the Methodist Church. My grandfather was the Rev. Dr. Thomas Charlesworth. My father was the Rev. Dr. Professor Arthur Charlesworth. Both were Methodist ministers. Living within a parsonage and hearing during each meal about the problems within the church, by the age of twelve I was leery of the institutional church. Thus, I am pleased to learn that the life and teaching of John Wesley reveal he also saw institutionalization as problematic.

I am convinced, therefore, that in this new millennium the Methodist Church will succeed if effectiveness is more important than institutionalism, if spirit takes precedent over form, if mission is perceived to be superior to maintenance, if innovation is allowed to dominate over convention, and if renewal is more important than continuity.

In the process we need to realize and emphasize the continuing importance of an institution, the necessity of form, the desire to attend to maintenance, the clarity evident in convention, and the need for continuity with our sacred traditions. In fact, I am convinced that continuity with the Wesleys and with Jesus and the earliest followers is the rudder that will guide the ship of the Church into the new millennium and past the Scylla and Charybdis. This is evident and possible—the Holy Spirit was far more powerful in the lives of Jesus, his followers, and the Wesleys than any set rules or institutional norms. This emphasis also, as Wesley knew, united the Methodists with all other Christians—especially the Orthodox—because of the uniting force of the Holy Spirit in all worship services where she reigns.

What then did Wesley mean by "the Church"? In his sermon "Of the Church," Wesley began by stressing that one might not be able to find a "more ambiguous word than this."[22] The church can be a building or an institution. The Church can also be defined as a gathering of the saints (as Paul did in Rom. 1:7). The Church has also been defined as a gathering of those who recognize they are sinners and need God's forgiveness and acceptance. Wesley would probably have wanted to include both definitions in his vision of the Church as a "body of people" that are "united together in the service of God."[23]

Both John and Charles Wesley would wish us to perceive that choosing only one of these options miscasts the Church. Thus the Church should be perceived as both a place where those who perceive a need for God's grace gather and also a place in which the saints, the elect of God, find God's presence.

The Wesleys' ecclesiology in light of new discoveries in Second-Temple Judaism

The term "Second-Temple Judaism" designates the world of Judaism in Palestine from 300 BCE to 70 CE. There were many groups of Jews, including the Baptist Groups, the Enoch Groups, the Essenes, the Samaritans, the Sadducees, the revolutionary groups which became Zealots about 66 CE, and, of course, the groups founded by Jesus from Nazareth. Among these groups the most powerful were often the Pharisees. Who were these Jews?

A cursory reading of John Wesley gives the impression that he was misled by some New Testament passages, especially in Matthew. Did Wesley imagine that the Pharisees were synonymous with hypocrites and were interested only in practical issues? In his "Upon our Lord's Sermon on the Mount" Wesley focuses on the Pharisees. He notes that the "Pharisees were a very ancient sect, or body of men, among the Jews; originally so called from the Hebrew word פרש—which signifies to *separate* or *divide*."[24] When Wesley wrote these words, no pre-70 CE Jewish text existed to indicate that he was correct. In the last few decades, however, we have known about a document found in Qumran Cave IV, *Some Works of the Torah*. This early Jewish document contains this Hebrew verb; and it clarifies why those at Qumran have *separated* from other Jews who control the Temple cult.

Wesley avoids the anti-Semitism or anti-Judaism unfortunately so typical of many sermons on the Pharisees. Wesley recognizes that the Pharisees were "the most eminent professors of religion," indeed the "wisest" and "the holiest of men."[25] Against those who would brand this group of Jews "a company of hypocrites," he judges:

> Some of them [the Pharisees] doubtless were [hypocrites]; men who had really no religion at all, no fear of God, or desire to please him; who had no concern for the honour that cometh of God, but only for the praise of men. And these are they whom our Lord so severely condemns, so sharply reproves, on many occasions. But we must not suppose, because many Pharisees were hypocrites, therefore all were so. No indeed is hypocrisy by any means essential to the character of a Pharisee. [*Works* 1:321]

This is sensitive, enlightening, and reveals Wesley's inner holiness; that is, he does not allow some passages in the New Testament, especially in Matthew, to mislead him to castigate and caricature the Pharisees. Methodists today who habitually vilify the Pharisees and assume that Pharisees and hypocrites are synonymous should listen to Wesley's perspective. Wesley even portrays the "stricter Pharisees" not as those who are legalistic, but as those who even give more to God than Torah demands.

Note Wesley's exegetical moves: When he reads that our righteousness must "exceed the righteousness of the Scribes and Pharisees" he does not proceed to portray these Jews as insincere or hypocritical. Rather, he elevates them by exploring how "our righteousness may exceed theirs." Many of Wesley's insights and judgments regarding the Pharisees harmonize with those of leading scholars who participated in the conference on Hillel and Jesus.[26] Wesley's appreciation of the Pharisees was very advanced for his day and is consonant with the widespread recognition today, among Jews and Christians, that the Pharisees of Jesus' day were often deeply religious, spiritually advanced, developed enlightened codes of morality, and that Hillel and Jesus often shared the same passion, commitment, and moral code. Quite startling is Wesley's use of the Pharisees in the Sermon on the Mount:

> A Pharisee . . . used all the means of grace. As he fasted often and much, twice in every week, so he attended all the sacrifices. He was constant in public and private prayer, and in reading and hearing the Scriptures. Do you go as far as this? . . . Ah, poor Christian! Shall not the Pharisee rise up in the judgment against thee and condemn thee? His righteousness is as far above thine, as the heaven is above the earth! [*Works* 1:323–24]

Of course, one cannot imagine Wesley being consistent on this point. He was not a philosopher of religion. He was an evangelist and a preacher. One expects him to stress that the Pharisee was interested only in external observations but that the Christian is devoted to internal purity also. He does so with the following advice: "But still the righteousness of a Christian exceeds all this righteousness of a Scribe or Pharisee, by fulfilling the spirit as well as the letter of the law; by inward as well as outward obedience."[27] He thereby sacrifices consistency and coherence to the rhetoric of a sermon that is intended to shock the reader, reveal the need for improvement, and elevate those called Christians, his audience, by lauding them. This sermonic development should not be divorced from his earlier emphasis on the first-century Pharisee whom he deeply admired and carefully represented.

Intermittently, John Wesley discloses that he studied Second-Temple Judaism. He must have read the pseudepigraphon called the *Testament of the Twelve Patriarchs*, a text his father advised young ministers to read for moral edification. It must be assumed that John Wesley followed this advice; he was the one who edited and published his father's work, *Advice to a Young Clergyman*.[28]

Wesley also must have known a remarkable amount about first-century Judaism in Jerusalem. For example, he pointed out that the earliest followers of Jesus did not have "any large place" in which so many could gather after Pentecost. He also judged, correctly, that these Jews would not have "been permitted to build one."[29]

The Dead Sea Scrolls. What Wesley could not have studied were the documents found hidden in eleven caves on the northwestern shores of the Dead Sea. Seven observations have been selected to reveal how these texts preserve Jewish insights that sometimes foreshadow Wesley's ecclesiology.

1) *Oneness in the Yahad.* Only at Qumran did the Hebrew word *yahad* obtain the specific meaning of those-who-have-united to prepare the Way of the Lord in the wilderness. Thus the best translation of this term brings out what is "common"; that is, Community. The *Rule of the Community* is so similar to the Methodist *Discipline* and was originally called *The Manual of Discipline*, even by Jewish experts on the Dead Sea Scrolls. The authors and compilers of this Qumran text clarify that it took over two years to enter into the *Yahad* and the New Covenant. Prefiguring some of Wesley's thoughts and words is the opening of the *Rule of the Community*. All those "devoting themselves to his truth"—and entering into the *Yahad* of God (or Community of God)—shall bring "all their knowledge, and their statutes, and discipline their strength according to the perfection of his ways" (1QS 1:11–12).[30]

Recall that Wesley stressed that the Church is a "body of people" that are "united together."[31] Harmonious with the Qumranites' concept of the *Yahad* is Wesley's claim that God's saints [for him, the Church] are those "whom God hath called out of the world," as "one body," possessing "one Spirit," and sharing "one faith, one hope," and "one God."[32]

2) *The heavenly dimension of the Community [= the Church].* The Holy Ones in the Community at Qumran imagined that their house was the "Holy House" in which "the Holy Ones" dwelt because the "Holy Spirit" dwelt with them. In the Hebrew Bible, or Old Testament, we find the concept of the Holy Spirit of God. At Qumran we find a development of that concept; only at Qumran do we hear about the Holy Spirit from God. Thus, one of Wesley's favorite terms, which he inherited from the New Testament, was developed at Qumran. Thus their Community was not separated from heaven; it was, as it were, an antechamber of heaven.

The Qumranites were the legitimate priests who left (in their own explanation) or were thrown out (the Hasmoneans' explanation) of Solomon's Temple. They believed that they had been called out of the Temple and into the wilderness by the Voice. Their interpretation of Isaiah 40:3 is as follows: "A Voice is calling, 'In the wilderness prepare the Way of the Lord.'" These thoughts adumbrate Wesley's concept of the Church. Recall that Wesley used the etymological meaning of *ekklesia* as "those whom God hath *called out of* the world."[33]

3) *Cosmic dimension of communal prayer.* Prayer at Qumran had cosmic dimensions and was aligned with the raising and setting of the sun. Note these words at the end of the *Rule of the Community*:

> As the day and night enters I will enter into the covenant of God,
> And as evening and morning depart I will recite his statutes. [1QS 10:10]

As "Sons of Light," Qumranites aligned their prayer with the daily movement of the sun, which was highlighted by a liturgical year defined by the solar calendar. This choice was both theologically and sociologically important, since the priests in the Temple followed the lunar calendar.

In contrast to Qumran, Wesley seldom uses the concept of "light." At one point he reveals his era and intellectual curiosity, stating that no one knows if the sun is "fluid or solid," and pondering if "light" flows in a continuous stream from the sun, is affected by gravity, or is free from "the general laws which obtain in all other matter."[34] Wesley did stress the cosmic dimension of prayer. Rather than defining a Methodist as one who holds certain theological opinions, or who stresses one belief over others, Wesley defines a Methodist as "one who has the love of God shed abroad in his heart by the Holy Ghost given unto him."[35] What Wesley called the Holy Ghost is strikingly similar to what the Qumranites knew as the Holy Spirit. Wesley stressed that the Methodist is one who prays unceasingly in very place and every moment, because "his heart is ever lifted up to God."[36] I imagine Wesley would have agreed with the Qumranites that in worship heaven meets the earth. Such thoughts were most likely in his mind when he stood and sang Charles Wesley's "Come, let us join our friends above," especially verse one:

> Come, let us join our friends a-bove
> Who have ob-tained the prize,
> And on the eagle wings of love
> To joys celestial rise.
> Let saints on earth u-nite to sing
> With those to glory gone,
> For all the servants of our King
> In earth and heaven are one.[37]

At Qumran the Holy Ones joined with angels in their chanting. The scroll entitled *The Angelic Liturgy* describes the yearly ritual by which the angels chant in heaven. The Wesleys would have resonated with that description, since "Maker, in whom we live," composed by Charles Wesley in 1747, extols heaven and earth joined in praise: "Let all the angel throng / give thanks to God on high, / while earth repeats the joyful song / and echoes to the sky."[38] While the Wesleys could not have known the concepts and ideas in The Angelic Liturgy, they inherited from the Roman mass, through Anglicanism, the concept of celestial worship experienced on earth.

4) *Realizing eschatology.* The Qumranites composed a collection of psalms or hymns. Because the opening words are almost always "I thank you, O Lord, because," the collection is called *The Thanksgiving Hymns.* In these hymns a futuristic eschatology is combined with a realizing eschatology.[39] The believer in the *Yahad* experiences in the present the joys and promises of God's future day. For example, the Qumranites had memorized, from years of chanting, the hymn that celebrated how the Trees of Life, planted by God through the Righteous Teacher, have sent out their roots to the spring that flows with "living water."[40]

This realizing dimension, known to the Qumranites, and celebrated in the liturgy developed by Rome, is also found in Charles Wesley's hymns. Note, in particular, the hymn entitled "Come, and let us sweetly join." In stanza two we find a realizing eschatology, even though one should not imagine the Wesleys were eschatological in the same way as the early Jews:

> Hand and hearts and voices raise,
> Sing as in the ancient days;
> Antedate the joys above,
> Celebrate the feast of love.[41]

5) *Angels are present in worship.* In the Dead Sea Scrolls we find another exceptional thought. The Qumranites imagined not only that heaven touched earth within the *Yahad*; they also conceived that angels joined them on earth in their worship services.[42] The author of the *Rule of the Congregation* warned about the necessity of purity in the *Yahad*, or "Congregation of the men of the name," because "holy angels [(are) in] their [Coun]cil" (1QSa 2:9).[43] This concept does not seem to be evident in John Wesley's thought, but he did argue that "every member" in the church is "holy, though in different degrees."[44] Perhaps this perspective opens the door for imagining that those made perfect by the Holy Spirit have moved from anthropology to angelology, or angelic status.

6) *The fruit of the lips replaces sacrifice.* The Qumranites originated within priestly circles in the Jerusalem Temple. Some were Sons of Aaron, others Levites. Having left the cult and sacrifices behind, they developed a concept that appears in the prophets. For the Qumranites, God wanted not sacrifices but the fruit of the lips. That odd expression is a metaphor for chanting praises to God. Note the *Rule of the Community*:

> As long as I live an engraved statute (shall be) on my tongue
> as a fruit of praise, the portion of my lips.
> I will sing with skill, and all my song (is) to the glory of God.
> The strings of my harp (are tuned) to the norm of his holiness,
> And the flute of my lips I will play in tune with his judgment.
> (1QS 10:8–9; cf. 4Q MS D Frg. 4 Col. 1:7–9 and 4QS MS F Frg. 1 line 1).[45]

Such a concept would please John and Charles Wesley, as they emphasized the singing of hymns in church. The first stanza of Charles Wesley's "Musician's Hymn" resounds similarly:

> If well I know the tuneful art
> To captivate a human heart,
>   The glory, Lord, be thine;
> A servant of thy blessed will
> I here devote my utmost skill
>   To sound the praise divine.[46]

7) *The concept of perfection is possible with the help of the Holy Spirit.* In this twenty-first century, John Wesley's concept of perfection makes little sense. In pre-70 CE Jewish communities, the concept is known and developed at Qumran. At Qumran, as with John Wesley,[47] the concept of sin is emphasized. But at Qumran, as with Wesley, the faithful person may obtain perfection in the present by means of God's help. The Qumranite, in contrast to Wesley, kept himself separate from others while emphasizing perfection: "I will not console those who are being obstinate until their way is perfect" (1QS 10:21).[48]

How is perfection possible? The Qumranite stressed that perfection is possible only by means of God's covenant loyalty:

> For my way (belongs) to Adam.
> The human cannot establish his righteousness;
> For to God (alone) belongs the judgment
> And from him is the perfection of the Way. (1QS 11:10–11).[49]

John Wesley would add to this concept the importance of prevenient grace.

These reflections on Qumran theology reveal faint images of John Wesley's ecclesiology. Even though he could not have read the scrolls that contain these ideas, they resonate with his attempt to reform the Church of England by returning to the original sources.

The differences between the Qumranites and Wesley are vast and can only be summarized. They were exclusive; he was inclusive. They were Jews, some of who were looking for the coming of two messiahs; he was a Christian who rejoiced in the advent of the Messiah. They developed theology; he was focused on Christology. Their dualistic and exclusive claims lead to an end in which they abandoned Qumran, perhaps looking back on dreams going up in smoke as Vespasian and his troops burned what they had imagined was "the House of Holiness." Christianity is not a triumphant Essenism: In discerning Christian origins, Jesus matters.

Yet, John Wesley emphasized that the roots of his ecclesiology ran deep into Judaism. He opined that leading scholars "have shown at large that our Lord himself, and all his Apostles, built the Christian Church as nearly as possible on the plan of the Jewish."[50] In light of what experts on Second Temple Judaism and Christian origins have learned in the past half century, Wesley is not only a genius. He is prescient.

To conclude this section, let us contemplate Charles Wesley's hymn "Lo the church with gradual light."

> 3.   Now she without spot appears,
>   For Christ appears again,
>   Sun of righteousness, he clears
>   His church from every stain,
>   Rising in full majesty
>   He blazes with meridian light:
>   All th' horizon laughs to see
>   The joyous heavenly sight.

It is impressive to note how many of the concepts and words in the hymn quoted ring of Dead Sea Scroll's terminology, especially "light" and the related concepts, and evidence the resonance that existed between John Wesley's attempt to reform the church according to Jewish models and the incarnation of those models at Qumran.

There is more that can be reported, but time will only permit a glimpse. Many scholars have rightly seen the origin of the offices and functions of deacon, elder, and bishop, well known from the later New Testament documents, in similar offices and functions with the hierarchical Qumran Community. However one evaluates the origin of these titles and offices, it is clear that Judaism is the major source.

The Wesleys' ecclesiology in light of research on Jesus and the earliest "Church"

In his ecclesiology, John Wesley sought to restore the spirit and beliefs of the earliest followers of Jesus. His renewal movement took its inspiration from the original genius of the first century, Jesus himself. He studied Hebrew and Greek to better access that genius and used them in his publications to help others access it also.

Jesus and "the Church." During the middle of the twentieth century, many NT scholars concluded that Jesus did not found a church and that the concept of the Church evolved and appeared only after Jesus' death and resurrection.

Over the past five decades, I and other New Testament scholars have argued that while the Greek term *ekklēsia* is only found in Matthew among the Gospels,[51] the concept of a "church" developed from Jesus' life and actions.

Jesus called sinners while they were sinners. He did not set extreme requirements on them, unlike the Qumranites and other Jews. He did not demand that they memorize a secret sectarian lore or adhere to a set of rules. He did not demand that they substitute earthen vessels for stone vessels so as to observe the increasing demands for purity. He also did not require his followers to enter a bath for ritual purification, a *mikveh*, so that they would be cleansed before entering his community. He did not demand that they be perfect physically, mentally, and spiritually, as did the Qumranites. Also, there were no rigid barriers to keep those within his group distant and pure from those outside it.

Jesus made demands on those who would join his group and follow him. They could not continue as sinners. They had to turn from their ways and commit all to God's Rule. Of course, such an alteration of life required major changes. He asked those whom he called to commit all their future to God and God's Rule; he warned all who heard him that they could not serve two masters. One entered into the community Jesus was forming instantly without having to pass any requirements or tests.

Jesus' call. Jesus called together a group of men and women who were experiencing the presence of God, especially in the healing miracles, and awaiting the full in breaking of God's Rule or the kingdom of God. Later in the New Testament, this movement developed into an institution with a hierarchical structure similar to the Qumran *Yahad*—the offices of deacons, elders, and bishops are similar to the leadership roles in the *Yahad*.

In many ways the movement John Wesley shaped within the Church of England was forged in the first century, within Judaism, and under the influence, directly or indirectly, of Jewish rules for administration, such as those found at Qumran.

With Second-Temple Judaism: Oneness. The Oneness—or Community— developed at Qumran is unique within Second-Temple Judaism. While most New Testament experts ignore the Gospel of John when discussing New Testament views on ecclesiology, it is evident that the author of the Fourth Gospel had a developed and sophisticated ecclesiology.[52] In a major chapter, John 17, the Fourth Evangelist depicts Jesus praying to his father, beseeching that "they may be one, as we are one" (John 17:11). The oneness perceived as essential for Jesus' Twelve might have been influenced by the Qumran Essene emphasis on Oneness, the *Yahad*. John Wesley could not have known that possibility, but he certainly was correct to emphasize that Jesus' words directed only to the Twelve stressed Oneness, since, as Jesus stated, only one person had been lost, Judas.[53]

Jesus' prayer not only highlights a major Johannine thought to oneness as having a divine archetype, but also clarifies that those whom Jesus has called together are an ecclesiological group. In this assembly his followers are one because they obey a new revealed commandment: they love one another as he had loved them (John 13). This is nascent ecclesiology, especially in a social setting in which the Johannine Jews are being thrown out of the synagogue because of their belief in Jesus (John 9). John Wesley was correct to stress, *passim*, that Christ's love given to the believer by grace is evident in the way the believer loves others and helps those in great need. This thought was shaped into Charles Wesley's "Jesus, Lord, we look to thee," and especially in stanza four:

> Let us for each other care,
> each the other's burdens bear;
> to thy church the pattern give,
> show how true believers live.[54]

Clearly, John Wesley claimed that Jesus founded the Church. This fact becomes obvious in his "Primitive Christianity":

> Jesus, from whom all blessings flow,
> Great Builder of thy Church below,
> If now thy Spirit moves my breast,
> Hear, and fulfil thy own request![55]

Three emphases. How shall we proceed to penetrate deeper into John Wesley's thoughts on ecclesiology? This will not be a clear road, since we have no set doctrine of the Church bequeathed to us by Wesley. As W. J. Abraham points out, "we do not find in Wesley a fully rounded account of the church that will cope with all the issues that have to be addressed theologically."[56]

For some theologians Wesley's lack of precision may seem distractive. For me it is attractive. We are free from a concrete system and may be guided by meditation and oneness with the Holy Spirit, who is present with us and clarifies that our attempts to define ecclesiology will always culminate in mystery and wonder. Again, our reflections are adumbrated in the *Rule of the Community*: "My eye beheld his wonders, and the light of my heart beheld the mystery of what shall occur and is occurring forever" (1QS 11:3).[57] I can imagine John Wesley would have been attracted to such thoughts. For example, in his sermon "On the Holy Spirit," preached in Oxford in 1736, Wesley argued that God is not only in heaven, a fact which will leave us with awe but cannot save, God is also on the earth "with us, and in us."[58] He proceeds to stress, using an eschatology that seems exceptional in the seventeenth century: "Everything in Christianity is some kind of anticipation of something that is to be at the end of the world."[59]

I) The mystery of commitment and assurance

The first emphasis in Wesley's ecclesiology is the mystery of commitment and assurance. In the mystery felt in the church, the believer finds confidence and assurance.

In the *Yahad* Qumranites claimed to experience the assurance of being called to prepare the Way of the Lord and thus being the Holy Ones called to enter God's "New Covenant." Similarly, in Wesley's reconstituted Church, believers evidence confidence and assurance. Abraham expresses this thought well:

> Faith was also a direct, experiential encounter with God through the Holy Spirit that brought awareness of the love of God in one's heart and released new moral energy to gain real victory over evil here and now. On this front Wesley stumbled into the doctrine of assurance through the internal working of the Holy Spirit in his heart.[60]

Wesley would be surprised to find evidence that his belief (obviously without Christology) was similarly articulated by the Qumranites; note the *Rule of the Community*: "From the fountain of his righteousness (is) my justice. A light (comes) into my heart from his wondrous mysteries" (1QS 11:5).[61] Many Methodists experience that same assurance when they rise and sing "Blessed Assurance."

The mystery of salvation breeds love of others. While the Qumranites had no missionary document or zeal and thought only within high constricting walls that kept out the impure and imperfect, Wesley was an itinerant missionary who, like Jesus, sought out the lost and marginalized in the interstices of society. The mystery of salvation demanded reaching out in love to others. Note how Wesley concluded his sermon "Of the Church":

> Above all things, let your love abound. Let it extend to every child of man: Let it overflow to every child of God. By this let all men know whose Disciples Ye are, because you "love one another." [*Works* 6.401]

God's love is inclusive and gladdens Earth and Sky. For Wesley the Church is a noun that denotes the universal, catholic, Church; that is, "all the Christians under heaven."[62] Wesley did not follow the definition of the Church of England whereby Christian groups were excluded in which the "word of God" may not be deemed "pure," and in which the sacraments may not be "duly administered." Wesley was more inclusive than the Church of England.

Placing emphasis always on the gathering of Christians, he based his concept on Scripture: "sometimes the word Church is taken in Scripture in" an "extensive meaning, as including all the Christian congregations that are upon the face of the earth. And in this sense we understand it in our Liturgy."[63] Wesley's comment helps clarify that John and Charles Wesley developed their theology not in systematic tomes but in liturgy; this dimension of Methodism is certainly shared with the Orthodox.[64]

In Wesley's day as in our own there was sickness, death, and suffering. For us there is more: the threat of another terrorist attack. In November 2002, over one year after the twin towers melted to the ground in New York and the Pentagon was hit in Washington, D.C., Osama bin Laden sent "A Letter to America" which contained condemnation of America and demands that if not met would result in "more disasters." He prophesied that "you will lose this Crusade that Bush began, just like the other previous Crusades in which you were humiliated by the hands of the *mujahadeen*, fleeing to your homes in great silence and disgrace."[65]

We know that we are under attack from some vehement, but not necessarily lunatic, fringes of Islam. Sometimes we are hated because of the loss of Andalusia, the re-conquests from the fifteenth century, 1948 (and 1967), and the presence of non-Islamic troops in the Middle East. Sometimes we are attacked because of our non-Muslim faith. Does Wesley offer any insight that may help us understand and solve this problem? I think so, and it may be found in his vision of a triumphant Church and an eschatological dream:

> At that time will be accomplished all those glorious promises made to the Christian Church, which will not then be confined to this or that nation, but will include all the inhabitants of the earth. "They shall not hurt nor destroy in all my holy mountain (Isaiah xi. 9)."[66]

Wesley did not restrict this hope to only those who are Christians. He had an inclusive vision not often appreciated because of his sometimes excessive and emotional focus on Christ. We shall clarify this point further but close this section by contemplating the thoughts in Charles Wesley's hymn "Lo the church with gradual light."[67]

1. Lo, the church with gradual light
     Her opening charms displays,
  After a long dreary night
     Looks forth with glimmering rays,
  Scarce perceptible appears,
     Until the Day-spring from on high
  All the face of nature cheers,
     And gladdens earth and sky.

II) The wonder of the Lord is the beginning of wisdom

The second emphasis in Wesley's ecclesiology is the idea that wisdom commences with a perception of God's awesome wonder. Abraham rightly points out that Christians are often driven to church "fearful of God."[68] Many have memorized the biblical adage that the beginning of knowledge is the fear of the Lord (Prov. 1:7). Actually, the Hebrew phrase יראת יהוה (*yir'at YHWH*) also denotes that one recognizes the awesomeness of the Lord and Creator. Recall Psalm 66:5,

> Come and see the works of God,
> Who is held in awe by men for His acts. [TANAKH]

The Hebrew "held in awe" is etymologically linked with *yir'at YHWH*; it is *nôrâ*. As the *homo religiosus* comes closer to God, the Creator, awe and wonder replace comprehension. Eloquence is replaced by silence.

At this point we should broach the issue of perfection in Wesley's theology, as it pertains to those in the church. W. J. Abraham's words are striking:

> Wesley's views of justification and regeneration do not sit well with many of our current cultural assumptions. His views on the quest for perfection and the possibility of certainty are even more difficult to swallow. Wesley believed that it was possible to achieve spiritual perfection and genuine certainty about God in this life.[69]

Obviously, W. J. Abraham's judgment of Wesley seems rational in our contemporary American context.

Is perfection possible? Is it only possible at the Day of Judgment? Wesley is clear. Perfection is possible, and it is possible in the present life, though his brother Charles disagreed with him in this matter. Wesley was convinced that justification and sanctification were "the gift of God." Wesley advised that four beliefs are necessary. First, one must believe that God has promised to save you from all sin, not just some of it. Second, one is to believe that God will "fill you with all holiness," not just a little holiness. Third, the Christian should also believe that God is able and willing to do this for his creature. And, fourth, one should believe that God "is not only able, but willing to do it *now*." Wesley is adamant about that final point: "Not when you come to die; not at any distant time; not to-morrow, but *to-day*." His brother Charles, however, saw the possibility of full perfection in union with God at the point of death.

Wesley turns his exegetical mind to Matt. 5:48, "Ye shall then be perfect." What do these words mean? Again note Wesley's answer: "The Apostle seems to mean by this expression, τέλειοι, ye shall be wholly delivered from every evil work; from every evil word; from every sinful thought . . . and ye shall be renewed in the spirit of your mind, in every right temper, after the image of Him that created you, in righteousness and true holiness."[70]

Our task is not to seek how Wesley's comments could make sense in his time or even in our time. The crucial issue to explore is if he has found something fundamentally true in our early Jewish sources and in Jesus' time. For Wesley, for Jesus, and for the Qumranites all things are possible with God's help and with the generative power of the Holy Spirit. For the Qumranites, the most perfect member of the *Yahad* ascends through anthropology to angelology (using Greek terms for Semitic concepts). When translating the Dead Sea Scrolls I cannot discern if *elim* means celestial beings or Qumranites. Why? That is because those in the *Yahad* claim to have been perfected as Holy Ones in the House of Holiness on earth because of the presence of the Holy Spirit.

John Wesley could not have had these insights into Second-Temple Judaism, but they do help us grasp his generative insight, which Methodists have judged to be not speculative but revelatory. His insight is twofold. First, Wesley, following Paul, emphasizes the depth of human evil in each of us. Second, he creates a new concept: prevenient grace. With God's gift of prevenient grace, anyone, indeed everyone, grasps the dire situation we are in and this is the beginning of salvation, justification, and sanctification. Abraham couches this complex thought with precision, "Wesley attempts to relieve the pain in the brain by claiming that God intervenes in everyone's life, giving them the grace that empowers them to say yes to his healing work in Christ."[71] This is brilliant, and Wesley's genius at this point is evident.

Thus, both at Qumran and in Wesley's Church the faithful obtain realizing eschatology. When the "living water" is obtained by those planted by God's Irrigator, the Righteous Teacher, the Holy One in the *Yahad* has, in the present, perpetual life. Likewise, when Jesus tells the Samaritan woman that he has "living water," he makes it clear that once one drinks of that water one has eternal life. Matthew's report that Jesus called us to be perfect (Matt. 5:48) is paralleled in John when Jesus, quoting Psalm 82:6, reminds his listeners that "you are gods" (John 10:34). John Wesley's concept of perfection is grounded in the biblical concept of *imago dei*.

Our thought progresses as we again imagine the world created by Charles Wesley's hymn "Lo the church with gradual light."

> 2. Fair as the unclouded moon,
>   With borrow'd rays she shines,
>   Shines, but ah! she changes soon,
>   And when at full declines,
>   Frequent, long eclipses feels,
>   'Till Jesus drives the shades away,
>   All her doubts and sins dispels,
>   And brings the perfect day.

III) The redemptive love of God and the fulcrum of inclusive grace

The third emphasis in Wesley's ecclesiology is the experience of God's redemptive love made possible by grace. This grace is offered in the present to all who recognize and confess their sinful nature.

Wesley may have known *The Fourth Book of Ezra* in which the despondency over Adam's sin reaches its peak in Early Judaism, following the burning of the Temple by Titus' troops. For this Jewish author, all descendants of Adam inherit this "evil heart" *(cor malignum)*. The author's voice becomes a scream, "O Adam, what have you done? For though it was you who sinned, the fall was not yours alone, but ours also who are your descendants" (4 Ez. 7:48[118]).[72] Surprisingly, a similar thought is found in Wesley:

No man loves God by nature, any more than he does a stone, or the earth he treads upon. What we love we delight in: But no man has naturally any delight in God. In our natural state we cannot conceive how any one should delight in him.[73]

The Jew who composed 4 Ezra had no answer. His questions are so deep and profound that one is allowed to watch Uriel admit ignorance. For Wesley, and for the anonymous Christian who edited this Jewish apocalypse by supplying opening and closing chapters, there is an answer. Observe Wesley's words that follow the above quotation: "To love God! it is far above, out of our sight. We cannot, naturally, attain unto it." How is love possible? In "God's Love to Fallen Man," Wesley argues forcibly that God has loved us and that empowers us to love, and especially to love others.[74] The sinner has a Savior, the Christ, who reveals and shares God's love and grace.

Common coin among theologians and biblical scholars today is the assumption that in the seventeenth century, and earlier, the English word for "love" was "charity." This misconception grows and allows experts to pontificate that the translations of the New Testament, beginning in the late forties to the present, simply restore the original meaning of the Greek not represented by "charity" in the King James Version of 1611. The numerous mistakes in such reasoning are removed by an attentive reading of Wesley's sermon "On Charity."[75]

St. Paul's word is ἀγάπη, exactly answering to the plain English word *love*. And accordingly it is so rendered in all the old translations of the Bible. So it stood in William Tyndale's Bible, which, I suppose, was the first English translation of the whole Bible. So it was also in the Bible published by the authority of King Henry VIII. So it was likewise, in all the editions of the Bible that were successively published in England during the reign of King Edward VI., Queen Elizabeth, and King James I. Nay, so it is found in the Bibles of King Charles the First's reign; I believe, to the period of it. The first Bibles I have seen wherein the word was changed, were those printed by Roger Daniel and John Field, printers to the Parliament, in the year 1649. Hence it seems probable that the alteration was made during the sitting of the Long Parliament; probably it was then that the Latin word *charity* was put in place of the English word *love*. [*Works* 7:46; italics his]

As every one should know, Paul penned one of the quintessential definitions of love. What did Wesley think "love" meant in 1 Corinthians 13? He is clear:

I am thoroughly persuaded that what St. Paul is here directly speaking of is the love of our neighbour. I believe whoever carefully weighs the whole tenor of his discourse will be fully convinced of this. But it must be allowed to be such a love of our neighbour, as can only spring from the love of God. And whence does this love of God flow? Only from that faith which is of the operation of God. . . .[76]

This text has been chosen to illustrate Wesley's point that the redemptive love of God flows from the believer to others because of the fulcrum of inclusive grace.

John Wesley perceived that the Church is where one forbears "one another in love." That means, in his words "sympathizing with them in their sorrows, afflictions, and infirmities; the bearing them up when, without our help, they would be liable to sink under their burdens; the endeavouring to lift their sinking heads, and to strengthen their feeble knees."[77] For Wesley these are not mere metaphors; they disclose the practical mission Wesley evidenced in his life, as he sought out those beyond the walls of a church.

Again, our thoughts are elevated, as we recall Charles Wesley's hymn "Lo the church with gradual light":

> 4.   Bright with lustre not her own
>   The woman now admire,
>   Cloath'd with that eternal Sun
>   Which sets the worlds on fire!
>   Bright she shall for ever shine,
>   Enjoying, like the church above,
>   All the light of truth divine,
>   And all the fire of love.

Summary

In summation, by revisiting John Wesley's ecclesiology with both Wesley's own words and Qumran and Jesus' time in view, we have learned much. Wesley's ecclesiology is constructed from the bottom up, defined by pneumatology, and inclusive. Wesley's thought is not constricting, lacking dogmas or walls. While it is not defined as a system, his ecclesiology is coherent and phenomenologically true—that is, it accurately re-presents the ecclesiological phenomena in which we live and have our being.

Our research has been independent. Does it clash or harmonize with the conclusions obtained by Wesleyan experts? Surprisingly, it parallels Outler's claim that classical Wesleyan ecclesiology is defined by unity, holiness, catholicity, and apostolicity.

In light of the crises facing all today on this fragile globe, it is well not only to recall Osama bin Laden's words quoted earlier, but it is imperative to cultivate the love for all others articulated by John Wesley. Wesley perceived that our globe is our mission. I am convinced that Wesley's ecclesiology is crafted so as to withstand the tsunami that may hit the little craft of the Church over the next millennium.

We Methodists do not crouch to peruse a dogma three centuries old; we gather and stand to sing that "The church's one foundation is Jesus Christ our Lord." Wesley's Church is an open world in which grace and wonder may abound. His ecclesiological reflections provide an openness that may evolve into the Church that includes all Abraham's children. His program and ecclesiology are harmonious with the origins of what would be called "Christianity;" that is, in the first century *euangelion* meant "good news."[78] Methodists join with others to share the good news received from God. In so doing, they should also learn from W. E. Sangster's ten new commandments that release the joy the People of the Book share, especially the final two:

> 9. Thou shalt enjoy peace. This peace shall not attach only to your
>   circumstances; it shall abide in your heart.

> 10. Thou shalt enjoy God; the knowledge that He is there and that He is
>   love; that He cares for all.[79]

T. A. Langford quotes these commandments and then adds wisely, "Joy persists through good and bad. It does not exist without a sense of the tragic; but it moves through the surface of life to basic foundations."[80] May the Methodist concept of Church be inclusive so as to share the joy and the mystery with all, especially those who are children of Abraham.

Conclusion

The Wesleyan holy space revisited. For Wesley the Church should be called "holy" for one reason. Here are his words: "The Church is called *holy*, because it *is* holy, because every member thereof is holy, though in different degrees, as He that called them is holy."[81] We have perused the adumbrations of this thought in the *Yahad*.

The future is bright for Wesley's concept of the Church. Four observations convince me of this conclusion. First, Wesley was focused on holiness and sought to help the individual grow spiritually. Second, this growth occurs within the Church where the believer experiences the presence of God's sanctifying love and feels the power of the Holy Spirit. Third, Wesley did not constrict us by defining the Church; he freed us to experience new dimensions of how and what ways we can experience God, especially as we gather to sing hymns of praise to our Creator. Fourth, Wesley's ecclesiology is now seen to be grounded in texts that he could not have know and thus his thought is anchored in the Jewish world that shaped the life and thought of the one he called his Savior. Wesley is important for our day and this new millennium precisely because of the power in experiencing the ancient commitment we share with Orthodox Christians and the present passion available in the mystery of God's love.[82]

In this new millennium we may find a way through the Charybdis of claiming Christians alone have the truth and the Scylla of compromising the foundational truths and invigorating zeal of authentic Christian faith. By steering this course we avoid creating a world in which terror dominates and allow the dawn of the age dreamed of by Isaiah, Jesus, John Chrysostom, the Wesleys, and Muhammad.

John Wesley's theology is an exceptionally good fit for the Church in the new millennium. Two aspects of his ecclesiology make this clear. First, he imagined the Church to be a universal Church, uniting all believers, and not constrained by a building or institution. While his original thoughts may have been focused only on believers in Christ, his concepts may be refocused to include all those People of the Book. Note a source for this development in Charles Wesley's "All Praise to Our Redeeming Lord":

> We all partake the joy of one;
> The com-mon peace we feel,
> A peace to sen-sual minds un-known,
> A joy un-speakable.[83]

As I have discussed our common heritage behind the ancient walls of Jerusalem, Jews and Muslims have made it clear to me that they also experience this unspeakable joy.

Secondly, John Wesley's ecclesiology is inclusive and not defined by orthodoxy or orthopraxis. His conclusion to the "Character of a Methodist" is programmatic and enlightening:

> And I beseech you, brethren, by the mercies of God, that we be in no wise divided among ourselves. Is thy heart right, as my heart is with thine? I ask no farther question. If it be, give me thy hand. For opinions, or terms, let us not destroy the work of God. Dost thou love and serve God? It is enough.[84]

For me, the "work of God" includes his revelations to Jews, Christians, and Muslims. With Wesley's perspicacity and focus we can come together and hope that the sons of Abraham—Jews, Christians, and Muslims—may reach toward each other and so define synagogue, church, and mosque as the Abode of God's People who love each other.

Endnotes

[1] The primary sources for this paper are Wesley's *The Works of John Wesley*, 14 vols. (Grand Rapids: Baker Books, 1996 [3rd ed.]). Other primary publications include Wesley's *Explanatory Notes upon the New Testament* and the 35 vols. entitled *The Bicentennial Edition of the Works of John Wesley*, whose initial editor was Frank Baker. Henceforth, *Works* = *The Works of John Wesley*.

[2] William Abraham, *Wesley for Armchair Theologians* (Louisville, KY: Westminster John Knox Press, 2005).

[3] Abraham, *Wesley for Armchair Theologians*, 83.

[4] I am indebted to R. P. Heitzenrater and C. R. Young for their studies of Eastern sources and the Wesleyan tradition, published in S T Kimbrough, Jr., *Orthodox and Wesleyan Spirituality* (Crestwood, NY: St. Vladimir's Seminary Press, 2002), 25–55.

[5] Here is a selected guide to recent publications on Charles Wesley: S T Kimbrough, Jr., *A Heart to Praise My God: Charles Wesley's Hymns for Today* (Nashville: Abingdon, 1996); S T Kimbrough, Jr., ed., *Charles Wesley: Poet and Theologian* (Nashville: Abingdon/Kingswood, 1992); S T Kimbrough, Jr. and Oliver A. Beckerlegge, *The Unpublished Poetry of Charles Wesley*, 3 vols. (Nashville: Abingdon/Kingswood, 1988, 1990, 1992); John R. Tyson, *Charles Wesley on Sanctification: A Biographical and Theological Study* (Grand Rapids: Zondervan Press, 1986); John R. Tyson, *Charles Wesley: A Reader* (New York and Oxford: Oxford University Press, 1989, 2001); and Carlton R. Young, *Music of the Heart: John and Charles Wesley on Music and Musicians* (Carol Stream, IL: Hope, 1995).

[6] *Works* 6:395.

[7] *Works* 6:396.

[8] See R. P. Heitzenrater's chapter in this volume. Outler and Heitzenrater are occupied with a doctrine of the church held by Methodists. I will focus here on John Wesley's concept of the church and on the original texts in their social and historical contexts.

[9] Abraham, *Wesley for Armchair Theologians*, 117.

[10] I express indebtedness to many insights obtained from M. Merleau-Ponty's works.

[11] *Works* 6:396. Reflecting his time, Wesley tended to judge the Church of Rome as not holy [*Works* 3:43] and to be inferior to the Church of England [*Works* 10.133–40]. He also has some harsh things to say about Knox and the members of the Church of Scotland [*Works* 3.253–54].

[12] *Works* 6:396.

[13] Ibid.

[14] Wesley quoted Origin in *Works* 8:93, 96, 97; 10.22, 27, 105, and 118.

[15] Wesley cited Augustine in *Works* 6:281, 323, 513; 7.170; 10.90, 91, 93, 94, 100, 111, 113, 118, 149, and 154.

[16] Wesley often used Chrysostom as an authority. See *Works* 8:92, 94, 95; 9:113; 10:1, 2, 265; 12:89.

[17] Wesley often discusses Calvin; he cites him in *Works* 10:206, 207, and 260 to 264.

[18] *Works* 8:42.

[19] The precise date is September 1745. See J. B. Richards, ed., *God of Our Fathers: Advice and Prayers of Our Nation's Founders* (Reading, PA: Reading Books, 1994), 5.

[20] Even though Wesley sometimes refers to the Church and other times to the church, I have tried to be consistent and use the lower case. This may help avoid the impression that Wesley had a set concept of "the Church."

[21] Abraham, *Wesley for Armchair Theologians,* 120.

[22] *Works* 6:392.

[23] Ibid.

[24] *Works* 1:319 [italics his].

[25] Ibid.

[26] See J. H. Charlesworth and L. L. Johns, eds., *Hillel and Jesus* (Minneapolis: Fortress, 1997).

[27] *Works* 1:324.

[28] See James H. Charlesworth, "The Wesleys and the Canon," Proceedings of The Charles Wesley Society 3(1996): 63–88, esp. 69.

[29] *Works* 6:392–93.

[30] Translation by Charlesworth in Princeton Theological Seminary, Dead Sea Scroll Project, vol. 1.

[31] *Works* 6:392.

[32] *Works* 6:396.

[33] *Works* 6:392 [italics his].

[34] *Works* 2:340.

[35] *Works* 8:341.

[36] *Works* 8:343.

[37] Charles Wesley composed this hymn in 1759. See Hymn 709 in *The United Methodist Hymnal* (Nashville: The United Methodist Publishing House, 1989); henceforth cited as *UMH.*

[38] Hymn 88 in *UMH.*

[39] Unfortunately, some leading experts continue to use the impossible concept of "realized eschatology," created by C. H. Dodd to nullify the thoroughgoing eschatology that A. Schweitzer attributed to Jesus. Dodd later lamented of his mistaken terminology and withdrew it. "Realizing eschatology" brings out the pregnant dimension of the breaking of the future eschaton into the present day.

[40] For further discussion, see Charlesworth, "An Allegorical and Autobiographical Poem by the Moreh Haṣ-Ṣedeq (1QH 8:4–11)," in *Sha'arei Talmon,* ed., M. Fishbane, et al. (Winona Lake, IN: Eisenbrauns, 1992), 295–307.

[41] Hymn 699 in *UMH.*

[42] See James H. Charlesworth, "The Portrayal of the Righteous as an Angel," *Ideal Figures in Ancient Judaism,* ed., G. W. E. Nickelsburg and J. J. Collins. *Septuagint and Cognate Studies* 12 (Chico, CA: Scholars Press, 1980): 135–151; see esp. 136.

[43] See Charlesworth and L. T. Stuckenbruck, *Rule of the Congregation,* 117.

[44] *Works* 6:400.

[45] Charlesworth, *The Rule of the Community,* ad loc. cit.

[46] *Hymns for Those that Seek and Those that Have Redemption in the Blood of Jesus Christ* (London: Strahan, 1747), Hymn 25, stanza 2.

[47] See esp. Abraham, *Wesley for Armchair Theologians,* 51.

[48] Charlesworth, *The Rule of the Community,* 47.

[49] Charlesworth, *The Rule of the Community,* 49.

[50] *Works* 7:275.

[51] The Greek word appears three times in Matthew but not in the other gospels. It appears 23 times in Acts and 62 times in the letters attributed to Paul. See R. Morgenthaler, *Statistik des neutestamentlichen Wortschatzes* (Zürich and Stuttgart: Gotthelf-Verlag, 1973), 93.

[52] See esp. J. Ferreira, *Johannine Ecclesiology,* Journal for the Study of the New Testament, Supplement Series 160 (Sheffield: Sheffield Academic Press, 1998); Ferreira points out that the ecclesiology of the fourth Gospel has not been sufficiently researched and the term "ecclesiology" is the best one to represent the Johannine concept of a "community of believers who are bounded together by their belief in the Revealer" (p. 14).

[53]*Works* 10:292.

[54]The hymn was composed in 1749; see Hymn 562 in *UMH*.

[55]*Works* 8:44.

[56]Abraham, *Wesley for Armchair Theologians*, 120.

[57]Charlesworth, *The Rule of the Community*, 47.

[58]*Works* 7:514.

[59]*Works* 7:515.

[60]Abraham, *Wesley for Armchair Theologians*, 35.

[61]Charlesworth, *The Rule of the Community*, 47.

[62]*Works* 6:393.

[63]Ibid.

[64]James H. Charlesworth, "Two Similar Spiritual Paths: Methodism and Greek Orthodoxy," in *Orthodox and Wesleyan Scriptural Understanding and Practice*, edited by S T Kimbrough, Jr. (Crestwood, NY: St. Vladimir's Seminary Press, 2005), 107–129.

[65]Osama bin Laden, "A Letter to America," in P. L. Williams, *Osama's Revenge* (Amherst, NY: Prometheus Books, 2004), 9–19.

[66]Wesley, "The General Spread of the Gospel," *Works* 6.287.

[67]Charles Wesley's hymn is from *Short Hymns on Select Passages of the Holy Scriptures*, 2 vols. (Bristol: Felix Farley, 1762), 1:298. I express appreciation to S T Kimbrough, Jr. for pointing me to this text, which is based on the Song of Songs 6:10:

> Who is she that shines through like the dawn,
> Beautiful as the moon,
> Radiant as the sun
> Awesome as bannered hosts? [TANAKH]

[68]Abraham, *Wesley for Armchair Theologians*, 64.

[69]Abraham, *Wesley for Armchair Theologians*, 83.

[70]*Works* 2:492.

[71]Abraham, *Wesley for Armchair Theologians*, 54.

[72]B. M. Metzger's translation in Charlesworth's *OTP* 1.541.

[73]*Works* 6:59.

[74]See *Works* 6:235.

[75]See esp. *Works* 7:46–47.

[76]*Works* 7:47.

[77]*Works* 6:399.

[78]In the second century, *euangelion* developed to mean "gospel."

[79]P. Sangster, *Dr. Sangster* (London: The Epworth Press, 1962), 150–151. I shall never forget the first time I heard the name "Sangster." My father had just returned from England, immediately after World War II. He had discussed theology with Sangster. Later at Lake Junaluska I met "Sangster" and heard him preach. No one seemed to note that a young boy had met this iconic preacher imagined from afar.

[80]T. A. Langford, *The Harvest of the Spirit* (Nashville: The Upper Room, 1981), 28. Quoting Tom, I recall the many years we shared together at Duke, from the time he was my teacher until our last days together as colleagues.

[81]*Works* 6:400 [italics his].

[82]Also, see the similar judgment of Abraham, *Wesley for Armchair Theologians*, 43. Note that Wesley was influenced by Bishop Erasmus (an Eastern Orthodox), and felt comfortable with pre-Nicene Christianity. Also note the words of Abraham: "Wesley . . . was Eastern Orthodox in that he saw human agents as genuinely acting through grace in the whole drama of salvation." Abraham, *Wesley for Armchair Theologians*, 103 [also see pp. 19, 42].

[83]Hymn 554 in *UMH*.

[84]*Works* 8:347.

5

Bulgakov and Florovsky: In Search of Ecclesiological Foundations

Sergei Nikolaev

Introduction

A friend of Father Georges Florovsky (1893–1979), E. L. Mascall, wrote that Florovsky once perplexed a group of theology students in England by starting his lecture talking about an "Orthodox lemon" and "Anglican zoology." Apparently, what Florovsky said to the students was "The Orthodox layman, when he first meets Anglican theology, thinks it is crypto-Nestorian; the Anglican layman, when he first meets Orthodox theology, thinks it is crypto-monophysite."[1] In a certain ironic way, this anecdotal situation describes the general predicament in which both Florovsky and Father Sergius Bulgakov (1871–1944) developed their theologies after 1922. These Orthodox theologians were among those who had to leave their native country of Russia in the first quarter of the twentieth century and pursue their academic careers in foreign countries and foreign languages.[2] If there was a doctrinal concern that guided the thoughts of both these theologians through their eventful careers, it concerned their new identities and their understandings of the Church.[3] Furthermore, in exile, both Bulgakov and Florovsky became deeply involved with the problem of disunity within Christianity and were among the early Orthodox leaders in the modern ecumenical movement.

Both Bulgakov and Florovsky found themselves addressing many similar sets of ecclesiological and ecumenical questions and analyzed them in similar ways. However, the conclusions they reached and the solutions they proposed in response to those questions differed significantly. These differences, and even disagreements, can be seen especially in the area where their ecclesiological thought is applied to ecumenical problems. In particular, these disagreements are apparent in the ecumenical actions each theologian proposed based on their respective ecclesiologies. Nonetheless, both Bulgakov and Florovsky were thoroughly rooted in the Orthodox tradition and were faithful representatives of it. Gaining an acquaintance with their thought and the details of their ecumenical disagreements can serve, if not as the source of solutions for the questions dominating present ecumenical thought, then at least as a way to immerse us in an environment in which the pursuit of the visible unity of the Church was a vibrant, creative, and urgent undertaking, with the hope of recovering parts of this robust ecumenical milieu for our time.

In this paper, I will characterize briefly the general principles that lie at the foundation of construing the ecclesiologies for both Bulgakov and Florovsky. Then I will discuss the ecumenical dimensions of their respective ecclesiologies. I will examine Florovsky's own practical proposals on how to work to resolve the problem of disunity in Christianity. I will finish my paper by assessing the legacy of Bulgakov's thought and Florovsky's thought for pursuing ecumenical questions in particular and questions of ecclesiology in general.

Bulgakov on the Church and ecumenism

In his last major theological work *The Bride of the Lamb*,[4] Bulgakov delineated three chief dimensions in understanding the nature of the Church: the essence of the Church (the ontological dimension of the reality of the Church), the Church as a sacramental and hierarchical organization (the empirical dimension of the reality of the Church, expressed in the fact of the historical existence of the Church), and grace (the interaction between the previous two). In these respects, the Church in the most general way can be described as

> the fulfillment of God's eternal plan concerning creation and the salvation, sanctification, glorification, deification, and sophianization of creation. In this sense, the Church is the very foundation of creation, its inner **entelechy**. The Church is Sophia[5] in both of her aspects, Divine and creaturely, in their interrelationship, which is expressed in their union. This union is a synergism, Divine-humanity *in actu*, in its eternal being and in its creaturely becoming.[6]

Hence, on the one hand, the Church is eternal as the Divine Sophia, and is outside of history and time; on the other hand, the Church as creaturely Sophia emerges in time and history. In St. Paul's letter to the Ephesians, Bulgakov saw support for his understanding of the Church as the foundation of creation. God "has chosen us in him before the foundation of the world . . . by Jesus Christ to himself, according to the good pleasure of his will, to the praise of the glory of his grace, wherein he has made us accepted in the beloved" (Eph. 1:4–5).[7]

In general, Bulgakov held that the term *church* is used in Scripture in two senses: (1) in the sense of *churches* in the plural, united by the unity of life, talking about communities of believers and (2) in the sense of the *Church* as this actual life, as one mystical essence.[8] It is precisely in this second sense that Scripture talks about the Church as the body of Christ, the temple of the Holy Spirit, and the Bride of Christ, according to Bulgakov.

The description of the Church as the body of Christ and the temple of the Holy Spirit importantly emphasizes the unity in the Church composed of multiple members.

> For as the body is one and has many members, and all the members of that one body, being many, are one body: so also is Christ. For by one spirit are we all baptized into one body, whether we be Jews of Gentiles, whether we be bond or free; and have been all made to drink into one Spirit (1 Cor. 12:12–13).[9]

Bulgakov pointed out that this and other ecclesiological texts typically describe the Church both in christological and pneumatological terms.[10] It is because the Church has this "dyadic character" that Christians are told that they are the body of Christ and the temple of the Holy Spirit, concluded Bulgakov. Consequently, one is impossible without the other, and any monistic ecclesiology is defective.[11]

What problems does Bulgakov's sophiological interpretation of ecclesiology resolve? In Eph. 1:23, Bulgakov pointed out, the Church as the body of Christ is described as "the fullness of him which fills all in all." This fullness cannot be applied to any creaturely being which is in a state of becoming, only to the life of God, the heavenly Church, the Divine Sophia. So the Church in the world cannot be described as "the fullness of him that fills all in all." Consequently, Bulgakov maintained that typical ecclesiology faces difficulty in this situation, whereas understanding the Church as the unity of the Divine Sophia and the becoming, creaturely Sophia resolves this question. The Church can be conceived as one body in reality, even though it has a creaturely becoming component.[12]

Bulgakov warned that there might be attempts to resolve the problem of unity and multiplicity by diminishing the ontological significance of this unity by turning it into a simile: like a body or similar to a body. In response to this threat, he insisted that

> the apostle speaks precisely about one body (Eph. 4:4–6), in direct relation with the unity of God. The Church is not a conglomerate, but a body; and as such, it is not quasi-one, but genuinely one, although this unity is not empirical, but substantial, ontological. Empirically it as yet only "increases with the increase of God" (Col. 2:19).[13]

The assertion that the Church is the body of Christ also implies that the Church, as the body of the true God and true man, is the Church as divine-human life.[14] The Church as Divine-humanity is a union of divine and creaturely principles without separation and without confusion. It is in this sense, the Church is a synergism where the divine principle descends to humanity and the human principle ascends to the divine.[15]

Ontologically, the limits of the Church coincide with the limits of the power of the Incarnation and Pentecost—there are no limits of the Church in the ontological dimension. The whole universe belongs to the Church in this sense. "The universe is the periphery, the cosmic face of the Church."[16] However, this description of the Church, while helpful to establish the essence of the Church, is not helpful for making apparent the interaction of the divine principle and the human principle in the Church. For this task, a distinction between the Church and the world outside the Church has to be made. In other words, an understanding of the Church in history has to be developed. It is in this dimension that the ecumenical questions take their shape.

For Bulgakov, the Church as a sacramental and hierarchical organization belongs to a concrete historical reality. The mystical Church facing human history inevitably takes on human relativity and limitedness. Consequently, it has to go on a path of certain development. Therefore, the Church in its phenomenal existence does not coincide with the noumenal Church. However, this circumstance does not mean that it is something negative. Without the phenomenal existence of the Church, the noumenal

Church would not be able to enter the time and history of the created world. Thus, the noumenal Church unavoidably connects with the forms of life in the world. This results, firstly, in the fact that the visible Church as a hierarchical and sacramental organization has limits that separate this Church from the rest of the world; it has a history. It appeared in the world at Pentecost, it has its own rules, and its structures appeared in history and develop in time. Secondly, it means that the power of the Church extends beyond the institutional Church: *ecclesia extra ecclesiae*.[17] The principle *ecclesia extra ecclesiae* in Bulgakov's ecclesiology is important not only from the point of view of understanding the nature of the Church, but also from practical ecumenical point of view.

The unity and oneness of the Church are among the dogmatic characteristics of ecclesiology. However, they are the characteristics that are based not on knowledge, but on faith, according to Bulgakov. Invisible unity, as the unity of Christ and the Holy Spirit, exists in the visible multiplicity of churches, where each has its own unique characteristics. In the empirical dimension of the Church, we deal only with the multiplicity of different local and national churches. The multiplicity of Christian churches is the result of disagreements, heresies, and splits, of which the split between the East and the West was the most damaging, according to Bulgakov.

When in ecumenical circles, the question arises how to bring the Christian churches together in one, as it existed originally, often people are seduced by the simplest, at first glance, solution; that is, all who are outside of the communion with the one true Church (each confession considers other confessions to be such) have to come back to the Church. At the same time, each confession considers its own historically developed church to be an adequate expression of the Church of the Nicene-Constantinopolitan, Apostolic, and Athanasian Creeds.

If you follow this simplified view of the ecumenical problem, all who are not in direct communion with the one Church are completely out of church life and deprived of grace. In such a view, there are no clergy or sacraments outside of one's own church. The problem of such a view is that it does not allow for a difference between non-Christian religions and Christianity outside of one's own church; that is, there is no distinction between the baptized and those who are not baptized. This situation, according to Bulgakov, contradicts ecclesial practice and the canon definitions, which always recognized how far a certain group was removed from the Church.

Bulgakov insisted that the Church distinguishes between Christianity and non-Christianity. The Church counts everything within the limit of baptism as its own. Heresies and schisms are possible only within the Church. Consequently, there exists an area for the Church outside of its limits, at its periphery, which is not within the limits of the Church but with which the Church has ecclesial connection. The visible Church includes the invisible Church not only outside this world but in this world as well.[18]

Florovsky on the Church

Through his involvement in ecumenical movement in the twentieth century, Florovsky had to examine his own understanding of the Church and come to a position that he believed was consistent with the Orthodox Church's position. Florovsky first became involved in ecumenical discussions in Paris in 1926 and later was involved in discussions in the late twenties and thirties at the Fellowship of St. Alban and St. Sergius in Oxford. He wrote of those experiences: "Both of these early ecumenical involvements of mine were of an informal character. By the nature of the circumstances there was not room for making decisions. It was a great advantage that the dialogue could be free and intimate, that one could be sincere and outspoken. We could meet each other in complete Christian freedom."[19] Thus, his involvement in early ecumenical discussions included primarily interesting, though sometimes heated, exchanges of ideas, and predated his publications on the Church and ecumenism.[20] However, by the time he attended the Second World Conference on Faith and Order in Edinburgh in 1937, he had already begun to work out his own Orthodox understanding of some of the issues that were central to the official ecumenical discussions.

One of the difficulties of working with the writings of Bulgakov and Florovsky is the vast quantity of their writings with repetitive or slightly varying content. Only very close analysis and discernment of the time of writing versus the time of publication can provide one with a sound way of determining a sequential development of their thought. This paper is not pursuing such an aim. Therefore, I take Bulgakov's and Florovsky's ideas as they presented them and use what clarifications they provide to flesh out any nuances explained in other works.

According to Peter Chamberas, Florovsky's ecclesiology presents a challenge to all Christians.

> The Orthodox Ecclesiology which Father Florovsky has systematically interpreted and elaborated for our time is precisely at this point most creatively challenging not only to Protestantism and Roman Catholicism but also to Orthodoxy in general, only because it is an Ecclesiology of the *Una Sancta,* the Catholic and Apostolic Church of Christ which is not a mere theological concept, but emphatically an historical reality existing in space and time with a definite eschatological dimension.[21]

Thus, although attempting to remain firmly within the Orthodox tradition, Florovsky, in facing new situations of the early twentieth century, came to a novel and creative formulation of the Church. It may have presented a challenge to Florovsky himself. Understanding Florovsky's ecclesiology is not easy, because many of Florovsky's works focused on highlighting the negative aspects of the ideas of others rather than a clear formulation of his own positive ideas.[22] Nonetheless, there are several articles that give us insight into his understanding of the Church.

According to Florovsky, it is difficult to have a definition of the Church. In fact, for more than fifteen hundred years the Church existed without a formal definition.[23] He did not find the earlier lack of a definition troublesome. In fact, Florovsky argued that there was no real need for a definition by the Early Fathers because "the most glorious *reality* of the Church was open to their spiritual vision."[24] Thus, he assumed that the Church Fathers did not need a definition because they all knew what the Church was in its most real sense. Naturally, this assumption is quite problematic to the twenty-first century mind. The fact that the circumstances under which these Fathers lived did not require a formal understanding of the Church was ignored entirely by Florovsky.

Nonetheless, based on his understanding of the self-evident nature of what the Church is, Florovsky argued that the Church can be understood only by being within the Church and participating in what he called the "Catholic mind." However, to participate in this experience of the "Catholic mind" of the Church, one must be in the Church. "The nature of the Church more likely must be represented and described, rather than defined. It is likely that even this description will be convincing only for those who are in the Church. The secret is revealed only by faith."[25] In this way, Florovsky created a closed definition that only those in the Church can know what the Church is, and even then, the representations and descriptions are based on experience and faith rather than any other foundation. Without personal involvement, the Church cannot be understood.

However, the experience cannot be individual, it must be in the community of the Church. "Personal convictions and even a lifestyle still cannot make a person a Christian."[26] The important aspect of the experience is that it is with membership in the community of the twelve apostles, "that is, in community with the Twelve and their announcement."[27] Moreover, "Christians are united not only among themselves, but before all else they *are one—in Christ,* and only this community with Christ makes the community of people first possible—*in Him.* The center of the unity is the *Lord,* and the power communicating and promoting the unity is the *Spirit.*"[28] However, this unity is not a human creation or even effected by people. Rather, it is the work of God. "Christians are arranged in this unity according to the Divine plan, by the Will and Power of God."[29]

Florovsky's description became more complex as he explains the relation of the community to Christ. Christ is the head of the Church. However, he is not in the Church nor is he over the Church. Rather, "The Church is *in Him.*"[30] However, belief in Christ is not sufficient to assure membership in the Church. "The Church is not simply a society of those who believe in Christ and follow Him or His commandments. It is a society of those who live and dwell in Him and in whom He Himself lives and dwells by the Spirit."[31] The members of this society have a new life and are set apart as different from others. Not only are their lives new, there are practices through which the unity is reinforced. These practices are the sacraments of baptism and the Eucharist.

> The unity of the Church is made complete through sacrament: Baptism and the Eucharist are two "social sacraments" of the Church, and in them the true sense of Christian "community" is continually revealed and imprinted. It can be said even more sharply: the sacraments constitute, establish the Church. Only in the sacraments does the Christian community transcend ordinary human measures and become the Church. Thus, the "correct administration of the sacraments" belongs to the very essence of the Church (to its *esse*).[32]

However, the Church is more than just a community of people united in Christ by God's will and unified by the sacraments. There are special attributes of the Church. The first that Florovsky noted was that of holiness. The Church is holy, a holy community. "The Apostle Paul with all obviousness uses the term 'Church' and 'saints' as connected and as synonyms. It is noteworthy that, in the New Testament, the name 'saint' is almost always used in the plural, that is, holiness by its internal meaning is social. For this name relates not to some human achievement, but to a gift, to consecration or to being made holy."[33] Holiness can come only from God, and, thus, it is God who makes the Church holy. However, more importantly, holiness cannot be achieved in isolation, only in the community that is the Church.

The Church is more than just a holy community. It is the body of Christ. "By the Spirit, Christians are united with Christ, are united in Him, are established in His Body. One body, that is the Body of Christ."[34] However, with the recognition of the fact that the Church is the body of Christ, Florovsky changed his initial choice of words. No longer did he want to call the Church a society or a community. Instead, he chose at this point to recognize that the Church was more like an organism. Thus, as an organism, "the Church is the body of Christ and His 'fullness.' "[35] Chamberas explained this passage as follows: "The Church then is Christ Himself as He lives and rules in His members, who in turn grow and are built up in and through Him. This intimate union which transcends the merely human dimension . . . is effected primarily in the eucharistic experience of the faithful who gather together with one accord and one mind in Christ and in the Holy Spirit."[36]

"The Church is the unity of charismatic life. The source of this unity is concealed in the sacrament of the Lord's Supper and in the mystery of Pentecost."[37] The Church, through apostolic succession, has historical continuity uniting the Church to Pentecost. Moreover, the Church has, as it were, "a double life—*in heaven and on earth*. The Church is a visible historical society and it is the body of Christ. It is both the Church redeemed, and the Church of yearning sinners."[38]

Thus, according to Florovsky, there is only one true Church. It is holy, and it has apostolic succession as its connection to the appearance of the Holy Spirit and to its historical continuation. The sacraments of baptism and the Eucharist are necessary activities in bringing about the unity within the body of Christ, "the organism of Divine Grace."[39] In *The Historical Problem of a Definition of the Church*, Florovsky wrote the following:

> One, holy, catholic, apostolic—these words are not independent of each other but intimately and organically interdependent. The Church is one by her "holiness"; that is, by the sanctifying grace of the Spirit. She is holy only because she is apostolic; that is, she is likened with the apostles in the living continuity of the charismatic life, disclosed in the mystery of Pentecost, which is the source of the Church's "holiness." She is catholic by the grace of the Spirit, which makes her one single body of the only Lord. Yet her unity is a unity in multiplicity, a living unity, as the Church is and must be—an image of the Holy Trinity, which is one God and the only God. Here is rooted the mystery of the Church catholic.[40]

The catholicity of the Church was the theme of another article by Florovsky.[41] In this article, Florovsky argued that the catholicity of the Church was not a geographical description, but rather an inherent part of its existence.

> The Church is catholic . . . because it is catholic all through and through, in any of its smallest parts, in any act and occurrence of its life. Catholic is the nature of the

> Church; the very fabric of the church body is catholic. The Church is catholic because
> it is the united Body of Christ, it is union in Christ, unity in the Holy Spirit, and that
> unity is the greatest wholeness and fullness.[42]

This catholicity is promoted in the commandment to love one's neighbor as one's self. Catholicity can be achieved only through love. All in the Church are called to strive for catholicity in love.

For Florovsky, the continuity of the Church was of great importance. He argued that the Church was an organism that transcended any particular time. This organic sense of active continuity is seen in apostolic succession, which because of Florovsky's understanding of the Church in time came to hold great importance for him. It is an example of the catholicity of the Church. "The catholic nature of the Church comes out especially brightly in the fact that the experience of the Church relates to all times. In the life and existence of the Church, time mystically is overcome, time, as it were, stops."[43] Time has little importance for the Church when considered in a broad sense. "The unity in the Spirit unites the faithful of all generations in a mystical way that defeats time. This unity that overcomes time appears and is uncovered in the experience of the Church, and most of all in the eucharistic experience. The Church is the living image of eternity in time. The experience and life of the Church are not interrupted or destroyed in time."[44]

Tradition, too, then plays an especially important part in the Church, because the "Church thinks about the past not as something that is no longer, but as something that is completed, that exists in the catholic fullness of the one Body of Christ."[45] However, only those in the Church recognize tradition as authoritative. Furthermore, tradition is not simply history, but rather, "the voice of God—not only the voice of the past, but the voice of eternity itself."[46] In this way, Florovsky's attention to the early church fathers becomes particularly important and clear. The transcendence of time and the entrance into eternity were the result of study of the church fathers and participation in the communion of saints. Furthermore, it provided stability for Florovsky in the midst of the changing and difficult present. "'Agreement with the past' is only a result of faithfulness to the whole; it is only an expression of the continuity of the catholic experience in the context of changing times."[47]

Furthermore, Florovsky asserted that, just as tradition has meaning and authority only within the Church where the Holy Spirit witnesses to its authority, Scripture too can be understood only within the Church. Neither Scripture nor tradition stands alone. When individual understanding or conscience takes priority over the Church in understanding tradition or Scripture, the Church is then hindered in its mission. Florovsky claimed that the "sin of the Reformation" was elevating individual conscience over the Church.[48] The call to *sola scriptura,* according to Florovsky, cannot find support in the Church, because the experience and tradition of the Church are vital to understanding how the Holy Spirit speaks through Scripture. With this view of the Reformation and of the Church, I turn to Florovsky's ideas on ecumenism.

Florovsky on ecumenism

From the information given above, it is clear that Florovsky believed tradition was a vital part of the Church. The elevation of the self over the Church, as Florovsky understood it, in the Reformation meant that individuals had placed themselves and their conscience over the body of Christ. For Florovsky, the submission of the self to the Church was one of the main activities of the Christian. Those active in the Reformation had rejected this most basic element of Christian life.

For more than two decades Florovsky worked actively in ecumenical discussions and in the establishment of the World Council of Churches. He came to realize that "There was actually no real agreement concerning the basic issue—the very 'nature' or true character of the unity which Christians are bound and called to seek."[49] Without a fundamental understanding of what the unity of the Church is or should be, little progress toward that goal could be made. Florovsky feared that unity might cease to be the goal, replaced by the goal of cooperation. "The ecumenical experience itself has shown that the encounter or confrontation of the divided Christian groups or communions, in their present state and form, cannot break through the deadlock of denominational diversity and of all sorts of isolationist prejudices unless the perspective is enlarged to include the whole scope of the Christian historical tradition."[50]

From these two passages, it becomes clear why Florovsky emphasized unity and tradition in his writings on the Church. In order to discuss Christian unity, it was necessary to have an understanding of what that unity is and/or should be. Additionally, calls for authority through tradition also needed to have a solid foundation for further discussion.

The position of the Orthodox Church that it is the one Church and that all other groups that call themselves the Church are incorrect was clear in Florovsky's writings.

> The Orthodox Church claims to be *the Church.* There is no pride and no arrogance in this tremendous claim. On the contrary, it implies a heavy responsibility. It is a constant reminder of inadequacy, a call to repentance and humility. In no way is it a claim to "perfection." The Church is still in pilgrimage, in travail, *in via.* She has her historic failures and losses; she has her unfinished tasks and problems. Nor is it just a claim. It is rather an expression of deepest conviction, of deepest spiritual self-knowledge, humble and grateful. The Orthodox Church is conscious of her identity through the ages, in spite of all historic trials and tribulations. She believes that she has kept intact and immaculate the sacred heritage of the early Church, of the Apostles and the Fathers, "the faith which was once delivered to the saints."[51]

In the article "The True Church," Florovsky affirmed that he, too, believes that the Orthodox Church is the true Church. "As a member and priest of the Orthodox Church, I believe that the church in which I was baptized and brought up *is* in very truth *the Church,* i.e., *the true* Church and the *only* true Church."[52] Because he believed that only the Orthodox Church had the right to call itself the true Church, his position concerning the ecumenical goal of unity was straightforward. There could be no reunion of churches. There was and is only one Church. "Christian reunion is simply universal conversion to Orthodoxy."[53] For him, there could be no reaching theological agreements with those who were not in the true Church.

According to Florovsky, the issue of ecumenism was first and foremost a Protestant problem, raised by Protestants due to the historical situation of their churches.[54] Thus, Florovsky questioned the involvement of the Orthodox Church in ecumenical activities. If, as he held, the only path to reunion was conversion to Orthodoxy, why participate? He came to view his participation not as an attempt to bring reunion by human means.

> I regard Orthodox participation in the Ecumenical Movement in the same way as missionary action. The Orthodox Church is specifically called to play a part in ecumenical exchanges of ideas, precisely because it is aware of its own role as guardian of apostolic faith and of Tradition in their full integral shape, and it is in this sense the only true Church since it knows that it holds the treasure of divine grace through the continuity of the ministry and apostolic succession; and finally because in this way it can claim a special place among divided Christianity. Orthodoxy is the universal truth, the truth for the whole world, for all the ages and all nations.[55]

Thus, Florovsky's ecclesiology was constructed to support his position concerning the identity of the Orthodox Church as the true Church. The emphasis on unity and on tradition and on historical continuity all strengthened his belief that reunion was not an issue that threatened the Orthodox Church. Rather, the value of the ecumenical movement was that it gave the Orthodox Church the opportunity to claim its identity as the true Church. It also, according to Florovsky, gave members of the Orthodox Church a forum in which to lead others who believed they were Christians into the "fullness" of the Church.

In evaluating his experiences in ecumenical discussions between 1926 and the 1960s, Florovsky claimed that much good had already come as a result of such interactions between representatives of different churches. He feared the exclusion of the Orthodox from future talks, but did not anticipate any significant moves toward reunion or unity in the near future.[56] His fears about Orthodox exclusion no doubt stemmed from his own stand concerning ecumenism, that the only unity that could exist would be conversion to the Orthodox Church. His view of the unlikelihood of much progress in reunion was no doubt related to the difficulties he had observed in the discussions over the period of his involvement in ecumenical activities.

Some points of tension

Having looked briefly at general ecclesiological and ecumenical positions of Bulgakov and Florovsky, it will be useful to look at some areas in which tension between Bulgakov and Florovsky's positions arises. In particular it might be helpful to look at the questions of the limits of the Church, and "partial intercommunion."

On the limits of the Church

Bulgakov deals with the question of the limits of the Church[57] in his programmatic ecumenical essay "By Jacob's Well."[58] In it Bulgakov challenges the dominant belief of the Orthodox Church that the limits of the historic Orthodox Church coincide with the limits of "the true Church," and all the other churches are "schisms and heresies." In the question of the relation of the historic Orthodox Church to non-Orthodox Christians Bulgakov sees a conflict between two religious authorities: "the harsh, unbending, unrelenting institutionalism of the one saving Church" and "a service in the Spirit, which 'bloweth where it listeth, and thou hearest the voice thereof, but knowest not whence it cometh, and whither it goeth (John 3:8).'"[59] In this essay Bulgakov argues that all Christian churches are, in fact, one body, one Church:

> The Church is one as life in Christ by the Holy Spirit is one. Only, participation in this unity can be of varying degrees and depths. Therefore, quite naturally, there are two aspects in the relation of Orthodoxy to non-Orthodoxy: a repulsion in the struggle of truth with an incomplete truth, and a mutual attraction of Church love.[60]

Attraction and repulsion, unity and division are all present in the Church. The way out of this antinomy of thesis and antithesis is not only "fuller realization of confessional differences" or only "growing consciousness of unity," but the understanding that "the Spirit of God" will transcend it "through a new kind of synthesis that is brought about, not by means of a new agreement or compromise, but by a new inspiration."[61]

According to Bulgakov's analysis the present situation in conceptualizing the Church suffered from overemphasizing the divisions in the Church at the expense of the actual unity already present. Consequently he seeks to highlight the limits of divisive elements in the Church and lift up areas that reveal unity. Prayer, the Word of God, the spiritual life, and the sacraments are the pillars of the actual Christian unity of the apparently divided Church.

Florovsky, on the other hand, is a representative of a different approach to resolving the ecumenical problem. In his later article Florovsky defends the view of Christian reunion as "universal conversion to Orthodoxy."[62] In "The Limits of the Church"[63] Florovsky finds the foundation for his ecumenical position in St. Cyprian of Carthage's doctrine of "a complete absence of grace in every *sect* [for Florovsky, in every non-Orthodox Church] precisely as a *sect*."[64] For Florovsky, reunion first of all includes "unity of mind" in the sphere of dogma.[65] Since all non-Orthodox Churches are "sectarians" or "heretics," the only reunion between the Orthodox Church and non-Orthodox churches is in fact the receiving of sectarians and heretics into the Church (Orthodox Church). "Is it in fact conceivable that the church should receive these or those sectarians and heretics into her own body not by way of baptism simply in order thereby to make their decisive step easy?"[66] In fact, relaxing the requirements for entry into the Church for sectarians and heretics is performing a disfavor to them from both the practical and theological point of view. The sooner a non-Orthodox believer realizes that he or she is not in the Church and has a desire to enter the Church, the sooner the Church will achieve unity.

The main problem with schism for Florovsky is the absence of love.[67] The fact that there is a schism already by its existence reveals that in this schism there is a will for disunity, and hence, no true love that seeks unity, for God is one. The problem with the sacraments in the sects is that they are valid, but not effective (unrealized).[68]

> It is the mysterious and even enigmatic sphere beyond the canonical limits of the church, where the sacraments still are celebrated, where hearts are often flame and burn in faith, in love, in works. It is necessary to admit this, but it is also necessary to remember that *the limit is real, that there is no union.*[69]

The facts in Bulgakov and Florovsky's arguments are similar but their judgments are diametrically opposite. For Bulgakov the most fundamental truth about the Church that its unity is real, the limits are only apparent; for Florovsky the limit is real, there is no union.

Partial intercommunion

Differences in understanding the nature of the Church resulted in the actual clash between Bulgakov and Florovsky when Bulgakov made a proposal for "partial intercommunion" between the Orthodox and Anglican members of the Fellowship of St. Alban and St. Sergius.[70] In a nutshell, Bulgakov conceives of the "partial intercommunion" as follows.

> It [intercommunion] started within the Fellowship among those Anglican and Orthodox members who, *on the basis of doctrinal agreement and understanding,* are prepared to go further *in manifestation of the unity experienced* between their Churches at the Anglo-Russian Conferences. *This does not commit other members of the Fellowship to participate in such an action.* It is . . . done on the personal responsibility of those Orthodox and the Anglicans in the Fellowship, who desire to do it. . . . a group of members of the Church, *who have already reached doctrinal agreement,* proceed to further action without waiting for the whole body of their respective Church to be prepared to share in this experience.[71]

Bulgakov's proposal at different points was opposed by some and supported by others.[72] Florovsky was, perhaps, one of the few members of the Fellowship who did not share the sensibilities of the majority but recognized the fundamental move that Bulgakov was arguing for and totally disagreed with it.[73] Florovsky expressed his original objections to Bulgakov's proposal in four main points:

(a) There is the greatest danger of taking the wrong road towards reunion, as Rome had.

(b) It is not sufficient to be in love and charity with all men, if this was mere human love. There is a lack of clarity as to the nature of a united Church.

(c) It is more difficult to be united in truth than in love.

(d) Could essential unity be achieved simply by agreement in formula and conditional ordination, having regard to psychological and spiritual differences between East and West?[74]

Florovsky's dominant criticism of Bulgakov's proposal accused Bulgakov of employing psychological reasons at the expense of intellectual and dogmatic ones.

Florovsky agreed with most of Bulgakov's points but denied his interpretation. There were two main areas in which Florovsky questioned Bulgakov's proposal. The first was whether Bulgakov's points, even in combination, were able to produce justification for practicing intercommunion in the Fellowship. The second was whether practicing partial intercommunion would be effective in fostering corporate reunion.

Florovsky clearly recognizes that the Fellowship has indeed experienced "love and charity" between members of the Orthodox and Anglican churches.[75] This is the starting point for Bulgakov's proposal. However, then Florovsky takes issue with Bulgakov's next step. For Bulgakov the fact that love, common prayer, and spiritual unity are experienced in the Fellowship is not a human achievement, it is a "revelation" from God.[76] "God calls us to action here and now."[77] The decision to practice intercommunion within the framework of partial reunion in the Fellowship is not a human initiative; it is a human response to God's call. "It is spiritually dangerous to continue forever in mere discussion of differences."[78] By postponing the actions of partial reunion and intercommunion we risk offending God. Florovsky cuts down this argument of Bulgakov's at the very root: the love and charity experienced in the fellowship is very nice but this is "mere human love."[79] Originally, Florovsky does not even address the question of doctrinal agreement, indispensable to Bulgakov's position, because his argument does not allow grounds for recognizing the presence of doctrinal agreement in Bulgakov's sense, since love and the experience of spiritual unity in the Fellowship are basically human feelings and emotions. In this way Florovsky denies revelation as a basis for Bulgakov's proposal.

Having challenged Bulgakov's claim of revelation as justification for his proposal, Florovsky attempts next to portray the proposal as unity "in love," opposing it to unity "in truth."[80] By dividing the realm of unity into love and truth, Florovsky characterizes Bulgakov's claims as void of truth, dogma, and, ultimately, reason, pushing Bulgakov's claims again to the area of psychological emotions and feelings. Instead, any discussion concerning reunion should start with "essential dogmatic accord," next it should be authorized by canonical authority, and only then should intercommunion possibly be considered, according to Florovsky.[81] Presupposed in this line of argument is the logic that if authorization does not come from canonical authority then the claims cannot belong to the realm of truth. Consequently, if the claim does not belong to the realm of truth, it raises the question of whether this claim is based on reason.

Finally, after depleting Bulgakov's proposal of its original meaning, Florovsky asks whether the proposal would contribute anything positive to the corporate reunion between East and West with their "psychological and spiritual differences."[82] In a way, Florovsky allows Bulgakov to apply his proposal to overcoming psychological differences between East and West; however, Florovsky argues there is no foundation in that proposal for effectively overcoming spiritual differences.

Even though Bulgakov was able to defend the integrity of his proposal for intercommunion and partial reunion, a majority of the Fellowship followed Florovsky in the concern that Bulgakov's proposal might precipitate the members of the Fellowship being denounced by their own churches.[83]

Conclusion

From this brief introduction to the ecclesiologies and ecumenical understandings of these two theologians, it is clear that at many points Florovsky and Bulgakov were in agreement. Almost all of their central points of ecclesiology are similar. The importance of the one, holy, catholic, and apostolic Church, of the Church as the body of Christ, the unity of the Church, the relation of the Church to time and eternity, and so on, all hold an important place for both of these men. It is striking that in being so close, their conclusions concerning ecclesiology and ecumenism were so different. What difference does it make?

Discussing the limits of the Church, Bulgakov insists that the unity of the Church is the real characteristic of its nature. Florovsky insists that the limits of the Church are fundamentally real, and there is no union. Both are talking about the fundamental nature of the Church. Is there more than one way of conceiving ecclesiology in the Orthodox tradition, or is it essentially one and the same way?

Clearly, in relation to the "partial intercommunion" Bulgakov and Florovsky showed that they themselves disagree about the practical application of each other's ecumenical understandings. Does it mean that their general ecclesiological constructions are also fundamentally different? Do Bulgakov and Florovsky hold fundamentally the same understanding of ecclesiology? Does Bulgakov's proposal of "partial intercommunion" indicate Bulgakov's "naivete and impatience"[84]? Or does his proposal indicate that Bulgakov's ecclesiological constructions substantially disagree with those of Florovsky, while both are faithful to the Orthodox tradition? What difference does it make for present ecumenical discussions? The complex legacy left by Bulgakov and Florovsky demands more careful, detailed analysis and still promises to be a fruitful area of discovery of the riches of the Orthodox theology, especially in the realm of ecclesiology and ecumenism.

Endnotes

[1] E. L. Mascall, "George Florovsky (1893–1979): Some Personal Memories," *Sobornost* 2:1 (1980): 69.

[2] At the St. Sergius Orthodox Academy in Paris both Bulgakov and Florovsky taught and wrote primarily in Russian. Florovsky, later, in the U.S., taught in English. Though "he became very fluent in English speech he never entirely mastered English pronunciation," recalls E. L. Mascall. Nonetheless, he was fluent enough to teach at Harvard University School of Divinity and Princeton University. Russian remained Bulgakov's primary language to the end of his life. Perhaps, this is one of the reasons why his works were not accessible to the non-Russian reading audience until recently.

[3] On this point see Peter A. Chamberas, "Some Aspects of the Ecclesiology of Father Georges Vasilievich Florovsky," in *The Heritage of the Early Church*, eds. David Neiman and Margaret Schatkin, 421–36 (Roma: Pont. Institutum Studiorum Orientalium, 1973) and L. A. Zander *Bog i Mir: Mirosozertsanie otsa Sergia Bulgakova [God and World: The Worldview of Father Sergius Bulgakov]* (Paris: YMCA Press, 1948).

[4] Sergius Bulgakov, *The Bride of the Lamb*, trans. Boris Jakim (Grand Rapids, MI: William B. Erdmann's Publishing Company, 2002). Originally published in Russian as *Nevesta agntsa. O bogochelovechestve*, chast' III (Paris: YMCA Press, 1945).

[5] This paper will not explicate Sophia and sophiology—a complex and controversial subject and the central aspect of Father Bulgakov's theological method, which was pursued by Father Bulgakov with the purpose of further development of the problematic of relationship between God as divine being and

the world as creaturely being. For the purposes of this paper, it will suffice to say that Father Bulgakov distinguished between Divine Sophia and creaturely Sophia. He described the Divine Sophia as "the life of God, the self-revelation of God" and "the heavenly Church" (Bulgakov, *Bride*, 257) and creaturely Sophia as "the world" and "the creation" (Bulgakov, *Bride*, 264). In relation to each other "the creaturely Sophia is the kenosis of the Divine Sophia. God's act of creating the world is a kenotic act within God first of all, in the general sense that God places alongside his absoluteness the relative being of creation. In that in his free and sacrificial love towards creation he kenotically engages in a relationship with it." (Bulgakov, *Bride*, 69). Quoted in Myroslaw Tataryn, "Sergius Bulgakov (1871–1944): Time for a New Look," *St. Vladimir's Theological Quarterly,* 42:3–4 (1998): 320, henceforth cited as *SVTQ*. For more thorough statements on Sophia see Sergius Bulgakov, *The Wisdom of God* (New York: Paisley Press, 1993) and Bulgakov, *Bride*. For a short summary, see the above-mentioned article of Father Myroslaw Tataryn, as well as Father Thomas Hopko, "Receiving Father Bulgakov," *SVTQ* 42:3–4 (1998): 373–385. For a longer treatment, see Zander, *Bog i mir.*

[6]Bulgakov, *Bride*, 253.

[7]Ibid., 254.

[8]Ibid., 255.

[9]Quoted in Bulgakov, *Bride*, 256.

[10]Bulgakov cites 1 Cor. 6:15, 19; 1 Cor. 12; Rom. 12.

[11]Bulgakov, *Bride*, 257.

[12]Ibid., 258.

[13]Ibid.

[14]Ibid.

[15]Ibid., 262.

[16]Ibid., 267.

[17]Ibid., 274.

[18] Sergii Bulgakov, "Tserkov' i 'Inoslavie'," *Put'* 4 (1926): 9–10.

[19]Georges Florovsky, "My Personal Participation in the Ecumenical Movement," *The Collected Works of Georges Florovsky, vol. 14: Ecumenism II: An Historical Approach,* ed. R. Haugh (Vaduz: Buchervertrieb-sanstalt, 1989), 170, henceforth cited as *Collected Works.*

[20]Florovsky's earlier writings that brushed on ecclesiology and ecumenism were primarily concerned with consequences of the Russian Bolshevik Revolution and exile.

[21]Chamberas, "Some Aspects," 421.

[22]Berdiaev in his review of Florovsky's book *Ways of Russian Theology,* focused attention on this aspect of Florovsky's writing. See Nikolai Berdiaev, "Ortodoxiya i cheolovechnost' " (Prof. Georgii Florovskii. *Puti russkogo bogosloviya*), *Put'* 53 (1937): 53–65. *http://www.krotov.info/engl/berdyaev/1937_424.html* Accessed January 2006.

[23]Ibid., 186.

[24]Ibid.

[25]Ibid., 187.

[26]Ibid., 188.

[27]Ibid.

[28]Ibid., 189.

[29]Ibid.

[30]Ibid.

[31]Ibid.

[32]Ibid., 189–190.

[33]Ibid., 190.

[34]Ibid., 191.

[35]Ibid., 192.

[36]Chamberas, "Some Aspects," 429–430.

[37]Georges Florovsky, "Tserkov': Ee priroda i zadacha," *Izbrannye bogoslovskie stat'* (Moscow: Probel, 2000), 193.

[38]Ibid., 196.

[39]Ibid.

[40]Georges Florovsky, "The Historical Problem of a Definition of the Church," *Collected Works,* 14:35–36.

[41]Georges Florovsky, "Kafolichnost' tserkvi," *Izbrannye bogoslovskie stat'* (Moscow: Probel, 2000), 141–158. For a version in English, see *http://www.fatheralexander.org/booklets/english/catholicity_church_florovsky.htm#n7,* accessed January 2006.

[42]Ibid., 144–145.

[43]Ibid., 148.

[44]Ibid.

[45]Ibid., 149.

[46]Ibid.

[47]Ibid.

[48]Ibid., 151.

[49]Ibid., 171.

[50]Ibid., 172.

[51]Florovsky, "The Historical Problem," 36.

[52]Florovsky, "The True Church," *Collected Works,* 13:134.

[53]Ibid.

[54]Florovsky, "The Quest for Christian Unity and the Orthodox Church," *Collected Works,* 13:136.

[55]Florovsky, "The Orthodox Contribution to the Ecumenical Movement," *Collected Works,* 13:161.

[56]Florovsky, "My Personal Participation in the Ecumenical Movement," *Collected Works,* 14:172–173.

[57]Some ideas of this and the next part of my paper come from my earlier article, "Spiritual Unity: The Role of Religious Authority in the Debates between Sergii Bulgakov and Georges Florovsky Concerning Intercommunion" *SVTQ* 49:1–2 (2005).

[58]Sergius Bulgakov, "By Jacob's Well" in *Sergius Bulgakov: A Bulgakov Anthology,* eds. James Pain and Nicolas Zernov (Philadelphia: Westminster Press, 1976 [Abridged]), 100–113; Russian original: Sergii Bulgakov "U Kladezia Iakovlia (Io. 4.23). O real'nom edinstve razdelennoi Tserkvi v Vere Molitve i Tainstve" in *Khristianskoe vozsoedinenie: ekumenicheskaia problema v pravoslavnom soznanii* (Paris: YMCA, 1933), 9–32.

[59]Quoted in Bulgakov, "By Jacob's Well," 101.

[60]Ibid.

[61]Ibid., 102.

[62]Georges Florovsky, "Confessional Loyalty in the Ecumenical Movement," in *Intercommunion,* ed. Donald Baillie and John Marsh (New York: Harper, 1952), 204–5; quoted in Chamberas, "Some Aspects," 433.

[63]Georges Florovsky, "The Limits of the Church," *Church Quarterly Review* CXVII (October 1933–January 1934): 117–31; Russian version: Georges Florovsky "O granitsakh tserkvi," *Put'* 44 (July–September 1934).

[64]Florovsky, "Limits of the Church," 117.

[65]Ibid., 121.

[66]Ibid.

[67]Ibid., 128.

[68]Ibid., 126–29.

[69]Ibid.

[70]For analyses of "partial intercommunion" see Anastassy Gallaher, "Bulgakov and Intercommunion," *Sobornost* 24:2 (2002): 9–28; Bryn Geffert "Anglicans and Orthodox between the Wars" (Ph.D. diss., University of Minnesota, 2003); and Nikolaev, "Spiritual Unity."

[71]Nicolas Zernov, "Some Explanations of Fr. Bulgakov's Scheme for Intercommunion," (1933?); Fellowship of St. Alban and St. Sergius Archives, Oxford, UK; Folder "N. Zernov's 1st Years of Work in England. Programmes of Fellowship. Bulgakov's Scheme for Intercommunion (1933)," 1.

[72]See "General Report of the Fellowship Conference, June 1933," *Journal of the Fellowship of St. Alban & St. Sergius* no. 20 (June–July 1933): 11–16; A. F. Dobbie-Bateman, "Partial Intercommunion: Summary of Positions as of 27th Nov. 1933," Fellowship of St. Alban and St. Sergius Archives, Oxford, UK; Folder "N. Zernov's 1st Years of Work in England. Programmes of Fellowship. Bulgakov's Scheme for Intercommunion (1933)," (November 27, 1933); "Discussion of Fr. Bulgakov's Proposal for Intercommunion," transcript of the Executive Meeting of the Fellowship from November 9, 1933; Fellowship of St. Alban and St. Sergius

Archives, Oxford, UK; Folder "N. Zernov's 1st Years of Work in England. Programmes of Fellowship. Bulgakov's Scheme for Intercommunion (1933)"; "Memorandum for the Annual Conference at High Leigh, June 26th–28th, 1934," Fellowship of St. Alban and St. Sergius Archives, Oxford, UK; Folder "N. Zernov's 1st Years of Work in England. Programmes of Fellowship. Bulgakov's Scheme for Intercommunion (1933)"; and "Report of Conference held at High Leigh, June 26–28, 1934 on 'The Healing of Schism,' " Fellowship of St. Alban and St. Sergius Archives, Oxford, UK; Folder "N. Zernov's 1st Years of Work in England. Programmes of Fellowship. Bulgakov's Scheme for Intercommunion (1933)."

[73]See Rowan Williams, ed., *Sergii Bulgakov: Towards a Russian Political Theology* (Edinburgh: T&T Clark, 1999), 269, n. 1 and Andrew Blane, *Georges Florovsky*, 65.

[74]Dobbie-Bateman, "Partial Intercommunion," in "General Report," *Journal of the Fellowship of St. Alban and St. Sergius* (June–July, 1933): 14–15.

[75]Dobbie-Bateman, "Partial Intercommunion," in "General Report," *Journal of the Fellowship of St. Alban and St. Sergius* (June–July, 1933): 2.

[76]"General Report of the Fellowship Conference," *Journal of the Fellowship of St. Alban and St. Sergius* (June–July, 1933): 12.

[77]Ibid.

[78]Ibid.

[79]Dobbie-Bateman, 1933, 2.

[80]Ibid.

[81]Ibid., Report of Conference Held at High Leigh, June 26–28, 1934 on "The Healing of the Schism," 1934.

[82]Dobbie-Bateman, "Partial Intercommunion," 2.

[83]See "Report of Conference."

[84]Florovsky, "Some Contributors to the Twentieth-century Ecumenical Thought," *Collected Works*, 14:212.

6

The Unity of Revelation and the Unity of Tradition

Dimitar Popmarinov Kirov

Revelation is a basic concept of the Christian faith. It is closely related to other fundamental concepts of Christianity, such as inspiration, truth, Holy Tradition, Holy Scripture, Christology, ecclesiology, pneumatology, and so forth. In this chapter I will attempt primarily to shape a vision of revelation as it issues from the experience of Orthodoxy. This experience reveals itself in the tradition, in the practical life of the Church. Therefore, in a way this will be an attempt at self-reflection—how one Christian perceives revelation in the Church, how it is expressed through the tradition, and how it is transmitted in history, and finally, what are its challenges today.

The unity of revelation

The idea of the existence of revelation is a purely religious notion. Its fullest expression is in the monotheistic religions. The unity of revelation is a biblical concept and is expressed as such in Christian theology. The main ideas of this unity are obvious from the teaching, doctrine, and practices of Christianity. In its depths, the unity of revelation leads to the certainty of attaining final truth—something given once and forever. In this sense, the unity, expressed in human vocabulary, has a historical and meta-historical dimension—its final solution is eschatological.

On the other hand, from the point of view of science, it is not possible to speak about revelation. For science, truth in large measure coincides with empirical data. Hence, the scientific approach more or less is defined by natural determinism. Revelation is put into the framework of history and is perceived only in a naturalistic, evolutionist way. This understanding presupposes that the Old Testament faith grows from primitive to higher forms. In this sense, revelation is apprehended predominantly as a concentrated, mythologized idea of God's presence in the world and his acts in the history. Therefore, revelation is somewhat like a process of growth of the self-consciousness of humankind.

From the point of view of the Old Testament, revelation has a personal character. It presupposes the relationship between at least two persons, an encounter between revealer and receiver. It is an intimate interpenetration of two personalities. As a consequence of this relationship, it touches many aspects of human nature. It starts with personal encounter (Ex. 3:14) and combines physical, physiological, psychological dimensions and culminates in spiritual heights. Therefore, revelation is accepted mostly on personal grounds; it is not usually a collective event. Despite the fact that God reveals mighty acts in the Old Testament to the people as a whole, those acts are a witness to God's activity but not necessarily to be considered "real" revelation. True revelation, as we speak of it here, transpires in God's encounter with the patriarchs— Moses, Joshua, the prophets, with chosen and charismatic persons. Understood in this manner revelation is akin to theophany.

For God's chosen people, revelation is of historical significance. The focal point of history is the Incarnation of God's Son and his saving mission (cf. Mark 14:49, 15:28; Luke 4:21, 24:27, 32; John 19:36; Rom. 4:3, 9:17, 10:11, 11:12; 1 Tim. 5:18). God revealed the whole truth in human and written form (John 10:35). This is the understanding of the Fathers of the Church. "For St. John Chrysostom, the Bible has its origin and existence in the Incarnation of the Son. 'As in the historical Incarnation the eternal Word became flesh, so in the Bible the glory of God veils itself in the fleshly garment of human thought and human language.' "[1] This reality presupposes the unity of revelation in history, as it is given to the human beings through the Scripture. Revelation, the foundation of the Scriptures and tradition, is not changeable; it is not dependent on the determinations of history and the development of humankind.

On the one hand, the unity of revelation is presupposed by the unity of God. The unity of God is implicit in God's oneness. God is revealed as One. One of the first revelations to humankind was that God is one (Deut. 6:4). Ancient Israel was chosen by God (Gen. 12:2–3) as a vehicle of revelation to the world. Monotheism, a central idea of the Old Testament, presupposes that the knowledge of God is possible only because God desires it. The knowledge that God is One is a common heritage of Jews and Christians. On the other hand, the unity of revelation in the New Testament is presupposed by the unity of the Trinity. This dogmatic formula, which is not rationally conceivable, is apprehended only through believing consciousness. The unity of revelation proceeds also from another dogmatic formula: the unity between the divine and human nature of Christ. These aspects of the faith are above all human reason, they are super rational but not irrational. Their certainty is based on spiritual experience, not on rational speculation.

At the same time, the Bible confirms that revelation is related to truth. Therefore, for Christians revelation is Christ-centered—Jesus Christ is the fullness of revelation, he is the final truth (John 14:6) and only through him is it possible to apprehend revelation. As a consequence, the unity of revelation in Christ presupposes that "Jesus Christ is the same yesterday and today and forever" (Heb. 13:8). This is why the truth is accepted by the believing society (the Church) through the final revelation in Christ.[2] Orthodox theology presupposes that revelation in tradition and in Scripture is not only a historically determined reality, but also is a spiritual reality, which is permanently actualized. It transcends all historical and natural determinism. This reality transpires through the relational aspects of the tradition and partly through the authoritative (ethical) character of Scripture, in the everyday life of the people.

In Orthodox theology, revelation is not simply an action between two or more persons, but with God. It is not simply the coincidence of two wills—of God and of human beings—or, only a historical event. It includes all of this but transcends every human notion. Through Scripture, revelation manifests eternity in history and beyond and at the same time makes eternity known to the human heart (Luke 24:3). Thus, revelation is not a static event, nor is it simply empirical data. Jesus Christ gives it totality. It becomes real and vital through the action of the Holy Spirit in the Church. Expressed in the Church, it becomes a historical phenomenon. Being historical, revelation is related to Holy Tradition. In this sense Holy Tradition is an external dimension of revelation, assuming different forms in diverse nations, cultures, and historical periods. Therefore, it is quite correct to speak about the unity of revelation in Holy Tradition and unity of revelation in the diversity of traditions. Hence, one must approach revelation in a holistic way. The relationship between revelation and tradition in Orthodoxy may be understood only in an ecclesiological way. Only by entering the Church through repentance and baptism and practicing the eucharistic life is it possible to perceive the unity and fullness of revelation. Only then is it possible to trace its diversity in the Tradition, as expressed through the traditions. Therefore, the holistic dimension of revelation assumes an ecclesiological understanding, which combines the christological and pneumatological.

Simultaneously, as mentioned above, revelation takes place in history—it becomes an objective reality, for it is given to human beings through Scripture and the Incarnation. As stated previously, revelation is not dependent on historical determination or the developments of humankind. But the unity of revelation depends on God's unity in the Holy Trinity. Thus, the unity of revelation presupposes the unity of the Church. This is why in the Nicene-Constantinopolitan understanding the Church is defined as one. Being realized in history, revelation expresses itself in the Holy Tradition and its forms, called "traditions." The Church through its Tradition (sacramental life), recognizes and actualizes real life from the mystical depths of revelation. So, in this way the Church canonizes and authorizes Scripture and Tradition and vice versa—Scripture and Tradition become the Church's authorities. Only in this way is revelation infallible. As human expression, revelation can be fallible. This is also true for the different practices defined as "traditions."

The unity of revelation in Holy Scripture as revealed in the Church

The Orthodox attitude towards revelation in Holy Scripture is not fixed dogmatically. It is the same with Holy Tradition. Nevertheless, in both of them revelation is accepted as a dynamic relationship. From the point of view of the New and Old Testaments the fullness of revelation is always centered in Jesus Christ. This centrality of Jesus Christ versus revelation is always actualized in his name through the Holy Spirit in the sacraments of the Church. The unity of revelation in the Scripture is not an abstract idea, it is not a philosophical notion, and it is revealed through the experience of the Church. As Fr. Dumitru Staniloae has written: the "cooperation of the Word of God and of the Holy Spirit can be observed, first of all, in revelation down to the time of its conclusion in Christ, and after that in the Church, in Scripture and Tradition."[3] In Holy Scripture the Church meets and recognizes, through her spiritual experience and teaching, the voice of God.

Going further, we can see on the one hand, that the unity of revelation in Scripture presupposes the unity and constancy of God. On the other hand, the unity of God in the Trinity presupposes the constancy and consistency of revelation. The constancy and consistency of revelation are also presupposed by revelation's eschatological aims. It is given by God in order to witness to the final truth revealed by Christ once and forever. The dynamics of the historical dimensions of revelation do not change the fullness of the revealed truth. In the historical process this truth can be interpreted in both correct and incorrect ways. This is the origin of the emergence of different sectarian groups and friction within the Church. The historical partiality of revelation, its empirical appearance, illustrates human diversity in accepting eternal realities. There is no human being who could receive the totality of revelation (Ex. 33:20; 1 John 4:12; 1 Tim. 6:16). The wholeness of revelation could be embodied only in the person of Jesus Christ. This is why on the altar of an Orthodox Church there is a permanent presence of Holy Scripture. It represents the presence of the truth among the believers in the Church. It represents also that believers are bearers of the revealed truth. This is why worshippers kiss the Scripture, venerating it. The fullness of this union between believer and revelation is expressed in its highest form when believers receive Holy Communion and, at the end of the liturgy, kiss the Scripture and return home. Only through this mystical union between God and human beings does it become possible for them to carry the burden of God's whole revelation.

According to Orthodox understanding there is not an external authority that can guarantee the truth given in revelation. The external forms (dogmatic formulas, canons, rules, and so on) are only instrumental. They are empty, if behind them is no real faith, which is met by God's grace, by the vital power of the Holy Spirit. In this sense it should be mentioned once again that revelation is not a static reality but a dynamic one. Despite its dynamic character revelation is given once and forever and cannot be changed. Its dynamism is preconditioned by human inconsistencies, by the sinful estate of humankind. Revelation is constant and consistent in its eternity, but is changeable in its expressions to people, or better said, in their spiritual perception. The fullness of revelation is comprehended more and more by believers as they ascend the spiritual ladder. Only through mutual interaction of the two wills—divine and the human—is it possible to comprehend revelation; it is a result of synergy between God and humankind—a common action between the Holy Spirit and the Son. Between them "exists a continuous reciprocity of revelation and both bring about a common revelation of the Father, and a common spiritualization of the creation."[4] This posture is close to the understanding of John Wesley, who saw the practical love of God as a way toward perfection. Following St. Paul's spiritual experience he writes: "He that being dead to the world is alive to Christ; the desire of whose soul is unto His name; who has given Him his whole heart; who delights in Him, and in nothing else but what tends to Him; who, for his sake, burns with love to all mankind; who neither thinks, speaks, nor acts, but to fulfill his will, is on the last round of the ladder to heaven...."[5]

For Orthodox Christians it is only the Church that mediates between God and the world. Therefore the Church, as a gift of God, comprehends revelation. The Church incorporates within herself, and at the same time reveals, the invisible God in Jesus Christ; through his humanity the Church reveals to the world eternal and final truth. Therefore, she contains within herself the final revelation—she holds the keys of the kingdom of God. She reveals God as One, and simultaneously as the Trinity. So, following New Testament revelation, it is obvious that the unity of God is not in mere oneness (as might be construed from the Old Testament) but in the Trinity. God, the Holy Trinity, is love. The unity of the Godhead is maintained through the constancy and consistency of divine love. The Gospel substantiates God's love— "God is love" (1 John 4:8, 16). In God love is perfect, therefore, it is permanent and unchangeable.

In human beings love is a task and a virtue to be attained through an enriched spiritual life. Observed from this perspective, soteriology is closely related to the idea of *theosis*. In its deepest sense soteriology is nothing more than an expression of the real, most high love of God. Soteriology is fulfilled in the act of love towards God. This is fulfillment of the first commandment of Christ (Matt. 22:37; Mark 12:30; Luke 10:27); and the second, to love one's neighbor (Matt. 22:39; Mark 12:31). So, to love God is the final goal of a Christian. Through love of God one becomes godlike and participates in *theosis* or deification. In the love of God and neighbor one affirms one's salvation. Therefore, the final self-revelation of God is Love, and as a result of the activity of God's love, revelation becomes a uniting force that moves from God to humankind and vice versa. Love leads to God and unites people with God and themselves to one another. This is also what the spiritual experience of the ascetics says. The contemporary St. Silouan the Athonite says, "real unity is possible only in love and through love."[6] Unity among people presupposes dynamic relations. It is not an abstract idea, but transforms mental ideas into spiritual *orthopraxis*. Therefore, revelation is related in its totality to Christ, while at the same time it mediates truth to the people. "Christ is the 'criterion' as to when the Holy Spirit is speaking in us and as to when our experience, 'inspiration,' is a false prophecy."[7] The Old Testament biblical law to love God, reconfirmed in the New Testament by Jesus Christ, makes the purpose of life and humankind theocentric. The orientation of the human mind towards God, to love God makes the human life theocentric. Through finding God's image in the other persons, society becomes theocentric. Then God abides in everyone and everywhere. This enables the spiritualization and transfiguration of the world.

The "fall" and tradition

The existence of the tradition, as we understand it today, is possible only as a result of the fall, of sin. With the fall of humankind, the whole cosmos, the universe, degenerated (Rom. 8:9ff.). Humankind is no longer in close relationship with God; God's face is far away. This alienation from God provokes a need of the manifestation of God's acts of love towards all creatures. People cannot see God any more; they see only divine attributes, or energies, in the natural world. Losing closeness with God makes people want to personify the divine energies in this world. Hence, the world becomes a variety of different natural forces (personalized pagan gods) that contradict each other. Consequently, the fallen state of human beings and their nature prevents them from seeing the basic unity of the world, its divine foundation. Only the acts of God in history, divine providence, and guidance prevent the world from falling apart. Believers seek to trace this activity of God, this providence, in the world. Tradition emerges through the revealing acts of God in history. In this sense tradition itself maintains and, at the same time, reveals the mystery of God, the Holy Trinity, among the people. As Benedict Englezakis notes: "The living and charismatic principle and reality of the tradition belong to the Revelation itself, is itself a divine gift and a divine manifestation, a divine work."[8]

From this perspective, tradition unites in itself all truth, revealed in Jesus Christ and leads to salvation through *theosis*. In the Eastern Church "the true and holy Tradition is not reduced only to a verbal and visible transmission of teachings, rites and institutions; but it is at the same time an invisible and actual communication of grace and sanctification."[9] Tradition allows the hidden *eidosis* of the whole universe, including the created and non-created realities, to become visible to the spiritual eyes. Therefore, tradition is more than a worldly phenomenon. It has the ability to transmit the intrinsic realities of the divine world among the people of the Church. It is God's initiative to manifest the Divine Self in history through divine grace. God's final manifestation is fulfilled in the Incarnation and permanently revitalized through the mystical life of the Church. As one of the legitimate and obvious consequences of the Incarnation in the Orthodox Church, tradition includes the practice of venerating holy images, icons. Iconography, as well as other art forms in the Church, shapes a large part of Orthodox Christian culture, possible only on the basis of tradition. In their endeavor to reach God, fallen human beings are searching for final reality, the reality that is firm and not shakable. This process creates the empirical side of tradition and enables the possibilities for the appearance of many traditions.

The rejection of tradition creates a one-sided vision of the world. The world becomes too mental, too rational, and too reductionist. Reductionism tends to multiply rational *empiria* and human beings feel lost. Mental desperation occurs when the mind realizes its frames of reference and limitations. We can trace this development in ancient Greek philosophy. St. Paul faced it in Athens—the Greeks did not believe him. Their skepticism was so intense that they wanted to perceive everything only through their minds—philosophy was for them the only possible means of understanding the world,[10] hence to understand the gods. Philosophers want first to understand and then to believe. The ancient Greeks did not believe their gods, so they had to initiate a philosophical process of understanding the world. Their initiative was based on the mind; they tried to rationalize the world. Hence, they reject Paul's perspective as foolishness (1 Cor. 1:20–25). In biblical revelation there is initiative on both sides—from God and from humankind. God's initiative, however, forestalls human initiative through divine grace. God comes closer to the people and reveals the Divine Self. People find, trust, and follow God. This is the process of *synergia*, of uniting God's will and human will. When the ancient Greeks lost faith in their gods, they tried reason. They wanted to believe after they understood. Today we often do the same. We try to understand the Bible, doctrine, etc., in order to believe. In Orthodox Christianity the conviction is still preserved that one must first believe in order to understand. This is in accordance with Paul's words that "we walk by faith, not by sight" (2 Cor. 5:7). We find similar perspectives in Methodist understanding and practice. John Wesley speaks of "enlightening our understanding" as a first step towards salvation.[11] One's approach to God begins with allowing of the Holy Spirit to enter the heart of the believer.

One of the challenges that Orthodoxy faced during the twentieth century was to explain itself to Western Christianity, to verbalize its own teaching and worldview. Among the major questions was "How does Orthodoxy understand tradition and its relationship to Scripture, the Church, Christian heritage (culture), and so forth"? Orthodox theology was radically challenged on the one hand by modern, Western biblical approaches to Scripture, to the texts themselves, to the content (the revelation), and history, and on the other hand, by new philosophical and social theories, such as liberalism, modernism, and secularization. These challenges were rather fruitful for Orthodoxy because they enabled it to re-examine its own heritage and to look back at its own patristic tradition. The answers were first of all needed for Orthodoxy and then for others. From this author's perspective, modern theological and biblical studies follow the old philosophical experience, trying first of all to understand, to apprehend through a rational approach, and thereafter to believe. As mentioned above, this way of thinking leads to subjectivity and skepticism,[12] alienation from God and no real and vital experience of God. This means that human beings rely first on themselves instead of God. This approach becomes too subjective and ecclesiology, christology, and pneumatology lose their meaning. Christ becomes only a human being, a historical figure to be treated only on empirical grounds, and the Church is turned into an earthly institution which minimally can provide some ideas of earthly benefits—to guarantee the social order and create a possible paradise on the earth.

This is a great problem for Orthodox churches in the post-communist world of today. There is an ongoing process of reversing priorities: Church and faith are considered by a great part of the society as something instrumental and ideological; they serve the ideology of the social order and become part of it. The Church and different Christian organizations are considered to be like all other secular institutions. Such an approach points to a lost spiritual relationship between theology and the Church. Theology is reduced to an ideology, and scriptural exegesis to a sort of philology preconditioned by philosophical assumptions. This situation occurs because it is taken for granted that the only possible solution is the rational approach.

To many contemporary theologians and theologies it is not easy to admit the relativity of the existing presuppositions in different theological assumptions. In much research of the Holy Scripture today the spiritual dimension is lost. Biblical research is based largely on rational and empirical presuppositions.[13] While biblical scholars may not reject it, often they do not like to admit the importance of a spiritual approach. Given the human philosophical or rational presuppositions, which shape much biblical interpretation, theology can easily become anthropocentric. Instead of God at the center of Scripture, one finds humankind. God becomes an abstract idea, no longer a personal God, One with whom one may talk (pray), even argue, agree or disagree. God becomes an idol of the mind. With this approach there can be the loss of the spirituality of tradition with its ecclesiological orientation.

The Tradition in the traditions

Following the Orthodox doctrinal heritage, Orthodox theology takes the stand that the totality of revelation is expressed through Holy Tradition and Holy Scripture. Holy Scripture is written Holy Tradition.

> The Orthodox do not consider tradition as something in addition to, or over against, the Bible. Scripture and tradition are not treated as two different things, two distinct sources of the Christian faith. Scripture exists within tradition, which, although it gives a unique pre-eminence to the Bible, also includes further developments of the apostolic faith—in the form of clarification and explication, not of addition. It is even more important that the Orthodox conception of Tradition, as distinguished from the various local or regional or even temporal traditions, is not a static entity but a dynamic reality, not a dead acceptance of the past but a living experience of the Holy Spirit in the present.[14]

Holy Scripture is canonized on the basis of Holy Tradition. Nevertheless, that part of the Holy Tradition that is not written remains Holy Tradition and consists in itself of the totality of the same revelation that is in Holy Scripture. Holy Tradition is transmitted in history through the Church and is preserved in the Church. Through it the realization of the organic unity between the ontological and empirical expression of revelation is fulfilled in living faith. It is an ongoing process of the verification of faith through the encounter and recognition of the truth in Scripture. This encounter is personal but not individualistic—it is always in the context of the Church. As Benedict Englezakis writes "Tradition is a dynamic principle of life, always young and always in need of rejuvenation, continuation, and progress.... The Tradition ... is not just history. It is revelation too, and not just revelation through history, but through history and word and theophany."[15]

In its sacramental life the Church is the recipient, guardian, and transmitter of revelation through Holy Tradition. In its sacramental life the Church unites the past generation with present-day church members. Through its mystical life she transcends the past and the future and makes them participants in the eschatological reality. Here it is important to cite comments of Fr. John Romanides:

> The believers receive without any hesitation the witness and teaching about God of the Prophets, the Apostles and the Saints, and they are satisfied with their words and thoughts. They avoid scientific and philosophical method of investigating God's grace and truth, because their spiritual leaders and fathers, the Prophets, the Apostles and the Saints were not intellectuals, who engaged in dialogue and search about the truth, but were eyewitness of the Godhead, Kingdom and glory of Christ ... [They] do not theologize in an abstract, intellectual way or dialectically, but spiritually, in the cloud of mystical Theology.[16]

This spiritual level is not possible for everybody; it is an ideal. Nevertheless, it is the core of Orthodox spirituality; it is the real way in which the Tradition is accepted and transmitted.

In this sense it could be said that Holy Tradition as revelation is always present in the different forms of the traditions, if they do not contradict the doctrine and the experience of real faith. It is important to note that if within the traditions a believing person recognizes his/her own faith, it is a sign that he or she is on a correct path. If the traditions contradict the teaching of the Church, this means that there is something wrong and the Church as an institution has the duty to preserve, to teach, and to cure. From time to time in Orthodoxy, problems arise out of diverse traditions that need decisions of the local church and, if necessary, of a convened council of the Church at large.

There follows an example of how a theological notion can provoke discussions among the believers and create problems, even temptations. Such a temptation may arise when believers attempt to answer a difficult spiritual question in an easy, rationalistic, or scholastic way. Very often the question is asked: Who will be saved and who not? Posed in this way the question is not solvable. It touches problems related to the correct transmission of Holy Tradition concerning the interpretation of the revelation of salvation. Temptation may emerge from the fact that Christians usually think that the main goal of the Christian faith is to bring persons to salvation. This purpose is proclaimed from the pulpit and is elevated to the highest task of life and Christian behavior. When this is emphasized as the sole Christian duty in life, self-sufficient within itself, it is a divergence from Orthodox teaching. It is an over-simplification of a very deep spiritual teaching. Understood in this way salvation is devalued and cannot be achieved. This perspective suggests that salvation includes something juridical, something that is possible only on a utilitarian basis. Salvation is put into the narrow framework of ethics, of moral behavior, of the relationship between people. It becomes more or less a function of social relations. The idea that the sole purpose of human existence consists in "saving" other persons significantly deviates from the central teaching of the Church. Christ's new order is to love God and one's neighbor. Salvation is only the consequence, the result of this love—of the endeavor to love God and to become perfect in this love (Matt. 5:48).

Tradition and the traditions as culture-formatting vehicles

One of the most valuable results of tradition is culture. Yet, there is reciprocal movement. Tradition produces culture and culture produces tradition. We can trace this in Old Testament Israel. The whole organizing process of the religious life of the Old Testament community is given in the Pentateuch. It is the same for the Church: the culture of a local church becomes a source of a local tradition. In this situation the local church culture is combined with the local social forms of life. Enlarging its influence, the culture is brought into homes and institutions and becomes an important factor in social life. This is an example of how culture influences society and extends itself. Thus it can be said that different cultures bring with themselves deep ideas often rooted in primitive cultic rites.

The Christian religion, as all other religious systems, grows through different internal contradictions and controversies. These usually lead to separations, exemplified in the Church by different confessions. Despite the fact that they have the same basic foundation, though often creating different attitudes about revelation, these different confessions create diverse forms of worship and rites. These differences often change worldviews, the understandings of religious community, and of spiritual sensitivity. There are changes of the experience of the higher spiritual realities and therefore different approaches to revelation emerge. In this sense culture appears to be an objectivized interpretation of revelation: it bears the stamp of culture.

Different traditions create different examples of culture. Culture is conveyed by literature, music, and other art forms. Therefore, culture needs interpretation, because it sustains itself, and within it are found the inner words of revelation. Culture, so to speak, witnesses to its roots, meaning, and tradition. In a reverse way culture leads back to tradition and revelation. Seen from this perspective, culture is preserved in different forms of tradition: language, literature, words, art, music, and architecture. Benedict Englezakis avers:

> Whoever says word, says language, and whoever says language, says tradition. For the word establishes a tradition in which it speaks . . . . The tradition is the interpretation of the word, in the sense that the word is significant only within the reality of the tradition. . . . I understand tradition organically, as a whole, which cannot be reduced to its elementary parts, the words, for it consists of the words *plus* their relations to each other as created and unveiled by the Spirit.[17]

Sometimes the same process of differentiation of traditions goes on in the same confession. As an example, the Orthodox culture, despite the fact that its roots and symbols are essentially the same, is different in its external appearance in different places. It depends on the local spiritual perception of revelation, of national character and psychology, historical circumstances, and other factors. This is a good example of how Holy Tradition becomes traditions. In this sense cultural forms are an interpretation, an exegesis of the very ideas that are hidden behind and within the traditions. It is an experience of common principles, of a common spiritual heritage and environment reinterpreted by certain historical, national, social, and linguistic determinants.

The role of the Church is very important in shaping the development of traditions into culture and vice versa. There is always a danger that local tradition may become something alien to the Church, to the tradition that gave it birth. The history of revelation in the Old Testament is marked by the endeavor for pure monotheism and the rejection of paganism and pagan faiths. The written form of revelation, the Scripture, provides its own means of self-interpretation. Therefore, in the history of Scripture the process of demythologization is quite obvious. The Old Testament scribes are trying to keep the essence of the message and to rid it of anthropomorphisms. This practice and tendency is clearly evident in the New Testament writings. At the same time, Holy Tradition is not like that; Tradition does not have a fixed codex. This is equally true of traditions.

As traditions become culture, or part of culture, they incorporate in themselves many external influences. In the traditions it is not possible to maintain a high level of church theology and dogmatic codification. As a result, the Church becomes more loosely connected and a new stage of mythologizing begins. A secondary culture emerges, which is built on a false interpretation of revelation. This is a sign of straying from the Church and revelation. The modern Russian scholar, Sergei Averintsev, describes this process as "secondary mythologizing." Such mythologizing is an ongoing process with which the Church is struggling throughout her entire history.

Today very often secondary mythology is vitalized through contemporary culture—movies, literature, paintings, and novels. Many elements of the Christian tradition are incorporated in such expressions of culture. They are conveyed through a fictional lens and misinterpret the tradition behind them. It is a continuing process of conscious rejection of the Church tradition, of reversing meaning and using it for the purposes of the new mythology. As a result a new, antichristian culture, which exploits the forms of Christian tradition, is born. The history of the Church and the history of Holy Tradition are presented in a false way, very often in a kind of caricature. The sense of the holiness of the world is lost and replaced by the sense that the world is nothing more then a place of different natural powers—the spirits of the fallen cosmos. Many of those ideas divert people from the real historical horizon and suggest pantheistic attitudes. In such a way revelation is rejected: God's presence in the world, God's providential and creative activity. "Revelation is part of the whole of God's economy and 'history of salvation.' Without history, the word is a chatter of men; without the word, history is a game of gods."[18] Therefore, it is vital for the Church to find the true means of transmitting to the new generation the real meaning of the traditions and the Tradition.

Today globalization enables the possibility of easy contacts and syncretic approaches towards different cultural patterns. In this jungle of ideologies and cultural trends, in this technological age, people need real answers from Christians. The rush after false gods means nothing else for Christianity than that Christians have lost the core of their traditions, i.e. the core of Holy Tradition, the correct interpretation of revelation. Nevertheless, Holy Tradition has a quality, which can assist today in a tremendous way: its essence is relational and hence it embodies the possibility of relationships. Its relational character presupposes revelation, revealing from one to another. As God reveals the Divine Self to people, so they must reveal themselves to one another. Through genuine relationships Christians will grow closer to each other and to God through the eucharistic life of the Church. The deeper we go into our traditions, the greater the opportunity to discover the true Tradition behind them.

Throughout history God uses all the means bearable by human beings, without hindering them but maintaining their freedom of choice, in order to reveal divine knowledge to them. Today the situation is not changed. The Church must find the appropriate answers to the challenges of external life in order to incorporate it and to bring it closer to authentic spirituality while transforming and transfiguring it. This goal may be fulfilled through the means of the traditions, as bearers and witnesses of revelation.

Conclusion

Today as the world experiences diverse "external unity" through technology, economics, and social and political change, the challenges facing Christianity are growing rapidly. Christians are becoming a minority; they cannot rely any more on external powers such as the state, big church institutions, or political influence. Therefore, there is a need to find mechanisms for solving problems in another way. Should this process be institutionalized or will such an institutionalization become yet another problem? This situation is not a new one; it has historical precedents. The globalization of today's world resembles the processes that appeared at the time of Alexander the Great. By conquering the East, Alexander mixed together many of the religious and cultural layers of that time. Something similar is happening today. We see different cultures meeting each other, causing the interpenetration and shaping of a new global society. Very often we call them different "traditions." As Christians we need to clarify the term "tradition" (with a capital "T" and a lower case "t") at least for ourselves. In the diverse reference books one finds different definitions of tradition for different Christian confessions. In a general way it is understood as "a complex of doctrines, practices, norms of behavior, cult and religious experience, handed down from the beginning."[19]

If we agree that we can speak in a general way for Protestant, Roman Catholic, and Orthodox confessional traditions, we can agree also that there are different traditions among those confessions. Thus, the question arises: Are those traditions something that unite or divide Christians? It is important to understand that other traditions must be viewed through the eyes of their members. One of the most interesting experiences is to understand the other and how she/he understands you. Here is an explanation by a non-orthodox writer of how the Orthodox understand tradition: "The concept of tradition is of capital importance to the Eastern Orthodox Church. For the Orthodox, tradition means in effect the life of the Holy Spirit in the Church, sustaining, quickening and directing all the Church's thought, prayer and activity. Tradition in this view cannot either conflict with or supplement Scripture, but must interpret it, and any doctrine or practice once securely established by tradition is virtually immutable."[20]

Without pretending to be perfect, this brief comment correctly represents the Orthodox attitude. But then one asks: Is it possible to understand each other in a verbal way—to express our ideas, theological notions, in a manner comprehensible to all? Is that enough? It would seem not! Unfortunately this is because we try to transform our traditions into the Tradition. This unfortunate practice leads to the phenomenon of understanding the Church itself as religion,[21] and simply accepting it as all other cultic societies in the ancient and present world, or even worse, merely as an ideological or societal institution.

Endnotes

[1]Veselin Kesich, "Criticism, the Gospel and the Church," *St. Vladimir's Seminary Quarterly* 10.3 (1966): 154.

[2]Following Orthodox understanding, it includes simultaneously Holy Tradition and Holy Scripture.

[3]Dumitru Staniloae, *The Experience of God* (Brookline, MA: Holy Cross Orthodox Press, 1994), 29.

[4]Ibid., 30.

[5]*John and Charles Wesley. Selected Writings and Hymns*, ed. by Frank Whaling (Mahwah, NJ: Paulist Press, 1988), 78.

[6]Archimandrite Sofroniy (Saharov), "*Pismo za edinstvoto na Tsarkvata*" ["A Letter About the Unity of the Church"] *Mirna* 25:139 (Sofia, Bulgaria: Prokrov Foundation, 2006): 139 [in Bulgarian].

[7]Ibid., 140.

[8]Benedict Englezakis, *New and Old in God's Revelation* (Co-publication: Cambridge: James Clarke & Co. and Crestwood, NY: St. Vladimir's Seminary Press, 1982), 10.

[9]Philaret of Moscow (1782–1867) cited by A. Scrima, "Révélation et Tradition dans la Constitution Dogmatique 'Dei Verbum' selon un point de vue orthodoxe," in B. D. Duprey, ed., *La Révélation Divine*, ii (Paris, 1968), 523–539. Cited in Benedict Englezakis, 10.

[10]In Orthodox theology there remains a suspicion of philosophy. It is considered more or less as an attempt of the human beings to reach God and to explain the Divine predominantly on the basis of the human intellect. This attitude provoked the great controversy that arose during the period of scholasticism and still exists today. This position presupposes the understanding that human beings can trust only in the human mind. God's revelation, grace, and so on, are effective only through their mental elaboration. However, the ancient biblical vision of the unity of world realities, the wholeness in the perception of the world, is still preserved in the East today. Orthodoxy maintains that only through the encounter of God and man is the revelation of the spiritual realities possible. For Orthodoxy theology is not philosophy; it is not love of human *sophia* (wisdom), rather it is the expression of God's love to human beings and vice versa. *Sophia* comes from God; it is divine and is imparted to persons through God's grace and their trust in God. Therefore, in the East there is no tension between belief and faith. *Philosophia* is not *ancila theologia*—both are incorporated into one vision, in the unity of the revelation.

[11]Geoffrey Wainwright, "Trinitarian Theology and Wesleyan Holiness," in *Orthodox and Wesleyan Spirituality*, ed. by S T Kimbrough, Jr. (Crestwood, NY: St. Vladimir's Seminary Press, 2002), 60.

[12]Veselin Kesich, 134.

[13]Ibid., 159.

[14]Petros Vassiliadis, *Eucharist and Witness* (Geneva: World Council of Churches and Brookline, MA: Holy Cross Orthodox Press, 1998), 11.

[15]Benedict Englezakis, 18–19.

[16]John S. Romanides, *An Outline of Orthodox Patristic Dogmatics* (Rollinsford, NH: Orthodox Research Institute, 2004), 87.

[17]Benedict Englezakis, 9.

[18]Ibid., 5.

[19]R. P. C. Hanson, "Tradition" in *A New Dictionary of Christian Theology*, ed., Alan Richardson and John Bowden (London: SCM-Canterbury Press, Ltd., 9th edition, 1996), 574, col. 1.

[20]Ibid., 575, cols. 1–2.

[21]Cf.: Petros Vassiliadis. "Holiness in the Perspective of the Eucharistic Theology," in *Orthodox and Wesleyan Spirituality*, 108.

7

Wesleyan Ecclesiology:
Methodism as a Means of Grace[1]

Richard P. Heitzenrater

At the Oxford Institute of Methodist Theological Studies in 1962, Albert Outler raised a few eyebrows with his lecture, "Do Methodists have a Doctrine of the Church?" The audience was not expecting the esteemed speaker to answer his own question with the hedging comment, "The answer 'yes' says too much; 'no' says too little. 'In a manner of speaking,' which is more nearly accurate than the other two, seems nevertheless equivocal."[2] But the audience on that occasion and two generations of Methodists since that day, have been intrigued and challenged by his and various other attempts to outline the manner in which Methodists understand themselves as a church.

Outler tried to outline what he called "the classical Methodist or Wesleyan ecclesiology" in four categories: unity, holiness, catholicity, and apostolicity, focusing on the acts of the gathered community of faith. This direction reached its logical conclusion in a 1987 consultation in Sweden with the topic, "The Church is Mission." There is a sense in which the Wesleyan movement in the eighteenth century was understood primarily as a particular mission within the structure of the Church of England. But the question remains whether Methodism as a church itself has a clearly understood separate ecclesiological identity.

The question was raised again forty years later at the Oxford Institute of 2002 by Dr. Thaarup, dean of the Överås Metodistkyrkans nordiska teologiska seminarium (Göteborg, Sweden) in a lecture on "The Praxis of Wesleyan Ecclesiology and the Effectiveness of the Methodist Mission in Scandinavia."[3] He contrasted the background of the Wesleyan movement in England with the subsequent development of the Methodist Episcopal Church in America, and then asked some probing questions about the nature of Methodism in Sweden. His paper looks at three defining elements of Methodism: its shape as a church, its nature as a small group movement, and its role as a mission to the world. Part of the problem, of course, is that Swedish Methodism is a derivative of the nineteenth-century American scene but planted in a context more similar to that of eighteenth-century Great Britain. The basic difference is the presence of an established church in Great Britain, which changes the social and ecclesiastical context and relationships.

During my teenage years, my father was pastor of the former "First Swedish M.E. Church" of Jamestown, N.Y., which historically has a largely Swedish population. Our

Methodist Church sat on a street corner one block away from the huge First Lutheran Church, part of the Augustana Synod, which was Scandinavian (the church in which my wife was raised). As you might guess, many of our Methodist members were Swedish. We had a Confirmation Class, just like the Lutherans. We had a Juletta Service just like the Lutherans. We occasionally sang hymns in Swedish, just like the Lutherans. Karen and I sang in the "A cappella Choir" in high school, which was directed by the Lutheran choir director, and we sang many religious works. That is as close as I have ever lived to an established religion on the American scene. But that situation does not come close to the actual situation in England, or Sweden, or Austria, or Spain, or many other places in the world, which have a religion that is politically or practically established.

The history of Methodism in America is not uniform, of course, and to characterize it as such is to miss the very real influence of regionalism on North American culture. The transition within Methodism from *movement* to *church*, from society to congregation, has been as variegated as the different regional environments into which the church has moved, as is the case within the spread of the Wesleyan movement around the globe. In every case, however, one common element in the transition from movement to church (often incomplete, one might add), is the tension, if not confusion, between a theological view of what the Church *is* and a functional view of what the Church *does*. One would assume that the theological view would have primacy, would be the grounding for action. There is a certain awkwardness in trying to move from function to principle, from activity to theological rationale. Contrary to appearances, however, I would suggest that in our heritage, there actually is a theological rationale that lies behind the functional view of the Methodist movement in the eighteenth century.

My purpose today, then, is to suggest a Wesleyan view of the Church and of Methodism that helps bring closer together the view of what the Church is and does, but focusing on the "is": Methodism as a means of grace.

First we have to say a few words about the traditional understanding of "church." Then we shall make a few definitional comments about "Methodism." Finally, we shall examine the meaning of "grace" and "means of grace."

Church

It is certainly true that Wesley spent very little time on the subject of ecclesiology, for (as he constantly reiterated) he was not interested in setting up a new church. He grew up in a traditional country parish church; he attended Christ Church Cathedral and St. Mary's University Church at Oxford; he went to St. Paul's Cathedral when he was in London—all of which were very good examples of the English understanding of what the Church was like. Wesley considered himself a faithful Church of England man until the day he died. In his mind, Methodism had a loftier goal. As he explained it, God raised up the Methodist preachers to reform the nation, especially the Church, and spread scriptural holiness across the land. The goal was to reform and renew the given institutions, not to replace them.

Wesley therefore generally accepted most of the Anglican tradition as the framework for his own thinking about the Church. When talking about the nature of the Church, he was often inclined to quote Article XIX, "Of the Church," from the Anglican Thirty-nine Articles:

> The visible Church of Christ *is* a *congregation* of *faithful* men in which the *pure word* of God is preached and the *sacraments* be *duly ministered* according to Christ's ordinance in all those things that of necessity are requisite to the same.[4]

This definition combines, to some extent, a view of what the Church is with what the Church does.

IS—a congregation of faithful people
DOES—the true Word is preached, and the Sacraments are duly administered

This definition, from the Thirty-nine Articles of Religion, provides the traditional principles for Wesley's adopted ecclesiology. But Wesley's principles do not always correlate precisely with his practice. One can almost always be assured that his praxis will take into account many contemporary cultural contextual conditions not necessarily anticipated by the framers of particular standards of doctrine, such as the Thirty-nine Articles. He always managed to stretch, emphasize, and heighten those elements of the matter that he felt needed special implementation to meet specific needs of the time.

Determining one's ecclesiology bears a methodological similarity to determining one's ethical perspective: that what one does in practice reveals what one actually holds in theory. Just as doing is related to being (what one does derives from who one is), so the Church's actions derive from what the Church considers itself to be.

The traditional Protestant doctrine of the Church, then, is somewhat limited in its conception of itself as a congregation of faithful who worship together (hear the Word and participate in the sacraments). Most churches consider themselves as more than just a worshiping community, though what they do may grow out of their common devotional practice, even if not consciously. But even within this somewhat minimalist and bare definition of the Church, Wesley seems to have a slightly variant understanding. While Article XIX talks about the visible church as a congregation of the faithful, in practice Wesley seems to have taken that view a bit further and considered the *true* Church as the *fellowship of believers*, a slightly more radical ecclesiology. Granted, when Wesley adapted the Thirty-nine Articles for the establishment of a Methodist Church in America, he replicated Article XIX, Of the Church, nearly verbatim. But the more radical view is implied in much of Wesley's practice within Methodism and is actually found now in the United Methodist Confession of Faith (dating from 1960 in the EUB tradition): "We believe the Christian Church is the *community* of all *true believers* under the Lordship of Christ. We believe it is one, holy, apostolic and catholic. It is the redemptive *fellowship*. . . ." This view seems to lean toward a more sectarian view of the Church (such as is found among the Mennonites and Amish) than the more catholic Anglican or Lutheran view. To have these two definitions side by side in our *Book of Discipline*—in the Articles of Religion and in the Confession of Faith—illustrates some of the present-day ecclesiological confusion and theological apathy in our denomination.

But before leaving the Anglican/Methodist definition, let us ask what "faithful" meant to Wesley—the congregation of faithful people. I recently spent a sabbatical leave trying to figure out the nature of "faithfulness," a term that we use frequently but seldom define. One obviously can understand what it means to be faithful to one's spouse, but what does it mean to be faithful within or to one's religious tradition? It obviously means more than not leaving it, in the negative sense, and more than just going to services, in a more positive sense. To assume that the phrase "faithful people" is equivalent to "true believers" (as found in the Confession), presents a much more sectarian view of religion, to which Wesley was opposed, in spite of the fact that he constantly made reference to the idea of "real Christians" as distinguished from "almost Christians" (a sometimes confusing distinction on which Wesley himself changes positions). Wesley comes very close to identifying faithful in a very literal sense: people who are full of faith. He refers to "faithful men" as "men endued with living faith," or "holy believers." In this sense, Wesley sees no apparent tension between an understanding of the Church as the congregation of faithful, or as the fellowship of believers, regardless of whether we see important differences in the two definitions.

Some of Wesley's lack of concern for precise definition on these matters can be explained by a careful examination of his conception of the nature and design of Methodism.

Methodism

The real tension in the eighteenth century was manifest in the way the church lived out its ecclesiology. In order to affirm one's acceptance of membership in the Church of England, one had to subscribe the Thirty-nine Articles as the list of one's own beliefs. One could not vote, attend university, hold public office, or generally participate fully in the civic life of the nation without subscribing the Articles. But Wesley had no subsidiary list of beliefs that were required of Methodists in order to join the movement. All that people had to profess, in order to join a Methodist society, was a "desire to flee from the wrath to come and be saved from their sins."

This simple desire was all that was required to join; but the requirements to keep one's membership in the Methodist society were a bit more complicated. Members must exhibit their desire for salvation by following three rules (the "General Rules"): avoid evil in every kind, do good of every possible sort to all people, and attend upon all the ordinances of God—that is, use the means of grace whenever possible.[5] During the early years of Methodism, Wesley was adamant in his assertion that true religion entailed more than being a good person, avoiding evil, and going to Church, and so forth. But he never denied that these represented the minimal expectations of a person aspiring to be a Christian. True religion might entail more than simply attending to the ordinances of God, but it cannot exist without that. (Just as he said that he was "a man of one book," yet later argued that one could not be a good preacher and read only the Bible).

These requirements for joining and maintaining one's Methodist status do not imply a doctrinal test but rather an eschatological focus with present implications.

That is to say, Methodism had a basic soteriological intent with specific expectations of the believer, including one's constant attention to using the means of grace. This soteriological focus was spelled out clearly by Wesley's statement in the Large Minutes of 1763, in answer to the question, "What was the purpose of God in raising up the Methodist preachers?" (Notice that the attention is focused on the preachers here.) The answer is well known and often repeated by Methodists in every cultural context: "to reform the nation, especially the Church; and spread scriptural holiness across the land."

This design presents an ambitious goal—reforming the nation and the Church. It also presents a very specific method—spreading scriptural holiness. This task is the primary responsibility of the Methodist preachers. In another place, Wesley presents the same focus in different terms. Listing his rules for the preachers in 1746, he says, "You have nothing to do but to save souls. Therefore, spend and be spent in this work. And go always, not only to those who want [i.e., need] you, but to those who want you most." Wesley spent a great deal of time focusing the work of the leadership of Methodism into what he considered the most efficient and effective possible organization to meet its soteriological goals.

One of the issues that became apparent in this organization was the nature and role of the preachers. In his sermon on "Prophets and Priests," or the nature of ministry in the church, Wesley makes it clear that the Methodist preachers do not displace the ordained clergy of the Church of England. Sacramental leadership requires ordination, and the Methodist preachers under Wesley did not have the educational certification required for the ordained priesthood in the Church. He thought they were certainly qualified, though not certified—his intent for and training of them was that they be "learned" in divinity. A well-furnished mind was one of Wesley's expectations for his preachers.

Prophetic ministry, however, had somewhat different requirements. The questions asked of those who felt they were called by the Holy Spirit to be Methodist preachers reveals Wesley's expectations rather succinctly: do they have the gifts, grace, and fruits necessary for the work?[6] Charles and John had some differences of opinion as to which of these requirements held priority over the others. When in doubt, John preferred that a preacher exhibit the grace of God in his life, while Charles was much more concerned about the talents and gifts of the prospective preacher. Both were convinced that the person should be able to exhibit the fruits of their calling in the lives of persons who had been changed by God working through their various ministries.

This view of ministry represents a more radical, spiritual view than that of the Church of England. Again, the Wesleyan view is quite ably stated in our definition of the Church in the Confession of Faith: it is the fellowship of believers in which the Word is *preached by persons called of God.* This specific reference to the movement of God's Spirit in the life of the believer, calling them to a vocation of preaching, is an essential part of a Wesleyan ecclesiology. And when Wesley talks about the role of the Holy Spirit in this process, and asks if these persons have exhibited the grace of God in their lives, he is calling attention to the most basic element of his ecclesiology, a focus on God's *grace*—as we have already seen in the expectation that the members use the means of God's grace at every opportunity.

We should remember at this point that Wesley's expectations for Methodism were not separate from his hopes for the Church of England. He was simply trying to help the Church fulfill its role and mission in the world. We can see this clearly in the basic point of his treatise, *The Character of a Methodist*. He raises the question, what is the defining mark of a Methodist? What is it that sets Methodists apart? He then runs through several obvious possibilities: their view of the Trinity; their view of Scripture; their view of Jesus; their view of worship? Of course, none of these things sets the Methodist apart from other Christians. Wesley then answers his own question. The Methodist is one who loves God and loves his neighbor. All right, he says, anticipating the reaction of the reader—but aren't these the normal expectations of all Christians? Why yes, he says, you have it right. These are the things that the Methodists actually do: love God and love their neighbor. What he is saying is that the genuine Methodist is simply a real Christian—he obeys the Great Commandment, by loving God and neighbor. Methodists actually do it.

Now we should remind ourselves that love of God and love of neighbor is the heart of what Wesley calls "holiness." So by defining the Methodist as one who loves God and neighbor, and the Methodist preacher as one who spreads scriptural holiness across the land, Wesley is saying that Methodism is simply trying to fulfill its role in renewing the Church in light of its basic intent. For Wesley, holiness was the heart of religion itself. As you know, he constantly equated happiness, or the goal of our creation, with holiness, and defined holiness as love of God and neighbor. In describing the "three grand doctrines" of Methodism, he described repentance as the porch of religion, faith as the door of religion, and holiness as "religion itself."

Love of God and love of neighbor become evident in the life of the church through two basic avenues: love of God through works of piety (worship, devotion) and love of neighbor through works of mercy (social concern). These are not to be understood as simply activities of individual Christians. Wesley recognized no solitary religion, that is to say no solitary holiness. Methodism is sometimes misunderstood as maintaining a focus on individual piety or individual holiness. But this is not Wesleyan. Wesley coined the term "social holiness" in order to counteract this misunderstanding of religion as simply individual piety. "Solitary religion," he says, " is not to be found [in the gospel of Christ]. 'Holy solitaries' is a phrase no more consistent with the gospel than holy adulterers. The gospel of Christ knows of no religion but social, no holiness but social holiness. 'Faith working by love' is the length and breadth and depth and height of Christian perfection. 'This commandment have we from Christ, that he who loves God [should] love his brother also;' and that we manifest our love 'by doing good unto all men, especially to them that are of the household of faith.' " This statement is a very good summary of Wesley's ecclesiology.

Wesley was also opposed to another view common among Protestants today. He despised what were called "gospel sermons" and the "gospel preachers" who preached them: "Let but a pert, self-sufficient animal that has neither sense nor grace, bawl out something about Christ, or his blood, or justification by faith, and his hearers cry out, 'What a fine gospel sermon!' Surely the Methodists have not so learned Christ. We know no gospel without salvation from sin." He goes on to say that preaching of the gospel must be accompanied by preaching the law—the expectation that the Christian obey the will of God. Christ came not to overcome the law, but to fulfill the law in his life of service to others. Grace does not do away with the law, but helps us to fulfill the expectations of God. Every command of God is a "covered promise"—an implied covenant. If God asks us to do something, God will help us fulfill that command. So when Christ says, "Be ye perfect," that is a promise that God will help us become perfectly loving.

Grace

When we say "grace," of what are we actually speaking? We use the term with great facility but with little actual understanding. It is often used in such a way as to imply some gift that God presents us to help cure problems or help us through hard times, such as medicine or a nutritional supplement. But grace is not a substance, a thing. Grace is relational—it is God's relationship with us, his activity in our lives, grounded in his loving attributes directed toward us. Wesley puts it very succinctly: grace "means that power of God the Holy Ghost which 'worketh in us both to will and to do of his good pleasure.'"

Grace is God's presence (that is to say, power) active in our lives. God's presence is always experienced (felt)[7] as power of some sort or other—not necessarily the ways in which we usually think of "power"—the exhibitions of might and glory and strength that humans equate with things powerful. There are other ways that power is evident: the powerful expressions of soft music in the final movement of Faure's *Requiem*, the power of a mother's hushed lullaby as she rocks her baby quietly in her arms. God's power can be experienced in a myriad of ways.

If we understand God's grace in this way, it helps us understand Wesley's soteriology more clearly as a theology of grace, as traditionally taught. God's presence/power enlightens us at the beginning (prevenient grace); God's presence/power judges our sinfulness (convicting grace); God's presence/power forgives our sins (justifying grace); God's presence/power empowers us (sanctifying grace). But these are not "four graces" or four different kinds of things. All of these are part of one reality—the grace of God, the power/presence of God working in our lives, to inform, convict, liberate, and strengthen us.

There are many other ways that we experience the grace or presence/power of God in our lives: redeeming, assuring, comforting, sustaining, directing, or perfecting us. We can also see how Wesley would say that we can only have faith through the grace or presence of God, which leads us into a sure trust and confidence and provides the evidence of things not seen, the assurance of which Wesley calls, "the witness of the Spirit with our spirit." This witness of the Spirit is yet another manifestation of God's presence/power (grace) in our experience.

Means of Grace

When we ask, what are the means by which we experience God in our lives, Wesley answers with two main categories: instituted means and prudential means. The instituted means are those traditional works of piety instituted by Christ and the Church through which we are brought into the presence of God: the Lord's Supper, fasting, prayer (and Wesley lists "religious conversation" in this group). These are the experiences that most Christians consider when they think of the "means of grace." But there are many more experiences through which we come into the presence of God, and Wesley refers to these as "prudential" means of grace, including those works of mercy through which we can experience the power of God in our lives, as Christians, as Methodists, as preachers, and as leaders. Wesley lists a few examples of these prudential means of grace:

> As Christians, following the arts of holy living (by rule, to grow in grace)
> As Methodists, attending class and band meetings regularly
> As preachers, meeting every society, leaders, and bands
> As Assistants, executing every part of your office

Wesley goes on to explain: "Some means result in no fruit, but some means always result in fruit: watching, denying ourselves, taking up our cross, *exercise of the presence of God*" (another way of expressing the reality of experiencing the power of God, grace, in our lives).

To these examples of prudential means of grace, we could add many other ways that people experience the presence and power of God: studying, preaching, teaching, singing, visiting the sick, the poor, the prisoners, and the elderly. Wesley explained the importance of understanding this aspect of Christian living as a means of grace very clearly to Miss March in 1776. She was a well-to-do woman whose upper class prejudices led her to be hesitant about actually visiting the poor, instead of simply sending them food, clothes, or money. She would much rather spend her time improving her mind, which Wesley generally would not discourage. But he saw an opportunity for her to grow in grace in new ways. He advised Miss March to value improving her knowledge, but as nothing compared to love.[8] He writes to her rather forcefully:

> Aim at love and you will not stop at the threshold of perfection. There are many blessings in life, but how do you improve them to the glory of God? And are you willing to know? Then I will tell you how. Go and see the poor and such in their own poor little hovels. Take up your cross, woman! Remember the faith! Jesus went before you, and will go with you. Put off the gentlewoman. You bear a higher character."[9]

Christ will go with you. Such visiting will be a means of grace to you as well as to them, for Christ will go with you to them. The presence/power of God will become known in your experience.

Methodism is designed by Wesley to help people experience the presence of God in their lives in many different ways. Both the organization and the program of their mission are designed with this purpose in mind. The organization of small groups in the Methodist societies, the classes and various kinds of bands, were designed to encourage prayer, Bible study, confession, and other works of piety to supplement the instituted means of grace found in the Church (the Sacraments). The activities of the Methodist societies also promote the prudential means of grace, seen in preaching, studying, helping the poor, and visiting the sick.

When we say that the Methodists helped the poor, we must remember that about two-thirds of the Methodists themselves were poor, about the same percentage as in British society as a whole. So the Methodists had a major task simply in taking care of the poor in their own societies. The one fact that is not often noticed is that about 4 percent of the members of the Methodist societies were in the highest economic level of society as a whole—namely, the rich. This percentage represents about twice as high a proportion as found in society in general. So that when Wesley talks about collecting food, money, or clothing for the poor, he is talking about asking those of the Methodists who had the means of providing these materials if they would give of their means to those who could not afford them. When he went "begging" on the streets, it meant that he was going to the homes of the rich in the society to help the poor. And his well-known rule as to money—earn all you can, save all you can, and give all you can—was applied in such a way that anyone was responsible for helping anyone else who was worse off than they, no matter how rich or poor they were. This approach was a way to express a communal approach to social problems, both within the Methodist societies and in the larger society.

The list of activities that Wesley organized shows that these are not just individual efforts. They include a host of institutional programs: medical clinics, loan programs, schools for children, subsidized housing for widows and orphans. These are community works of mercy, organized by Methodists, first for their own members but also for other people in the larger society of the time. In this very real way, Wesley's view of holiness, love of God and love of neighbor, works of piety and works of mercy, using the means of grace, becomes embodied in Methodism, which he views as the place where the Church can experience the grace, presence, power of God in ways that represent genuine Christianity in its organized form—the Church. Thus, Methodism itself became a means of grace, a religious community in which people could experience the power and presence of God's love, the part of the Church that was experiencing what the Church was intended to be.

We could give other examples of ways that people experience God's presence and power through means that are not traditionally understood as "instituted" means, but must surely be understood as "prudential" means of grace. Listen to a great performance of Handel's *Messiah*, with such magnificent sections as the soprano solo, "I Know That My Redeemer Liveth." You will find it difficult not to be moved by the presence of God. My wife and I sing in the 140-voice Duke University Chapel Choir, and every year we sing G. F. Handel's *Messiah* three times. A choir member told me an incident that happened a few years back on the Friday evening of *Messiah* weekend. A young Marine from Camp Lejeune, a few miles east of us, was visiting a friend on campus, who talked him into going to the performance—the soldier said he could only stay until eight o'clock, since he had to catch a bus back to the base. But once the performance started, he was captured by the power of the music and the message, and sitting there in the pew, was transformed by the power of God's loving presence and became a Christian. He subsequently went to Divinity School and is now a Methodist minister in Florida. He discovered in the experience that God can work through music—music can be a means of grace—and God's presence and power can change a person in such a circumstance.

Wesley often speaks of the reality of grace in the midst of the Methodist activities, recording often in his Journal, "and God was with us." Methodism was and can be a means of reforming and renewing the Church, not just by what we decide to do, but by our becoming channels of God's grace and responding to God's presence and power in us and in the world. Wesley saw Methodism itself as a means by which God's presence could become more vital in the lives of individuals, in the fellowship of believers, in the Church, and in the nation or the world.

Wesley himself, to an exceptional extent, tried to live constantly in the presence and power of God, attending always to the ordinances of God, understood as widely as possible. This approach is evident in the question he asked himself every hour: Have I said or done anything without a present or previous perception of its direct or remote tendency to the glory of God? His constant attempt to remain open to the grace of God in the life of the church can be seen in his encouraging people to "exercise the presence of God." And Methodism, as the extended shadow of Wesley himself, can be seen as a movement organized to be a collective means of grace to members and to the world.

Wesley would be one to admit that he (or we) might not always feel the constant presence of God, especially when we become solitary or prideful in our religious experience. But he also was aware that even in those moments, we remain a member of the community of faith and that God does not abandon us.[10]

At end of life, we see his final testimony to the reality of grace at the heart of the Christian life in the community of faith. His lifelong spiritual pilgrimage in the presence of God lies behind his witness to the reality and priority of God's grace encapsulated by his last words, "The best of all is, God is with us."

Endnotes

[1]This paper was originally delivered as The Källstad Lecture at the Överås Metodistkyrkans nordiska teologiska seminarium, Göteborg, Sweden, May 24, 2005.

[2]Albert C. Outler, "Do Methodists Have a Doctrine of the Church?" in Dow Kirkpatrick, ed., *The Doctrine of the Church* (Nashville: Abingdon Press, 1964), 11.

[3]See: *http://oxford-institute.org/site/2002papers/2002–8Thaarup.pdf.*

[4]Author's italics for emphasis.

[5]*The Nature, Design, and General Rules* lists examples of the ordinances of God: "the public worship of God; the ministry of the word, either read or expounded; the supper of the Lord; family and private prayer; searching the Scriptures; and fasting, or abstinence.

[6]See Wesley's understanding of the ministry of the Church of England in his "Address to the Clergy," which reflects his requirements for Methodist preachers.

[7]See Wesley's letter to him mother in 1725, where he expresses a conviction that if one is forgiven of sins by God, one must surely sense or feel it.

[8]See Wesley's comment, "Knowledge without love is but learned ignorance."

[9]See Wesley's letter to Miss March, June 1776.

[10]See his letter of June 1766, to Charles: "This is the mystery. . . ."

Wesleyan Ecclesiology: Charles Wesley's Understanding of the Nature of the Church

S T Kimbrough, Jr.

Like his brother John, Charles Wesley did not write extended treatises on ecclesiology. Clearly both of the brothers accepted the premise of Article XIX of the Articles of Religion of the Church of England, which stated: "The visible Church of Christ is a congregation of faithful men, in which the pure word of God is preached, and the sacraments duly administered according to Christ's ordinances in all those things that of necessity are requisite to the same." Therefore, neither felt the need to write ecclesiological treatises. Both, however, express at times explicit views of the Church. Charles does so especially in his hymns and sacred poems, which reflect his belief in the apostolicity, catholicity, unity, and holiness of the Church, attributes of the Church I explore in this chapter.

The nature of the Church

Apostolicity is at the heart of Charles Wesley's theology of the Church.[1] In *Short Hymns on Select Passages of the Holy Scriptures* (1762)[2] he suggests a strong adherence to the principle of apostolic succession, namely, the historic line of ordained clergy that originated in the New Testament but was rooted in the priesthood of Moses and Aaron, and passed down through the ages via the early church.

> Impower'd thro' Moses's hallowing hands,
> Aaron before the altar stands,
>   The consecrated priest of God!
> Jesus *his* officers ordains:
> And thus the *Christian* priest obtains
>   The gift of elders' hands bestowed.[3]

Wesley held fast to apostolic succession, within which the Church of England stood, and he was clear that the separation from Rome did not originate as an ecclesiastical one. Charles's posture on apostolic succession led him to oppose his brother John's "ordination" of superintendents ("bishops") for America in 1784.

Hebrews 5:4, "No man taketh this honor unto himself, but he that is called of God, as was Aaron," precipitates the above-quoted lines, expressing in part Charles Wesley's sentiments on ordination. The second stanza of the same hymn makes clear his opposition to dissenting views.

The *catholicity* of the Church is also emphasized strongly by Charles Wesley. While the Church is the body of Christ and includes those who believe in him and follow him, Wesley envisions

> A church to comprehend
> > The whole of human race,
> And live in joys that never end
> > Before thy glorious face.[4]

The all-encompassing "whole of human race" is the Wesleyan view of the Church universal. From Charles Wesley's perspective the Church universal is not, however, merely an "earthbound" church. As God's Church, it is not limited to time and space.

> One family we dwell in him,
> > One church above, beneath,
> Though now divided by the stream,
> > The narrow stream of death.[5]

In "Christ from whom all blessings flow" he also makes very explicit the *unity* of the Church.

> Many are we now, and one,
> We who Jesus have put on;
> There is neither bond nor free,
> Male nor female, Lord, in thee.
>
> Love, like death, hath all destroyed,
> Rendered all distinctions void:
> Names and sects and parties fall;
> Thou, O Christ, art all in all![6]

Earlier in the same poem he prays, "Join us in one spirit, join." Wesley knows that unity resides in God's grace: "Jesus, united by thy grace, / and each to each endeared." The Church of Jesus Christ is a grace-united church.

Holiness is also a distinctive aspect of the nature of the Church. Wesley formulates a prayer that should be the constant prayer of the Church in any age—to reform the nation and spread scriptural holiness throughout the land:

> Jesus, we wait to see
> > That spotless church of thine,
> The heaven-appointed ministry,
> > The hierarchy divine;
> > Command her now to rise
> > With perfect beauty pure,
> Long as the new-made earth and skies
> > To flourish and endure.[7]

How does the Church demonstrate or live out its apostolicity, catholicity, unity, and holiness? If it exists by God's grace, it is a means of the realization of that grace in the world. John Wesley understood the Church to be a fellowship of believers, a redemptive fellowship, which impacted not only its members, but also the community at large. Thus the Church is defined not only by what it is but by what it does— how it implements what it is by nature. In the *General Rules* one learns that Methodist believers are to avoid evil, do good, and attend to the ordinances of the church. Thus, it is not surprising to find Charles Wesley emphasizing how the Church realizes its nature.

> Let us for each other care,
> Each the other's burdens bear;
> To thy church the pattern give,
> Show how true believers live.[8]

For Charles Wesley, at the heart of the realization of all aspects of the Church's nature is love of God and love of neighbor.

He does not perceive of the Church, however, as being perfect. No, it is imperfect, because it is filled with those going on to perfection. One of his finest poems, "Lo, the church with gradual light," illustrates this understanding. In it Wesley describes the Church's penultimate state on earth despite its eschatological character. The church endures "a long dreary night." The penultimate reality of the Church is like the moon, which shines with the borrowed rays of the sun. Like the moon, the Church has frequent eclipses. It is only the light of Jesus Christ that dispels the darkness. The Church's eschatological hope, however, is that Christ will come again to purify it.

> Now she without spot appears,
> For Christ appears again,
> Sun of righteousness, he clears
> His church from every stain.[9]

Wesley continues his interpretation of the eschatological hope of the Church with these words:

> Bright she shall for ever shine,
> Enjoying, like the church above,
> All the light of truth divine,
> And all the fire of love.[10]

The Church is also born of the Spirit, united in Christ, and in the Eucharist one experiences the "perfect harmony" of the Church.

> Who thy mysterious supper share,
> Here at thy table fed,
> Many, and yet but one we are,
> One undivided bread.[11]

Wesley emphasizes the centrality of *theosis* in the mystical body at the table. We are "One with the Living Bread Divine." Our hearts, minds, and spirits all meet and are joined in Jesus. As intimate as the bond in Christ may be on earth, however, it is but a foreshadowing of the close tie that shall bind the Church eternal.

> And if our fellowship below
>> In Jesus be so sweet,
> What height of rapture shall we know
>> When round his throne we meet.[12]

Wesley stresses the unity of the mystical body of the Church in these words.

> Born of the Spirit and the word,
> Are we not brethren in the Lord,
> Flesh of his flesh, bone of his bone,
> His body mystical and One![13]

Wesley writes numerous poems about the unity of the body of Christ, indeed it is a primary theme of his life and ministry. He prays some of the most eloquent prayers for Christian unity to be found in the English language.

> Make us of one heart and mind,
> Gentle, courteous, and kind,
> Lowly, meek in thought and word,
> Altogether like our Lord.[14]

And

> Giver of peace and unity,
>> Send down thy mind, pacific Dove;
> We shall then in one agree,
>> And breathe the Spirit of thy love.[15]

Finally, Charles Wesley emphasizes that the Church is called to mission. In the inspiring poem "Give me the faith which can remove / The mountain to the plain," he articulates many dimensions of the Church's commitment to mission. In one stanza, however, he defines a two-fold purpose, timely for the Church in any age. All of the members of Christ's body, the Church, commit

> To spend and to be spent for them
>> Who have not yet my Savior known,
> Fully on these my mission prove,
> And only breathe, to breathe thy love.[16]

The two-fold purpose is: (1) evangelism, the sharing of the good news of Jesus Christ, and (2) living a life of personified love as a eucharistic community. One fulfills both purposes in the context of the fellowship of the Church, not in isolation. Wesley emphasizes that the community moves forward in witness and mutual support in God's mission.

> He bids us build each other up;
> And gathered into one,
> To our high calling's glorious hope
> We hand in hand go on.[17]

One finds similar resonances of the fellowship of believers moving forward in witness and mission in these lines:

> Help us to help each other, Lord,
> Each other's cross to bear;
> Let each his friendly aid afford,
> And feel each other's care.

> Help us to build each other up,
> Our little stock improve;
> Increase our faith, confirm our hope,
> And perfect us in love.[18]

The Church is born by grace and sustained by love. In a poem with the title "A Prayer for Persons Joined in Fellowship" Wesley emphasizes over and over the role of love as the only possible sustenance of the Church.

> Still let us own our common Lord,
> And bear thine easy yoke—
> A band of love, a threefold cord
> Which never can be broke.[19]

He prays for the loving mind of Christ. He prays to be made perfect in love, and that "In earth, in paradise, in heaven, / Our all in all is love."

The book of the Church: Holy Scripture

At the heart of the life of the Church, the faith and practice of its members, is the Church's sacred book, the Bible or Holy Scriptures. From the early *Hymns and Sacred Poems* [1740] through to later writings such as the two-volume work *Short Hymns on Select Passages of the Holy Scriptures* [1762], we discover Charles Wesley's understanding of the authority and efficacy of the Bible.

It is the persons of the Holy Trinity, particularly the Holy Spirit, that unseal the meaning of the Holy Scriptures. In a poem to which Wesley gave the title "Before Reading the Scriptures" he invites the Holy Spirit, who is the "Source of the old prophetic fire, / Fountain of life and love" to inspire our hearts. The community of faith stands in historical continuity with the prophets inspired by the Holy Spirit to write and speak the truth to God's people. The Holy Spirit continues to shed light on the truth of the Word. It enables the reader to sound "The depths of love divine." Hence, in this hymn Wesley adjures all readers of the Bible to invite the Holy Spirit to illumine the Word before every reading.

A similar prayer is found in the hymn, "Come, divine Interpreter." On one's own it is impossible to grasp all the mystery of the Holy Scriptures. Hence, one prays:

> Come, divine Interpreter,
>> Bring me eyes thy book to read,
> Ears the mystic words to hear,
>> Words which did from thee proceed,
> Words that endless bliss impart,
> Kept in an obedient heart.[20]

Wesley's confidence in the power of the Holy Spirit to reveal the true meaning of the sacred text is so strong that he avers: against it all doctrine and experience may be tested. Reflecting on Isaiah 8:20, he writes:

> Doctrines, experiences to try,
> We to the sacred standard fly,
> Assur'd the Spirit of our Lord
> Can never contradict his word:
> Whate'er his Spirit speaks in me,
> Must with the written word agree;
> If not: I cast it all aside,
> As Satan's voice, or nature's pride.[21]

There is a sufficiency in the Word that completes humankind.

> All thy word without addition
>> Renders us for glory meet,
> Fits us for the blissful vision,
>> Makes the man of God complete.[22]

It also makes us wise unto salvation.

> If faith in our dear dying Lord
>> The sacred instrument applies,
> The virtue of his hallowing word
>> Shall make us to salvation wise,
> Wise our high calling's prize t'attain,
> And everlasting glory gain.[23]

He also discovers in Ezekiel 37:3–4, the power of the divine energy of the Word.

> All-good, almighty Lord,
>> Thou know'st thine own design,
> The virtue of thine own great word,
>> The energy divine.[24]

There is a sense in which Wesley places confidence in the literal Word.

> Trusting in the literal word,
> We look for Christ on earth again:
> Come, our everlasting Lord,
> With all thy saints to reign.[25]

Did Charles Wesley then take the Bible literally? Yes, in the sense that he believed that the promises of God in Holy Scripture could be trusted completely. God will fulfill them. However, when one reads his response to John 6:63, one is unlikely to conclude that he is a biblical literalist.

> The word in the bare *literal* sense,
> Tho' heard ten thousand times, and read,
> Can never of itself dispense
> The saving power which wakes the dead;
> The meaning *spiritual* and true
> The learn'd expositor may give,
> But cannot give the virtue too,
> Or bid his own dead spirit live.[26]

One of the texts that reveals the foundational perspective of Charles Wesley's hermeneutic and approach to the Holy Scriptures is "Whether the Word be preached or read." Without faith, says Wesley, the Word may be preached or read, but may be nothing but empty sounds and dead letters. It may be unprofitable and vain unless one hears by faith. He pleads for the spirit of the Word not the letter, which can be deadly.

In fact, says Wesley, those who "On the bare Word rely" are "wretched comforters." He asks, "What are the all verbal promises?" They are "Nothing to me, till faith divine / Inspire, inspeak, and make them mine." He would read the Holy Scriptures with "appropriating grace" bestowed by Jesus, who can open his eyes "to see" and his heart "to know." Thus, he gains assurance in faith.

As stated above, Wesley knows without question that it is the Holy Trinity that unseals the sacred book. Hence, in responding to 2 Timothy 3:15, he prays:

> Jesus, the Spirit of faith bestow,
> Who only can thy book unseal,
> And give me all thy will to know,
> And give me all thy mind to feel,
> Filled with the wisdom from above,
> The purity of heavenly love.[27]

If there is a foundational text for a Wesleyan *lectio divina*, perhaps it is found in the poem that begins with the words, "The table of my heart prepare." The Scripture to which Wesley is responding is Deuteronomy 6:4–7. The poem is a six-stanza prayer for the complete saturation of one's life with the Holy Scriptures. In stanza 1 he avers that if one is totally absorbed in them and God writes their precepts on the table of the heart, one will discover that "All things are possible to love." Here one finds the goal of Charles Wesley's biblical hermeneutic—the discovery of the possibilities of love.

1. The table of my heart prepare,
        (Such power belongs to thee alone)
   And write, O God, thy precepts there,
        To show thou still canst write in stone,
   So shall my pure obedience prove
   All things are possible to love.

2. Father, instruct my docile heart,
        Apt to instruct I then shall be,
   I then shall all thy words impart,
        And teach (as taught myself by thee)
   My children in their earliest days,
   To know, and live the life of grace.

3. When quiet in my house I sit,
        Thy book be my companion still,
   My joy thy sayings to repeat,
        Talk o'er the records of thy will,
   And search the oracles divine,
   Till every heart-felt word is mine.

4. O might the gracious words divine
        Subject of all my converse be,
   So would the Lord his follower join,
        And walk and talk himself with me,
   So would my heart his presence prove,
   And burn with everlasting love.

5. Oft as I lay me down to rest,
        O may the reconciling word
   Sweetly compose my weary breast,
        While on the bosom of my Lord
   I sink in blissful dreams away,
   And visions of eternal day.

6. Rising to sing my Saviour's praise,
        Thee may I publish all day long,
   And let thy precious word of grace
        Flow from my heart, and fill my tongue,
   Fill all my life with purest love,
   and join me to thy church above.[28]

In stanza 2 Wesley prays to the first person of the Trinity, "Father, instruct my docile heart," for this will make him an able instructor of his own children who will learn early in life "To know, and live a life of grace."

The benefits are not only for one's role as a parent: one is personally enriched; the Bible becomes one's "companion." A companion is a friend who accompanies you through all of life's experiences. One is in conversation with this intimate companion.

One talks "o'er the records of [God's] will" and searches them carefully until the words of the Holy Scriptures are one's own words.

Charles Wesley dreams of the divine words of the Bible becoming the only subject of his conversation. Literally he wants to walk and talk with this daily companion so that he will "burn with everlasting love." He would lie down to rest at the end of the day "sweetly composed" by the reconciling Word. He would rise to sing his Savior's praise and all day long he would proclaim the good news of salvation.

In the last stanza of this poem there is one of the most eloquent statements of the goal of Wesleyan biblical hermeneutics. One does not interpret the Holy Scriptures in a binding, restrictive way so as to control oneself and the community of faith by legalism. One reads the Scriptures and praises the Savior, one becomes so absorbed in the words of Holy Writ that the "precious word of grace" flows from the heart and fills the tongue. All of this has one goal—that one's life may be filled "with purest love" and joined to God's Church.

The sacraments of the Church

For Charles Wesley the Church is unequivocally a sacramental church.[29]

Baptism

Certainly his hymns for the sacrament of baptism are lesser known than his hymns for the sacrament of Holy Communion, for which he composed an entire volume, *Hymns on the Lord's Supper* (1745).

The hymn, "Truly baptized into the name," written in response to Acts 19:5, "They were baptized in the name of the Lord Jesus," is important for the way in which Charles weaves so many central facets of Wesleyan theology into eight lines.

> Truly baptized into the name
> Of Jesus I have been,
> Who partner of his nature am,
> And saved indeed from sin;
> Thy nature, Lord, through faith I feel,
> Thy love revealed in me;
> In me thy full salvation, dwell
> To all eternity.[30]

In this poem he speaks in the first person on behalf of the baptized. The opening two lines simply state the fact of baptism: "Truly baptized into the name of Jesus I have been." The next four lines, however, focus on *theosis,* participation in the nature of God. Wesley states that through baptism he has become a partner of God's nature: "Who partner of his nature am / And saved indeed from sin." The awareness of salvation from sin is, of course, central to Wesleyan theology.

Lines 5 and 6 emphasize the faith experience. Charles Wesley uses the verb "feel" to express how he experiences God's nature: "Thy nature, Lord, through faith I feel, /

Thy love revealed in me." God's nature is love and this is what Wesley senses within himself. Such love is the expression of "full salvation," which is eternal.

In a second hymn, "Come Father, Son, and Holy Ghost,"[31] which bears the original title, "At the Baptism of Adults," one discovers the foundational elements of a Wesleyan theology of baptism.

1. Come, Father, Son, and Holy Ghost,
        Honour the means injoined by Thee,
    Make good our apostolic boast,
        And own thy glorious ministry.

2. We now thy promised presence claim,
        Sent to disciple all mankind,
    Sent to baptize into thy name:
        We now thy promised presence find.

3. Father in these reveal thy Son,
        In these for whom we seek thy face,
    The hidden Mystery make known,
        The inward, pure, baptizing grace.

4. Jesu, with us thou always art,
        Effectuate now the sacred sign,
    The gift unspeakable impart,
        And bless thine ordinance divine.

5. Eternal Spirit, descend from high,
        Baptizer of our spirits thou,
    The sacramental seal apply,
        And witness with the water now.

6. Oh! that the souls baptized herein,
        May now thy truth and mercy feel,
    May rise, and wash away their sin—
        Come, Holy Ghost, their pardon seal.

In the opening lines Wesley affirms that all Christian baptism is Trinitarian. The Holy Trinity has enjoined baptism, which connects the Church of every age with the age of the apostles. Through baptism the community of faith claims the "promised presence" of God, for it is sent to disciple humankind and to baptize in God's name.

Wesley follows the above affirmations with a three-fold prayer to the Holy Trinity. He prays that the Father will reveal the divine Son, Jesus, in those who are baptized, and will make known the "hidden Mystery"—"The inward, pure, baptizing grace." Baptism is a grace-filled act, which no one can fully comprehend. Even if God makes known the "hidden Mystery," this does not mean that one can fully grasp its meaning.

Wesley prays to Jesus, who is always present with us, to make the sign of baptism effective and to impart the "unspeakable gift." What does he mean by the language of "hidden Mystery" and "unspeakable gift"? What is to be revealed? What is to be imparted? Precisely what Wesley says in the first baptismal hymn above—God's nature, which is love.

Finally, Wesley prays to the Holy Spirit to descend and seal the sacrament and witness with the water. Baptism of water is accompanied by the baptism of the Spirit. The Holy Spirit is the "baptizer of our spirits." Once again Wesley turns to the verb "feel," for baptism is experiential. He says one "May now thy truth and mercy feel." How does one *feel* two such abstract concepts as truth and mercy? Through the sense of sharing in God's nature, love, one knows the truth and mercy in God's redemptive act in Christ. One rises and feels one's sins washed away.

Eucharist/Holy Communion/Lord's Supper

There can be no question about the importance of the sacrament of Holy Communion for Charles Wesley as pertains to Christian theology and practice, and his understanding of the nature of the Church. He and his brother John devoted an entire volume of poetry, *Hymns on the Lord's Supper* (1745), one of his most significant compositions and publications, to multiple facets of this subject. It continues to have an impact in the church, particularly ecumenically. It has been studied by a number of writers, such as J. Ernest Rattenbury, *The Eucharistic Hymns of Charles Wesley* (London: Epworth Press, 1948). See also Geoffrey Wainwright's Introduction to the publication of the facsimile reprint of the first edition of *Hymns on the Lord's Supper* (1745) (Madison, NJ: The Charles Wesley Society, 1995, second printing 2001), and volume 2 of *Proceedings of The Charles Wesley Society* (1995), a volume that celebrated the 250th anniversary of the publication of *Hymns on the Lord's Supper*, with articles addressing these hymns from various denominational perspectives. Charles Wesley also wrote a brief prose document on the necessity of Holy Communion, which has recently been published in Kenneth Newport's *Sermons of Charles Wesley.*[32]

While the volume, *Hymns on the Lord's Supper* (1745), carries both brothers' names on the title page, it is generally accepted that John wrote the introduction and appropriated the material from Daniel Brevint's treatise on Christ's sacrifice and Charles wrote the sacred poems or hymns.

In one selection, "Constant Communion," Charles Wesley lays out the mandate for regular, if not daily, practice of the reception of Holy Communion by all believers. In the brief prose document mentioned at the conclusion of the preceding paragraph, he makes the case from Scripture and tradition to support the view of constant communion, and holds the Church of Rome, Luther, Calvin, and the Church of England responsible for the decline in the practice of Holy Communion. "The Church of England is blameable for infrequency of Communion as well as her Presbyterian neighbours." He believed most sincerely that members of the Church of England are "indispensably held to the same duty by the plain positive injunctions of our own church."[33]

Charles Wesley was convinced that

> we may take for granted that we have evident Scripture on our side for the necessity
> of celebrating the Eucharist every Lord's Day. That we have Christian antiquity to

support us in the same doctrine, I believe none of the opponents of this practice will be so hardy as to deny.... We have the testimony of St. Luke in several passages of his Acts of the Apostles, of St. Paul in his first Epistle to the Corinthians, of Tertullian, St. Justin the Martyr, the *Apostolic Constitutions*, and lastly of the Roman Pliny to prove that the Holy Eucharist is to be celebrated every Lord's Day at the least.... both Scripture and tradition do give plain evidence for the necessity of making at least a weekly oblation of the Christian sacrifice, and of honouring every Lord's Day with a solemn public celebration of the Lord's Supper.[34]

In the poem "Constant Communion" Wesley begins by stating that "true followers" of Christ in the early church were those who continued in the regular practice of Holy Communion. They fulfilled their duty: "They kept the Eucharistic feast." But in his own day he asks in stanzas 10 and 11:

> Where is the pure primeval flame,
>> Which in their faithful bosom glowed?
> Where are the followers of the Lamb,
>> The dying witnesses for God?
>
> Why is the faithful seed decreased,
>> The life of God extinct and dead?
> The daily sacrifice is ceased,
>> And charity to heaven is fled.[35]

Wesley earnestly prays for God to "Restore the daily sacrifice," for lack of regular practice of Holy Communion is what quenches the spark of love among the faithful.

> Sad mutual causes of decay,
>> Slackness and vice together move,
> Grown cold we cast the means away,
>> And quenched our latest spark of love.[36]

In his poem "Come to the feast, for Christ invites" he goes one step further in his argument for "constant communion." He believes strongly that no one has the right to determine the non-necessity of the Eucharist, or for that matter its necessity. This is not a matter of human decision.

> 'Tis not for us to set our God
>> A time his grace to give,
> The benefit whene'er bestowed,
>> We gladly should receive.[37]

In Charles Wesley's view whether or not to administer Holy Communion with constancy is not for either clergy or church councils to determine. He maintains that both Scripture and tradition expect at least the weekly reception of the sacrament. Hence, if one is faithful to the mandate of Scripture and the practice of tradition, one will receive the sacrament at least once a week.

How can the Eucharist be a means of God's grace? He acknowledges that it is an incomprehensible mystery. One of his forms of address for God in these poems is

"God incomprehensible." He queries how one may presume to grasp the incomprehensibleness of God and the mystery of power transmitted through the Eucharist. He does not shrink from asking how the bread and wine become instruments of God's grace, but avers that he "Need not know the mystery." What he does know, however, is that his blindness has been removed and now he can see. What he sees is not a resolution of all questions about the mystery but a glimpse of divine, pardoning, self-giving love poured out for him. This is the vision of the eucharistic experience.

Wesley speaks of the "unfathomable grace" mediated through the bread and wine. Who can possibly explain how through them one is filled with "all the life of God"? Once more we see Wesley's emphasis on *theosis*.

> Let the wisest mortal show
> How we the grace receive;
> Feeble elements bestow
> A power not theirs to give.[38]

It is at the eucharistic table that one experiences that God indeed will "Unseal the volume of [divine] grace, / And apply the gospel-word."

Time and again Wesley emphasizes that the central focus of Holy Communion is the experience of love, the love of God. His constant eucharistic prayer is:

> Our needy souls sustain
> With fresh supplies of love,
> Till all thy life we gain,
> And all thy fullness prove,
> And strengthened by thy perfect grace,
> Behold without a veil thy face.[39]

God's love, experienced at the sacred table, has power to unite the members of Christ's body, the Church. Thus, the Eucharist is the key to community.

> 'Tis here his closest love unites
> The members to their Head.[40]

"God is love" and love is thus the most powerful force in all creation. It alone truly unites those who are estranged, alienated, and divided.

It is at the table of the Lord that the divisions of the Church are overcome. Thus, Wesley prays,

> We thirst for the Spirit
> That flows from above,
> And long to inherit
> The fullness of love.[41]

The eschatological hope of the Eucharist is that the fullness of God's love will overcome all separation and fragmentation and unite the body of Christ, the Church, as one people. Wesley expresses this hope in these words:

> Sure and real is the grace,
>> The manner be unknown;
> Only meet us in thy ways
>> And perfect us in one.[42]

In speaking of the early church and its practice of constant communion, Wesley recalls:

> O what a flame of sacred love
>> Was kindled by the altar's fire![43]

In regular attendance at the altar of the Lord in Holy Communion the flame of sacred love was kept alive. The context of the early church's existence was the daily reception of "The tokens of expiring love." What a picture of the Church of Christ in any age—aflame with sacred love at its eucharistic celebrations!

The Eucharist is for Wesley, unequivocally, a Trinitarian meal. All persons of the Trinity share in the meal as one Godhead.

> Father, Son, and Holy Spirit
>> Sav'd by Thee
>> Happy we
> Shall thy throne inherit:
> Here our heavenly banquet tasting.
>> In thy love
>> Joy we prove
> Ever, ever lasting.[44]

As in the invocation of the Holy Spirit in the liturgical *epiklesis*, historically a part of most traditional eucharistic celebrations, Charles Wesley offers prayers of invitation to the Holy Spirit to be present in the experience of Holy Communion. At this Trinitarian meal and experience, Wesley asks the Holy Spirit to be the spark of human memory, awareness, and conscience at the table of the Lord.

> Come, thou everlasting Spirit,
>> Bring to every thankful mind
> All the Savior's dying merit
>> All his suffering for mankind.[45]

Wesley refers to the Holy Spirit as the "Divine Remembrancer." Once again he uses the verb "feel" as he asks, "Let us feel thy (Holy Spirit's) power applying, / Christ to every soul and mind." Thus, those communing receive the atoning grace via the Holy Spirit.

More specifically Wesley refers to the power of the Holy Spirit shedding its influence over the bread and wine: "Thy life infuse into the bread, / Thy power into the wine." The goal of the infusion is unmistakable: LOVE.

> Effectual let the tokens prove,
>> And made by heavenly art
> Fit channels to convey the love
>> To every faithful heart.[46]

How does one prepare for this experience of God's grace and love, union with Christ, all the life of God, and the visitation of the Holy Spirit?

In a poem based on Christ's command, "Do this for my sake," Wesley spells out quite definitively how believers are to prepare for the Eucharist.

In stanza 1 he asserts that those who desire to commune are to be filled with calm expectation. Like the man waiting for healing at the pool of Bethesda, one expects the grace of God to be revealed in the Supper of the Lord.

In stanza 2 Wesley lists the disciplines that properly prepare one for Holy Communion:

> With fasting and prayer
> My Savior I seek,
> And listen to hear
> The Comforter speak;
> In searching and hearing
> The Life-giving Word
> I wait thy appearing,
> I look for the Lord.[47]

Before coming to the table, we are to fast, pray, await the voice of the Holy Spirit, diligently study the Scriptures, and be attentive to the proclamation of the Word that gives life. With such preparation we await the appearance of the Lord in the Eucharist. As believers we do all these things because we hope "to inherit / Thy fullness of love." We do all these things because, when we come to the Lord's Supper

> 'Tis here we look up
> And grasp at thy mind,
> 'Tis here that we hope
> Thine image to find;
> The means of bestowing
> Thy gifts we embrace
> But all things are owing
> To Jesus's grace.[48]

Even if believers prepare themselves in all the disciplines Wesley mentions, the disciplines themselves do not guarantee the experience of the fullness of God's love and grace at the table, for "all things are owing / To Jesus's grace."

Conclusion

Since Charles Wesley's life was centered in the worship of God, it is not surprising that he composed numerous hymns for specific times of worship. In the Church of England there were two major forms of the liturgy: the daily office (Morning Prayer and Evening Prayer) and the Eucharist (on Sunday or other days). Both the daily office and the Eucharist were liturgically adjusted to the cycle of the Christian year according to the Book of Common Prayer. There were, of course, occasional services held for events such as marriage, death and resurrection, and special feast days.

How were Charles's hymns for the opening and closing of worship and for the morning and evening used by the Wesleys, since the eighteenth century worship of the Church of England was not characterized by hymn singing? When would the hymns designated for the opening and closing of worship and for morning and evening have been used? While one cannot give definitive answers to these questions, it is highly likely that they were used in the Societies and members were also encouraged to use the texts for private devotions as well.

The hymn "Come, let us join with one accord" which bears the title "For the Lord's Day" is a superb summary of Wesley's understanding of the Christian's doxological vocation. Wesley immediately connects the earthly community of faith with the heavenly community of faith. He says "Come, let us join with one accord / In hymns around the throne." The earthly voices of worship unite with the voices of eternity in singing God's praise. God set aside at creation a day for rest and praise of the divine. Even so, Wesley bids all believers:

> Not one, but all our days below,
>   Let us in hymns employ;
> And in our Lord rejoicing, go
>   To his eternal joy.[49]

The doxological life is a life of constant praise of the Creator for creation and life itself.

Wesley does not forget that the "constant praise" of which he speaks is praise of the Holy Trinity. He exclaims: "Praise to the great Three-One be given / By all on earth, and all in heaven."

The hymn "Blest be the dear uniting love" with the title "At Parting," is indicated as being for the closing of worship. Throughout the development of the Methodist movement this text was used for funerals and memorial services. It is, however, one of Wesley's finest ecclesiological statements.

1. Blest be the dear uniting love
        That will not let us part;
    Our bodies may far off remove,
        We still are one in heart.

2. Joined in one spirit to our Head,
        Where he appoints we go,
    And still in Jesus' footsteps tread,
        And do his work below.

3. O let us ever walk in him,
        And nothing know beside,
    Nothing desire, nothing esteem,
        But Jesus crucified.

4. Closer and closer let us cleave
        To his beloved embrace;
    Expect his fullness to receive,
        And grace to answer grace.

5. While thus we walk with Christ in light,
   Who shall our souls disjoin?
   Souls, which himself vouchsafes to unite
   In fellowship divine!

6. We all are one who him receive,
   And each with each agree;
   In him the One, the Truth, we live;
   Blest point of unity!

7. Partakers of the Savior's grace,
   The same in mind and heart,
   Nor joy, nor grief, nor time, nor place,
   Nor life, nor death can part:

8. But let us hasten to the day
   Which shall our flesh restore,
   When death shall all be done away,
   And bodies part no more.[50]

Even though the members may be separated from one another, they are nevertheless "one in heart." They are also "Joined in one spirit to our Head," Christ. The members do the work of Christ on earth.

They have a constant companion and constant communion, as they meet at the table of the Lord and follow in the footsteps of Christ; they "ever walk in him." And, above all else, they desire and esteem nothing but Jesus crucified.

As the members come closer and closer together and expect to receive the fullness of Christ, Wesley says that in their relationships "grace [is] to answer grace." What a pattern for the life of the Church and its members! They respond to one another always with grace. They are responding to God's grace in Christ by answering grace with grace. What if all those claiming to be part of the Church of Jesus Christ actually lived by the principle for all relationships of "answering grace with grace"? Divisions, disunity, denominational aggrandizement, and selfishness would rapidly diminish.

The unity of the body of Christ rooted in God's grace cannot be disjoined by anyone or anything, for God in Christ has created a divine fellowship. With reminiscences of St. Paul, Wesley writes:

We all are one who him receive,
   And each with each agree;
In him the One, the Truth, we live;
   Blest point of unity!

Partakers of the Savior's grace,
   The same in mind and heart,
Nor joy, nor grief, nor time, nor place,
   Nor life, nor death can part.[51]

Endnotes

[1]The following section is not an exhaustive study of the four emphases apostolicity, catholocity, unity, and holiness in Charles Wesley's writings but rather a selection of passages that illustrate the presence of these emphases in his literature.

[2]*Short Hymns on Select Passage of the Holy Scriptures* (1762), 2 vols. (Bristol: Felix Farley, 1762); henceforth cited as *Short Hymns* (1762).

[3]*Short Hymns* (1762), 2:351, Hymn 685.

[4]*Short Hymns* (1762), 1:392, Hymn 1160; based on Isa. 66:21–23: "I will also take of them for priests and Levites, saith the Lord. For as the new heavens and the new earth, which I will make, shall remain before me, saith the Lord, so shall your seed and your name remain. And it shall come to pass, that from one new moon to another, and from one sabbath to another, shall all flesh come to worship before me, saith the Lord."

[5]*Funeral Hymns* (London: [Strahan], 1759), Nr. 1.

[6]*Hymns and Sacred Poems* (London: Strahan, 1740), 195; henceforth cited as *HSP* (1740).

[7]*Short Hymns* (1762), 1:392, Hymn 1160.

[8]*Hymns and Sacred Poems*, 2 vols. (Bristol: Felix Farley, 1749), 1:248; henceforth cited as *HSP* (1749).

[9]*Short Hymns* (1762), 1:298, based on the Song of Solomon 6:10: "Who is she that looketh forth as the morning, fair as the moon, clear as the sun, and terrible as an army with banners!"

[10]Ibid.

[11]*Hymns on the Lord's Supper* (Bristol: Felix Farley, 1745), 138, Hymn 165; henceforth cited as *HLS* (1745).

[12]*Hymns for those that seek and those that have Redemption in the Blood of Christ* (London: Strahan, 1747), Nr. 32; henceforth cited as *RH* (1747).

[13]*Short Hymns* (1762), 2:392, Hymn 767; based on 1 Pet. 2:17: "Love the brotherhood."

[14]*HSP* (1749), 1:248; original text: Gentle, courteous, and kind = Courteous, pitiful, and kind.

[15]*Hymns and Sacred Poems* (Bristol: Felix Farley, 1742), 271; henceforth cited as *HSP* (1742).

[16]From "Give me the faith," *HSP* (1749), 1:300, stanza 2.

[17]*RH* (1747), Nr. 50.

[18]*HSP* (1742), 83.

[19]Ibid., 86.

[20]*Short Hymns* (1762), 2:412, Hymn 821; based on Rev. 1:3: "Blessed is he that readeth, and they that hear the words of this prophecy, and keep those things which are written therein."

[21]Ibid., 1:310, Hymn 973.

[22]Ibid., 1:89, Hymn 278; based on Deut. 4:2: "Ye shall not add unto the word which I command you, neither shall ye diminish ought from it, that ye may keep the commandments of the Lord your God which I command you."

[23]Ibid., 2:337, Hymn 663.

[24]Ibid., 2:51, Hymn 1273; based on Ezek. 37:3–4: "Can these dry bones live?"

[25]Ibid., 2:56, Hymn 1284.

[26]Ibid., 2:249, Hymn 429. The italics are Wesley's.

[27]Ibid., 2:337, Hymn 663.

[28]*Short Hymns* (1762), 1:91–93, Hymns 287–92. Each stanza is originally written in the above sequence but as a separate poem.

[29]This section is not an exhaustive examination of Charles Wesley's views on the sacraments but rather illustrates his strong adherence to both. He was a strong advocate of infant and adult baptism and constant communion.

[30]*The Unpublished Poetry of Charles Wesley*, 3 vols., ed. by S T Kimbrough, Jr. and Oliver A. Beckerlegge (Nashville: Abingdon/Kingswood, 1988, 1990, 1992), 2:389–390, based on Acts 19:5: "They were baptized in the name of the Lord Jesus."

[31]*HSP* (1749), 2:245.

[32]Kenneth G. C. Newport, ed., *The Sermons of Charles Wesley, A Critical Edition, with Introduction and Notes* (Oxford: Oxford University Press, 2001), 277–86.

[33]Ibid., 282.

[34]Ibid., 286.

[35]*HLS* (1745), 140, Hymn 166, stanzas 10 and 11 of a 22-stanza hymn.

[36]Ibid.

[37]*HLS* (1745), 44, Hymn 60.

[38]*HLS* (1745), 41, Hymn 57.

[39]*HLS* (1745), 30, Hymn 40.

[40]*HLS* (1745), 43, Hymn 60.

[41]*A Short View of the Differences between the Moravian Brethren, Lately in England, and the Rev. Mr. John and Charles Wesley* (1748).

[42]*HLS* (1745), 41, Hymn 57.

[43]*HLS* (1745), 139, Hymn 166.

[44]*Hymns on the Trinity* (Bristol: Pine, 1767), Hymn 37.

[45]*HLS* (1745), 13, Hymn 16.

[46]*HLS* (1745), 51, Hymn 72.

[47]*A Short View of the Differences between the Moravian Brethren, Lately in England, and the Rev. Mr. John and Charles Wesley* (London: Strahan, 1745), 19; a hymn based on Isa. 64:5, "Thou meetest those that remember thee in thy ways."

[48]Ibid.

[49]*Hymns for Children* (Bristol: Felix Farley, 1763), Nr. 62.

[50]*HSP* (1742), 159–160.

[51]Ibid.

9

Understandings of Ecclesiology in United Methodism

Russell E. Richey

United Methodism defines itself and exhibits its ecclesial sensibilities with four books. Two of these, the Bible and hymnal, one finds in the pew and in the homes of the Methodist faithful. One finds the other two, *The Book of Discipline* and *The Book of Worship*, in the studies of ministers or in church libraries.[1] Each characterizes or shapes the church in a distinct way. All are important. Each plays a role in the drama of the church's daily life.[2] The *Discipline* and *Book of Worship* work off stage, so to speak, determining how the play unfolds, who acts, and what instructions are followed. The Bible and hymnbook script Methodist life together. The latter scripts rituals from birth to death, and at Sunday morning worship, structures the weekly praise of God and specifies the Psalms to read and the hymns to sing. The former—studied downstairs by all ages in Sunday school, always read upstairs and now frequently in accordance with the uniform lections—scripts life lived in Christ. The four books— Scripture, hymnbook, *Book of Discipline*, and *Book of Worship*—define how United Methodists do church.[3] In "practicing" church, Methodists have in their own way lived out what the church more generally has held to be important ecclesial understandings. I shall attempt to take note of those at first mention with **bolding**, marking key Wesleyan or Methodist ecclesial notions in the same manner, thereby identifying how and where Methodism imbeds its ecclesiology in its practices and as guided by these books.

1. Foundations

Wesley's transmittal

John Wesley conveyed each of these aforementioned books to the little North American Methodist movement at the point of the movement's becoming church. His "Large Minutes," the governing instrument of the British movement, constituted the basis of the first *Discipline*.[4] Compiled out of the decisions of the "governing" conferences of Wesley with his preachers, the "Large Minutes" and the American version thereof, the *Discipline*, provided a quasi-constitution for the reformist Methodist

movement, specified its distinctive practices and gatherings, and outlined its ministerial tasks and duties. *A Collection of Psalms and Hymns for the Lord's Day*[5] was
appended to the *Discipline* (in its first, 1785 edition). *A Pocket Hymnbook* appeared the
next year, one in a long series of hymnbooks for the Methodist people. The Wesleys
had selected verse from Charles and structured and organized the collection to guide
the faithful in the way of salvation.[6] Rich in scriptural citation and allusion,[7] it put
biblical motif and Wesleyan doctrine on Methodist lips. It began with hymns entreat-
ing the sinner to turn to God and followed with several sections posing the consequences of one's actions, either with God in heaven or in death and hell. A second part
contrasted formal and inward religion. In a third part, the Wesleys located hymns
evocative of repentance, conviction, conversion and perseverance. Part four, the
longest with ten sections, exhibited 261 hymns for Christians struggling towards perfection. The final part featured hymns for Methodist societies and classes.

The Book of Common Prayer (BCP) was dear to the Wesleys, and John had edited
and digested it into the *Sunday Service of the Methodists in North America*. Despite the
latter's apparently restrictive title, it provided a full set of rituals—morning prayer,
evening prayer, weekday litany, Sunday service, Eucharist, two baptismal rites, marriage, and orders for communion of the sick, burial and ordination services for deacons, elders and superintendents. It also included a brief lectionary and twenty-four
Articles of Religion, excerpted from Anglicanism's Thirty-nine.[8]

A letter from Wesley conveyed these documents and authorized the establishment of the new church. Addressed to the two bishop (superintendent) designees and
their brethren, "To Dr. COKE, Mr. ASBURY, and our Brethren in NORTH AMER-
ICA," it instructed the young church: "They are now at full liberty, simply to follow
the Scriptures and the Primitive Church."[9] The injunction to follow Scripture was
hardly needed but it did effectively found the new church with the fourth book.

With Scripture, hymnbook, discipline, and book of worship, Wesley made provision for the movement that would call itself the Methodist Episcopal Church. By reference, inclusion, and allusion, these books pointed to other standards: Twenty-five
Articles of Religion (adapted from the Thirty-nine and one added to the twenty-four
that Wesley had isolated); Wesley's *Sermons*; his *Explanatory Notes upon the New Testament*; and the General Rules, a set of injunctions and disciplines by which
Methodists might hold themselves and one another accountable for the ethical life
and chart their way towards the knowledge and love of God (practices largely echoed
in the *Discipline*). These standards also figured (and figure) in the definition of
Methodism and of the Methodist way of life, but they tended to be less the day-to-day,
week-to-week, traveling companions for Methodists in their pilgrim's progress. Scripture, hymnbook, discipline, and book of worship were made to travel.

The books and their ecclesial import

We should register two points about these books and their ecclesiological import.
First, one can draw a rough correspondence between the four and the putative Wesleyan quadrilateral—*Scripture, experience, reason* and *tradition*.[10] To be sure, we might
rightly connect each of the books with all parts of the quadrilateral, as we will illus-

trate in the paragraph immediately below. But each book had, as well, a special force with respect to one of these Methodist epistemological impulses. Second, the four pulled early American Methodism in ecclesially different directions, one might say, in one of two opposing ecclesiological directions. Each book, its primary quadrilateral association, and its early ecclesial significance deserve remark.

The hymnal standardized a particular Methodist *experience*, providing poetic scripts for the Methodists to follow towards perfection. Its phrasing, images, themes, and organization captured and charted the ups and downs of the pilgrim's progress from the first stirrings of grace in the sinful soul through to the blessing of holiness. Though the hymnal featured the **"evangelical doctrines,"** its verse comprehended the range of Christian experience, the whole task of the church, and the full catholic creedal witness. Rich in scriptural citation and allusion, offering the tradition's doctrinal consensus, and ordering the Christian walk in a rational though poetic style, the hymnal, like the other books, could and should be recognized as evidencing all parts of the quadrilateral.[11] Most Methodists would have missed the hymnal's epistemological or methodological quadrilateral complexity.[12] For them it fed experience—the quiet private devotion and the fervid communal song. And it did so with exacting attention to Arminian doctrines predicated upon **free grace**, the goal of **holiness**, and the resources of Wesleyan spirituality or, as Methodists would have described it, **piety** and discipline.

The *Discipline*, and the various authoritative texts which it included or referenced, gathered Methodist experience and belief, individual and collective, into *reasonable* order. If the *Discipline* can be said to have exhibited the *reason* aspect of the quadrilateral, it did so in a peculiarly Wesleyan fashion, indeed, in an American Wesleyan fashion. The *Discipline* offered a practical *reason*; an ordered rule of life—individual and corporate; a set of regimens or **"disciplines"** for life in the kingdom; and the structures, offices, polices and procedures by which to follow those dictates.[13] This was not reason in the mode of John Locke and his Age of Reason colleagues, neither that of Thomas Aquinas and the great tradition of scholasticism, nor even that of John Wesley himself who could address *An Earnest Appeal to Men of Reason and Religion* and *A Farther Appeal to Men of Reason and Religion*. No, this was a practical reason that American Methodists referenced when in 1787 they refashioned their version of the "Large Minutes," now termed *A Form of Discipline . . . Arranged under proper Heads, and Methodized in a more acceptable and easy Manner*. The "rationality" of the *Discipline* would only increase over time, the product of Methodism's rapid growth, consequent structural complexity, problem-solving and missional diversification.

The *Discipline*, like the "Large Minutes," set forth the ordered life for the people, including what Wesley specified as the instituted **means of grace: prayer, searching the Scriptures, the Lord's Supper, fasting** and **Christian conference.** By the latter, he meant conversation about the good life, not the structures of governance. The *Discipline*, however, supplied the latter as well, outlining the responsibilities and prerogatives of each of the connectional levels, and of several ministerial offices: **bishops, presiding elders, traveling elders, traveling deacons, local preachers, exhorters, stewards** and **class leaders.** Here was the three-fold ministry augmented by the distinctively Wesleyan offices, all **connected** as essential cogs in a missional system. The first four offices itinerated broadly, the latter four more locally.

These two books, hymnal and *Discipline*, one for the believer's purse, the other for the preacher's saddle bag, pulled one towards a discrete Wesleyan identity, inward or more accurately, "connectionally." They provided Methodists a Wesleyan grammar for the Christian life, a Wesleyan missional ecclesiology.[14] The 1787 *Discipline* made that missional ecclesial assertion explicit as it defined Methodist **purpose**:

Of the Rise of Methodism (so called) in Europe and America.

Quest. 1. What was the Rise of Methodism, so called, in Europe?

Answ. In 1729, two young Men, reading the Bible, saw they could not be saved without Holiness, followed after it, and incited others so to do. In 1737, they saw likewise, that Men are justified before they are sanctified: but still Holiness was their Object. God then thrust them out, to raise an holy People.

. . .

Quest. 3. What may we reasonably believe to be God's Design, in raising up the Preachers called Methodists?

Answ. To reform the Continent, and spread scripture Holiness over these Lands. As a Proof hereof, we have seen in the Course of fifteen Years a great a glorious Work of God, from New-York through the Jersies, Pennsylvania, Maryland, Virginia, North and South Carolina, even to Georgia.[15]

"**To reform the continent and spread scripture holiness over these lands**" refined John Wesley's agenda for the American context. This mantra, despite its inward pull, did not yield a sectarian spirit—though such claims have occasionally been made— but instead an **evangelical or missionary connectionalism** or **denominationalism**. Not sectarians, Methodists did not withdraw from a sinful world but sought to transform it. They would transform it revivalistically, by bringing in the sheaves and in witnessing against sins, individual and social. What exactly would they transform? Note their ambitions, hardly those of a sect, but instead quite impressive territorial or geographical ambitions, indicated in the church's commitment to reform the entire continent. They began, moreover, with a passion to take on the most intractable of American dilemmas, that of race. They began with a commitment to African Americans and their freedom.[16]

Methodists undertook this transformative endeavor with Wesley's methods: the class-quarterly meeting-conference structure; exacting disciplines for both members and preachers; an elaborate schema of local and **itinerant ministries**; and Wesley-like **itinerant general superintendents (bishops)** with powers to appoint preachers to circuits or stations.[17] These practices, sung about in Wesleyan verse and performed in the directives of the *Discipline*, implicitly carried an ecclesiology, a **missionary** and **connectional** conception of the church. But as practices, as practical or experimental divinity, Methodism's gatherings, rituals, offices and strategies did not yield very clear and concise theory.[18] Methodists became better at doing church than articulating an ecclesiology. Here and there one can find statements or discussions out of which a more formal **missionary** and **connectional** ecclesiology might have developed, but only in recent years have Methodists pursued that project.

* * *

If hymnbook and *Discipline* produced an implicit expansive missional denomina-tionalism, Bible (*Scripture*) and *Sunday Service* (*tradition*) claimed Wesley's Anglican heritage and proclaimed Methodism's **catholic identity**. They pushed outward, ecu-menically. Although early Methodists may have been insecure in and frequently unclear about this ecumenical identity, it nevertheless defined the movement. It was there by received tradition and by continued practice.

The *Sunday Service* provided the Methodist Episcopal Church with the rights and rites for their middle name. Instructing the Americans of its dependence on the BCP, Wesley asserted in the preface to the *Sunday Service*:

> I believe there is no LITURGY in the World, either in ancient or modern language, which breathes more of a solid scriptural, rational Piety, than the COMMON PRAYER of the CHURCH of ENGLAND.

Wesley conceded that he had shortened the *Supper*, omitted a few sentences from *Bap-tism* and *Burial*, and dropped some holy days and psalms.[19] But far more impressive than the abridgements and omissions was Wesley's preservation of the substance and structure of the BCP.

Appropriately, those gathered in 1784 at the organizing Christmas Conference decided to call their new ecclesial entity the Methodist **Episcopal** Church, a name that they patented before the Protestant Episcopals did. They communed to Cranmerian cadences for **Eucharist** and **baptized** with the Triune formula. They ordained **deacons, elders and bishops** with ritual little altered from the BCP and lived into Anglicanism's **threefold ministry**. Although they could not claim apostolic succession and early and often found themselves defending the legitimacy of their orders, Methodist Episco-pals nevertheless sustained **an orderly laying-on of hands** from John Wesley onwards. Methodists did diverge from Anglicanism in positing that bishops were **not a third order**, a stance occasioned if not necessitated by John Wesley's extra-ordinary venture in ordaining Thomas Coke who then ordained Asbury. Asbury's refusal to accept ele-vation to the episcopacy solely on Wesley's appointment and insistence that the Amer-ican preachers be invited to assent, established the principle that **bishops be elected in conference**.[20]

Methodist formal definitions of the Church and sacraments remained those in the BCP, the (Anglican) **articles** and the **creeds**. The Church manifested itself in **faithful congregations where the pure Word was preached and the Sacraments administered according to Christ's ordinance**. The Church defined itself with the classic "notes" or "marks"—**one, holy, catholic, and apostolic**. Church by the book! So, in providing this book, these books, Wesley intended to anchor the American branch of his movement liturgically in the church to which he remained loyal. This was, to reiterate, a church that deserved its middle name. It sustained its continuity with the *tradition* of its birth.

To be sure, Methodists did not exhibit much of what later would be deemed Anglican practice and polity. However, their patterns were rather more in accord with what had been the actual practice of those colonial Anglicans who, with the Wesleys, had worried about the ethical and spiritual estate of the land and who had, in many instances, found common cause with the Methodist preachers up until 1784. Indeed, the Devereux Jarratts experienced Methodist organization as a separate church and a violation of what had been, they thought, a Wesleyan covenant to work together for the reformation of the Church.[21]

* * *

The American Methodists sustained John Wesley's immersion in Scripture, aided in the understanding thereof by his *Explanatory Notes upon the New Testament,* an American edition of which they published as early as 1791.[22] Wesley had instructed the American Methodists in 1783:

> Let all of you be determined to abide by the Methodist doctrine and discipline, published in the four volumes of *Sermons* and the *Notes upon the New Testament,* together with the Large Minutes of conference.[23]

The Americans, particularly the preachers, were perhaps even more than Wesley himself *homo unius libri,* people of one book, the Bible.[24] They lived with it, inscribed it on their hearts, and guided their lives by its examples, teaching and precepts. The preachers preached from it, frequently multiple times a day, often leaving in their journals little more than the notation of the text used. When for reasons of distance or weather, they wanted for a congregation and opportunity to expound the Word, they would note that as a "dumb day."

And they understood their movement, their ministry, their ecclesial order as biblically scripted. They were and remained particularly conscious of the grounding of itinerancy in Scripture. It was, they believed, the pattern of Jesus himself and of the apostles. To that theme, Bishop Asbury returned again and again, insisting that both Methodist bishops and preachers adhered to the **apostolic, itinerant plan of ministry**. In parting instructions to his junior bishop, William McKendree, Asbury insisted that they, like the apostles of the Bible, were "apostolic bishops" for like they "we have both planted and watered, and do water still."[25] He explained that it was the Methodists who had recovered the apostolic plan of ministry:

> This leads me to conclude that there were no local bishops until the second century; that the apostles, in service, were bishops, and that those who were ordained in the second century mistook their calling when they became local and should have followed those bright examples in the apostolic age.
>
> . . . .
>
> It is my confirmed opinion that the apostles acted both as bishops and traveling superintendents in planting and watering, ruling and ordering the whole connection; and that they did not ordain any local bishops.
>
> . . . .
>
> My dear bishop, it is the traveling apostolic order and ministry that is found in our very constitution. No man among us can locate without order or forfeit his official standing. No preacher is stationary more than two years; no presiding elder more

than four years, and the constitution will remove them; and all are moveable at the pleasure of the superintendent whenever he may find it necessary for the good of the cause.

Methodism's immersion in Scripture did not distinguish it from other Pietist movements, and its appreciation thereof did not distinguish it from Protestants generally. Indeed, Methodists knew themselves to be a movement united in common endeavor with all who lived and loved Scripture. This unitive impulse, in its earliest North American expression, one might term "evangelical" rather than "catholic." Among the groups with whom Methodists experienced the greatest commonality were the United Brethren and Evangelical Association, two groups with roots in Reformed-Mennonite and Lutheran Pietism respectively, with their own distinctive evangelical-Reformation ecclesiology and with a strong confessional orientation. They shared much with the Methodists, including a unitive spirit, and over time grew even closer, eventually combining with one another and later with the Methodists to form United Methodism. That union, as we will note below, connected the new church with the major branches of the Protestant Reformation, with its diverse ecclesial principles, and with a confession of faith, occasionally updated, with a clear articulation of the classic "notes" of the Church.

* * *

The two unitive commitments, one Anglican, the other Pietist, tugged the Methodist Episcopal Church in different directions—either back towards their English roots or forward into the Protestant endeavor to Christianize America—though the difference in the two options would become more marked as the Protestant Episcopal Church gravitated away from the shared evangelicalism. Initially both Scripture and *Sunday Service* situated the distinctive Wesleyan ecclesial patterns and the energetic, competitive Methodist itinerant ministries within shared Protestant visions of the Church.[26]

2. Transformations

The Quadrilateral: A literary evolution?

Over the course of two centuries, Methodism's four books, Methodist ecclesial sensibilities, and the service that the several books rendered underwent interesting and significant shifts. Tradition suffered in the rough and tumble of evangelistic, frontier oriented, camp-meeting-dominated Methodism. This trend surfaced early, in the Methodist decision to abandon its book of worship, the *Sunday Service of the Methodists in North America*. Jesse Lee explained why in his early, first-person narrative of the American church, *A Short History of the Methodists*.

> [T]he prayer book, as revised by Mr. Wesley, was introduced among us; and in the large towns, and in some country places, our preachers read prayers on the Lord's day: and in some cases the preachers read part of the morning service on Wednesdays and Fridays. But some of the preachers who had been long accustomed to prayer extem-

pore, were unwilling to adopt this new plan. Being fully satisfied that they could pray better, and with more devotion while their eyes were shut, than they could with their eyes open. After a few years the prayer book was laid aside, and has never been used since in public worship.[27]

As Lee noted, revivalistic evangelicalism trumped the prayer book. At times and in places, Methodism behaved like a continuous camp meeting. The camp meeting did suit Methodist polity—Methodist practice of church—quite nicely. In the nineteenth century, Methodists routinely placed their warm weather quarterly meeting in a camp meeting.[28] By locating in a camp meeting the circuit's—the local church unit's—official or business meeting, Methodists embraced, albeit informally, a revivalistic modality of being Church. Experience, conversion, revivalism thus upstaged tradition.

However, Methodist Episcopals did not and could not give up rituals for the Supper, baptism, ordination, or marriage. Indeed, though the *Sunday Service*, as book for pocket and pew, did not define Methodism's devotional life, the above services, typically and as appropriate, would be enacted at the high point of the church's worship calendar, the two-day quarterly meeting. When camp meetings emerged, as I have already noted, Methodists located the quarterly meeting there, the Lord's Supper being one of its high water marks.[29] Whether two days in colder weather or elongated into a week or more in a summer camp meeting, the **quarterly meeting** functioned as an enacted or dramatized BCP for Methodists. There the entire array of officers would gather, including the bishops if they were anywhere close, and there the circuit did its business. It exercised discipline, including conducting trials if necessary. It collected "quarterage" to supply the common salary for all the traveling ministers. It licensed or renewed licenses to preach, made recommendations about ordination, and filled local offices. That was the Saturday agenda. Sunday wedded rituals of the BCP to distinctive Methodist practices. The day opened with the **Love Feast**, restricted to members, followed by preaching, the Lord's Supper, more preaching, baptisms if indicated, memorials when required. In the quarterly meeting, Methodism was most fully Church, offering to those gathered the preached word, the sacraments and discipline or order.

Over the course of the nineteenth century, Methodism freed stations from its circuits, appointed educated preachers to those congregations, built substantial churches to house the middle-class populations that filled its urban pews, and increasingly edged its way into the Protestant establishment. Such "improvements" spawned protests, various movements that hoisted a holiness banner and/or defended the camp meeting to call Methodism back to its commitment to the marginalized. Schisms took some of the protesters out of the church, but others remained to voice complaints as Methodism gained in respectability and gravitated towards more formalized worship.

Methodists tracked Anglican reforms and kept up-to-date versions of the ritual available to preachers in the quadrennially produced *Discipline*.[30] On the popular level and over the course of the nineteenth century, Methodists gradually reclaimed traditions that had been important to the Wesleys, including liturgical practices and entire services that could hardly be managed without a published order in congregant's hands, much less with the preacher's eyes shut. This reclamation went on more in the urban and upscale congregations than in rural areas, but was modeled for all preachers in annual conferences. In 1905 the Methodist Episcopal Church and the Methodist Episcopal Church, South formalized that trend by including both an "Order of Worship" and a Psalter in the jointly published *Methodist Hymnal*.[31] And in 1945, the new Methodist Church [MC], which united in 1939 the Methodist Episcopal Church [MEC], the Methodist Episcopal Church, South [MECS] and the Methodist Protestant Church [MPC], revisited Wesley's recrafting or remodeling of the BCP. *The Book of Worship for Church and Home* provided a BCP-like full set of services. A sequel *Book of Worship* appeared in 1965 and *The United Methodist Book of Worship* in 1992.[32] With each of these successive liturgical efforts, save this most recent, Methodism reasserted its connection to the BCP and enriched its sense of tradition as mediated through Anglicanism.

Bible, Discipline, *Hymnbook*

Scripture, reason and experience—and their literary expressions of Bible, *Discipline* and hymnbook—found an easier path into the life of the young Methodist movement and into its ecclesial sensibilities. Wesley had exhorted his preachers and people to read and had made ample provision for their reading in his many publications. The American Methodists carried on that program, even under frontier conditions. They created a surrogate Wesley, in the person and office of Book Agent, who took responsibility for an aggressive publishing and distributing campaign of popular literature and eventually serials. Preachers functioned as regional sales representatives for the publishing enterprise. Colporteurs they were, with responsibilities to push the product, handle sales, collect and forward receipts, and in every way cultivate the reading and buying habit.[33] They kept a percentage of the profit, in some instances, substantially augmenting what was otherwise a meager annual salary.[34] Available records indicate significant sales of catechisms, pious memoirs, spiritual guides, Bibles, hymnals and *Disciplines* and much more modest sales of weightier items by Wesley or his theological successors. In one particularly profitable year (1814), Benjamin Lakin sold 1314 items. Hymnals constituted 413 of that total, *Disciplines* 505.[35] So the Methodist movement put pocket hymnals and mass-produced Bibles into the laps of the people. The preachers, if not all the laity, had carried a third book, the *Discipline*. Their saddlebags reputedly came with Bible, hymnbook and *Discipline*.

The canon of Scripture, of course, did not change nor, one might argue, has Methodism's effort to be faithful to it. The modes of that fidelity have evolved, taken on complexity, found institutional niches, but nevertheless sustained the twofold commitments inherited from Wesley. He wanted his people and preachers to be students of the Bible. From the laity he expected daily reading, the small group (class) for study and prayer, hymns and sermons for interpretation and personal witness through testimony in the Love Feast. He expected the same from the preachers but also careful study of his commentary, *Explanatory Notes upon the New Testament*, a formally defined touchstone of orthodoxy drawn from what he regarded as the best scholarship of the day.

On the popular level, today's United Methodists have *Disciple Bible* plus an incredible array of other adult biblical resources from the United Methodist Publishing House (Cokesbury and Abingdon). Cokesbury makes similar provision for all other age groups. The clergy typically own the *Interpreter's Bible* and are acquiring the *New Interpreter's Bible*. Or if the *IB* and *NIB* are not to taste, Abingdon features several other commentaries itself and its distributing arm, Cokesbury, offers series from other publishers as well. The digitally inclined can discover the incredible array of United Methodist biblical resources through the Publishing House and other denominational agencies—biblical guides, commentaries and devotional materials. Since the days of class meeting and *Explanatory Notes upon the New Testament,* through today's *Disciple Bible* study series and *New Interpreter's Bible* there are almost two centuries of Methodist leadership in the Sunday School as a medium for popular instruction and of Methodist endeavor to stay current with biblical scholarship. Over that period Methodists had lived into the ecumenical promise of Scripture, becoming a denomination that spans the center of American Protestantism from moderate evangelicalism to progressive liberalism.

Both hymnals and *Disciplines* have undergone dramatic changes since leaving John Wesley's hand. Initially, the *Discipline,*[36] titled to reflect "The Large Minutes" from which it derived—"Minutes of Several Conversations Between The Rev. Thomas Coke, LL.D. The Rev. Francis Asbury And Others ... Composing a Form of Discipline For the Ministers, Preachers and Other Members of the Methodist Episcopal Church in America"—functioned as a guide to corporate Christian life. It served the gathered community as the hymnal served the individual believer, as rules for the pilgrim's progress. It really was a source of discipline. Though addressed to the preachers, through them it instructed the faithful as well, concerning dress, behavior, intermarriage, slavery, distilled beverages, means of grace, devotional practices, life together, and belief—in short, the way of salvation. Initially an action pamphlet, the *Discipline* grew gradually as Methodist expansion required enhancements to the simple missional imperatives inherited from Wesley and as the church saw reason to specify more clearly its belief, structures, authority and governance. In 1788, 1789 and 1790, the church annexed to the *Discipline* "some other useful Pieces," Arminian essays by Wesley against Calvinist doctrines of predestination and unconditional perseverance, and others explaining Christian perfection and baptism. In 1792, Methodists signaled the purpose the *Discipline* plays in setting forth reasoned belief by re-titling it *The Doctrines and Discipline of the Methodist Episcopal Church.*

Over time much of the explicitly doctrinal content of the *Discipline* eroded or to be more precise was "outsourced," specified as authoritative but separately published. This change in one of Methodism's key books, sometimes interpreted as the church's loss of theological fiber, might better be construed as the consequence of ecclesial maturation. Ecclesial maturation led to a sharper constitutional awareness, most notably in the General Conference of 1808, which passed "**Restrictive Rules**" protecting Methodist **doctrine, conference structure, episcopacy and "General Rules."**[37] Ecclesial maturation led to the rapid growth of a publication empire, which produced or reproduced theological as well as devotional, historical and instructional materials in abundance. Ecclesial maturation led to ever-greater organizational complexity and therefore required greater specificity and precision in the *Discipline.*[38]

For a variety of reasons, then, the *Discipline*, over time, kept doctrine to a minimum and let polity flourish. In 1972, as we will note below, consequent to the uniting of the Evangelical United Brethren and the Methodists and in the face of the challenge of putting together confessional and doctrinal traditions that drew on the Anglican, Calvinist, Lutheran and Anabaptist Reformations, a Theological Commission brought in, and General Conference adopted, a rich theological apparatus. Revised in 1988 (and referenced below), this Disciplinary apparatus now plays a decisive role in orienting the church, and particularly those undergoing the ordination process, towards United Methodist doctrine and theology as witness to the church's apostolic and catholic faith.[39]

American Methodists began with a hymnal filled with Charles Wesley's verse, a poetic guide to the *via salutis*, the way of salvation. In the latest hymnal, that of 1989, only 7% of the hymns come from Charles (52 of 734). Successive hymnals have seen a steady erosion of Wesley's hymns. Or to put it more constructively, successive hymnals have made increasing space for hymns expressive of the religious impulses of the day and/or the larger Christian witness. However, almost from the start, American Methodist leaders, like their British counterparts, struggled to keep the faithful faithfully singing Charles's hymns. The first American-generated hymnbook, the *Pocket Hymn Book* of 1786, drew on hymnals by Robert Spence as well as by the Wesleys.[40] Soon music reflecting the African American experience, camp meetings and revivals, singing schools and the Sunday School competed with that bearing the Wesleyan imprimatur. *A Collection of Hymns and Spiritual Songs Selected from Various Authors by Richard Allen, African Minister* appeared in 1801. Camp meeting hymnals appeared soon thereafter. With such popular alternatives the official or authorized hymnals, which appeared regularly (for the *MEC*: 1786, 1802, 1808, 1821, 1836, 1849, 1878, 1905) had to contend.[41] Worship wars are hardly new.[42]

3. United Methodism

A new church

In 1968, The United Methodist Church [UMC] was created, bringing together The Evangelical United Brethren Church [EUB] and The Methodist Church [MC], and uniting into one the heritage and traditions that had informed the Evangelical Association, the United Brethren, the Methodist Protestants and the two Episcopal Methodisms. The first two of these had united with one another in 1946, the latter three with each other in 1939.[43] The '68 union connected the new church with the major branches of and **diverse ecclesial principles of the Protestant Reformation**, through the UB with the Anabaptist and Reformed, through the EA with the Lutheran, through the Methodists with the Anglican reformations. The larger question of how the new church brought into harmony the practices, policies and polity of these several denominational impulses lies beyond the scope of this enquiry. We do, however, need to take note of the doctrinal, specifically ecclesiological, challenge represented in this union. In 1968, the uniting conference and UMC *Discipline* met this challenge by positing the congruence of doctrine of the two predecessor churches and of the tersest expressions thereof, of the EUB "Confession of Faith" and the Methodist "Articles of Religion." Not content to leave it there, General Conference established a "Theological Study Commission" with a broad mandate, including the possibility of "a contemporary formulation of doctrine and belief."[44]

The Commission chose not to craft a new confession, creed or set of articles but instead to embrace the EUB **Confession** and Methodist **Articles** and place within the *Discipline* a long doctrinal-theological disquisition. Revised in 1988, this section now constitutes Part II of the *Discipline*, "Doctrinal Standards and Our Theological Task." Accordingly, Part I of the *Discipline*, the Constitution, continues both Articles and Confession (Para 3, Article III) and revises the "Restrictive Rules" to protect both statements of belief. The Constitution also includes important ecclesial and ecumenical affirmations, as we note below. However, it is this Part II, which governs the reception and interpretation of these two standards, the General Rules and Wesley's *Sermons* and *Explanatory Notes upon the New Testament*, which figures most prominently in United Methodist ecclesial understanding. One section, Para 101, treats "Our Doctrinal Heritage," covering "Our Common Heritage as Christians," "Basic Christian Affirmations," "Our Distinctive Heritage as United Methodists," "Distinctive Wesleyan Emphases," "Doctrine and Discipline in the Christian Life," and "General Rules and Social Principles." The following section, Para 102, attends to "Our Doctrinal History." Then follow the standards—the Articles, Confession and General Rules—reproduced in full, and declaratory statements indicating where the authoritative *Sermons* and *Explanatory Notes upon the New Testament* may be acquired. Having identified and ordered Methodist doctrine, the *Discipline* in a fourth section, Para 104, "Our Theological Task," sets forth guidelines for drawing on doctrine in the church's efforts to think theologically. Important now in Methodism's practice of theology and especially in ordination processes, this section posits a distinction between doctrine and theology, sets forth characteristics of United Methodism's theological task, describes the quadrilateral and its hermeneutics, identifies challenges to theology, and concludes with a discussion of the church's ecumenical commitment.[45]

United Methodism's four books

"Doctrinal Standards and Our Theological Task," a feature of *Disciplines* since 1972, sets forth distinctively Methodist and Wesleyan belief vigorously and clearly. It does so within an explicitly ecclesiological and ecumenical framework, a point we explore in some detail in a separate section below. This conjoining of the Wesleyan and the ecumenical represents an important development, not a surprising development, perhaps, but nevertheless an important development. Not surprising given Methodism's investment in the ecumenical enterprise and also, as we have noted, the shift of the other specifically Methodist books, hymnal and book of worship, in addition to discipline,[46] in that ecumenical direction.

The current *Hymnal* (1989) gathers the best of the church's praise, whether recent or ancient. Supplementary volumes have followed so as to capture the "The Faith We Sing" and "Global Praise" of the church, the best of its music, the best of its verse. The

Hymnal (1989) also features the liturgies used commonly in congregational life, reflecting as we note below, the ecumenical liturgical consensus. In addition, United Methodists understand the two sacraments, baptism and the Lord's Supper, as rites for the whole church—baptism, inherently ecumenical, and Eucharist, so now nuanced, often with the Wesleyan gloss that it is a converting ordinance.[47]

The two books, then, that had once looked inward and towards a distinctively Wesleyan identity—the *Discipline* and *Hymnal*—now sustain that identity within a clearly catholic context. Insofar as these two books retain their function as the quadrilateral principles of reason and experience, respectively, they point now, as do Scripture and tradition, towards Wesleyan or Methodist belief as part of a common Christian faith.

The United Methodist Book of Worship also repositions its witness to Methodism's tradition(s) within an ecumenical context. Eucharist can still be celebrated with the beautiful phrases of Archbishop Cranmer, but that liturgy, setting IV, now functions as an alternative in the *Book of Worship* (1992) (and in *Hymnal* [1989]), as in BCP. The *Book of Worship* (1992) no longer orients Methodism exclusively towards its Anglican past but rather more broadly to the catholic tradition generally or perhaps one might say to the Anglican-Methodist reception of the catholic tradition. From beginning to end, from its initial setting out of "The Basic Pattern of Worship" to its concluding rites for missionaries and deaconesses, the *Book of Worship* (1992) draws into United Methodist life the best liturgical wisdom and practices of the twentieth-century liturgical and ecumenical movements. The witness of the BCP remains, but is now surrounded by worship patterns reflective of the great tradition of the church and its global expression today.

The *Book of Worship* (1992) still indicates the place of tradition, in its widest sense, in United Methodist life. Some areas of the denomination and some congregations have become liturgically self-conscious to a remarkable extent. In such places, worship draws significantly and imaginatively on the *Book of Worship* (1992). There congregations experience the church year, the lectionary, the rich array of special services, a high degree of liturgical self-awareness and albs and stoles. The trend is sufficiently prominent as to have worried Thomas Langford who complained that a once preaching church had become a liturgical church.[48] Still, large sectors of United Methodism function out of lower church paradigms, in some cases now re-energized with the so-called "contemporary" styles of worship and music and a church-growth ecclesiology. The *Book of Worship* (1992) continues therefore, as ecclesial touchstone and provides one clue to United Methodism's ecclesial self-understanding. Its use signals orientation towards ecclesial self-understanding and catholicity predicated on the long Christian tradition. Its non-use often signals investment in more evangelical, missional and present-oriented forms of Christian unity.

Scripture functions, one might argue, in Methodist/Wesleyan understanding, to orient believers towards the common witness of the church and the unity realized and promised in Christ. Such an affirmation and a direction clearly inform United Methodist scholarly and devotional attention to the Bible. The clear commitment, within sectors of United Methodism, to hold together critical scholarship and piety— nicely epitomized in the *Disciple Study* Bible series and *The New Interpreter's Bible*, both products of The United Methodist Publishing House—orients this fundamental or primary epistemological criterion, one might insist, towards the other three aspects of the quadrilateral, a point that the *Discipline* itself makes explicitly.[49]

Counterpoint

However, the ecumenical convergence represented in current versions of Methodism's four books does not command the loyalty and adherence of the entire church. The culture wars, ignited within North American society, also blaze across United Methodism. They blaze especially brightly over Scripture and its relation to other authorities. A conservative or evangelical wing of Methodism—actually comprising diverse religious impulses, but achieving some unity through allegiances to a single seminary, an alternative missionary society, separate presses, collaborative media and web sites, distinctive funding mechanisms, an entity that behaves like the Congregation for the Propagation of the Faith, and a common insistence on a closed creed as well as closed canon—reads the Bible as yielding quite fixed doctrines.[50] Scripture, this sector of Methodism seems to suggest, speaks univocally and once-and-for-all-times. So, spokespersons in this camp insist, Scripture and Scripture alone should settle matters deemed doctrinal, like abortion and homosexuality.

Experience, reason, and tradition thereby lose their capacity to function interactively and transmissively with respect to Scripture, and to bear forth and address the inspired Word to specific times and contexts. Only Scripture can be inspired. Some in this wing of United Methodism, not surprisingly, have little use for the notion of a quadrilateral, even in its post 1988 version with the guarantees of the primacy of Scripture: "Scripture is the primary source and criterion for Christian doctrine." This camp tends to pit Scripture against other authorities. It offers a new modality of Wesleyan inwardness, a loyalty to the Wesley of one book, the Bible. It permits, if not actually encourages, a disuse of the other books. Particularly where energized by church growth or mega-church doctrine, it prefers power-pointed contemporary worship to the *Book of Worship* (1992), the praise chorus to the *Hymnal* (1989), and congregational prerogative to the connectional structures and processes that the *Discipline* describes and prescribes. The *Discipline* as a law book, however, this wing of United Methodism finds still serviceable, indeed, vital in the war they wage for Methodism's soul. Still, one could say this wing pits the one book, the Bible, over against the other three.

One detects in this conservative-evangelical Methodist stance a somewhat different ecclesiology than that represented in the current versions of the four books, different than that I am positing as ecumenical Methodism, different than that outlined immediately below. This wing of the church certainly claims the Wesleyan missional emphasis, indeed, it makes mission, understood as disciple-making, the primary, even sole task and purpose of the church, a conviction recently legislated into the *Discipline*. It leavens mission not with the "Christ the transformer of culture" spirit that has been a hallmark of American Methodism but with a "Christ against culture" style but AChrist of culture@ nature [**SIC!**]. It does so in the conviction that in so doing it, rather than ecumenical United Methodism, is the more faithful to Wesley. Accordingly it launches a critique, sometimes quite harsh, against the agencies and leadership of United Methodism. It does so convinced that the "missional" rather than the "catholic" requires the church's energy and focus in today's world. Its spirit is non-catholic and its style non-connectional. Or, to be more generous, it reserves its catholicity for counterpart conservative wings of other denominations and in concert with them builds its own connectional structures. Like the larger evangelicalism so suffused with Calvinist practice, it has begun to put a premium on the creedal and confessional shibboleths.

4. Missional ecclesiology

The official stance

In its official stance, Methodism's four books continue, in their own way, to sustain indebtedness to John Wesley—the Wesleyan commitment perhaps more salient post-1968 than before—but the important yet diverse heritages mediated through the EUB have helped reduce the distance or tension between that Wesleyan ecclesial self-understanding and that oriented towards the larger Christian witness. In lessening that tension or achieving the new balance, the four books function, where they are all used, with some degree of harmony. Their harmony owes to the long-term developments to which we have alluded, rather than the formal enunciation of a quadrilateral hermeneutic or epistemology. Nevertheless, the quadrilateral, tersely described in *Disciplines* since 1972, provides United Methodists a language with which to grasp and explain this common focus. And, in various ways, the *Discipline* has become more explicit about Methodism's doctrinal commitments.

Discipline: catholic spirit

After 1968 and especially after 1972, the new church imbedded within the *Discipline* expressions of a catholic spirit and pointers towards an ecumenical ecclesiology, understanding the bringing together of traditions representing the major strands of the Protestant Reformation as an opportunity for still greater unity. That ecumenical, unitive or catholic commitment defines United Methodism—in its structure, policy and program, indeed, in its very Constitution—in the following ways.

> The Preamble to the Constitution (Part I) situates the newly constituted church within the universal church.

> Article III of the Constitution incorporates and Articles I and II of the Restrictive Rules protect the Articles of Religion, John Wesley's adaptation of the Thirty-nine Articles and the Confession of Faith, from the Evangelical United Brethren Church, thereby defining the church in classic Reformation terms (Articles) and claiming its classic marks or notes, "one, holy, apostolic and catholic" (Confession).

> Article IV of the Constitution on the "Inclusiveness of the Church" proclaims The United Methodist Church "a part of the church universal" and commits it to overcoming all those forces and factors which divide the human family.

Article VI of the Constitution on "Ecumenical Relations" affirms "As part of the church universal, The United Methodist Church believes the Lord of the church is calling Christians everywhere to strive toward unity. . . ."

United Methodism also builds this ecumenical, unitive or catholic commitment into its structure, policy and program elsewhere in the *Discipline*—in particular:

"Our Doctrinal Heritage" in Part II locates United Methodism within the "common heritage with Christians of every age and nation" and sets out "Basic Christian Affirmations" which United Methodists confess with all Christians.

This statement concludes that "With other Christians, we declare the essential oneness of the church in Christ Jesus." It illustrates that ground of and commitment to unity, affirming, "This rich heritage of shared Christian belief finds expression in our hymnody and liturgies. Our unity is affirmed in the historic creeds as we confess one holy, catholic, and apostolic church. It is also experienced in joint ventures of ministry and in various forms of ecumenical cooperation.

. . . "Our avowed ecumenical commitment as United Methodists is to gather our own doctrinal emphases into the larger Christian unity, there to be made more meaningful in a richer whole."

"Our Doctrinal History" begins by insisting that the church's constitutive traditions "understood themselves as standing in the central stream of Christian spirituality and doctrine," characterizes the church's vocation as "catholic spirit," and concludes by positing the recovery, updating and reinvigorating of "our distinctive doctrinal heritage—catholic, evangelical, and reformed—as essential to both evangelism and ecumenical dialogue."

"Our Theological Task" ends with a section on "Ecumenical Commitment" insisting that "Christian unity is not an option" but is mandated theologically, biblically and practically "a gift to be received and expressed."

"The Ministry of All Christians," Part III of the *Discipline*, evokes the ecumenical consensus of Vatican II, COCU, BEM that all baptized are called to ministry. Appropriately it situates important United Methodist rubrics—the Journey of a Connectional People, Servant Ministry, Servant Leadership, Called to Inclusiveness, and the Fulfillment of Ministry Through The United Methodist Church—within the narration of the longer and larger story of God's covenantal initiatives and of the Church's mission.

Part V, Chapter One, "The Local Church," in framing the church's global mission makes provision for cooperative parishes and ecumenical shared ministries.

The rubric on "Church Membership," para 214, states "The United Methodist Church is a part of the holy catholic (universal) church, as we confess in the Apostles Creed." The next paragraph affirms "A member of any local United Methodist church is a member of the denomination and the catholic (universal) church."

The episcopal or superintending office is assigned a number of tasks, among them, "to seek and be a sign of the unity of the faith" and "to exercise the discipline of the whole Church" (para 404) and specifically "To provide liaison and leadership in the quest for Christian unity in ministry, mission, and structure and in the search for strengthened relationships with other living faith communities" (para 414).

The General Commission on Christian Unity and Interreligious Concerns, and its corresponding boards or officers on jurisdictional, conference, district, and congregational levels, are charged explicitly to exercise "ecumenical leadership" towards Christian unity and dialogue with others faiths, cultures and ideologies.

The *Discipline* acknowledges UMC membership explicitly in several "Interdenominational Agencies"—World Methodist Council, the Consultation on Church Union (COCU), the National Council of Churches, the World Council of Churches, the Commission on Pan-Methodist Cooperation and the American Bible Society—and assigns UMC leadership therein to the bishops and GCCUIC leadership (para 2401).

United Methodism's formal commitments to unity and catholicity set impressive standards and directions, and accord with the role United Methodism and its predecessor denominations have exercised within the ecumenical movement. Methodism has been a major ecumenical player. At this writing, Methodists head both the National and World Council of Churches. In the past, Methodists have played leadership roles in COCU, and in many unitive efforts at regional, national and global levels. Over recent decades, United Methodism has invested much in bilateral dialogues, such as the one for which this essay is crafted.[51] The catholic language of the *Discipline*, the prominence of Methodists in ecumenical endeavor, and the clear commitment of the church's leadership to dialogue give the appearance of ecclesiological single-mindedness and coherence. In actual practice, various kinds of unities beckon the church. United Methodists work on different fronts, the genuine laborers for unity and catholicity remain few, the church at all levels voices more commitment than it proves willing to honor. Some within the denomination express open hostility to ecumenical efforts and many remain absolutely oblivious to investments long made. The important tension with which the denomination began, a ecclesiological tension lived out by John and Charles Wesley between the church's catholic and its missional self-understanding remains present, indeed highly politicized. That tension may be obscured, forgotten, neglected, and overlooked in ecumenical conversation in Methodist self-representation—in efforts to mirror our conversational partners or as a stratagem towards unity. The ecclesiological tension should not be obscured. It constitutes a gift of Methodism to the larger Church, when really kept in tension.

Discipline: missional commitment

The missional understanding of the church remains prominent in the two books where it has been most salient from the start, *Discipline* and *Hymnal*. Both nicely exhibit the tension, now both sides of the tension, within which United Methodism does church. The unitive side of this tension we have described above. The missional is equally prominent.

The *Discipline* devotes four paragraphs of the "Preamble" to the church's unity, but affirms in a fifth, "The church of Jesus Christ exists in and for the world, and its very dividedness is a hindrance to its mission in that world." The "Restrictive Rules" continue the protection to Methodism's distinctive, missional understanding of episcopacy or superintendency, as itinerant and general in character. Several articles within the Constitution delineate the nature and tasks of the conferences of United Methodism and para 31 identifies the annual conference as "the basic body in the Church." In so defining the Church connectionally and at that level which admits into ordained ministry, at which ordination occurs, and from which ministries proceed and ministers sent, United Methodism sustains Wesley's missional ecclesiology. The *Discipline* treats the understanding and tasks of ministry that flow from this ecclesiology. But from this definition flow Methodism's distinctive itinerant and appointive commitments. Part II on "Doctrinal Standards and Our Theological Task," as we have noted, accents Wesleyan practical, soteriological and missional emphases within the shared catholic heritage.

The missional understanding becomes more marked in Part III, "The Ministry of All Christians," subtitled "The Mission and Ministry of the Church." Para 120, "The Mission" proclaims

> The mission of the Church is to make disciples of Jesus Christ. Local churches provide the most significant arena through which disciple-making occurs.

The "Rationale for our Mission," immediately following, begins:

> The mission of the Church it to make disciples of Jesus Christ by proclaiming the good news of God's grace and thus seeking the fulfillment of God's reign and realm in the world. The fulfillment of God's reign and realm in the world is the vision Scripture holds before us.

The phrasing attempts to hold justification and justice, evangelism and social transformation, in tension, but the adequate development of the latter missional emphasis really is to be found in the next major *Disciplinary* section, Part IV.[52] Part III does set the mood by reference to and exegesis of Matthew 28:19–20. As of the 1996 *Discipline*, III also enunciates a theme of servant ministry and servant leadership, stating that this calling figures prominently in the office of the permanent deacon but belongs also to the laity and is added as well to that of the elder and therefore of bishops. The full implications of an adequate theology for servanthood need to be more fully developed, especially since the church made this missional addition, a fourth, to the traditional three—word, sacrament, and order.[53]

Another section in III, para 138, declares the church to be "Called to Inclusiveness." That mission of the church, to be agent and anticipatory of the kingdom and of the redemption of the world, the *Discipline* develops quite fully in Part IV, "Social Principles," pp. 95–122. This long treatise recalls early Methodism's social witness (including antislavery), notes the 1908 elaboration and adoption by the MEC of a social creed (other predecessor denominations following later) and develops United Methodism's contemporary social commitments under six rubrics, "The Natural World," "The Nurturing Community," "The Social Community," "The Economic Community," "The Political Community," and "The World Community." The principles are to guide United Methodist attitudes and practices with respect to the world outside the church. They also apply within, touching matters of marriage, divorce, sexuality, family violence, sexual harassment, abortion, care at the end of life, and suicide. General Conference has chosen to locate more fully developed stances on both internal and external concerns in a now huge, quadrennially produced tome, *The Book of Resolutions*. One might wish that this could be added as a fifth book defining United Methodism and exhibiting its ecclesial sensibilities. However, despite its official status, United Methodist laity and clergy seemingly make little use of it. Fortunately, they are more likely to heed the injunction that appears with the "Social Creed" in the *Discipline* that the creed be available to the people and used in Sunday worship. A variant of the creed appears in the *Hymnal* (1989), to be used as an affirmation of faith.

The *Discipline* continues efforts to balance evangelism and social concern, mission and catholicity in the remainder of what has now become a long book. Part V on "Organization and Administration," for instance, begins the treatment on "The Local Church" with successive paragraphs, the first of which affirms by definition, "The **local church** provides the most significant arena through which disciple-making occurs." The next paragraph, treating the local church's function, declares, "The church of Jesus Christ exists in and for the world. It is primarily at the level of the local church that the church encounters the world."

The *Hymnal* (1989) achieves the same balance, at least in part explaining its wildly successful introduction and congregational adoption. It retains the favorites derived from Methodism's revivalistic and holiness past, like Fanny Crosby's "Pass Me Not, O Gentle Savior," "Blessed Assurance," "I am Thine, O Lord," and "Rescue the Perishing." It includes social gospel hymns by Harry Emerson Fosdick and Frank Mason North, civil rights songs, and verse from across the world. Alongside Methodism's missional anthems can be found chants ancient and modern, from the Community of Taizé or Byzantium.[54] Like the *Discipline*, the *Hymnal* (1989) invites United Methodists to claim their distinctive voice but to sound it loudly for the Church catholic.

Conclusion

United Methodism's four books define it and exhibit its ecclesial sensibilities. Most United Methodists have ready access to only two of them, the Bible and *Hymnal* (1989). The other two, *The Book of Discipline* and *Book of Worship* (1992), some Methodists have never seen. Nevertheless, each can, and I think should, work for and work itself into the drama of the church's daily life. The *Discipline* and *Book of Worship* (1992) function off stage determining how the play unfolds, who acts, and what instructions to follow. Bible and *Hymnal* (1989) script Methodist life together.

For present life together, especially life in congregations, the four books, where effectively used, orient Methodists towards the Word, mediate United Methodism's traditions, including particularly its Wesleyan heritage, offer experiential expressions of the faith once delivered, and order belief and practice accordingly. The books evidence United Methodism's actual use of quadrilateral ways of knowing Christ and being Christ-like. They also show, in their convergence, a convergence clearer now than in earlier days, how the four-fold epistemology or hermeneutic yields a common focus. And the common focus in the four books orients United Methodism to the classic marks or notes of the Church—its **oneness**, its **holiness**, its **catholicity** and its **apostolicity**. Methodism nuances those marks in its own distinctive fashion as connectional, disciplined, ecumenical, missional. Its books claim these Wesleyan nuances or understandings, but point as well towards the received ecclesiological doctrines of catholic Christianity.

In these four books, the catholic and missional, the high liturgical and fervid evangelical that the Wesleys held so curiously together come again into tension. The four books beckon United Methodists who press to one extreme or the other to reclaim balance and live our distinctive witness. Scripture, hymnbook, discipline, and book of worship, define how United Methodists do church. This may not be ecclesiology in its most familiar, doctrinal form. But in structure and practice, in office and program, United Methodists nevertheless live faithfully into the ecumenical ecclesial consensus, adding what they affirm to be an apostolic commitment to mission. Methodists offer a *via salutis* to augment the tradition's *ordo salutis* and an ecclesiological *via* to augment the tradition's ecclesiological *ordo*.[55]

Endnotes

[1]The full titles are: *The Book of Discipline of the United Methodist Church, 2000* (Nashville: The United Methodist Publishing House, 2000); *The United Methodist Book of Worship* (Nashville: The United Methodist Publishing House, 1992); and *The United Methodist Hymnal* (Nashville: The United Methodist Publishing House, 1989). The first is revised and a new version published after each General Conference, typically quadrennially.

[2]See Karen B. Westerfield Tucker, *American Methodist Worship* (New York: Oxford University Press, 2001).

[3]For an effort to set out standards of United Methodist doctrine by their official level of authority, see Scott J. Jones, *United Methodist Doctrine: The Extreme Center* (Nashville: Abingdon Press, 2002), 43–56. Jones distinguishes ten texts that fall into three levels. First are the constitutional standards, which include items embraced in the *Discipline* (Constitution, Articles, Confession and General Rules) plus infrequently used but official standards, Wesley's "Standard Sermons" and *Explanatory Notes Upon the New Testament*. At a second level he places contemporary statements, namely other parts of the *Discipline* and the wonderful but rarely used *Book of Resolutions*. At the third level he locates *Hymnal* and *Book of Worship* that he terms liturgy. In his formulations, he recognizes the degrees of authority represented but draws on all three levels. For a simpler schema, compare Ted A. Campbell, *Methodist Doctrine: The Essentials* (Nashville: Abingdon Press, 1999), "Appendix 2," 116–22. See also Thomas C. Oden, *Doctrinal Standards in the Wesleyan Tradition* (Grand Rapids: Francis Asbury Press of Zondervan Publishing House, 1988). The discussion that follows addresses the issues they raise.

[4]*Minutes of Several Conversations Between the Rev. Thomas Coke, LL. D., the Rev. Francis Asbury and others, at a Conference, Begun in Baltimore, in the State of Maryland, on Monday, the 27th of December, in the Year 1784* (Philadelphia: Charles Cist, 1785). For the text of the first *Discipline* in parallel columns with the "Large Minutes" see Jno. J. Tigert, *A Constitutional History of American Episcopal Methodism*, 3rd. ed. (Nashville: Publishing House of the Methodist Episcopal Church, South, 1908), 532–602.

[5]See Carlton R. Young, *Companion to The United Methodist Hymnal* (Nashville: Abingdon Press, 1993), 94–95.

[6]See *The Works of John Wesley, 7, A Collection of Hymns for the use of the People called Methodists*, ed. Franz Hildebrandt and Oliver A. Beckerlegge, with the assistance of James Dale (Nashville: Abingdon Press, 1983). Unless otherwise indicated, reference is to this critical edition begun as "The Oxford Edition of the Works of John Wesley," continued as "The Bicentennial Edition of the Works of John Wesley" by Abingdon Press, 1984–. The series began with Oxford, 1975–83.

[7]To some extent, it would function for Methodists as the Book of Common Prayer (BCP) did for Anglicans.

[8]*John Wesley's Sunday Service of the Methodists in North America*, with an introduction by James F. White (Nashville: Quarterly Review, 1984).

[9]Russell E. Richey, Kenneth E. Rowe and Jean Miller Schmidt, *The Methodist Experience in America: A Sourcebook, II* (Nashville: Abingdon Press, 2000), 1784a, 72. Hereinafter this volume is abbreviated *MEA*.

[10]See Ted A. Campbell, "The 'Wesleyan Quadrilateral': The Story of a Modern Methodist Myth," and Albert C. Outler, "The Wesleyan Quadrilateral—In John Wesley," in Thomas A. Langford, ed., *Doctrine and Theology in The United Methodist Church* (Nashville: Kingswood Books/Abingdon Press, 1991), 154–61 and 75–88; W. Stephen Gunter et al., *Wesley and the Quadrilateral: Renewing the Conversation* (Nashville: Abingdon Press, 1997); Scott J. Jones, *John Wesley's Conception and Use of Scripture* (Nashville: Kingswood Books/Abingdon Press, 1995); Scott J. Jones, *United Methodist Doctrine: The Extreme Center*; and Walter Klaiber and Manfred Marquardt, *Living Grace: An Outline of United Methodist Theology*, translated and adapted by J. Steven O'Malley and Ulrike R. M. Guthrie (Nashville: Abingdon Press, 2001), 17–92.

[11]See the scriptural annotations, the rubrics and indexes, and the theological acuity clearly evident in *The Works of John Wesley, 7, A Collection of Hymns for the use of the People called Methodists*.

[12]The quadrilateral as a construct does not come into Methodist usage until the late twentieth century.

[13]I owe this formulation to my colleague, Thomas Frank.

[14]For an overview of Wesley's theology and theological development accenting its missional and salvific character, see Kenneth J. Collins, *John Wesley: A Theological Journal* (Nashville: Abingdon Press, 2003).

[15]*Form of Discipline, for the Ministers, Preachers, and Members of the Methodist Episcopal Church in America* (New York: W. Ross, 1787), 3. Compare the earlier (1784) formulation, lacking the second assertion, actually lacking points (2) and (3) of Methodist purpose, in the first *Discipline*, in Tigert, *Constitutional History*, 535.

[16]On early Methodism's antislavery witness and the retreat therefrom, see A. Gregory Schneider, *The Way of the Cross Leads Home: The Domestication of American Methodism* (Bloomington and Indianapolis: Indiana University Press, 1993); Christine Leigh Heyrman, *Southern Cross: The Beginnings of the Bible Belt* (New York: Alfred A. Knopf, 1997); John H. Wigger, *Taking Heaven by Storm: Methodism and the Rise of Popular Christianity in America* (New York and Oxford: Oxford University Press, 1998); Cynthia Lynn Lyerly, *Methodism and the Southern Mind, 1770–1810* (New York and Oxford: Oxford University Press, 1998); Dee E. Andrews, *Religion and the Revolution: The Rise of the Methodists in the Greater Middle Atlantic, 1760–1800* (Princeton: Princeton University Press, 1999); Donald G. Mathews, *Religion in the Old South* (Chicago and London: University of Chicago Press, 1977); H. Shelton Smith, *In His Image, But . . . : Racism in Southern Religion, 1780–1910* (Durham: Duke University Press, 1972); and my *Early American Methodism* (Bloomington and Indianapolis: Indiana University Press, 1991).

[17]One gets a nice overview of the Methodist missionary system through the day-to-day activities, the scenes described, and the instructions of its itinerant apostle and chief bishop, Francis Asbury. For the day-to-day activity of missionary itinerancy, see all three volumes of *The Journal and Letters of Francis Asbury*, ed. Elmer T. Clark, 3 vols. (London and Nashville: Epworth Press & Abingdon Press, 1958). This work is cited hereinafter as *JLFA*. For a recent review of Asbury at the center of Methodism's missionary system, see Darius L. Salter, *America's Bishop: The Life of Francis Asbury* (Nappanee, IN: Francis Asbury Press of Evangel Publishing House, 2003).

[18]On this dimension of Wesleyan theology, see Robert E. Cushman, *John Wesley's Experimental Divinity: Studies in Methodist Doctrinal Standards* (Nashville: Kingswood Books/Abingdon, 1989); Thomas A. Langford, *Practical Divinity: Theology in the Wesleyan Tradition* (Nashville: Abingdon Press, 1983); Scott J. Jones, *United Methodist Doctrine: The Extreme Center* (Nashville: Abingdon Press, 2002), pp. 61, 71–77, 241–97); Kenneth J. Collins, *A Real Christian: The Life of John Wesley* (Nashville: Abingdon Press, 1999).

[19]*Sunday Service*, p. A 1. White's "Introduction" and "Notes" provide more extensive documentation of Wesley's changes to the BCP.

[20]For the first sustained defense of Methodist ecclesiology, ministry and episcopacy, see the annotated *Discipline* produced by bishops Thomas Coke and Francis Asbury, *The Doctrines and Disciplines of the Methodist Episcopal Church in America* (Philadelphia: Henry Tuckniss, 1798) and excerpts in Richey, Rowe

and Schmidt, MEA, II, 1798. Wesley's ministry laid the essential foundation of what became the Methodist style of episcopacy, and in many ways that foundation has remained intact in America, Gerald F. Moede, "Bishops in the Methodist Tradition: Historical Perspectives," *Episcopacy: Lutheran-United Methodist Dialogue II*, eds. Jack M. Tuel and Roger W. Fjeld (Minneapolis: Augsburg, 1991), 52–69, 58. For an overview and assessment of the office, see James E. Kirby, *The Episcopacy in American Methodism* (Nashville: Kingswood Books/Abingdon Press, 2000); Thomas Edward Frank, *Polity, Practice and the Mission of The United Methodist Church*, updated edition (Nashville: Abingdon Press, 2002), 229–53; and Norman Woods Spellmann, *The General Superintendency in American Methodism, 1784–1870*, Ph.D. Dissertation, Yale University, April 1961.

[21]See *The Life of the Reverend Devereux Jarratt*, foreword by David L. Holmes, series editor Barbara Brown Zikmund (Cleveland: The Pilgrim Press, 1995; first published 1806), especially Letter II, penned in 1794, pp. 47–78 and particularly 61–70.

[22]Early American editions of John Wesley's *Explanatory notes upon the New Testament*, included: Philadelphia: Printed by Joseph Crukshank, sold by John Dickins, No. 43, Fourth-Street, near the corner of Race-Street, 1791; A two-volume version published by Ezekiel Cooper and John Wilson, William C. Robinson, printer, 1806; published by Daniel Hitt and Thomas Ware, for the Methodist Connection in the United States, John C. Totten, printer, 1812; published by J. Soule and T. Mason, for the Methodist Episcopal Church in the United States, Abraham Paul, printer, 1818; New-York: published by T. Mason and G. Lane, for the Methodist Episcopal Church, at the Conference Office, J. Collord, printer, 1837; New-York: Published by T. Mason and G. Lane, for the Methodist Episcopal Church, at the Conference Office, J. Collord, printer, 1839; New York: published by G. Lane & P.P. Sandford, for the Methodist Episcopal Church, at the Conference Office, J. Collord, printer, 1844.

[23]John Telford, ed., *The Letters of the Rev. John Wesley*, 8 vols. (London: Epworth, 1931), 7: 191; Nathan Bangs, *A History of the Methodist Episcopal Church*, 4 vols., 12th edition (New York: Carlton & Porter, 1860), 1: 148. For the case for the continued authority of the *Notes*, see Oden, *Doctrinal Standards in the Wesleyan Tradition*, 15–68. The sales of the *Notes* must have been primarily to the preachers as they were minuscule in comparison to the movement of other Methodist books, particularly the hymnals. See midwestern sales records in William Warren Sweet, ed., *Religion on the American Frontier. 1783–1840, IV, The Methodists: A Collection of Source Materials* (New York: Cooper Square Publishers, Inc. 1964; originally published by the University of Chicago, 1946), 698–706.

[24]For Wesley's self-identification, see *The Works of John Wesley*, I: 105, the Preface to the 1746 edition of *Sermons on Several Occasions* and *The Works of John Wesley*, 3: 504. On Wesley's understanding and use of Scripture, see Jones, *John Wesley's Conception and Use of Scripture.*

[25]August 5, 1813, "A Valedictory Address to William McKendree," *JLFA*, 3: 475–92, 475, 480. Several pages into the address, Asbury began to appeal by extensive citation to Thomas Haweis' *History of the Church of Christ*, on the basis of which he posited the apostolic character of Methodist episcopacy.

[26]For recent efforts to review Methodist ecclesiology, typically with reference to its Wesleyan foundations and their catholic import, see Ted A. Campbell, *Methodist Doctrine: The Essentials* (Nashville: Abingdon Press, 1999), 64–79; Scott J. Jones, *United Methodist Doctrine: The Extreme Center*, 241–74; Walter Klaiber and Manfred Marquardt, *Living Grace: An Outline of United Methodist Theology*, section 4, 311–417; and Theodore Runyon, *The New Creation: John Wesley's Theology Today* (Nashville: Abingdon Press, 1998).

[27]Jesse Lee, *A Short History of the Methodists* (Baltimore: Magill and Clime, 1810; facsimile edition, Rutland, VT: Academy Books, 1974), 340.

[28]The placement of camp meeting in quarterly meeting can be seen in the quarterly meeting records reproduced in Sweet, ed., *The Methodists: A Collection of Source Materials*. I have explored the relation between camp meeting and quarterly meeting in *The Methodist Conference in America: A History* (Nashville: Kingswood Books/Abingdon Press, 1996) and in *Early American Methodism* (Bloomington: Indiana University Press, 1991).

[29]See *The Methodist Conference in America: A History, Early American Methodism*, and Lester Ruth, *A Little Heaven Below: Worship at Early American Methodist Quarterly Meetings* (Nashville: Kingswood Books/Abingdon Press, 2000).

[30]See Karen B. Westerfield Tucker, *American Methodist Worship* (New York: Oxford University Press, 2001).

[31]Young, *Companion to The United Methodist Hymnal*, 112–13.

[32]See Tucker, *American Methodist Worship*, 3–30.

[33]See James Penn Pilkington and Walter Newton Vernon, Jr., *The United Methodist Publishing House: A History*, 2 vols. (Nashville: Abingdon, 1968 and 1989).

[34]For an illustration of this point and documents that sustain the argument of this paragraph, see Sweet, ed. *The Methodists: A Collection of Source Materials* (1946), 709, 680–709.

[35]Ibid., 706.

[36]Tigert, *Constitutional History*, 463, 533. Tigert examined the titles and contents of the early *Disciplines* in Appendix I, 463–76.

[37]*MEA*, II, 1808.

[38]Richey, *Methodist Conference in America*, traces this evolution.

[39]For exploration of the 1972 statement and its 1988 revision, see Langford, ed., *Doctrine and Theology in The United Methodist Church*.

[40]Young, *Companion to The United Methodist Hymnal*, 97–108.

[41]For the stemma of MEC, MECS, MPC and MC hymnals, see Young, *Companion to The United Methodist Hymnal*, 94–95; for EUB, 81–82. See also *MEA*, II, 29–30.

[42]See Thomas G. Long, *Beyond the Worship Wars: Building Vital and Faithful Worship* (N.P.: The Alban Institute, 2001).

[43]For the terse, official narrative of this union and the histories behind it, see *The Book of Discipline of the United Methodist Church*, 2000, 9–20, 50–59.

[44]Albert C. Outler, "Introduction to the Report of the 1968–72 Theological Study Commission," in Langford, ed., *Doctrine and Theology in The United Methodist Church*, 20–25. The entire volume, on which this discussion draws, attends to the 1972 Commission and 1988 Committee and the resultant doctrinal-theological disciplinary sections. See also Frank, *Polity, Practice and the Mission of The United Methodist Church*, 141–57.

[45]See the final section below on the ecclesiological and ecumenically ecclesiological import of the *Discipline*.

[46]*The Book of Discipline of the United Methodist Church*, 2000, *The United Methodist Book of Worship*, 1992; henceforth cited as *Book of Worship* (1992); and *The United Methodist Hymnal*, 1989; henceforth cited as *Hymnal* (1989).

[47]United Methodists divide as to whether the "open table" extends universally or to the baptized. See E. Byron Anderson, *The Meaning of Holy Communion in The United Methodist Church* (Nashville: GBOD/Discipleship Resources, 2000); Gayle Carlton Felton, *This Gift of Water: The Practice and Theology of Baptism among Methodists in America* (Nashville: Abingdon Press, c1992); ———, *By Water and the Spirit: Making Connections for Identity and Ministry*, The Christian Initiation Series (Nashville: GBOD/Discipleship Resources, 2003); also on web at http://www.gbod.org/worship/articles/water_spirit/; ———, "The Holy Mystery: A United Methodist Understanding of Holy Communion," Holy Communion Study Committee; Lester Ruth, *A Little Heaven Below*.

[48]Langford enunciated such claims several times in conversation or discussion.

[49]*The Book of Discipline of the United Methodist Church*, 2000, 78–79.

[50]See Leon Howell, *United Methodism @ Risk: A Wake-up Call*, Study Guide by Bishop C. Dale White and The Rev. Scott Campbell (Kingston, NY: Information Project for United Methodists, 2003).

[51]On Methodist participation in the various ecumenical conversations, see Geoffrey Wainwright, *Methodists in Dialog* (Nashville: Kingswood Books/Abingdon Press, 1995).

[52]However, as the "Counterpoint" discussion indicates, not all United Methodists hold these two aspects together. The more progressive wing of the church believes that the conservatives slight justice and social transformation. The conservative wing believes that the progressives slight justification and evangelism.

[53]On issues and problems related to this concept, see Frank, *Polity, Practice and the Mission of The United Methodist Church*, 162–68.

[54]Young, *Companion to The United Methodist Hymnal*.

[55]See Jones, *United Methodist Doctrine: The Extreme Center*, 246–70 and Campbell, *Methodist Doctrine: The Essentials*, 64–79.

10

The Holiness of a Human Being:
A Mark of Christian Spirituality

Tamara Grdzelidze

I felt compelled to write this chapter on the holiness of the human being for two reasons. On the one hand, I was captivated by the image of holy people as depicted in hagiographical texts, especially two eleventh-century Georgian sources that I was translating from Georgian into English. On the other hand, I was already aware of some fruits of the Orthodox-Wesleyan encounters from which I learned that the Wesleyan outlook on holiness and perfection, in many ways, is close to the tradition of the Eastern Church Fathers. Such observations as "Wesley came nearer to the Eastern doctrine of synergism then most of Western theologians, largely through his reading of Chrysostom" by Dr. Frances Young,[1] pushed me to consider the possibility of similar patterns of living out holiness in everyday life. In the article of Dr. Young we also learn that John Wesley and the Macarian homilies had "a common emphasis on the impetus towards perfection as the goal of the Christian life, a common emphasis on the Incarnation and the Holy Spirit as the sources of perfection, and a common stress on the love of God."[2] Chrysostom and Macarius were well known to the people whose everyday lives I examined in the course of my translations. Another supporting source for my deliberations came from an article on "Trinitarian Theology and Wesleyan Holiness" by Geoffrey Wainwright, where I learned that "full salvation, entire sanctification, perfection, perfect love in the Wesleyan understanding did not coincide with the Calvinists and Lutherans of his day." "Wesley knew, of course, that *God's love has been poured into our hearts through the Holy Spirit which has been given to us* (Rom. 5:5) and he was reluctant to set limits to what God might accomplish in us."[3]

In a description of the lives of the Athonite saints, there is clarity about the holiness—to which all created in the image of God are called—experienced every day throughout their lifetimes and even expected and experienced after their deaths. In the lives of the saints, this expectation is associated with their presence in this world after death. Generally, hagiographers share the common conviction that departed holy people protect those now on their spiritual journey.

The hagiographers intend to give an account of the spiritual journey that is a description of the lives of holy persons, thus presenting a dynamic picture of the human response to divine grace. I gather that in Wesleyan spirituality, holiness, as grounded in divine love, is also a dynamic concept rather than a static one, it is a perfection set in motion while stillness comes within "the house of God" (Ps. 42:4).[4]

In what sense is holiness a sign of human perfection? How is holiness revealed in everyday life? This chapter attempts to find points of convergence and divergence on the holiness of a human being in Wesleyan and Orthodox theologies and to address these highlighted issues within a wider framework of Christian spirituality. A very first impression, when reading texts so very different culturally and chronologically, is of their convergence on a synergistic approach: in order to reach salvation, human effort must respond to God's grace. The central role of a spiritual guide, a teacher or spiritual father in one's spiritual journey also finds its counterpart in Wesleyan spirituality, I believe, in the way in which the call for holiness is communicated to believers through hymns and sermons: the spirit of the words moves between the invocation involved in hymns and the didactic content of sermons. On the other hand, there are a number of ways of expressing the holiness in the lives of the Athonite saints that are less likely to be found in Wesleyan texts, for example, miracles and prophecy and the veneration of the body of the saint. However, in some cases modern Methodist scholarship traces similar trends, for example, the significance attributed by John Wesley to relics.

My sources for examining holiness in Wesleyan spirituality are rather limited: I shall refer to John Wesley's sermon, "On Working Out Our Own Salvation"[5] and to a section of hymns on "Christian Holiness" from *The Methodist Hymnbook* (1933).

For Orthodox sources, I refer to two Georgian hagiographical texts from the eleventh century, *The Life of St. John and St. Euthymius the Athonites*[6] and *The Life of St. George the Athonite.*[7] Both saints lived on Mount Athos and were abbots of the Georgian monastery of Iviron at various periods of the eleventh century. Their role in the life of the Church of Georgia was immense. They undertook the translation of "the holy books"—as they are named in the *vitae*—and thus introduced into the life of the Church of Georgia the standards and norms accepted on Mount Athos.[8]

Holiness in Wesleyan spirituality

Let us now look at the Wesleyan view of the holiness of a human being. The above-mentioned sermon by John Wesley expounds on two verses from St. Paul's epistle to the Philippians: "Work out your own salvation with fear and trembling: for it is God that works in you, both to will and to do of his good pleasure" (Phil. 2:12–13).

In Wesley's sermon the spiritual life of the faithful person is seen as a matter of development or progress, going from repentance (the same as "convincing grace") to perfection in divine love. "We know and feel that the very first motion of good is from above, as well as the power which conducts it to the end."[9] The *alpha* and the *omega* of the good in a human being is God, but all good is given with the view of working out one's own salvation, as John Wesley wrote: "we grow up in all things into him that is our head till we attain the measure of the stature of the fullness of Christ" (here he refers to Matthew 13:31–32 and Ephesians 4:13). In this context John Wesley referred to two key words in the salvation history that Wesleyans know as "the way of salvation":

justification and sanctification. The former enables human beings to be restored to God's favor, and the latter enables human beings to be restored to God's image.[10] The question remains, however, as to how one might work out one's own salvation? How can the contemplative knowledge of God be transformed into the practical life? Here John Wesley, with his wide command of the Scriptures, sets the ground for a practical solution: learn to do good rather than evil (Isa. 1:16–17), hasten to do good works faithfully and mercifully (Titus 2:14), continue to reflect upon good and bad by reading the Scriptures, never miss an opportunity to partake of the Lord's Supper and to meet the Lord, be prepared to do good to all around you (Gal. 6:10), both to their souls and bodies, which means to take up one's cross daily (Luke 9:23) and do all that brings you closer to God, even if it is a difficult task, "grievous to flesh and blood." Then one reaches perfection and walks in the light.[11]

This code of behavior for achieving holiness and perfection coincides in many ways with the tasks and regulations given by the Fathers of the Church to their spiritual children. The most remarkable aspect of the Wesleyan code is its emphasis on continuous work and reflection for goodness and the quest for the Eucharist. In other words, the code speaks of the *theologia activa* lived out in the light of contemplative theology and mystical theology.[12] Salvation is the work of God: "Apart from me you can do nothing" (John 15:5), the most frequently used biblical reference in the *Philokalia* (the principal collection of spiritual writings of the Orthodox Church). At the same time, the sanctification of the human will is also essential for salvation, as the Macarian Homilies testify: "God, out of respect for the free will, does not do/save on his own but according to the will of man."[13] Divine grace and human freedom are complementary, as Vladimir Lossky says, "The Eastern tradition never separates these two elements: grace and human freedom are manifested simultaneously and cannot be conceived apart from each other."[14] The grace given by God demands a free response on the part of human beings, and it is never the other way around: grace comes first and the human response follows. The human co-operation with God is also the work of the Holy Spirit and therefore salvation is not a mere theory or ideology—when Simeon says, "My eyes have seen your salvation" (Luke 2:30), he is looking at the infant Jesus.[15] "Faith in two natures and two wills of the incarnate Saviour implies that the spiritual way, understood as an 'imitation of Christ,' involves the convergence or synergy of divine grace and human freedom."[16]

John Wesley stressed the impossibility of human salvation apart from a kind of co-operation: "If he did not work it would be impossible for you to work out your own salvation."[17] Although God is the cause of holiness, it is only through the practical application of the Lord's commandments and of the biblical tradition that human beings can work out their own salvation: we return to God the love he gave to us in the first place. "Stir up the spark of grace which is now in you, and he will give you more grace."[18] The synergy to which John Wesley refers may have been of Augustinian origin,[19] but we shall see that this is not far from the model of the perfection and holiness known in eleventh-century monastic spirituality on Mount Athos and Byzantium.

The hymns from the section on "Christian Holiness" in *The Methodist Hymnbook* (1933) are almost entirely by Charles Wesley but also include hymns by a few other authors. The very first hymn in this section, "Eternal Light! Eternal Light" (544) is by Thomas Binney (1798–1874), in whose text the energies of God are referred to as "the spirits that surround the throne" of God, "the uncreated beam," and "A Holy Spirit's energies." The hymn also offers human beings a way to "rise to that sublime abode," to the eternal lights, to the eternal love. As we read or sing the hymn, its practical theology ("an offering and sacrifice") and the divine energies ("A Holy Spirit's energies") "prepare us for the sight of holiness above."

After Hymn 544 there follow twenty-two hymns by Charles Wesley and a few by other authors. What strikes me about these hymns is their call for self-cleansing ("a humble, lowly, contrite heart, / believing, true and clean," 550:3) and praise of the omnipotence of God through whom extraordinary things are possible for human beings ("All things are possible to me," 548:1). When Charles Wesley says, "Take my body, spirit, soul: / Only Thou possess the whole," he speaks of ceasing to do one's own will when arriving at the source of holiness, where one stands in the light facing God:

> My will be swallowed up in Thee;
> Light in Thy light still may I see,
> Beholding Thee with open face;
> Called the full power of faith to prove,
> Let all my hallowed heart be love,
> And all my spotless life be praise. (Hymn 553:4)

In everyday life, however, holiness is more often seen in "the depths of humble love" (Hymn 555:4). In my opinion, Charles Wesley places a very strong emphasis on the human plea for divine intervention for cleansing and purity of heart: "Purge me from every evil blot" (562:3), "Cleanse me from every sinful thought" (562:3), "Give me a new, a perfect heart" (562:4). If God comes down to cleanse our souls, then we are able to open our hearts to him, so that he can fill the "heart with purity" (564). His call for redemption from sin is so eager that it brings him very close to expressing the "spiritual strife" of the monks desiring to be rid of earthly delights and thus reach what they call *apatheia*, liberation from worldly passions. But the hymns, apart from that by Thomas Binney, do not explicitly use a synergistic approach. It is true that the examination of the "humble love" on the part of the faithful may well explain the absence of the synergic approach, as the latter must be implied in the human call to the Savior.[20]

Humility, work for the good, restraint from worldly passions

What is it that shows the holiness of a person? How do others detect holiness? How does doing good and ceasing from evil, as John Wesley highlights it, become a part of everyday life? The answers to these questions will be found in the above-mentioned *vitae* of the Athonite monks, as described by eyewitnesses. Euthymius and George were eventually canonized in the Church but their canonization should not have influenced the authors in their treatment of the persons under discussion as holy people. Even though both *vitae* have one or two passages with a description of supernatural realities (miracles performed either by the holy people or over their bodies), the bulk of the narrative describes the holiness of the persons via their endless labors in humility and fervent prayer.

The most striking features of hagiography are the saints' familiarity with holiness, and the accessibility and ease of holy people that emanates from their own reverence and simplicity when facing the holy. Holy people live and lead everyday lives among others who, in most cases, acknowledge their worthiness and understand it as the grace of God. In both *vitae*, the hagiographers show that the holiness of the saint is part of their entire life, whether it involves a prayer read out over a sick monk or a punishment meted out to an unruly brother.

What is the ultimate goal in recollecting the lives of holy people? An answer to this question is found in the *Life of St. George the Athonite*. The text reads as follows:

> And what is the praise of God? Glory and the praise of His saints, telling stories of their lives and activities either in written form or orally so that the other nations shall learn too and Fathers will tell these stories to their children.[21]

As a coenobitic settlement, the Georgian monastery of Iviron cherished human labor as an existential imperative for a community. However, in Iviron as elsewhere on Mount Athos, there were a great number of hermitages where the main occupation of the solitary monks was prayer, and there were many episodes in which their prayerful lives are brought into the narrative. Prayer is also a kind of labor, a spiritual endeavor. Hagiographers pay tribute to both of these expressions of human perfection, but the primary task of their descriptions remains the recording of the example of one's life in prayer, humility, and labor as a paradigm for those seeking salvation.

In the above-mentioned *vitae* of the Athonite monks there are a few marks of holiness that characterize the milieu of these holy men. Among such marks we can name spiritual guidance, predicting the future, the capability of communicating without a common language, and special qualities attributed to the body of a holy person after their demise.

a) Spiritual guidance

In everyday life, holy persons often give spiritual guidance. However, they also seek guidance from another person, and they never cease to be guided in matters of spiritual perfection.

Who is a spiritual guide and what is the spiritual life that we shall be hearing about during this presentation? The spiritual life is a practical expression of the theoretical foundation necessary for a virtuous life. The words "practical" and "theoretical" are chosen here on purpose, as etymologically they belong to the world of the Greek Church Fathers. The Fathers believed that *praxis* should not lack *theoria*.

The Orthodox tradition attributes a critical role to a spiritual master, usually addressed as a spiritual father. This is a person who serves as a model to younger and less experienced monks and helps them discern their thoughts—not necessarily their sins or transgressions, but their thoughts in general—as good or evil. From the *vitae* of St. Euthymius and St. George, we learn that the Athonite tradition highly respected the values of the monastic life adopted in Alexandria that reached the following gen-

erations under such names as John Climacus, Barsanuphius, and John and Doroth-
eos of Gaza. The Georgian texts from Mount Athos utilize a specialized vocabulary
from this tradition: a spiritual father is considered a "healer," "mediator," one who possesses "insight, discretion, lack of worldly passions, and gentleness tempered by sever-
ity."[22] In the *Life of St. George the Athonite* we read that his personality could be
compared with the figure of Moses:

> Indeed, it was the divine providence in this matter, since He knows everything in
> advance and sees the future [of human beings] as if it were the present, as it is [in
> the story] of Moses who had to leave his own land to become a prophet (Ex. 2:1), or
> [in the story of] Abraham whom God called away from his home [in Haran and
> brought to Egypt] to make a covenant with him (Gen. 12:15). It has been [true] about
> many holy persons: when they wish to approach God, in the first place they go away
> from their homeland and friends so that they can find [their] true call and will of
> God.[23]

Before becoming a teacher and saving the souls of others, George went through a long
journey himself, ascending slowly the ladder of spiritual growth, just as Moses, who
was the image of the spiritual leader *par excellence*. Towards the end of the narrative
the hagiographer tells a story of George gathering eighty people, mostly young
orphans, in Georgia and taking them to Mount Athos to be brought up in the community of the Georgian monks. George, his *Life* tells, became the source of God's
mercy for their souls, "saving them through twofold nourishment just as Joseph in the
past saved the Egyptians, and Moses led the souls entrusted to him out of the sea of
hunger."[24]

Patristic writings, especially those of the tradition shaped by such Church Fathers
as John Chrysostom, Athanasius of Alexandria, Evagrius of Pontus, Macarius, the
Cappadocians, John Climacus, the above-mentioned Alexandrian monastics, and
Maximus the Confessor, provide a coherent but not homogeneous teaching on the
twofold life of monks as a means of spiritual growth and salvation. In the *Chapters on
Knowledge*, Maximus the Confessor said: "All immortal things and immortality itself,
all living things and life itself, all holy things and holiness itself, all virtuous things and
virtue itself, all good things and goodness itself, all beings and being itself, are clearly
found to be works of God." Things that have their beginning in time by participation
are here differentiated from those that did not begin in time—there was never a time
when virtue, goodness, holiness and immortality did not exist. "God is creator of all
life, immortality, holiness, and virtue, for he transcends the essence of all which can
be thought and said."[25]

The ladder of perfection of a human being is as follows: faith and love of God
generate *fear*, and fear brings about *humility* that creates *gentleness*, and such a person
keeps *commandments*, which in turn leads to *purification* followed by *illumination*;
after this is the movement to what the Fathers called the *inner chamber of mysteries*. A
ladder of spiritual perfection is a standard vision shaped by these church fathers. They
often expressed the degrees of perfection differently, but their content was uniform.
What does each stage of perfection mean? The line of perfection known to the tradition that nourished the monastic ideal in Iviron is that of progress from deeds to

gnosis. On Mount Athos, at Iviron, according to the regulations, some monks did only manual labor and even those who did intellectual work had to do a routine of manual labor: there was no exemption from this requirement.

The Studite influence on Mount Athos is a widely accepted fact. The Byzantine Emperor John I Tzimiskes (969–976) sent the Studite monk Euthymius to Mount Athos to adjudicate disciplinary matters.[26] Although the mission of the Studion was different, as it was a monastery in a city, the main principles of its communal life were transplanted to Mount Athos. One of the remarkable characteristics of the Studite tradition was a serious concern for education and a good library. It was also marked by a strong interest in the spiritual guidance of monks.

From the tenth century on, Mount Athos became a place of imperial monastic foundations, and the Byzantine emperors were eager to back the Athonite monasteries. The Studite tradition came to dominate matters of spiritual life.

In the *Testament* of Theodore, the Studite superior, it is said:

> I acknowledge that the monastic life is lofty and exalted, even angelic, pure of every sin on account of its perfect way of life. It is clear that the monastic life must be ordered according to the ascetic rules of the holy Basil the Great and not by half measures so that some in one place choose some rules and let others go. For, one cannot choose to lead this life lawfully in some other fashion without the three revealed orders of the divine ladder.[27]

Theodore's *Testament* No. 27 says:

> Stick to obedience until the end so that you will "obtain the unfading crown of righteousness (1 Pet. 5:4; 2 Tim. 4:8). Led by humility, you should always deny your own will and pattern yourselves only after the judgements of your superior. If you keep in mind these things and if you should guard them to the end, you will enjoy the eternal blessings.[28]

The two future abbots Euthymius and George joined the monastic life of Iviron in different ways. Euthymius was taken as a child to Mount Athos by his Father John and was brought up in Great Lavra (the very first monastic foundation on the Mountain) in the milieu of monks. Some of these monks were about to found a new haven of spiritual life. Athanasius, the abbot of Great Lavra, was close to the imperial court and the place was not at all short of generous gifts from the capital.

When George the Athonite turned 25 years old, his *Life* tells us, he "bowed his head to the sweet yoke of monasticism." The first thing on his mind was to find a teacher and a spiritual guide since he knew that without a spiritual guide there is neither life for the soul nor a monastic path. Thus he found, in between the rocks on Mount Mirabilis, George the Recluse, "pure as pigeon and undefiled as dove, a man of the heaven and an angel on earth, entirely estranged and detached from worldly concerns and abiding with God in his mind." When the Recluse saw the goodness of George's soul and his gifts, he rejoiced with great joy and encouraged George to stay on Mount Mirabilis. Then he instructed George to follow up the work of his great fellow countryman Euthymius, in other words, to continue the translation of the holy books into the Georgian language. George was advised to go to Mount Athos, where Euthymius had lived and worked all his life, and conform himself to the literary and spiritual traditions he would find there.

When George as a young man arrived at the Holy Mount, he intended to follow the will of the master and immediately begin his translation of the holy books, but instead he started his life in the monastery in extreme self-discipline, fasting and prayer, in humility and peace, in obedience and endurance, and most of all in self-denial. For a while he behaved like a simple and illiterate person, serving and obeying all the brethren. For several years he "humbly executed all the lowest jobs while remaining with a lowered head and mournful; although by the physical sight he could see the outside world, by the spiritual sight he invisibly experienced the invisible glory of God which only few may achieve." Here the text points out that one may invisibly experience the glory of God while executing the lowest jobs. The *vita activa* and *vita contemplativa* are not separated in time but go hand by hand.

One day the spiritual Father George the Recluse learned that his disciple had neither been ordained nor had been translating the holy books. He sent another of his disciples from the Black Mountain with a message of discontent for George's not executing his will. But the blessed monk George behaved so not out of disobedience to his master but because of disregard for himself, for he remembered the Lord's saying: "All who humble themselves will be exalted" (Matt. 23:12). Also as the Fathers say: "The mother of all passions is vainglory."[29] After having read the letter, George had to accept the will of his spiritual father. He then accepted the honor of priesthood with tears and sighs, reverence and fear. This particular episode clarifies that even spiritual persons such as George are in need of guidance in order to fulfil the will of God and avoid falling into a trap.

From the *Life of St. Euthymius*, as described by St. George the Athonite, we learn that according to the rule of Father Euthymius, who never spoke loudly or abusively as he was adorned by the virtues, in a case of hostility among the brothers (fierce argument or tearing each other's beard or fighting) the problem was solved with sweet and agreeable words either by a quotation or by saying himself:

> My sons, if I allow you to go ahead with it, first you will damage your soul and also the rules in the monastery will be abused. As by God's providence I happened to be your judge and supervisor, I cannot let you go ahead without punishment because otherwise, as you know, you will be severely punished in the age to come. If I give you some instruction here that you will gratefully accept, I have faith in God that you will be spared of His eternal judgement.[30]

b) Predicting the future, seeing through one's thoughts and intentions

One of the remarkable signs of holiness, according to the hagiographic writings, is predicting the future, seeing either one's own departure from this world or an event that will take place after many years.

The holy Father George, the author says, had the grace of prophecy. At the time when Queen Theodora ruled the Greeks, she asked Bagrat, the king of the Abkhazs to give her his daughter Martha so that she could raise Martha as her own child. King

Bagrat happily sent his daughter Martha. However, by the will of God, Queen Theodora passed away at that time. Queen Mary, the mother of King Bagrat, was in Constantinople, and Father George was there too on his own business. As soon as Queen Theodora passed away, Martha, the daughter of Bagrat, arrived at the royal court. When the holy monk saw Martha, he predicted her future in front of all saying: "All of you know that today one Queen departed but the other one has arrived." After spending some time there, Martha was taken back to her own land, but some time later, by the demand of the royal family, she was brought back again as a daughter-in-law. Then those who remembered the prophecy of the monk saw it was fulfilled and thanked God for allowing the saints to predict things for those who follow his will. Thus Queen Mary, when Father George visited her, said: "Father, your prophecy has been fulfilled, one you have prophesied for Martha."[31]

Father George was aware of his own departure from this world. It occurred as he brought eighty orphans from Georgia to Mount Athos. On the way to the Holy Mountain Father George and his entourage visited the king. The text reads as follows:

> On the day of the Nativity of St. John the Baptist Father George, together with the other brethren, went to Constantinople, to the monastery of the Studion, venerated the head of the holy Forerunner and received the communion of the holy mysteries of Christ and thanked God. Then we went to our *metochion* and Father George was having fever but we thought that the travel caused it, as he had walked all day long. It was his habit to walk when going to the holy places for prayer. There Father George commanded us: "Prepare the orphans for presenting them to the King. If we do not see the King today, we will have no opportunity tomorrow." We could not understand the power of his words, what they were supposed to mean but obeyed and did so.[32]

When the king arrived and Father George presented the orphans, he said:

> Blessed King, these orphans I have gathered in Georgia and taught them the name of God; but now I present them to your royal highness, bring them up according to your judgement and have mercy upon them so that they pray for your soul and for the long and prosperous life of your children. It is to you that I entrust these orphans, after having entrusted them to God, because you will not see me any more. Then the King told the orphans to recite the Hours but Father George clearly commanded us to sing the departing prayer of St. Simeon the Elder which says: *the Lord sits in a chariot of the Cherubims*, and *Let us depart in Peace*. By this prayer George declared his departure, although no one could understand at that time, neither the King nor others. However, when he departed the next day everybody, as if woken up from sleep, thanked God who did not hide from the holy one his own departure.[33]

c) Communication without a common language

This miraculous sign occurs when two persons meet, see each other and recognize in one another something that establishes an extra means of communication between them. The venerable priest Gabriel the Iberian and the holy monk Leon the Great of Rome had a strong spiritual affection for each other. When Leon visited the Fathers on Mount Athos, he founded a cell nearby, the cell of Father Gabriel. And these two

did not share a common language. At twilight they were going out of their cells, praying and proclaiming the words of God until dawn. They did so at every vespers during the visits of Leon. And the monks of Iviron were astonished saying that "every time
Leon the Great arrived [to Mount Athos] they acted with the priest Gabriel as
described above and witnessed that everything was possible and trustworthy through
their holiness as both of them were great and perfect before God."[34]

d) The body of the departed becomes a source of miracles

Lightness of the corpse of a departed holy person is recounted in the *Life of St. George
the Athonite*. The body of the departed Father George showed his great mercy upon
Panteleimon, the youngest among the orphans. As the child walked barefoot during
the journey, he got a thorn into his foot. When he stopped to sit on his heels and get
out the thorn, suddenly the cart with the corpse of the newly departed Father George
ran over the young child.

> When we saw it, we started crying lamenting over the child as we thought that the
> child had been killed, but, instead we had to thank kind God for his mercy and for
> the grace of the divine man who, even after his departure from this world protected
> and guarded his orphans and thus bestowed mercy upon them! As it was mentioned,
> the cart ran over his back but the child immediately rose up while we were looking
> for him under the cart. And he said: "Behold, let me get out the thorn." And we asked
> him: "Are not you in pain?" And he answered: "I have not even noticed that the cart
> ran over me." Since he was a child, it was how he commented.[35]

Thus the grace of the corpse of the departed holy person made the fact unnoticeable
for the child. "Now—the author continues—he is a grown up and himself tells this
great miracle and glorifies God, maker of the miracles, and preaches about the grace
of the holy Father George."[36]

Conclusions

The *vitae* of St. Euthymius and St. George describe the spiritual life of the Athonite
monks but the authors emphasize most the truth described. Leading a spiritual life in a
monastery is nothing other than seeking one's own salvation. Monastic spirituality
interprets the grace of God granted to human beings as the way to salvation, a way in
which human response has a very significant role to play. The invisible glory of God can
be seen through the everyday struggle, labor and prayer assumed in obedience and
humility. Thus the *vita activa* is the foundation of the *vita contemplativa*. They are inseparable in the monastic life. Perfection and holiness belong to the existential reality of
monastic communities: every struggle, whether in thought or in deed, has its value on
the way to salvation. The hagiographers show very clearly that the concern of Church
Fathers for the obedience of monks and the role of a spiritual guide are also a part of
that reality which seeks salvation and shapes the holiness of the non-monastic saint.

     The main source of holiness, perfection, or salvation is God, but divine grace
works in cooperation with human beings out of respect for their free will. Holiness as

described in the *vitae* of the saints reveals this response on the part of a human being: keeping the Lord's commandments, and living out the divine love.

John Wesley clearly sympathized with the synergistic approach, and thus accepted that the *vita activa* and the *vita contemplativa* are inseparable, but his expressions of the bond between the two are very different from those explored above. My analysis may be insufficient for far-reaching conclusions on the *measure* of Wesleyan use of the patristic sources. However, it seems very clear that Wesleyan spirituality *has a close affinity* to the spirituality of the Eastern Church tradition, an affinity that is grounded in the writings of the early church fathers and in the ascetic life, of which the exegesis of the Scriptures was a vital part.

Endnotes

[1] Frances Young, *Orthodox and Wesleyan Spirituality*, S T Kimbrough Jr., ed. (Crestwood, NY: St. Vladimir's Seminary Press, 2002), 168.

[2] Ibid., 164

[3] Ibid., 63.

[4] Maximus the Confessor writes: "For great is the distance and many are the levels of knowledge through which the soul must pass before it reaches 'the place of miraculous tabernacle, the house of God itself, with the voice of exultation and thanksgiving, and the sound of feasting' (Ps. 42:4) . . . 'The place of the miraculous tabernacle' is a dispassionate and untroubled state of virtue in which the Logos of God adorns the soul like a tabernacle with the varied beauties of the virtues." Second Century on Theology, *The Philokalia*, The Complete Text compiled by St. Nikodimos of the Holy Mountain and St. Makarios of Corinth, trans. from the Greek and eds. G. E. H. Palmer, Philip Sherrard, Kallistos Ware, vol. 2 (London: Faber and Faber, 1981), 77–78, 157. In the above-mentioned description of the lives of St. Euthymius and St. George the prevailing picture is to show them in labor, actually doing physical work, in contrast to what we learn about many hermitages scattered around Iviron where some holy people were mainly busy with prayer and contemplation.

[5] *The Works of the Reverend John Wesley, A. M.*, ed. Thomas Jackson, 14 vols. (London: Wesleyan Conference Office, 1872), 6:506–513.

[6] *Zveli qartuli agiograpiuli literaturis zeglebi* (in Georgian language; English translation of title: *Monuments of the Ancient Georgian Literature*), vol. 2, ed. Ilya Abuladze (Tbiilisi, 1967), 38–100.

[7] Ibid., 101–207.

[8] The role of Mount Athos in the spiritual history of Byzantium from the eleventh century onwards, as well as for the tradition of the Orthodox Church in general, is of very great significance but goes beyond the scope of this paper.

[9] *The Works of the Reverend John Wesley, A. M.*, I:4, in Jackson 6:509.

[10] Ibid., II:1, in Jackson 6:509.

[11] Ibid., II:4, in Jackson 6:510–511.

[12] It is not easy to say whether the final step of the spiritual journey of the saints is love or gnosis. The Fathers of the Church in the eleventh century seem not to differentiate love and gnosis. The virtuous life demands everyday struggle followed with the rewards at every stage of the journey; gnosis and love make equal contributions towards the final destiny.

[13] *Les Homelies de saint Macaire*, XXXVII, 10, ed. by Abbaye de Bellefontaine, coll. "Spiritualité orientale," 1984, 309.

[14] Vladimir Lossky, *The Mystical Theology of the Eastern Church Fathers*, trans. from French by a small group of members of the Fellowship of St. Albans and St. Sergius (Cambridge: James Clarke & Co., Ltd., 1991), 197.

[15] Kallistos Ware, *L'ile au-dela du monde* (Paris: Éditions du Cerf, 2005), 107.

[16] Kallistos Ware, introduction to John Climacus, *The Ladder of Divine Ascent*, trans. Colm Luibheid and Norman Russell (Mahwah, NJ: Paulist Press, 1982), 19.

[17]Wesley's sermon "On Working Out Our Own Salvation," III:3, in Jackson 6:511–512.

[18]Ibid., III:6, in Jackson 6:512–513.

[19]"*Qui fecit nos sine nobis, non salvabit nos sine nobis*"—he that made us without ourselves, will not save us without ourselves. Augustine, Sermon 169, xi (13) as quoted by Wesley, *The Works of John Wesley*, 208.

[20]Hymn 570 may be the one exception. Therein Charles Wesley asks the Lord to "stamp" him with the "Spirit's seal"—the latter must be the divine energies implanted in the creation.

[21]*Monuments*, 102.

[22]Kallistos Ware, ibid., 42.

[23]*Monuments*, 119.

[24]It is not difficult to find a connection between this passage and *The Ladder of Divine Ascent*: "Those of us who wish to get away from Egypt, to escape from Pharaoh, need some Moses to be our intermediary with God, to stand between action and contemplation, and stretch out his arms to God, that those led by him may cross the sea of sin and put to flight the Amalek of the Passions." Step 1, ibid., 75. The passage has the following comment, footnote 4: cf. Ex 17:11–13: "In the battle between the Amlekites (passions) and Israelites (souls under a spiritual director) prevailed as long as the arms of Moses (the guide) were held raised in prayer by Hur (action) on one side and Aaron (contemplation) on the other. Action (*praxis*) is the ascetic struggle to practice the virtues and overcome the passions. It is the necessary foundation for contemplation (*theoria*), which is the direct apprehension or vision of God by the intellect."

[25]George C. Berthold, *Selected Writings by Maximus the Confessor* (Mahwah, NJ: The Paulist Press, 1985), 50. The influence of the Cappadocian tradition on perfection of the human being in Maximus is clear but it goes beyond the scope of this paper. See Anthony Meredith, *The Cappadocians* (Crestwood, NY: St. Vladimir's Seminary Press, 1995), 61: "Virtue is not only the condition of the possibility of knowledge, knowledge also serves as a step towards greater moral perfection. . . . The moral life is the precondition for knowing God, and when we grow in knowledge, this must mean a change in our own lives."

[26]*Byzantine Monastic Foundation Documents: A Complete Translation of the Surviving Founders' Typika and Testaments*, eds. John Thomas and Angela Constanides Hero, vol. 1, Dumbarton Oaks Studies, XXXV (Cambridge, MA: Harvard University Press, 2001), 69.

[27]Ibid., 76, i.e. renunciation, freedom from desire and solitude, as John Climacus suggests in his treatise: PG 88, 632A–672B.

[28]Ibid., 80.

[29]Maximus the Confessor, *Chapters on Love*, 3:60. See also Evagrius of Pontus, *Praktikos* 53: "All harmful thoughts spring from self-love." PG 79, 1145.

[30]*Monuments*, 72–3.

[31]Ibid, p.177

[32]Ibid., 182

[33]Ibid., 183.

[34]Ibid, p.66.

[35]Ibid., 199.

[36]Ibid., 199.

PART 2

Ecclesiology and Eschatology

11

The Eschatological Dimensions of the Church

John Behr

Any serious reflection on the Church—those gathered in the Spirit as the body of Christ, awaiting their Lord and Savior—must take account of the issue of eschatology: How can we claim to be the body of Christ, and say that he has not yet come, that we are awaiting his coming from the heavens? (I and II Thess.; Phil. 3:20–21) What kind of existence do we have now, if our lives are hid with Christ in God and our true citizenship is in the heavens? (Col. 3:3; Phil. 3:21) Christian existence, individually and collectively, is always bound up in this eschatological tension, usually characterized as "already, but not yet."

However, the very ease with which we use this formula ("already, but not yet") indicates how little we have thought it through. We tend to think of it as fairly clear and straightforward: Christ has come once already, when he worked out our salvation through his Incarnation and Passion, and he will come again—his "second coming"—to bring all things to a close. This is what we usually think when we say with the Nicene-Constantinopolitan Creed: "and he will come again," although, strictly speaking, the clause there: καὶ πάλιν ἐρχόμενος should not be translated as "he will come again" but as "he is again coming."

While various figures from the early centuries do write about the second coming, there is very little written on the topic of an "eschatological tension." Rather than speaking in terms of a tension between "already" and "but not yet," ancient authors more usually speak in a different framework—in terms of the tension between being in Adam and being in Christ, between dying to this world and being reborn, or recreated in a new life in Christ.

Another topic to which the Eastern Fathers devoted little direct reflection, as Vladimir Lossky pointed out, was the Church. Ecclesiology never really became a regular item of theological reflection, at least until the last couple of centuries, when it became a distinct theme in Orthodox theology, with its own importance, no doubt largely because of increased ecumenical encounters. (How can we, as divided Christians, speak of the one Church?) Beginning with Fr. Nicholas Afanasiev and now, most notably with Metropolitan John (Zizioulas) of Pergamon, the typical manner in which Orthodox tend to speak about the Church is in terms of a "eucharistic ecclesiology." So, I will begin with a brief review of this characteristic manner and perception of the eschatological dimension of the Church, before noting some limitations and offering an alternative approach.

Eucharistic ecclesiology

The basic intuition of Afanasiev's eucharistic ecclesiology is that "where there is a eucharistic assembly, there Christ abides, and there is the Church of God in Christ" ("Una Sancta" [1963] 495). This is paraphrased by Zizioulas in a shortened form (leaving out the connecting term) as: "wherever the Eucharist is, there is the Church."[1] As the title of his doctoral work suggests—*The Unity of the Church in the Divine Eucharist and the Bishop During the First Three Centuries*—Zizioulas grounds his ecclesiology in the life of the Church during the first three centuries, as *he* finds it. For him,[2] the Church is manifest in this world when all the Christians of a particular region or city come together, assemble, in the same place (*epi to auto*) on a particular day, especially Sunday, the Lord's Day, to break bread.

Unlike the various societies that existed in the Roman world—the *collegia,* or associations, or schools—the Christian eucharistic communities were distinct, in that they transcended race or profession, natural or social divisions: they came together as Christians—not as Jews or Greeks, males or females, adult or child, rich or poor, master or slaves, but simply as Christians, a third race, as it were, the true Israel or elect of God. This assembly, the *synaxis,* is *the only one* in that particular place, and as such, it is the *whole Church.*

In other words, they came together as a *catholic community,* the whole people of God to perform the work of God, the *leitourgia,* specifically, the eucharistic offering, in which the Church "experiences that which is promised for the *parousia,* namely the eschatological unity of all in Christ."[3] As it says in the *Didache* (late first, early second century):

> Just as this loaf was scattered over the mountains and having been brought together was made one, so let your Church be gathered from the ends of the earth in your Kingdom (*Didache* 9.4).[4]

The catholicity of the eucharistic gathering is also manifest, for Zizioulas, in its structure, with the one bishop of the assembly positioned on the throne behind the one altar, standing "in the place of God" or as "the living image of Christ," and seated round about his throne, the presbyters, with the deacons standing by the bishop helping him in his celebration, and in front of him, the "people of God"—a distinct order of the Church, initiated by the rites of baptism and chrismation, and without whom there is no eucharistic assembly. The bishop thus expresses in himself the "multitude" of the faithful in that place: he is the one who offers the eucharistic gifts to God in the name of the Church, thus bringing to the throne of God the *whole body of Christ.*

Zizioulas corrects two "errors" that he perceives in Afanasiev. First, the self-sufficiency of each local eucharistic assembly as a complete and "catholic" church.[5] For Zizioulas, this is rather the local church, the diocese gathered under its bishop. Second, the interdependence of each local church—the simultaneity of the one and the many; each local church is what it is only in communion with every other local church, so that each embodies the fullness of the Church rather than being merely part of it.

Zizioulas also corrects an error he perceived in Lossky's work, which spoke of the economy of the Spirit as being subsequent to the economy of the Son. For Zizioulas, the work of the Spirit and the work of Christ are interdependent: for it is only as the One anointed by the Spirit that Christ is who he is; there is no Spirit until given by Christ, but also no Christ until the Spirit is at work—in his resurrection, baptism, or conception. Similarly: the liturgical practices of baptism and chrismation go together, even if, historically, there have been various practices about which comes first.

It is significant that the arena in which Zizioulas works out the relationship between Christology and Pneumatology is not Trinitarian theology proper (as does, for instance, Dumitru Staniloae), but ecclesiology, and, specifically, eucharistic theology.[6] Working with the dictum that the works of the Trinity are indivisible but not undifferentiated, Zizioulas argues that the distinct role of the Son is having "become history," while the role of the Spirit is "to liberate the Son and the economy from the bondage of history."[7] The Spirit is "the *beyond* history," acting in history "in order to bring into history the last days, the *eschaton.*"[8] For Zizioulas, it is the Spirit that supplies eschatological dimension to the Church in her experience of communion: it is the Spirit that enables the Church to be the body of Christ, a corporate person, a body which, as expressed in the Eucharist, already manifests the presence of the *eschaton* in its communal being, a mode of being that transcends this world and its time.

All of this has become commonplace in recent years, but there are serious questions to be raised about it, centering on the question of whether the Church becomes exclusively identified with or as the "eucharistic gathering." Zizioulas begins with an identification of the Church with the eucharistic assembly, and then defines the roles of Christ and the Spirit in terms of this, so allowing no space outside the eucharistic context in which the Church, as the body of Christ, manifests the Spirit. His descriptions of the experience of communion and the *eschaton* are almost exclusively restricted to the celebration of the Eucharist.

> The Eucharist had the unique privilege of reuniting in one whole, in one unique experience, the work of Christ and the Holy Spirit. . . . It was only in the Eucharist that the dialectical relationship between God and the world, between the *eschata* and history, was preserved without creating dangerous polarizations and dichotomies.[9]

But making the Eucharist the exclusive place of unity actually introduces all sorts of problematic polarities and dichotomies. For instance, Zizioulas asserts categorically that "the notions of 'sanctification' and 'spirituality'" that lie behind monasticism have "never become a decisive aspect of *ecclesiology* in the East."[10] It is, he continues, only the liturgy, the Eucharist, that determines ecclesiology. So, for Zizioulas, it is only in terms of the eschatological *koinonia*, given by the Spirit to the eucharistic community, that the Spirit plays a role in the Church.

Staniloae, on the other hand, because he does not define the relationship between the Son and the Spirit in the particular arena of the Eucharist, is able to recognize the presence of the Church outside the liturgical assembly: the prayers of believers in their homes and elsewhere are, for him, still the prayers of the Church. Personal spirituality and holiness are integral to ecclesiology. Personal prayer and asceticism do not necessarily lead to individualism (which seems to be behind Zizioulas' rejection of these elements from ecclesiology); in fact, their purpose is precisely to remove egoism, so that we can indeed come together as one body.

More could be said, but more to the point is the fact that identifying the Church exclusively with the eucharistic assembly does not allow for seeing the Church elsewhere. Eucharistic ecclesiology has had an undoubtedly positive effect of increasing ecclesial awareness during the twentieth century and an increased participation in the Eucharist—the "eucharistic revival" —but it has also had a negative effect in two respects.

First, the "eucharistic revival" that has accompanied such ecclesiology has emphasized participation in the Eucharist to such an extent that it often overshadows, if not obscures, the perpetual baptismal dimensions of Christian life; baptism, rather, is regarded as the necessary preliminary step into body, which celebrates the Eucharist.[11] Taken to its extreme, this results in a community of, in Fr. John Erickson's phrase, "eucharistic pagans"—members of the Church who participate in the Eucharist but do not otherwise have any consciousness of the life in death that is the Christian life in this world. As John Erickson puts it:

> We forget that the Eucharist is but a foretaste of the kingdom, not its final realization. And then, this tendency towards a realized eschatology begins to creep from the Eucharist into other aspects of church life, so that the church *qua* church comes to be seen as perfect in every respect. Its dependence on Christ, and him crucified, is forgotten. We want the glory and forget the cross.[12]

Second, it results in a view that sees life outside the Orthodox Church, defined as coextensive with participation in her celebration of the Eucharist, in uniformly negative terms. As George Limouris put it (in a paper delivered to the WCC, no less):

> The boundaries of the body of Christ depend entirely on the eucharistic life. Outside that life, humanity is ruled by alien powers. Separation and destruction can only be averted by those who unite in Christ and prepare themselves for the joint assembly of the eucharist.[13]

In this perspective, not only do the Orthodox regard themselves as being or belonging to "the one true Church," but they deny the designation "Church" to any other body gathering together in the name of Christ: outside the Orthodox Church, "humanity is ruled by alien powers"—a very different, and questionable, claim.

More recent work has tended to emphasize the importance of "baptism" for ecclesiology, pointing out that the "one baptism for the remission of sins" is not simply a gateway to be passed through as we enter into the "one Church" and then left behind. Rather, the paschal dimension of baptism must characterize the totality of the Christian life, shaping and informing every aspect of it, until we are finally raised in Christ. As Aidan Kavanagh puts it,

> The whole economy of *becoming* a Christian, from conversion and catechesis through the Eucharist, is thus the fundamental paradigm for *remaining* a Christian. . . . The paschal mystery of Jesus Christ dying and rising still among his faithful ones at Easter in baptism is what gives the Church its radical cohesion and mission, putting it at the center of a world made new.[14]

We must never forget that the Eucharist is not simply a celebratory act of communion, but is a paschal banquet: by eating the bread and drinking the cup, we "proclaim the Lord's death until he comes" (1 Cor. 11:26), and this demands of us our own participation in the life through death manifest by Christ.

However, we must be careful not simply to substitute one sacrament for another; to say that baptism, instead of the Eucharist, is foundational for ecclesiology, or even the two together. That would be to take our current, phenomenological experience of the "Church" as the starting point, and then define the Christian mystery in terms of it, which can ever only result in idolatry. Rather, as the quotation from Kavanagh suggested, what is needed is a particular orientation: one that sees the whole of Christian life, and the Christian Church herself, in terms of a perpetual baptismal/eucharistic/paschal participation in the mystery of Christ.

This reminder regarding the importance of our own participation in the mystery of Christ, is similar, and related, to the point with which I began: that the early church did not really express the eschatological tension in terms of "already, but not yet," but rather in terms of our dying to this world to live with Christ. So, I would like to turn back to the early centuries, to consider again how they spoke of the coming of Christ and how they spoke of the Church.

Christ as the "Coming One"

It might seem unnecessary to examine how we speak of the "coming of Christ," but it seems that our familiarity with the language of a "first coming" and a "second coming" obscures a vitally important point. We tend to use these terms as if they were referring to two distinct things: the first regarding the past—what happened two thousand years ago; and the second regarding what will happen at some unknown point in the future—an eschatological drama with a different content yet to be unfolded. Theology does not divide up that easily: what the apostles and evangelists proclaim about Christ does not simply lie in the past, merely a matter of history, and our discussion about what is to come is not uninformed by what is given in Christ. Even for the evangelists, who proclaimed Christ's coming, he remains, because he *is*, "the coming one": "Are you the coming one, or should we look for another?" (Matt. 11:3).

This description of Christ, as "the coming one," is of course grounded in the Old Testament expectation of the coming Messiah, the blessed one who comes in the name of the Lord (Ps. 117:26 LXX; Matt. 21:9; John 12:13). But it also reflects the manner in which the disciples, in the first three Gospels, come to know who Jesus is. Apart from the confession of Peter on the road to Caesarea Philippi (Matt. 16): "You are the Christ, the Son of the Living God"—a confession that Peter did not really understand, as he then attempted to prevent Christ from going to Jerusalem to suffer (and so gets called "Satan")—apart from this episode, the disciples are remarkably slow in coming to know Jesus Christ as the eternal Son of God. Whatever the disciples heard about Jesus' birth from his mother, or about his baptism from others, whatever divine teachings they themselves heard from his lips or miracles they saw him doing with their own eyes, —even seeing him transfigured on the mountain in glory—they still abandoned him at the time of the Passion (in the Synoptics; the Gospel of John is different, a difference to which I will return), and Peter even denied him: "I do not know this man," he said three times (Matt. 26:70). Neither, for that matter, did the empty tomb persuade them, nor even the resurrectional appearances: when he appears, they didn't recognize him, but instead told him about the tomb having been found empty (Luke 24:22–24)!

Only when the crucified and risen Christ opened the Scriptures, to show how it was necessary for him to have gone to his Passion to enter his glory, only then did the disciples' hearts begin to burn, so that they were prepared to recognize him in the breaking of bread (the key locus for "eucharistic theology/ecclesiology"). But once he is recognized, the crucified and risen Lord disappears from their sight (Luke 24:31). At the very moment when the disciples finally encounter Christ *knowingly*, he passes out of their sight! We are left in anticipation of his coming; the one of whom we previously had no comprehension appears and disappears, or appears in his disappearance, creating in us a desire for his coming, a trace of his presence. As Augustine put it in the *Confessions* 11.2.4: "Through him you sought us when we were not seeking you, but you sought us that we might begin to seek you." And so, as the Apostle Paul puts it, we now "forget what lies behind and strain forward to what lies ahead," responding to "the upward call of God in Christ Jesus" (Phil. 3:13–4), knowing that our "citizenship" is not here on earth, but "in heaven," from which "we await our Savior, the Lord Jesus Christ" (Phil. 3:20–21). The "first coming," such as it is, cannot be easily separated from the "second coming." From the beginning, Christians have been waiting for the coming of their Lord, not for a "second coming," as something distinct from and other than a "first coming," but simply for his coming, his *parousia*, his presence.

The encounter with Christ is thus always eschatological and is itself the content of the *eschaton*. It is spoken of in apocalyptic terms: the crucified and risen Christ, who opens the books of the Scriptures to show how they all spoke of the necessity of his having suffered before entering his glory (Luke 24:27), is the slain Lamb who alone is able to open the scroll (Rev. 5), so that we can now see how all these things were written "for our instruction—for us, upon whom the end of the ages has come" (1 Cor. 10:11).

Having the Scriptures opened to them in this way, the apostles and evangelists used the language of Scripture to proclaim the coming one, the one who was crucified "in the last days" and who, likewise, was born "when the fullness of time had come" (Gal. 4:4)—again, an eschatological event, with the account of his birth being grounded in the account of his Passion: "to the tomb corresponds the womb,"[15] as Augustine put it, a point made so clear in the iconography for the feast of the Nativity.

The crucified and risen Christ, proclaimed in this way by the apostles "in accordance with Scripture," is thus the starting-point and end-point of theological reflection—he is the Alpha and the Omega (Rev. 1:8); he is the one by whom all things are created, and the end towards which all things tend, being recapitulated in him as the head of all things, and this, indeed, is the plan of God from all eternity (Eph. 1:9–10).

Yet this eternal plan is known only at the end: "He was destined before the foundation of the world, but was made manifest at the end of time for your sake" (1 Pet. 1:20).

The beginning and the end of all things not only coincide in Christ and as Christ, but, as St. Irenaeus puts it, he is the beginning who appears at the end.[16] Christ is revealed, in this way, at the end, and so we, in the present, are still in the process of "learning Christ," as the Apostle Paul puts it (Eph. 4:20). We look back to the last image that we have of Christ in this world, his cross and Passion, as preached by the apostles "in accordance with Scripture," yet stretch forward to encounter the eschatological Lord.

The birth of Christ and the motherhood of the Church

This is the "eschatological tension" in which Christians live. Thus having explored more deeply the unity of the "first" and "second" coming, we can now perhaps see new depths in our participation in the mystery of Christ, and how and why the Church was spoken of, from the earliest times not as a " eucharistic assembly" but as Mother or Virgin Mother, the matrix (or "womb") in and through whom the people called by God are born again to be the body of Christ and the temple of the Spirit, thus making the eschatological Lord present.

The Apostle Paul who proclaims, as we have already heard, that the Son of God was born from a woman "when the fullness of time had come" (Gal. 4:4)—an eschatological event—also announces, a few verses later, that by the proclamation of the gospel, he is himself "in travail until Christ be formed in you" (Gal. 4:19); in those, that is, as he puts it elsewhere, whom he (though this time as a father) has "begotten through the Gospel" (1 Cor. 4:15). He continues by explaining how this is so, applying the words of Isaiah to Sarah, in an allegory in which she represents the Jerusalem above, our free mother:

> Sing, O barren one, who did not bear; break forth into singing and cry aloud, you who have not been in travail! For the children of the desolate one will be more than the children of her that is married, says the Lord (Gal. 4:27; Is. 54:1).

Although modern scriptural scholarship would separate this verse, as a distinct oracle, from what it identifies as the fourth hymn of the Suffering Servant (Is. 52:13–53:12), they are united in the liturgical tradition of the Orthodox Church: Isaiah's words about the one who is bruised for our iniquities and pours out his soul unto death are read only at the Vespers of Holy Friday, and they conclude with the joyful proclamation that the barren one will give birth. Again, the Passion of Christ is the basis for how we speak of the birth of Christ, a birth that cannot be separated from his birth in those who now have the heavenly Jerusalem as their mother, the barren Virgin who, as a result of the Passion of Christ, becomes a Virgin Mother.

This Pauline theme of the birth of Christ in those who receive the Gospel is also eschatological in its orientation: it is only brought to completion when the coming Christ arrives. As Paul puts it: "We now await our Savior, the Lord Jesus Christ," then he adds, "who will change [n.b. the future tense] our lowly body to be like his glorious body" (Phil. 3:20–21).

John the Theologian also affirms that "when he appears we shall be like him, for we shall see him as he is" (1 John 3:2). In the Passion of Christ, as described by John, we can see these themes of motherhood and sonship developed further. Here, the Passion is again the moment of revelation: "When you have lifted up the Son of Man, then you will know that I AM" (John 8:28), and it is described in terms we usually associate with the second coming: "Now is the judgment of the world; now shall the ruler of this world be cast out; and I, when I am lifted up from the earth, will draw all men to myself" (John 1:31–32). But in the Passion, in this the "spiritual Gospel," Christ is not abandoned, as he is in the Synoptics. Instead, we have the scene usually depicted in iconography, with his mother and the beloved disciple standing at the foot of the cross (together with his mother's sister, Mary the wife of Cleopas, and Mary Magdalene, though in iconography these others usually recede into the background, if they are there at all). On the cross Christ does not cry out, as in the other Gospels, "My God, my God, why have you forsaken me" (Matt. 27:46; Mark 15:34; cf. Ps. 22:1), but instead addresses his mother and the Beloved Disciple: "Woman, behold your son," and to the disciple "Behold your mother" (John 19:26).

While the Beloved Disciple is traditionally identified with the evangelist himself, this is not actually an identification made by the Gospel of John; the only identification made here is that the one who stands by the cross of Christ and is not ashamed of him is the Beloved Disciple. Moreover, Christ does not say to his mother, "Woman, behold another son for you in my place," but simply "Behold your son": the faithful disciple standing by the cross becomes identified with Christ—the son of Christ's own mother—putting on the identity of Christ, as Christians do in baptism, so that the barren one now indeed has many children, as we heard Isaiah announce.

Given all of this scriptural reflection and imagery regarding the birth of Christ (the coming eschatological Lord) in those who receive the gospel by putting on the identity of Christ and becoming sons of the previously barren Woman, it is not surprising that Christians have, from the beginning, spoken of the Church as "Mother" or "Virgin Mother." This is done, for instance, in a very eloquent manner by *The Letter of the Churches of Vienne and Lyons*, which describes in graphic detail the sufferings of the Christians of Gaul during the persecutions around the year AD 177.[17]

During the first round in the arena, some of the Christians "appeared to be unprepared and untrained, as yet weak and unable to endure such a great conflict." About ten of these, the letter says, proved to be "stillborn" or "miscarried," causing great sorrow to the others and weakening the resolve of those yet to undergo their torture.[18] However, these stillborn Christians were encouraged through the zeal of the others, especially the slave girl Blandina, the heroine of the story, who was hung on a stake to be devoured by the wild beasts but who appeared to the other Christians as the embodiment of Christ: "In their agony they saw with their outward eyes in the person of their sister the One who was crucified for them."[19] After describing her suffering, the letter continues:

> Through their continued life the dead were made alive, and the witnesses (martyrs) showed favor to those who had failed to witness. And there was great joy for the Virgin Mother in receiving back alive those who she had miscarried as dead. For through them the majority of those who had denied were again brought to birth and again conceived and again brought to life and learned to confess; and now living and strengthened, they went to the judgment seat.[20]

The Christians who turned away from making their confession are simply dead; their lack of preparation meant that they are stillborn children of the Virgin Mother, the Church. But strengthened by the witness of others, they also were able to go to their death, and so the Virgin Mother received them back alive, finally giving birth to living children of God.

Baptism and Eucharist

This eschatological orientation of our present lives as Christians—directed towards the coming Christ, taking up our cross daily, ultimately to die in a good confession of Christ, so that we are born again into the fullness of life, as fully human beings, putting on the identity of Christ himself—all of this offers a very comprehensive and profound vision of the Church, as the Virgin Mother in and through whom Christ is born, and born in us.

This eschatological orientation of our lives, as an act of witness, also provides the broader picture for understanding the sacraments of baptism and Eucharist. Although baptism is a specific, sacramental event, in which we sacramentally die to the world, we *are* still living in this world and *still* have sin and death working in us, and will continue to do so until our actual death, in witness to Christ, at which point we will be born again into the newness of life, putting on, fully, the identity of Christ.

One of the most vibrant witnesses to this is St. Ignatius of Antioch, who, although being taken in chains across the empire, considered that he had not even yet begun to be a true disciple of Christ. And he implores the Christians at Rome not to interfere with his coming martyrdom:

> I seek him who died for our sake. I desire him who rose for us. The pains of birth are upon me. Suffer me, my brethren; hinder me not from living, do not wish me to die. . . . Suffer me to receive the pure light; when I shall have arrived there, I shall become a human being (*anthrōpos*). Suffer me to follow the example of the passion of my God. (Ign. *Rom.* 6)

Undergoing death in witness to Christ, who himself is the "perfect human being" (Ign. *Smyrn.* 4.2) or the "new human being" (Ign. *Eph.* 20:1), produces a birth into a new life for St. Ignatius, allowing him to emerge as Christ himself, a fully human being. Again beseeching the Romans to keep silent rather than intercede on his behalf, he asserts: "If you are silent concerning me, I am a word of God; but if you love my flesh, I shall be only a cry" (Ign. *Rom.* 2.1). By undergoing the same martyr's death as Christ, the suffering God, St. Ignatius hopes to attain to the true light, to true humanity after the stature of Christ, and so to be a word of God, rather than only an inarticulate cry.

Similarly, when St. Irenaeus asserts: "The glory of God is a living human being,"[21] he means specifically the martyr—the one who no longer lives by the strength of this world, but by the strength of the Spirit.[22] Just as the encounter with the coming Christ coincides with his disappearance from sight, so also the manifestation of a living human being, a true disciple of Christ, one who has become truly the body of Christ—this coincides with the moment at which they in turn depart from this world to be with God, to become a word of God.

The Eucharist, likewise, is intimately connected to the paschal dimensions of our baptismal lives, in such a way that we can, in turn, see our dying to this world and birth to the next in eucharistic terms. When writing to the Romans, St. Ignatius describes himself as being the "wheat of God, ground by the teeth of wild beasts," so that he "may be found to be the pure bread of Christ" (Ign. *Rom.* 4.1), a clear eucharistic allusion. St. Irenaeus develops this imagery more fully:

> Just as the wood of the vine, planted in the earth, bore fruit in its own time, and the grain of wheat, falling into the earth and being decomposed, was raised up by the Spirit of God who sustains all, then, by wisdom, they come to the use of humans, and receiving the Word of God, become eucharist, which is the Body and Blood of Christ; in the same way, our bodies, nourished by it, having been placed in the earth and decomposing in it, shall rise in their time, when the Word of God bestows on them the resurrection to the glory of God the Father, who secures immortality for the mortal and bountifully bestows incorruptibility on the corruptible.[23]

By receiving the Eucharist (as the wheat and the vine receive the fecundity of the Spirit) we are prepared (as we also make the fruits into the bread and wine) for the resurrection effected by the Word. At that resurrection, just as the bread and wine receive the Word and so become the Body and Blood of Christ, the Eucharist, so also our bodies will receive immortality and incorruptibility from the Father. The paschal mystery that each Christian enters by baptism is completed in their resurrection, celebrated as the Eucharist of the Father.

I have reviewed the way in which the eschatological dimension of the Church is being treated in recent Orthodox ecclesiology, specifically "eucharistic ecclesiology," and considered its limitations, and I have also demonstrated how we are able to speak about the coming of Christ, and how the Church is spoken of, related to baptism and the Eucharist. I hope that I have opened up a horizon that offers not only a broader and deeper understanding of the mystery of Christ and the coming of the eschatological Lord to his Church, the Virgin Mother, but also more fruitful space for further dialogue.

Endnotes

[1]J. Zizioulas, *Being as Communion* (Crestwood, NY: St Vladimir's Seminary Press, 1985), 24 (hereafter *BC*).

[2]*BC*, 150 ff.

[3]Ibid., 144.

[4]Ibid.

[5]Ibid., 24.

[6]For a full consideration of this issue, to which the following paragraphs are indebted, see Calinic (Kevin M.) Berger, "Does the Eucharist Make the Church? An Ecclesiological Comparison of Staniloae and Zizioulas," *SVTQ* 51.1 (2007): 23–70.

[7]Ibid., 130.

[8]Ibid.

[9]Ibid., 21.

[10]Ibid., 131.

[11]Zizioulas: "Baptism, Chrismation or confirmation, and the rest of the sacramental life, are all given in view of the Eucharist. Communion in these sacraments may be described as 'partial' or anticipatory communion, calling for its fulfillment in the Eucharist" ("The Church as Communion," *SVTQ* 38.1 [1994]: 15).

[12]See especially J. Erickson, "Baptism and the Church's Faith," in C. E. Braaten and R. W. Jenson, eds., *Marks of the Body of Christ* (Grand Rapids: William B. Eerdmans, 1999), 44–58, at 57.

[13]G. Limouris, "The Eucharist as the Sacrament of Sharing: An Orthodox Point of View," in *Orthodox Visions of Ecumenism*, ed. by G. Limouris (Geneva: WCC Publications, 1994), 254.

[14]*The Shape of Baptism* (Collegeville, MN: Liturgical Press, 1978), 162–163.

[15]St. Augustine, *On the Trinity*, trans. Edmund Hill, *The Works of St. Augustine, A Translation for the 21st Century*, vol. 5 (Brooklyn, NY: New City Press, 1991), 4.2.9.

[16]Irenaeus of Lyons, *Against the Heresies*. Irénée de Lyon, *Contre les Hérésies*, Livre I, Livre II, and Livre III, ed. and French trans. A. Rousseau and L. Doutreleau, SC 263–4, 293–4, 210–11 (Paris: Éditions du Cerf, 1979, 1982, 1974); *Against the Heresies* (henceforth = *AH*) 1.10.3.

[17]Eusebius of Caesarea, *Ecclesiastical History*, ed. and trans. by K. Lake, LCL, 2 vols. (Cambridge, MA: Harvard University Press, 1989), 5.1–2; henceforth cited as *EH*.

[18]Ibid., 5.1.11.

[19]Ibid., 5.1.41.

[20]Ibid., 5.1.45–6.

[21]*AH* 4.20.7; Livre IV, ed. and French trans. A. Rousseau, B. Hemmerdinger, L. Doutreleau, and C. Mercier, SC 100 (Paris: Éditions du Cerf, 1965).

[22]Cf. *AH* 5.9.2; Livre V, ed. and French trans. A. Rousseau, L. Doutreleau and C. Mercier SC 152–3 (Paris: Éditions du Cerf, 1969); English trans. ANF 1 (1885; repr. Grand Rapids: William B. Eerdmans, 1987).

[23]Ibid., 5.2.3.

12

The "Penultimate" Nature of the Church – the *Eschaton* Is Not Yet!

Frances Young

And if our fellowship below
in Jesus be so sweet,
What heights of rapture shall we know
when round his throne we meet.

Charles Wesley

New Testament studies were once dominated by eschatology: by the puzzle that Jesus apparently proclaimed the immediate presence of the kingdom of God and yet clearly the coming of the kingdom still belonged to the future; by the tension in the writings of St. Paul, commonly referred to as the "now and the 'not yet,'" whereby he could address his converts as already "saints," sanctified as well as justified in Christ—already "sons of God," and yet keep exhorting them to "become what they already are"; by the oscillation in the Gospel of John between the future gift of eternal life and its present reality. The documents of the New Testament ring with a sense of fulfillment, yet point to a future in which the prophecies will come to full fruition. The Church in the New Testament, it was often suggested, was an anticipation of that future, a new creation within the old, in the world but not of the world, in receipt of the first-fruits of the Spirit, yet awaiting redemption, caught between two aeons as the coming of Christ initiated the turning of the ages.

There can be little doubt that this perspective has affected recent statements on ecclesiology made by the British Methodist Church. I quote from *Called to Love and Praise* (1999), a document expressing the judgment of the Conference on the doctrine of the Church, framed with a view to standing as such for some years (as had the previous statement of 1937):

- The Church has been brought to birth, but has not yet attained its fullness. It comprises a pilgrim people seeking to enter, and to help others enter, the fullness of God's kingdom.

- [T]he Church, a pilgrim people journeying towards the End, must testify to, celebrate, and hope in the God who remains active in his creation, working out his purpose for its salvation.

- A Christian way of living in anticipation of the coming reign of God remains difficult to sustain both for individuals and for the Church as an institution. This has been true from the beginning. The New Testament does not know of a perfect Christian community, and human sinfulness has not diminished with the passage of time. The life of the Church is continually eroded by it. . . . Seeking the true reign of God means facing the temptations which Jesus himself endured and triumphed over: the temptation to live for bread and not for the word of God; the temptation to test God and require that God perform according to our wishes; to acquire power instead of to offer true worship.

- While the Eucharist "prefigures and images the life of the kingdom of God" and indeed, "in a sense, makes the Church," this "rite which powerfully expresses unity has become a source of disagreement."

- So the affirmation of the Church as "one, holy, catholic and apostolic" provokes the observation that "the Church continually fails. Often, these characteristics are barely discernible in the Church's life, and repentance is an ever-present requirement."

- At the same time, as expressed in Charles Wesley's lines, "Fortified by power divine, / The Church can never fail." Such belief in the "indefectibility" of the Church does not mean believing that it already has that "perfection without spot and wrinkle" (Eph. 5:27), which belongs only to the end of time. It means believing in a God who perseveres in re-creation, and who provides the essential means of grace in word and sacrament . . . .The saints on earth remain on pilgrimage, journeying towards and praying for an ever fuller expression of unity, holiness, catholicity and apostolicity.[1]

My question is: to what extent has this "now but not yet" perspective had any serious impact on the doctrine of the Church over the intervening centuries? Is it just an observation of recent New Testament scholarship, now taken up by a British Methodist Church leadership trained in the period when it was a standard topic? Or does it have roots in John Wesley's understanding of Church? Is there a deeper lineage in the Fathers? My hunch is that Eastern Orthodoxy and Methodism have a similar kind of realistic and pragmatic view of the Church as it exists on earth, by contrast with Western Christianity's tendency towards ideological ecclesiology, particularly as expressed in Roman Catholic tradition. I suspect that in both cases it is the outcome of a lively awareness of the whole of creation as God's concern, and of the sense that the whole creation falls short of the glory of God. The Church's business is to facilitate return to God's purposes, and this is in process rather than accomplished. The question is: do the sources substantiate such a view?

By way of preliminary comment, I might observe that a cursory consideration of the Fathers, as taught in early Christian doctrine courses, would seem to point in that direction. When it comes to the doctrine of the Church, textbooks and teachers focus on Latin authors, noting: (1) Cyprian's exclusive statements: "*Extra ecclesiam nulla salus*—there is no salvation outside the Church" and "The one who does not have the Church as his mother cannot have God as his Father," together with his treatise, *De*

Unitate Ecclesiae—On Church Unity; and (2) Augustine's struggles with Donatist claims to be the true Church. So in what has been the standard textbook for a couple of generations, J. N. D. Kelly comments:

> It is customarily said that, as contrasted with that of the West, Eastern teaching about the Church remained immature, not to say archaic, in the post-Nicene period. In the main this is a fair enough verdict, at any rate so far as concerns deliberate statements of ecclesiological theory.[2]

He quotes from Cyril of Jerusalem, commenting, "These are time-honoured commonplaces." Certainly it is interesting that no Eastern treatise on the Church as such immediately leaps to mind, and comments on the nature of the Church are largely to be found incidentally in the course of discussing other matters. The Church is not a subject in the *Five Theological Orations* of Gregory the Theologian—other doctrinal issues are far more pressing. Yet it would be very strange if the major Greek Fathers provided us with no reflection on the Church. They do, of course; you simply have to search for it. And I would argue that that search turns up material that does indeed suggest a pragmatic and realistic sense of the Church's penultimate state on earth, despite its ultimately eschatological character.

With no dogmatic treatises on ecclesiology to turn to, a sensible place to start might be texts concerned with canonical rulings. Such texts are of course pragmatic in their very character, but they might imply a vision of the nature of the Church for which ordinances are being made. Since the *Apostolic Constitutions* incorporates a number of earlier texts and appears to belong to the fourth century—the high period of early Greek patristic literature—we will focus on this text first, despite its lack of clear long-term influence. It is, of course, a text of importance to those scholars interested in church order and liturgy, and we may note first that the prayers found in Book VIII include, after the consecration, intercession for the Church spread throughout the world and "purchased with the precious blood of Christ," that God will preserve it unshaken and free from disturbance "until the end of the world"; and for "this people" that God will make them "a royal priesthood and a holy nation."[3] Earlier, among the intercessions, a similar prayer for the Church asks that "God would preserve and keep it unshaken, and free from the waves of this life, until the end of the world, as founded upon a rock."[4] Further prayers ask that God look down on "this flock" and keep them firm and blameless, "that they may be holy in body and spirit, not having spot or wrinkle." God is addressed as "their protector, helper, provider and guardian, their strong wall of defense, their bulwark and security."[5] These prayers imply that, while the Church's life is anchored in God and will reach safe harbor in the End, for the moment it needs divine assistance to withstand the storms and temptations of earthly existence, and it may potentially fail if not given divine protection.

Based as they are in Scripture, the various images of the Church found in these prayers are anticipated in the earlier books. The picture of the "flock" with the bishop as "shepherd" keeps recurring, with warnings that one "scabbed sheep" may infect the rest, and long quotations from Ezekiel and elsewhere alerting people to the existence of bad shepherds.[6] Much of the discussion assumes that Old Testament passages about Israel, whether about its sin and sedition or its worship and priesthood, apply directly to the Church.[7] Indeed, the Church is taken to be a "holy nation," "God's people": "You, therefore, are the holy and sacred Church of God, enrolled in heaven, a royal priesthood, a holy nation, a peculiar people, a bride adorned for the Lord God, a great Church, a faithful Church." As escapees from the ten plagues, who have received the Ten Commandments, learned the law, kept the faith, and believed in Jesus, they should offer tithes and sacrifices, now understood to be the prayers, thanksgivings and eucharistic offerings. Bishops are their high priests, presbyters their priests, and deacons are instead of Levites, not to mention readers, singers, doorkeepers, deaconesses, widows, virgins, and orphans—this being the list of those supported by the tithes. He who is above all these is the High Priest, Christ, to whom all the offerings belong.[8] They are a people who were once not a people.[9]

The biblical image of the vineyard also appears, and the catholic Church is called "God's plantation," containing those who are (among other things) heirs by faith, partakers of the Spirit, free to call God "Father," enjoying the benefits of the "sprinkling of the precious blood of Christ" and the promises of God.[10] People are exhorted not to leave the Church for the polluted temple of the heathen or the synagogues of Jews or heretics— how would they answer for it on the Day of Judgment? Scriptural warnings are quoted: they should not call things holy which God calls profane, or make unclean what God has sanctified. The Church is "the daughter of the Highest, which has been in labour pains for you by the word of grace, and has formed Christ in you, of whom you are made partakers, and thereby become his holy and chosen members, not having spot or wrinkle, or any such thing; but as being holy and unspotted in the faith, you are complete in him, after the image of God that created you" (Eph. 5:27).[11] The bishop is charged with treating those who cause disturbances and division in the Church as superfluous members of the body, to be amputated as a surgeon deals with physical excrescences—for the Church is a perfect body, with sound members who believe in God, in the fear of the Lord and in love.[12] The bishop is a physician.[13] It was because of the dangers the Church would face that bishops were given oversight at the Apostolic Council in Jerusalem.[14] Implicit throughout is a tension between the Church as a "safe haven of tranquility"[15] and as a vessel tossed on the storms of sin and heresy.

Indeed the most striking feature of this compendium of texts is its description of the assembling of the Church, for it takes the ship metaphor as its basis. The building is to be long, with its head to the east, so as to be like a ship. The bishop is the commander, so his throne is to be placed in the middle, with the presbytery on each side of him and the deacons standing by, for they are like the mariners and managers of the ship. The laity are all set in their proper places and order, men and women apart, young and old in their special places—the metaphor now shifting to the sheepfold. But the ship imagery is not abandoned: the doorkeepers and deaconesses keep watch like sailors over men and women respectively, and the bishop speaks after the presbyters, "as being the commander."[16] We may recall the hints found earlier: besides the expression, "a safe haven of tranquility," there was the prayer that the Church may be "free from the waves of this life, until the end of the world."

Now this focus on the Church as a ship is by no means a peculiarity of this text. A trawl through the letters of Basil of Caesarea reveals its persistent use, especially when Basil is appealing for help in the face of heresy and schism. A few examples will suffice:[17]

- The times are difficult, "having need of a great helmsman because of the continual storms and floods which rise against the Church (LXXXI).

- In the face of enemy attacks, "the Church has given up the struggle, like a ship in mid-sea buffeted by successive waves" (XC).

- Basil requests prayers "in order that the holy God may some day grant calm and repose to our concerns here, and may rebuke this wind and sea, so that we can find rest from the tempest-tossing and confusion in which we now find ourselves, ever waiting to be plunged utterly into the deep" (XCI).

- Advising a bishop, Basil says, "Like a wise helmsman who has assumed the command of a ship, rise superior in your resolution to every blast that is stirred up by the winds of heresy, and preserve your ship unsubmerged by the briny and bitter waves of error, awaiting the calm which the Lord will cause as soon as a voice is found worthy of rousing him to rebuke the winds and the sea" (CLXI).

- "No-one in his right mind would board a boat without pilot, nor entrust himself to a Church in which those who sit at the helm are themselves causing the billows and the tossing" (CCX).

In many other letters we find the metaphors of being "tossed about," of potential "shipwreck" of "continual storms," "fierce tempests," "floods," "torrents" and "a sea of evils," of the need for someone reliable to hold the tiller[18]—almost to the point of this cluster of expressions becoming dead metaphors. The *eschaton* certainly is not yet!

Now it might be objected that letters are bound to reflect a pragmatic viewpoint, and we should look elsewhere for Basil's serious understanding of the Church. I grant the point, but in his work *On the Holy Spirit* we find exactly the same metaphor. The present condition of the Church is compared to a naval battle, fought by people who cherish a deadly hate against each other, with long experience of naval warfare and eager for the fight:

> See the rival fleets rushing in dread array to the attack. With a burst of uncontrollable fury they engage and fight it out. Imagine the ships driven to and fro by a raging tempest, while thick darkness falls from the clouds and blackens the scene . . . Suppose the sea swollen with billows and whirled up from the deep, while a vehement torrent of rain pours down from the clouds and the terrible waves rise high. From all sides the winds beat on one point where the fleets are dashed against one another.[19]

Basil goes on to speak of combatants becoming traitors or deserting, sailors split into parties, utter confusion "from howling winds, crashing vessels, boiling surf, and the yells of the combatants," of inability to hear a word from admiral or pilot. They cannot cease from the struggle to get the better of one another, driven as they are by the mad love of glory, while their ship is actually sinking into the deep. Basil turns from this rhetorical picture to the unhappy reality of the Church's tempest and the shaking of every foundation, wondering who could make a complete list of the wrecks, when we see churches, crews and all, dashed and shattered upon the sunken reefs of heresy. The metaphor lives on as he laments the darkness that has settled upon the churches, and the divisions amongst its leaders.

Basil's letters also reveal his use of the other common metaphors traced in the *Apostolic Constitutions*, such as the flock and its shepherds.[20] The idea of the body and its members recurs, with the suggestion that the body is sick, like Basil's own body, or suggesting that "to unite these parts and bring them together in the harmony of a single body belongs to him alone, who by his ineffable power grants even to dry bones a return once more to flesh and muscles."[21] The idea of correcting or healing hidden maladies before facing the Day of Judgment[22] is frequent enough almost to become another dead metaphor, and is a reminder that the eschatological perspective generates a pragmatic realism about the life of the Church on earth. Healing and restoration is required.

As soon as we move into other texts of this period we find the same biblical metaphors of the flock and the body: for example, John Chrysostom, *On Priesthood*, and, not surprisingly, his homilies on the Corinthian letters; and Gregory of Nazianzus, *Oration II: In Defence of his flight to Pontus*. Gregory is all too aware that God has providentially united people in the Church so that they may form one perfect body, worthy of Christ our Head, but this requires pastors and teachers to rule and guide, as the soul or intellect functions in the body; while Chrysostom recognizes that Paul is exhorting the Corinthians to realize in the Church's life the united body he embodies—honoring the poor and the shameful in their midst, living out the ideals of mutual support and equality, getting rid of envy and jealousy which are the root of all evil. Chrysostom seems to recognize that the perfect body is not yet attained.

So far then we have found this eschatological tension present, if not named, in Greek texts of the fourth century. Is it also present when discoursing on the affirmations of the Creed? Let us turn to the *Catechetical Homilies* of Cyril of Jerusalem, dismissed as merely conventional by Kelly. In the eighteenth homily Cyril reaches the clause "one holy catholic church."[23] He says it is called "catholic" because it extends over all the world, from one end of the earth to the other; but he also gives other reasons: because it teaches universally and completely all the doctrines people need to know about things visible and invisible; because it subjects the whole human race, educated and uneducated, to godliness; because it universally heals all kinds of sins, whether of soul or body; and because it possesses every form of virtue and every kind of spiritual gift. He then discusses the term *ecclesia*, suggesting that it is used because the Church calls forth and assembles all humanity, that it is a scriptural word, proved by much quotation of texts, but that, since this is a common word used for many other gatherings, some of them dens of wickedness and heresy, the addition of these adjectives is important. The holy Church, he says, is the mother of us all and the spouse of Our Lord Jesus Christ, the figure and copy of the Jerusalem, which is above, in which God has set every kind of wisdom and virtue. In former days she crowned martyrs, now she receives honors from kings, while she alone transcends the boundaries of earthly kingdoms.

Here then Cyril would seem to be making a strong eschatological claim. Particularly interesting is his wide-ranging definition of the word "catholic." Yet, that in itself implies a process of teaching and healing, and elsewhere he affirms that the need for teaching relates to the fact of temptation, and suggests that the Church is Christ's school, gathered around the Scriptures.[24] Furthermore, the Holy Spirit is the Church's helper and teacher, guardian and sanctifier, a mighty champion on our behalf, and pilot of the tempest-tossed, who leads wanderers to the light, presides over combatants, and crowns the victors.[25] Cyril warns and encourages his catechumens: the Christian life remains one of struggle as long as one is in the body. However, he is confident that the Holy Spirit keeps the Church on track, and the Church's teaching enables its members to struggle through to victory.

It is time we turned to Wesley. One thing he has in common with the Greek Fathers is a sense of the individual's struggle to attain to the perfection promised in the New Testament.[26] Yet alongside this sense of struggle was his doctrine of Christian perfection, the affirmation that the New Testament promises must mean that perfect love is attainable, at least within the limitations of a person's creatureliness and maturity. This seems to capture in its own way the eschatological tension that is the subject of our exploration. But what about the Church? Wesley has much to say about the impossibility of being a Christian on one's own, of the need of fellowship; clearly the road to Christian perfection must lie in the company of others. But what does he understand by Church, and can Church be said to be in any sense an eschatological reality in process of realization?

For Wesley himself, specific debate about Church is found in controversial writings dealing with accusations that his actions were schismatic. From such material it is clear that he identified the Church of England as the Church in England, and that he never intended his societies to be "Church"; at the same time, however, he was profoundly critical of the then present state of the Church of England, clearly perceiving much of what went on as failing to embody Church as he understood it from the New Testament. In other words, he recognized in practice if not in name what we have called the "eschatological tension" between the "now" and the "not yet." Let us turn to some texts.

At the first annual conference of 1744, on June 27th the following questions were discussed:[27]

- What is the Church of England?
- What is a member of the Church of England?
- What is it to be zealous for the Church?
- How are we to defend the doctrine of the Church?
- Do [certain of the Thirty-nine] Articles agree with Scripture?
- How shall we bear the most effectual testimony against that part of the clergy who either preach or live contrary to the doctrine of the Church of England?
- How should we behave at false or railing sermons?
- How far is it our duty to obey the bishops?
- Do we separate from the Church?

- What do they mean who say, "You separate from the Church"? Or do you not weaken the Church? Or do not you entail a schism on the Church? That is, is it not probable that your hearers after your death will be scattered into all sects and parties, or that they will form themselves into a distinct sect?

The report, of course, answers each one by one, and to some extent one follows from another in a way obscured by picking out the questions. However, to quote the full text would be too extensive, and the implications of the questions are clear. Wesley quotes the twentieth Article to show that the "visible Church of England is the congregation of English believers in which the pure word of God is preached and the sacraments duly administered." He then defines a member of the Church of England as "a believer hearing the pure word preached and partaking of the sacraments duly administered by the Church." Being zealous for the Church means being earnestly desirous of its welfare and increase, and, he insists, its doctrines are defended "by our preaching and living." Problematic clergy are to be confronted in writing (to sum up in brief the response to the dilemmas posed), and the bishops are to be obeyed in all things indifferent. Wesley will not accept that "we separate from the Church," for "we hold communion therewith for conscience sake, by constant attending both the word preached and the sacraments administered therein." He cannot understand the questions of his opponents, "unless by the Church they mean themselves, i.e. that part of the clergy who accuse us of preaching false doctrines." It is clear Wesley himself will not countenance schism, and believes his followers will not separate even after his death "unless they be thrust out."

The position indicated by these bare questions and responses could be filled out with material from a sermon published first in *The Arminian Magazine* of 1786.[28] Wesley takes as his text Eph. 4:1–6:

I beseech you that ye walk worthy of the vocation wherewith ye are called, with all lowliness and meekness, with longsuffering, forbearing one another in love; endeavouring to keep the unity of the Spirit in the bond of peace. There is one body, and one Spirit, even as ye are called in one hope of your calling; one Lord, one faith, one baptism, one God and Father of all, who is above all, and through all, and in you all.

In the face of many different usages of the word, what Wesley does is to go back to the New Testament to discern there a sense of "Church." He finds the word used of a congregation, of a body of people united in God's service. The word is used in the plural because there were too many to meet in one place, but the singular is also used for the catholic or universal Church. He identifies the Church with the saints, that is, holy persons assembled for worship, who constitute one body, and have one Spirit, one hope, one Lord, one faith, one baptism, one God and Father of all. He then argues that part of this great body of the universal Church may be a national Church, such as the Church of England. A smaller part may be the Christians in a particular town, while two or three "gathered together in his name" (Matt. 18:20) are a Church in the narrowest sense. Thus he establishes that the marks of the true Church, universal or local, are to be found in the characteristics set out in the text from Ephesians, and he shows this is consistent with the nineteenth Article of the Church of England.

So, he goes on, the Church of England consists of the members of the universal Church who happen to inhabit England: in other words, they have the characteristics set out in the text, one Spirit, one hope, one Lord, and so on, adding two others from the nineteenth Article, namely that the pure Word of God is preached and the sacraments duly administered. Those congregations where this is not the case are "no parts either of the Church of England or the Church catholic," though Wesley is chary of pushing that too far because the Roman Catholic Church could hardly be excluded from the Church catholic. Yet for him, as a good Protestant, there were problems with regard to whether the doctrine preached there was scriptural and with respect to the "superstitious modes of worship" there practiced.

Nevertheless, the second part of this sermon goes back to the opening sentence of the verses quoted, insisting that only people with the qualities of lowliness, meekness, longsuffering, forbearing one another in love, and keeping the unity of the Spirit in the bond of peace can really be said to belong to the one body. Most people fall far short of this, yet it is only possible to be living members of the Church if that is how we are. The Church is called holy and catholic because it is holy, because every member is holy. So this excludes not only the Sabbath-breaker, the drunkard, the whoremonger, the thief, and the liar, but also everyone under the power of anger or pride, or who is a lover of the world. The real members of the Church should see that they walk holy and blameless in all things. Ultimately Wesley's idealistic assertions about the Church in the face of reality, like his views on Christian perfection and the struggle towards it, demonstrate a sense of eschatological tension. The Church of England is the Church, and yet it falls far short of what it is meant to be.

In *An Earnest Appeal to Men of Reason and Religion,*[29] another controversial piece re-published a number of times over his lifetime, Wesley makes the same assumptions about the nature of the Church, asking how what he does can be said to destroy the Church. Not living faith, nor preaching, nor the due administration of the sacraments is undermined; rather they are in fact reinforced. He answers the charges that he does not observe the canons, that he leaves the Church, divides the Church, undermines or destroys the Church by insisting that the practice of Christian life has improved in England. Wherever we look in his published sermons, we usually find the same assumption that what is meant by "Church" is the Church of England.[30] Controversy, however, did tempt him to modify his view of the Church of England: note his confession in the sermon "On the Catholic Spirit."

> I know it is commonly supposed that the place of our birth fixes the Church to which we ought to belong; that one, for instance, who is born in England ought to be a member of that which is styled the Church of England and, consequently, to worship God in the particular manner which is prescribed by that Church. I was once a zealous maintainer of this, but I find many reasons to abate of this zeal. I fear it is attended with such difficulties as no reasonable man can get over—not the least of which is that if this rule had took place, there could have been no reformation from popery, seeing it entirely destroys the right of private judgement on which the whole reformation stands.[31]

Wesley clearly has deep reservations about what he nevertheless continues to regard as "the Church" in England. His reading of the New Testament presents to him a vision of gathered "saints," which he does not find in the national Church of his time. Wesley clearly has a sense of what the Church should be, alongside a recognition that what he identifies as the Church does not live up to it.

This implicit tension is made explicit in some passages where the Church is not directly Wesley's subject. His sermon on "Scriptural Christianity" recognizes that very soon tares were sown among wheat, and Satan found a seat even in the temple of God. The story of "increasing corruptions of the succeeding generations" Wesley regards as so well known that he does not have to tell it. Despite this, however, he is sure that Satan cannot make the truth of God fail, and he surveys the possibility of a Christian world, quoting Scripture at length to show what it would be like, including Isaiah's prophecies of swords beaten into ploughshares and the Apostle's vision of the fullness of the Gentiles and all Israel being saved. "Suppose now the fullness of time to be come, and the prophecies accomplished," he says, describing a world without war or civil discord, full of righteousness and peace. But he ends the sermon with "a plain, practical application," asking where the Christians live, "where is the country the inhabitants whereof are all thus filled with the Holy Ghost?" He challenges his hearers, whether secular magistrates or clergy, mature scholars or young students (preaching at Christ Church, Oxford): "what probability, what possibility, . . . is there that Christianity, scriptural Christianity, should be again the religion of this place?" His climax is "Lord, save, or we perish!" And earlier he has inquired, "how soon the righteous Judge may say, 'I will no more be entreated for this people'?" The sense of "now" and "not yet" is clear in this sermon.[32]

So too in the second of his series on the Sermon on the Mount: Wesley is speaking of the Beatitudes, and pleads, "O God! How long?" after sketching the reality of Christian kingdoms desolating one another with fire and sword, Christian armies sending each other quick into hell, Christian nations "all on fire with intestine broils, party against party, faction against faction," Christian cities, where there is deceit and fraud, oppression and wrong, robbery, and murder, Christian families, torn asunder with envy, jealousy, anger, and Christian churches at war with one another, converting sinners by burning them alive, anathematizing one another—and the Protestant churches are as bad when it comes to persecution! Yet Wesley urges hope—"It is your Father's good pleasure yet to renew the face of the earth. Surely all these things shall come to an end, and the inhabitants of the earth shall learn righteousness." The prophecies of Isaiah figure again: "they shall not hurt or destroy in all His holy mountain." So comes the exhortation:

> Be thou part of the first-fruits, if the harvest is not yet. Do thou love thy neighbour as thyself. The Lord God fill thy heart with such a love to every soul, that thou mayest be ready to lay down thy life for his sake! May thy soul continually overflow with love, swallowing up every unkind and unholy temper till He calleth thee up into the region of love, there to reign with Him for ever and ever!

This is one of the more dramatic passages lamenting the present state of the world. But a trawl through Wesley's sermons shows time and again that he both urges the possibility of genuine Christianity here and now, lives filled with the love of God shed abroad in our hearts through the Spirit, and at the same time accepts the reality that even the saints can be tempted and do fail,[33] while the ultimate fulfillment of God's promises lies in heaven. The wise man

> knows the world: the place in which he is to pass a few days or years, not as an inhab-
> itant, but as a stranger and sojourner, in his way to the everlasting habitations; and
> accordingly he uses the world as not abusing it, and as knowing the fashion of it
> passes away.[34]

Wesley has a very conventional reading of the New Testament when it comes to the destiny of the soul—either for hell or heaven. He does not lack a future eschatology, for all his talk of the "inner kingdom" that can be a reality already. So I would argue that implicit in his work is the eschatological tension now recognised in New Testament scholarship and taken up in recent statements about the Church adopted by the British Methodist Conference; and, again implicit, is the idea of the saints that make up the true Church being on pilgrimage:

> . . . [I]n our whole lives, we are moving straight toward God, and that continually;
> walking steadily on in the highway of holiness, in the paths of justice, mercy and
> truth.[35]

"Outward religion" is worth nothing. Just belonging to the Anglican Church is not enough, for holiness of heart is required, "heaven opened in the soul."[36] One thing is to be pursued "to the end of time—the enjoyment of God in time and eternity"; but that necessitates, in this life, striving, agonizing, entering in at the straight gate, taking up the cross daily, "a constant and continued course of general self-denial!"[37] The sermon on "The Marks of the New Birth" affirms that the eschatological promises of the New Testament may be realized here and now in the life of the believer, but one of the marks is hope, a hope that "overflows, in the depth of affliction," a hope sustained "in heaviness through manifold temptations," as I Peter put it, a hope that ultimately the trial of faith will redound to praise, honor and glory when Jesus Christ appears.[38]

It is time to bring this argument to a close. I suggested at the start that maybe Eastern Orthodoxy and Methodism have a similar kind of realistic and pragmatic view of the Church as it exists on earth, by contrast with the tendency towards ideological ecclesiology in Western Christianity, particularly as expressed in Roman Catholic tradition. I guessed that in both cases it could be the outcome of a lively awareness of the whole of creation as God's concern, and of the sense that the whole creation falls short of the glory of God, so that the Church's business is to facilitate return to God's purposes, and this reality is in process rather than accomplished. To confirm these hunches fully I would need to explore Western ecclesiology to provide the contrast. Suffice it to say that discussion of the Vatican II statement, arrived at through intense debate and recognised as a genuine change and advance on the Council of Trent, would need to nuance my argument,[39] but only because it has moved the Roman Catholic Church towards an awareness of the impossibility of an imposed ideology of ecclesiastical perfection in the conditions of this penultimate world. I would also need to explore further the way in which both traditions take God's concern with the whole *oikoumene* with the utmost seriousness; and also say more about the fact that the individual saint's progress towards the perfection promised by God is an important element in both traditions, demonstrating further the way in which that permits the recognition of failings in the Body's members, alongside the affirmation of the ultimate wholeness of the Church, given by God in Christ. But I think enough material has been found to substantiate the basic claim I made at the start. Our traditions alike recognise that the End is not yet, while celebrating the fulfillment of God's promises already in process and the anticipation of the *eschaton,* partially if not wholly, experienced in the life of the Church.

Endnotes

[1] *Called to Love and Praise* (1999) 1.4.4; 2.1.11; 2.1.10; 2.4.8, 12, 13.

[2] *Early Christian Doctrines,* 2nd edition (London: A. & C. Black 1960), 401.

[3] *Les Constitutions Apostoliques* in *Sources Chrétiennes,* ed. Marcel Metzger, 3 vols. (Paris: Éditions du Cerf, 1985, 1986, 1987), Greek text with French translation. Complete English trans. in *Ante-Nicene Christian Library,* vol. 17, ed. by A. Roberts and J. Donaldson (Edinburgh: T. & T. Clark, 1870), VIII.12; henceforth cited as *Apostolic Constitutions.*

[4] *Apostolic Constitutions,* VIII.10.

[5] *Apostolic Constitutions,* VIII.11.

[6] *Apostolic Constitutions* II.15–20; cf. VI.18.

[7] *Apostolic Constitutions* II.21 ff, 25; cf. VI. 1–5.

[8] *Apostolic Constitutions* II.25.

[9] *Apostolic Constitutions* III.15.

[10] *Apostolic Constitutions* I.1; cf. II.15.

[11] *Apostolic Constitutions* II.61.

[12] *Apostolic Constitutions* II.43.

[13] *Apostolic Constitutions* II.20.

[14] *Apostolic Constitutions* VI.12.

[15] *Apostolic Constitutions* II.20.

[16] *Apostolic Constitutions* II.57.

[17] In each case the reference to the letter quoted is given in brackets in the text. See St. Basil, *The Letters,* in 4 vols., Loeb Classical Library, Greek text and English trans. by Roy J. Deferrari (Cambridge, MA: Harvard University Press, 1926, 1928, 1930, 1934).

[18] For example, XCII, CLXIV, CXCVII, CCXXVI, CCXL, CCXLII, CCXLIII, CCLVI.

[19] Basile de Césarée, *Traité du Saint-Esprit,* ed. B. Proche (Paris: Éditions du Cerf, 1947). English trans. in *Nicene and Post-Nicene Fathers* series II, vol. viii, trans. Blomfield Jackson (Oxford and London, 1895), xxx.76. The Greek text is found in *Sources Chrétiennes.*

[20] E.g. CCXLIII.

[21] XXX, LXVI; cf. XXIX, LXXX, LXXXII, XC, CLVI, CLXIV, CCIII, CCXLIII.

[22] E.g. CXXV; cf. CXIII.

[23] *Catechetical Homilies:* Greek text: *S. Patris Nostri Cyrilli Hierosolymorum Archiepiscopi Opera quae supersunt Omnia,* ed. W. K. Reischl and J. Rupp (Munich, 1848–60). English trans. by L. McCauley and A. Stephenson, in *The Works of Saint Cyril of Jerusalem I and II,* Fathers of the Church series vols. 61 and 64, (Washington, D.C.: Catholic University of America Press, 1967 and 1970), 18.22–27; henceforth cited as *Cat. Orat.*

[24] *Cat. Orat.* 4.1 and 33.

[25] *Cat. Orat.* 16.14, 19; 17.13.

[26] Frances Young, "Inner Struggle: Some Parallels between the Spirituality of John Wesley and the Greek Fathers," in *Orthodox and Wesleyan Spirituality,* S T Kimbrough, Jr., ed. (Crestwood, NY: St. Vladimir's Seminary Press, 2002), 157–172.

[27]Quoted from Albert Outler, ed., *John Wesley* (A Library of Protestant Thought, New York: Oxford University Press, 1964), 141–143.

[28]Outler, 308–317.

[29]Outler, 385–424.

[30]For example, "Justification by Faith," V.iii.5; iv.3; "The Witness of the Spirit," X.ii.4; "The Means of Grace," XII.ii.1. References are to the collection of 44 sermons first published in 1746, "to which reference is made in the Trust-deeds of the Methodist Chapels, as constituting, with Mr. Wesley's *Notes on the New Testament*, the standard doctrines of the Methodist Connexion" (London: Epworth Press, 1944).

[31]XXXIV of the 44, i.10.

[32]Sermon IV of the 44; see especially ii.9, iii.1–6; iv.1–11.

[33]For example, Sermons XV.ii; XXXV.i.8; XL, XLI.

[34]Sermon XXVIII of the 44, the 13th on the Sermon on the Mount, ii.2.

[35]Sermon XII of the 44, "The Means of Grace," 12.

[36]Sermon XXVIII.iii.1, 3; cf. Sermon XII "On the Means of Grace."

[37]Sermon XIII of the 44, "On the Circumcision of the Heart," i.12; ii.7.

[38]Sermon XIV of the 44, ii.1, 5.

[39]*Vatican II on The Church*, ed. Austin Flannery, O.P. (Dublin: Scepter Books, 1966); cf. Hans Küng, *The Church* (London: Burns and Oates, 1968).

PART 3

Ecclesiology and Sacred Space

13

Methodist Ecclesiologies and Methodist Sacred Spaces

Ted A. Campbell

Introduction and background

Methodists originated as advocates of a religious renewal movement, part of the Evangelical Revival in the British Isles in the eighteenth century. Frank Baker and others have documented the process by which Methodists organized themselves as "churches," but, for our purposes, it is sufficient to say that Methodist identity has been shaped by a critical ambiguity about whether Methodists should think of themselves primarily as a church or as a religious movement.[1] This ecclesiological ambiguity, I will argue, is reflected in the architecture of Methodist worship spaces. Some Methodist worship spaces reflect the needs of a religious movement; others reflect an understanding of "church" in the fuller and more ecumenical sense of the term. Others, yet again, offer a "hybrid" space which itself reflects this ecclesiological ambiguity.

Methodist ecclesiologies

I begin with the issue of Methodist ecclesiologies. In the 1960s Dr. Albert C. Outler wrote an essay asking the question, "Do Methodists Have a Doctrine of the Church?" His answer was, essentially, no—Methodists have a strong sense of the *mission* of the Church, but not really a "doctrine of the Church" beyond that inherited from Anglicanism.[2] At the risk of differing with one of my mentors, I shall argue that John Wesley and subsequent Methodists have had a doctrine of the Church, but it is what we might describe as a "bipolar" understanding of the Church, moving freely between an inherited Anglican conception of the Church and a rather different understanding of the Methodist community as a "religious society." This "bipolar" understanding of the Church, I will argue, can be seen in Wesley's distinction between "instituted" and "prudential" means of grace, in Wesley's distinction between "ordinary" and "extraordinary" ministries, in the relationship between the Methodist Love Feast and the Eucharist, and in Methodist doctrinal standards as they evolved in the eighteenth and nineteenth centuries.

Methodist Ecclesiologies: What was inherited

John Wesley and the Methodist movement inherited an understanding of the Church from the Church of England and the Reformed tradition, which held a great deal of influence over eighteenth-century Anglicanism. An Anglican article of religion, inherited from the Augsburg Confession, states that the Church is constituted by three things: a) faith, b) preaching, c) the due administration of the sacraments.[3] The Reformed tradition had added discipline ("church censures") to these three elements in the Westminster Confession of Faith (which Wesley sometimes cites as being authoritative for Anglicans).[4] To these historic definitions one may compare Wesley's general definition of the Church of England as "that body of people, nominally united, which profess to uphold the doctrine contained in the Articles and Homilies, and to use Baptism, the Lord's Supper and Public Prayer, according to the Common Prayer Book."[5]

I recognize that these four characteristics—faith, preaching, sacraments, and discipline—would not be sufficient to define "church" for Eastern Orthodox Christians. Indeed, they would not suffice to define "church" for many Anglicans (for example, those who insist episcopal succession is a necessary attribute). But they do provide a baseline for understanding doctrines of the Church as they developed in Methodist circles in the eighteenth and nineteenth centuries, and in what follows I will take them as such, as a way of testing Methodist understandings of the Church and then as a way of interpreting Methodist "sacred spaces."

Methodist ecclesiologies: "Instituted" and "prudential" means of grace

Having inherited this understanding of "church," however, there was critical ambiguity in the ways in which John Wesley and subsequent Methodists described their own movement, with regard to its identity as a "church" or as a part of the "Church." In the first place, ambiguity is revealed in John Wesley's understanding of "instituted" and "prudential" means of grace.

In the document we historically call the "Large Minutes," John Wesley distinguished between "instituted" and "prudential" means of grace.[6] The "instituted" means include prayer, "searching the Scriptures," the Lord's Supper, fasting, and "Christian conference," by which Wesley meant carefully guarded conversation with other Christians. The "prudential" means include rules that individual Christians might make to be kept with the help of their societies, attending class and band meetings, occasions on which preachers could meet with society or class members, and even more specific items such as abstaining from meat or late meals, drinking water, and temperance in the use of wine and ale.

Although the "Large Minutes" do not elaborate on Wesley's terms, it seems clear enough that the "instituted" means were practices instituted in Scripture, from the beginning of the Christian community, and that are binding on the Church in all times and places (for example, see Wesley's argument about these practices in the sermon on "The Means of Grace").[7] The "prudential" means, by contrast, include specifically and distinctively Methodist practices, things not "instituted" in Scripture but which were found to be prudentially helpful by Methodist people. Therefore, the distinction John

Wesley drew between "instituted" and "prudential" means of grace confirms a pattern in his thought by which he distinguished what is commonly Christian from those things that marked the distinctive mission of the Methodist movement. In other words, Wesley identifies the Methodist people as a distinct religious movement whose "prudential" practices supplemented those of the broader Christian community.

Methodist ecclesiologies: "Ordinary" and "extraordinary" ministries

A parallel pattern lies in the distinction John Wesley drew between "ordinary" and "extraordinary" ministries in the sermon "Prophets and Priests" (sometimes entitled "The Ministerial Office").[8] Outler's introduction to the sermon explains that the sermon attempted to justify Wesley's appointment of lay preachers by distinguishing "priests" (those who are ordained to celebrate the sacraments) from "prophets" (those who preach God's word).[9] It becomes a complicated argument: Wesley goes on to state that the prophets are divided into "extraordinary" and "ordinary" ones. Nevertheless, Wesley makes clear his conviction that the Methodist preachers had a distinct calling: they should be considered "As *extraordinary messengers*, raised up to provoke the *ordinary* ones to jealousy."[10]

Herein I discern what I believe to be a consistent pattern in John Wesley's thought, a distinguishing between that which is common to Christian communities in general, and that which distinctly defines the Methodist ethos. Common to Christian communities are historic doctrines, especially those defined in the creeds, the "instituted" means of grace and the "ordinary" ministries of the churches. Distinctive of the Methodist community (and again, this may denote the Evangelical movement very broadly, not just the Wesleyan part of the movement) are the doctrines that describe the "way of salvation" (centering on repentance, faith and holiness), the "prudential" means of grace found experimentally helpful to the Methodists, and the "extraordinary" work of itinerant preachers, including lay preachers and, by the 1770s, women preachers.

Methodist ecclesiologies: Love feast and Eucharist

A third sign of the "bipolar" nature of Wesleyan ecclesiology lies in the unusual relationship between the Love Feast and the Eucharist in the early Methodist movement. From his studies of Christian antiquity, John Wesley knew that ancient Christians "broke bread" together in a common meal associated with the Eucharist, and his "Plain Account of the People Called Methodists" (1748) indicates that Methodists had taken up the practice of the Love Feast, following the example of the primitive church.[11] He does not give the Moravians any credit in this tract, although he was aware of the renewed Love Feast as Moravians had practiced it. The Love Feast eventually became the defining act of Methodist unity, practiced quarterly in a rotation involving one quarterly love feast for men, one for women, and then a "promiscuous" or mixed love feast sometimes associated with the renewal of the covenant.

In addition to his belief that the Love Feast was related to early Christian practice of the Eucharist, John Wesley also believed that the eucharistic discipline of the early Christian church involved the use of "commendatory epistles" by which one bishop would recognize a Christian from another Christian community, and on the basis of which the visitor might be received into eucharistic communion. In the "Plain Account of the People Called Methodists," Wesley argued that the use of class tickets to identify Methodist members was consistent with the ancient practice of identifying communicants.[12] The distinctive aspect of the Methodist practice was that Wesley and the early Methodists used class tickets to control access to the Love Feast, whereas in ancient Christian practice, it was access to the Eucharist proper that was controlled by commendatory letters. In this case, Wesley seems to have justified the application of an ancient eucharistic practice to the Methodist practice of Love Feast and, as we have seen, Wesley did believe the Love Feast to have originated in the eucharistic practice of the early church. You may recall that on one occasion in Georgia in 1737 John Wesley attempted to enforce the Anglican Church's long disused canons controlling access to the Eucharist but, to my knowledge at least, he never attempted to control access to Eucharist at any point after his close encounter with Sophia Christiana Hopkey.

This leads me to reflect on John Zizioulas' thesis that the Eucharist defines the Church *per se*.[13] It is fascinating to think of the Church of England as defined by eucharistic communion, as is generally consistent with John Wesley's definition of the Church of England cited above, and the Methodist societies as defined by "communion" or fellowship in the Love Feast. The two are related in a complex and unusual way, but again this juxtaposition of discipline of the Love Feast and discipline (or lack of discipline) of the Eucharist might supply another instance of the "bipolar" ecclesiology lurking behind the shadows of Wesley's thought.

Signs of Methodist ecclesiologies: Doctrinal standards

A fourth area that reveals the ambiguity in Methodist understandings of the Church has to do with the doctrinal standards adopted at different points by the Methodist movement, and subsequently by Methodist churches, as the movement evolved into separate churches. The earliest Methodist doctrinal standards were those prescribed in the "Model Deed" that John Wesley drew up in 1784. These were John Wesley's own sermons and his *Explanatory Notes upon the New Testament*. To these we might add the "General Rules" which defined the earliest Methodist societies. Although the *Explanatory Notes upon the New Testament* were not as consistently utilized as doctrinal standards, John Wesley's sermons and the General Rules defined the distinctive teachings and ethos of the early Methodist movement, the sermons giving the content of the "way of salvation" and the "General Rules" giving the ethos that shaped Methodist life. We might also say that the hymnal, *A Collection of Hymns for the Use of the People Called Methodists* (1780), also served as an informal doctrinal standard, organizing Charles Wesley's hymns in such a way as to reinforce the "Way of Salvation" that was the consistent content of Methodist preaching.

When Methodists began to evolve into a church in North America in the 1780s, a different set of doctrinal standards was needed. At this point, John Wesley provided a revision of the Anglican Articles of Religion, condensed from 39 to 24, and a revision of the Book of Common Prayer under the title *The Sunday Service of the Methodists in North America.* Though condensed, the Articles of Religion summarized the teachings of the early Christian councils (at least, the first four councils) and significant insights from the Protestant Reformation (i.e., the reform of the Church *sola scriptura* and salvation *sola gratia*). The Prayer Book revision offered historic liturgies for Eucharist, baptism, and morning and evening prayer.

Given the four necessary attributes of the Church according to the Reformed tradition (faith, preaching, sacraments, and discipline), we might say that the Methodist movement was born in the 1730s and 1740s out of a desire to revive discipline (in small groups using the "General Rules" as a guide) and preaching (the itinerant preaching and preaching in other informal settings characteristic of early Methodists). By the 1780s, Methodists had added the two other elements of the Church, namely, the codification of their faith in the Articles of Religion, and the liturgy (and the provision for ordained ministers) that enabled them to celebrate the dominical sacraments. Nevertheless, even though all four elements constitutive of "church" were present from the 1780s in North America and from the 1790s in the British Isles, Methodists carried a strong memory of their origins as a religious movement, and they flourished in North America and elsewhere in the 1800s as a vigorous revival movement with complex and often ill-defined relationships to other ecclesial bodies.

Methodist sacred spaces

The previous section considered Methodist ecclesiologies as stated in formal doctrinal standards. But how were these understandings of the Church received in Methodist life? Church architecture can reveal a great deal about how Christian communities envision their life as a church, so we now turn to ask how these developing Methodist understandings of the Church might be reflected in the worship spaces or other "sacred spaces" adopted by Methodist people.

Wesley's sacred spaces

The first worship spaces built as a result of the Wesleyan movement were "preaching houses" (for example, the Preaching House in Bristol, built in 1740) and were intended solely for the proclamation of the Word, not for sacramental worship. This reflected Wesley's early reliance on the sacraments of the Church of England and his insistence that the Methodist movement was not a church separate from the Church of England. Although the Bristol preaching house had a rectangular shape, early Methodists in the lifetime of John Wesley would build fourteen preaching houses with a distinct octagonal shape. Karen B. Westerfield Tucker argues that although the octagonal shape may have been adopted for practical and aesthetic reasons, John Wesley was also aware of the octagonal shape of many early and medieval Christian baptismal fonts, and may have associated this shape with the work of Christian initiation.[14]

In 1749, John and Charles Wesley purchased an abandoned Huguenot place of worship on West Street in London. Since this chapel had been consecrated in the Middle Ages, its altar could be legitimately claimed as fulfilling canonical requirements for celebration of the Eucharist in the Church of England. The "new chapel" that John Wesley built on City Road in London, and which was dedicated on All Saints Day, 1779, reflects a different pattern. The chapel itself is almost exactly square, and is divided into thirds by two rows of columns. An apse situated at the front of the chapel confirms that Wesley's intention in building this chapel was to imitate the style of the Constantinian basilica, the pattern Wesley knew as the most primitive example of Christian architecture from his study of Peter King (*Primitive Christianity*) and other authors. As Frank Baker points out in his study of *John Wesley and the Church of England*, this was a space that was specifically designed for sacramental worship, with a table in front of the pulpit. But Baker also points out that the pulpit towered over the Lord's Table. With the addition of a gallery to the format of the basilica, City Road Chapel had the appearance of a preaching house with a significant accommodation of eucharistic worship.

Methodist sacred spaces: Informal spaces

Wesley's Chapel on City Road in London and the early preaching houses built by Methodists were in some ways exceptional. The most common worship spaces for early Methodist people were the informal settings in homes and outdoors (especially in North America) where Methodists prayed and preached. Methodists built some chapels and small church buildings from the early 1800s in Britain and in North America (e.g., the Lovely Lane Chapel in Baltimore), and early American Methodist *Disciplines* insisted that these worship spaces should be "plain and decent" spaces, in other words, not ornamented.[15] The pattern of "cottage worship" or worship in informal structures, led by lay stewards, involving Scripture reading, prayers, and the singing of hymns (but not celebration of Eucharist) was well suited to such informal worship spaces as private homes or meeting halls provided. When ordained Methodist clergy (circuit-riding preachers in North America) were present to celebrate the Eucharist and other traditional rites (such as baptism), they most often utilized these simple, informal worship spaces.

But although these Methodist worship spaces were informal settings, we should not conclude that they were devoid of reverence or lacking a sense of sacred presence. Indeed, accounts of Methodist worship, even of lay-led informal prayer services, often commented on the "solemnity" or reverence felt by worshipers. The sense of sacred presence was given not so much by the space itself as it was given in the manners in which prayers were said and Scriptures were read, manners that involved facial expressions, tones of voice, and other means of speaking, and in some cases trembling or other bodily expressions of reverence. In some cases, there was a sense that religious gatherings in homes or in simple structures marked a return to the primitive simplicity that characterized the earliest Christian gatherings (for example, as described in Acts 2:46).

Methodist sacred spaces: The camp meeting as sacred space

The advent of camp meetings marked a critical development in Methodist worship spaces in North America. Although camp meetings were traditionally said to have originated with the Cane Ridge meeting in Kentucky in 1791, historical studies by Leigh Eric Schmidt and Marilyn Westerkamp in the 1980s showed that American camp meetings continued a much longer tradition of Scottish and Scots-Irish Presbyterian quarterly communion celebrations. Two things need to be said about the earlier Presbyterian pattern that Methodists were to take up. In the first place, these meetings were in fact eucharistic in their origins. Both Schmidt and Westerkamp point out that Scottish and Scots-Irish quarterly communions often involved worship in outdoor spaces, due to the size of congregations that would attend.[16] Secondly, Marilyn Westerkamp points out that these "sacramental seasons" dramatized the understanding of the "order of salvation" (*ordo salutis*) that had developed in the Reformed tradition, with a pattern of preaching that began with repentance, continued with preaching on justification, then concluded with preaching on sanctification and glorification. The celebration of Eucharist was the culmination of this cycle of preaching and represented the fellowship with Christ restored in the believer's sanctification and glorification.

As Methodists took over the format of camp meetings, both the Eucharist and Love Feast were celebrated. But the focus of the camp meeting was on preaching of the "way of salvation," and the physical layout of the camp meeting assembly area came to be a sacred space representing the stages on the way of salvation. The altar rail, originated the point for receiving Holy Communion, came to represent the surrender of oneself in conversion and entire sanctification. The "mourner's bench" (or "anxious bench," as it was decried by the theologians of the Mercersburg movement) was placed in front of the altar rail and represented the experience of spiritual "awakening" that typically preceded conversion in understanding of the "way of salvation." In a weekend format, one might expect a sermon on sin, awakening and repentance on Friday, sermons on conversion and assurance on Saturday, and preaching on sanctification (including entire sanctification) on Sunday. The older pattern of cottage worship could be carried on within the context of the camp meeting in the form of small groups (typically separating women and men) that met on the camp meeting grounds, but the camp meeting assembly came to be the central focus of the event.

This distinctive form of sacred space left a lasting impact on Methodist architecture and indeed on the architecture of Evangelical churches in the United States. As the older camp meetings gave way to urban revivals in the late nineteenth century, the camp meeting assembly was institutionalized as the Evangelical auditorium (one thinks, for example, of the old Ryman Auditorium in Nashville, which was built originally as an Evangelical auditorium).[17] A contemporary example in the United Methodist Church would be The Woodlands United Methodist Church, north of Houston. This is one of the largest congregations in our denomination, and when the congregation recently built a new church facility, they decided to have a somewhat smaller traditional "chapel" space (more along the lines of what I will call "Methodist Gothic") and a larger assembly or auditorium space. This larger space is, with the notable omission of the mourner's bench, the format of the camp meeting assembly, updated to accommodate contemporary video and audio technologies. The rising prominence of "contemporary worship" has brought about a revival of the camp-meeting assembly space in the last two decades.

Methodist sacred spaces: "Methodist Gothic"

In the late nineteenth century, after the Civil War in the United States, Methodists began to build worship spaces that were much more clearly "churchly." I'll refer to this movement as "Methodist Gothic." Although the Gothic revival in church architecture began in the 1830s (the Chapel of the Cross in Chapel Hill, North Carolina, is a very early example, from the late 1830s), it came to prominence after the Civil War among old-line Protestant denominations in the U.S. It was originally associated with Tractarianism (among Anglicans) or with the Mercersburg theology (among Presbyterians in the United States) and in this early form it represented a reaction against revivalistic religion. But by the 1870s, versions of Gothic were being widely adopted, even in white-frame rural churches that began to sport windows with pointed arches (an example would be the current building for O'Kelly's Chapel, built in the late 1860s and now a United Church of Christ church building, near Durham, North Carolina).

The significance of Gothic for Methodists was that it represented an unequivocal attempt to claim the identity of "church" in the fullest sense of the word. Gothic had simply come to look like "church," like a traditional Christian space for worship. The development of Gothic coincided with Methodist prominence in urban areas and Methodists' growing sense of identification with Western culture and learning.[18] Thus, the main building for Garrett Biblical Institute in Evanston, Illinois, built in 1924 and celebrated in a whole issue of *Western Architect* magazine in 1925 as the "pride of the North Shore," is completely Gothic and complete with rich and elaborately documented medieval symbolism, such as the seal of Lincoln College, Oxford, over one of its doors. It would appear that Methodist congregations vied with each other in this period in their attempts to develop sophisticated church architecture. How could one trump the Gothic style? We might consider the Italian Renaissance architecture of the Lovely Lane Methodist Church in Baltimore, designed by architect Stanford White and completed in 1884, as an assertion of architectural sophistication in this period.

I would interpret the importance of Methodist Gothic as representing the high point of a more churchly or traditional ecclesiology in Methodist church life. It represents Methodists' growing involvement in the ecumenical movement and, closely related to this, the movement for liturgical renewal in the twentieth century. By the 1950s many Methodist churches were built with "split chancels," that is, with separate pulpit and lectern, reflecting a growing emphasis on the use of the lectionary in Sunday worship. In many cases in this period, Methodist churches were built with altars at the very back of the church, reflecting Catholic traditions from the Middle Ages—ironically, within a decade of Catholics' decision to bring the altars out toward the congregation.

Methodist sacred spaces: "Hybrid" spaces

I would complicate this simplified scheme of Methodist sacred spaces by noting what we might call "hybrid" spaces, that is, Methodist church architecture that reflects a combination of the elements noted above. In some cases, these hybridizations reflected simple alterations: the Lovely Lane Church in Baltimore (1884) was built on an Italian Renaissance pattern, but also sported theater-style seats and an astronomically correct representation of the night sky in the ceiling of the dome. Much more thorough-going as an example of hybrid space would be the so-called "Akron Plan" of church architecture, following the pattern of First Methodist Church in Akron, Ohio, in 1872.[19] The Akron Plan combines elements of Gothic style (pointed arches) with fixtures from the urban evangelical auditorium. It is a basically square building, oriented towards one corner where there is a chancel platform. Around the opposite two sides is a wrap-around gallery, and behind the seats in the main floor and the gallery are rooms that could be enclosed as Sunday-School meeting spaces or could be opened up to the main sanctuary for additional seating for worship. Other examples of hybrid spaces could be given, perhaps most notably the use of "modular" arrangements of church interiors since the 1970s that allow for very different configurations of worship spaces.

The Akron Plan and other Methodist examples of hybrid spaces allow for the ambiguity inherent in Methodist ecclesiologies. They combine elements of an "auditorium" architecture, characteristic of a revival movement, with elements of more traditional worship space, characteristic of a fuller understanding of the meaning of "church." They can even be reconfigured to serve the needs of different uses, and these reconfigurations may also reflect the ambiguities inherent in Methodist ecclesiologies. The problem inherent in the use of such a hybrid space is the jarring movement between different forms of sacred space. (Think of ushers busily reconfiguring Sunday School rooms into worship space in an Akron Plan church on a Sunday morning between Sunday School and worship.)

Conclusion

Methodists originated as a religious movement that presupposed existing church structures, and only later added elements necessary to configure themselves as "churches." They were, I am inclined to say, an "accidental" church and I would argue that they remain incomplete apart from identity within the broader Christian community. Methodists, in short, have never definitively decided if they are a religious movement or a "church" commensurate with other communities that claim to be churches. Some of the more creative proposals for Methodists as related to the ecumenical movement involve our rediscovering our identity as a religious movement within the broader Christian community.[20]

Methodist worship spaces have evolved from the "cottage" and other informal worship spaces of early Methodist gatherings to the camp-meeting assemblies of the nineteenth century to the "Methodist Gothic" architectures of the late nineteenth and early twentieth centuries. We continue to evolve new forms of worship spaces as Methodist churches, for example, adopting post-modern forms of church architecture. This evolution of sacred spaces reveals some spaces that reflect the nature of a religious movement (like the evangelical auditoriums of the late nineteenth century) and others that reflect the fuller sense of "church" (represented in what I have called "Methodist Gothic" architecture). The use of "hybrid" spaces uniquely reveals the ambiguity inherent in Methodist ecclesiologies.

Hidden within this narrative, however, is what I have come to think of as a broader pattern in Evangelical Christian cultures, and that is the evolution from a more radically independent community identity towards a more ecclesial self-identity that is more closely linked to the identity of historic Christian churches. When Pentecostalism originated in the early twentieth century, for example, it had a strongly independent self-identity as being the truest, indeed perhaps the only true, fulfillment of the church as depicted in the Acts of the Apostles. From this radically independent identity, however, Pentecostals have evolved over the last three or four generations of leadership towards a self-identity that is much more closely linked to that of other churches. Pentecostal historians at the Society for Pentecostal Studies (SPS), for instance, will speak of "Two Thousand Years of Pentecost," that is, how they have come to understand the Pentecostal emphasis on the gifts of the Holy Spirit expressed throughout the history of the Christian community. Some Pentecostal churches today have printed orders of service that indicate the point in the service at which gifts of the Spirit (such as speaking in unknown tongues) will be exercised. Some Pentecostal congregations utilize the Apostles' Creed in worship, and some affirm both the Apostles' Creed and the Nicene Creed (with the *filioque* clause) among their doctrinal statements.[21] These are intriguing developments for Pentecostal churches. But United Methodists, I hasten to point out, did not have the Nicene Creed in our church literature until it was incorporated into *The Methodist Hymnal* of 1964.[22] The Methodist pattern of evolution towards a more traditional Christian ecclesiology is a pattern that is replicated as new Evangelical movements emerged and differentiate themselves from other churches, in their first generations of leadership, then begin to knit themselves back together in the broader Christian community in later generations of leadership. It is nuanced, in the case of Methodists, by John and Charles Wesley's clear commitments to historic Christian doctrine and liturgy, but is nevertheless a pattern that I discern in the evolution of Methodist ecclesiologies and Methodist sacred spaces.

Endnotes

[1]Frank Baker, *John Wesley and the Church of England* (Nashville: Abingdon Press, 1970).

[2]Albert C. Outler, "Do Methodists Have a Doctrine of the Church?" in Dow Kirkpatrick, ed., *The Doctrine of the Church* (Nashville: Abingdon Press, 1964), 11–28.

[3]Anglican Articles of Religion 19 (cited in John Leith, ed., *Creeds of the Churches* [Atlanta: John Knox Press, third edition revised, 1982], 273).

[4]Westminster Confession of Faith, chapters 25 and 30 (cited in Leith, 222 and 227).

[5]Cited in Frank Baker, *John Wesley and the Church of England*, 327.

[6]"Large Minutes," question 48 in Thomas Jackson, ed., *The Works of the Reverend John Wesley, A.M.*, 14 vols. (London: Wesleyan Conference Office, 1873), 8:322–324; hereafter cited as "Jackson, *Works*."

[7]John Wesley, sermon on "The Means of Grace," 3–6 in Albert C. Outler, ed., *Sermons* (Bicentennial Edition of the Works of John Wesley), 4 vols. (Nashville: Abingdon Press, 1984–1987), 1:379–380; hereafter cited as "Outler, *Sermons*."

[8]Sermon "Prophets and Priests," in Outler, *Sermons*, 4:75–84.

[9]Outler's introduction, in Outler, *Sermons*, 4:73–74.

[10]In Outler, *Sermons*, 4:79. Outler notes that Wesley was here recollecting (not quite accurately) the Minutes of the annual conference of 14 May 1746.

[11]"Plain Account of the People Called Methodists" VI: 5 (in Jackson, 8:258–259; and in John Telford, ed., *Letters of the Rev. John Wesley, A.M.* ["Standard Edition" of the Works of John Wesley, 8 vols. (London: Epworth Press, 1931)]; hereafter referred to as "Telford, *Letters,*" 2:302).

[12]"Plain Account of the People Called Methodists" IV: 3, in Jackson, *Works,* 8: 257.

[13]John D. Zizioulas, *Being as Communion: Studies in Personhood and the Church* (Crestwood, NY: St. Vladimir's Seminary Press, 1985), 20–23, 143–169.

[14]Karen B. Westerfield Tucker, " 'Plain and Decent': Octagonal Space and Methodist Worship," in *Studia Liturgica* 24 (1994), 136–141.

[15]Cf. Karen B. Westerfield Tucker, *American Methodist Worship* (Oxford and New York: Oxford University Press, 2001), 239–243.

[16]Marilyn J. Westerkamp, *The Triumph of the Laity: Scots-Irish Piety and the Great Awakening, 1625–1760* (New York: Oxford University Press, 1988); Leigh Eric Schmidt, *Holy Fairs: Scottish Communions and American Revivals in the Early Modern Period* (Princeton, NJ: Princeton University Press, 1989).

[17]On the development of the auditorium style of architecture among Methodists, cf. Tucker, *American Methodist Worship*, 243–251.

[18]Cf. Tucker, *American Methodist Worship*, 252–256.

[19]Jesse A. Earle and Dorothea Derrig, "Akron, Ohio," in Nolan B. Harmon, ed., *Encyclopedia of World Methodism* (Nashville: United Methodist Publishing House, 1974), 1:73.

[20]Geoffrey Wainwright, "Ecclesial Location and Ecumenical Vocation" in M. Douglas Meeks, ed., *The Future of the Methodist Theological Traditions* (Nashville: Abingdon Press, 1985).

[21]I observed the use of the Apostles' Creed at the Yoido Full Gospel Church in Seoul, Korea, in May of 2005. The Cathedral in the Pines Christian Center in Beaumont, Texas, an Assemblies of God congregation, has a handout sheet for visitors indicating their beliefs, including the full texts of the Apostles' and Nicene Creeds.

[22]Although the doctrinal claims of the Nicene Creed are affirmed in the Articles of Religion, which North American Methodists have affirmed since 1784.

PART 4

Ecclesiology and the Role of Women

14

Ephrem the *kitharode* and Proponent of Women: Jacob of Serug's Portrait of a Fourth-century Churchman for the Sixth-century Viewer and Its Significance for the Twenty-first-century Ecumenist

Kathleen McVey

I have chosen as my contribution to this consultation the traditions concerning St. Ephrem's establishment and promotion of women's choirs. Ephrem (ca. AD 305–373) was a pioneer in creating a large corpus of hymnody—the largest by far that survives from the fourth century.[1] Although his hymns strongly influenced subsequent Syriac traditions, and to a lesser degree also influenced the development of hymnody in other traditions, basic historical work is still needed to evaluate his contributions to Christian hymnody.[2] In the broad spectrum of both Wesleyan and Orthodox traditions throughout the centuries, hymnody has played an especially significant role. It has provided a means for composers and singers to glorify their God and for singers and listeners to receive instruction in the faith. Elucidating Ephrem's role in the early history of Christian hymnography and of women's choral singing should contribute to our understanding of the shared history of the Christian communities at the center of Orthodox and Wesleyan ecclesiology. This is the first of two important and hopefully relevant aspects of this chapter.

The focus of my presentation today is a *mêmrâ* (ܡܐܡܪܐ, a metrical homily) on Ephrem the Syrian,[3] attributed to Jacob of Serug (AD 449–521).[4] Although the homily is among the earliest sources pertaining to Ephrem's life, apart from the claim that Ephrem established women's choirs, its biographical data are minimal.[5] Yet, several scholars have drawn attention to it because of Jacob's affirmation of women as redeemed equally with men and their consequent right to express themselves by singing in the public liturgy of the Church.[6] Jacob attributes these views to Ephrem and asserts that they were the basis for his establishing women's choirs to sing his hymns (*madrâshê* ܡܕܪ̈ܫܐ). Neither the validity of that attribution nor the content and purpose of Jacob's *mêmrâ* has received a comprehensive discussion.[7] Clearly this homily deserves further study to discover its broader historical, theological and exegetical context as well as to assess the historical validity of Jacob's claims about Ephrem's contributions to the performance of Christian hymns. I propose to begin that undertaking here. It is a good historian's task, but why present the material here at this ecumenical gathering?

Neither Orthodox nor Wesleyan tradition excludes women from participating in liturgical song today. So Jacob's concern to defend that practice and to claim St. Ephrem's posthumous support for his own views may seem at first a quaint matter of the past, an interesting historical moment at best. The way in which Jacob argued his position, as we shall see, raises interesting issues about the equality of men and women. Although his concern was to defend the existence of women's choirs, his choice of scriptural arguments to defend that practice anticipates some current justifications of women's ordination to eucharistic ministry. Contemporary Orthodox and Methodist understandings on this point differ significantly. My primary intention here is to elucidate Jacob's concerns and motivation within his sixth-century context. Thanks to his approach to the issue of his day, the discussion here will address, indirectly, the contested issue of women's ordination and the scriptural arguments underlying it. In this regard, as well, I hope the paper will be useful.

I will begin with (1) an overview of Jacob's *mêmrâ*, his claims about Ephrem, and his literary, exegetical and theological themes. (2) Then I will survey the evidence about women's choirs in the early church in general and the arguments against them in Greek and Latin sources. Here we will see that the Pauline injunction to silence plays a role in the opposition to women's singing. The next section (3) will show how Jacob's use of "second Eve" Mariology is rooted in Syriac tradition and leads him to an alternative view. (4) Next will be a survey of the evidence prior to Jacob's time (beginning with Ephrem's own witness to himself and then the testimonies of fourth- and fifth-century authors) about Ephrem and his musical accomplishments, focusing especially on the evidence concerning his establishment of women's choirs to sing his *madrâshê*. (5) Finally, I will consider some possible motives for Jacob's composing this homily in praise of Ephrem. I will leave it to the reader to decide whether to pursue the discussion of this paper purely in historical terms or to expand it into current theological and ecclesiological matters.

(1) Jacob's mêmrâ, his claims about Ephrem, and his literary, exegetical, and theological themes

Jacob begins his homily with a rhetorical introduction, a virtuoso display of metaphor and epithet. Amid the flurry of images a few stand out: he is painting a portrait, indeed, an icon of the saint. By his actions and by his teachings both spoken and sung, Ephrem is an athlete in the contest against heresy, the mouthpiece of Truth, and a *kitharode* of the house of God.

The main theme, which occupies the central section of Jacob's *mêmrâ*, is that Ephrem's role as the originator of women's choirs makes him a second Moses for women and a champion of truth against heresy.[8] Jacob weaves an intricate exegetical and hagiographic fabric. On the one hand, he gathers biblical strands celebrating in music and song God's victories as holy warrior. On the other, he paints an image of

Ephrem as combatant for truth over against heresy, enlisting women to sing songs of praise, songs of thanksgiving for salvation from idolatry, and songs of doctrinal disputation.

Jacob begins by addressing Ephrem himself[9] with a typological interpretation from the Psalms:

> Behold, your name is written mystically in the Book of Asher
> where David called you "Ephrem, my helmet."

Jacob alludes to Psalm 108:

> My heart is steadfast, O God, my heart is steadfast;
> I will sing and make melody.
> Awake, my soul!
> Awake, O harp and lyre!
> I will awake the dawn.
> I will give thanks to you,
> O Lord among the peoples,
> And I will sing praises to you among the nations.
> . . .
> Be exalted, O God, above the heavens
> . . .
> Give victory with your right hand, and answer me,
> So that those whom you love may be rescued.
> God has promised in his sanctuary:
> ". . . Ephrem is my helmet;
> Judah is my scepter.
> . . .
> Over Philistia I shout in triumph."[10]

The Psalmist's allusion to "Ephrem . . . my helmet," Jacob says, is not only a reference to Ephrem bar Joseph; it is also a foreshadowing of the Christian saint's role as a champion of truth:

> When he spoke of Ephrem, the son of Joseph,
> he was mystically looking to you with the eye of the Spirit.
>
> Therefore [right] Teaching calls you "my helmet,"
> for she was raised up by you to conquer all [false] doctrines
>   in the contest.[11]

Jacob's choice is apt not only because Ephrem's name happens to be mentioned, but more importantly because the psalm celebrates with song and instrumental music the defeat of Israel's enemies. Similarly Ephrem's hymns are a celebration of Christian truth over false teachings. Jacob enlarges his argument by describing Ephrem's particular contribution to the struggle for truth: his encouragement of women to participate in liturgical song. This he portrays both as a radical departure from custom and as fully consonant with the Christian gospel:

> By you even our sisters were strengthened to give praise,
> for women had not been allowed to speak in church.[12]
> Your instruction opened the closed mouths of the daughters of Eve.
> The gatherings of the glorious (church) resound with their melodies!
> A new vision that women will speak the gospel—
> they are called teachers in the congregations!
> It is an entirely New Age, a sign of your teaching
> that there in the kingdom men and women will be equal.
> Your effort made the two sexes into two harps,
> and men and women began to give glory together.[13]

In the first lines above, it appears Jacob briefly alludes to the Pauline prohibition of women's speaking in church:

> As in all the congregations of the saints, women should remain silent in the churches. They are not allowed to speak, but must be in submission, as the Law says. If they want to inquire about something, they should ask their own husbands at home; for it is disgraceful for a woman to speak in the church.[14]

But in the following verses Jacob ignores this text insofar as it is a New Testament teaching and treats it instead as having a bearing only on women before the time of Christ. For he explicitly represents as Ephrem's teaching the idea that in the kingdom, men and women will be equal, that a New Age has already begun, and that a sign of that New Age is the end of women's silence and the beginning of their being called as teachers who will speak the gospel.

It appears Jacob intends only to say that women should sing the hymns composed for them, not that they should preach or teach in a more literal sense. Yet his fundamental hermeneutical stance is that men and women will be equal in the kingdom of God and that the New Age of the gospel, which has already begun, has immediate practical implications for women in a liturgical context. He ends his apostrophe to Ephrem with a comparison that anticipates the theme of the next section of the *mêmrâ*:

> You resemble Moses, leader of the tribes,
> Who gave tambourines to the young girls in the wilderness.[15]

At this point Jacob turns to the fifteenth chapter of Exodus, the celebration of the Israelites after the crossing of the Red Sea. As with Psalm 108, the setting is celebration for the victory of the Divine warrior on behalf of his people. Comparison of the victory at the Red Sea with the victory of the cross leads into a comparison of the Song of Moses with Ephrem's musical compositions. This passage serves as an opportunity for Jacob to portray Ephrem as "a second Moses for women" in that he has freed them to sing aloud in gratitude for their deliverance from idolatry.[16]

Jacob draws out the parallel between Moses, who "instructed the daughters of his nation not to refrain from the required praise," and Ephrem, who taught the "Aramean women," that is, the Syriac-speaking Christian women, "sweet melodies to give praise."[17] First he emphasizes the similarity of Ephrem to Moses. Then he stresses the greater glory of deliverance through Christ and, as a consequence, the greater magnitude of the praise of the Christian women led by Ephrem. Jacob leaves no room for doubt about which is the greater saving act and hence which is more deserving of glorification:

> Greater is this glory than that one (then)
> For greater also is the deliverance that is now brought about.
>
> By that deliverance the sea was torn asunder before the daughter of Jacob;
> By this one of ours, graves are bursting open by the power of our Lord.
>
> Then Pharaoh the king was drowned because [his heart] was hardened,
> But now Death is swallowed up and extinguished by Life.
>
> Then a staff in the riven seas built bulwarks,
> But now a cross in solid rocks has worked stupendous deeds.
>
> Then a path in the seas was broken through and the tribes crossed over,
> But now the devouring pit is broken through and the nations are emerging.
>
> That deliverance put to death the living of Egypt,
> But this one of ours made the dead rise up from [their] graves.
>
> Then from a staff fled the floods that were gathered,
> But now a cross has overthrown the numerous idols.
>
> Then arose the proud bride from the sea
> And the Hebrew women played the tambourines to give glory,
>
> But now that the redeemed Church has bathed in baptism,
> Our sisters play the chants of Ephrem to make joyful sounds.
>
> Which glory is greater than the other, oh hearers;
> Compare [them] in the rectitude of your minds.[18]

Having established the superiority of deliverance in Christ, Jacob is free to describe at dramatic length the power of deliverance worked by God through Moses.[19] This portion of the homily culminates in the description of the Israelites' song of praise and thanksgiving to the God who saved them.[20] Jacob elaborates the biblical account by having Moses address the women with explicit emphasis on their inclusion in God's saving act and their consequent mandate to "beat the tambourines before the Savior who freed His people" and to "shout out praise with [their brothers and fathers] in a loud voice."[21] Since all have been saved together by "El, the mighty warrior," all are to sing praise in unison:

> You, like your husbands, have seen stupendous deeds and wonders.
> In their company give glory by your hosannas to El, the mighty warrior.
>
> One deliverance was accomplished by God for you and for them;
> Let one praise arise from your mouths.[22]

Jacob has not only enlarged Moses' role to make his point about the religious equality of women, he has also, paradoxically, omitted Miriam and her song. In Exodus
15:20–21 it is Miriam who sings while the women dance and play the tambourines:

> Then Miriam, the prophetess, the sister of Aaron, took a timbrel in her hand; and all
> the women went out after her with timbrels and dancing. And Miriam sang to them:
> "Sing to the Lord, for he has triumphed gloriously; the horse and his rider he has
> thrown into the sea."

In depriving Miriam of her role, Jacob has taken one further step in the trend
within the history of the biblical text itself. The original victory song and dance of the
women under Miriam's leadership was first supplemented by a more elaborate version attributed to Moses, then eclipsed by it.[23] It has been shown that such victory celebrations by women are an established phenomenon within the context of early
Israelite religion and that they have endured in some traditional Middle Eastern societies even into the twentieth century.[24] If this continuity extends to Jacob's world, why
would he seek to circumscribe Miriam's role in his own celebration of women's role
in Christian liturgy? We will return to this issue later.

At this point in the *mêmrâ*, Jacob turns to Ephrem, whom he depicts as inten-
tionally emulating Moses in, as it were, the "new key" of Christ.[25] After contemplating, in clear counterpoint to the deliverance brought about through the staff of Moses,
the deliverance effected by the cross of Christ, Ephrem deliberately imitates Moses by
choosing to compose hymns (*madrâshê*) for virgins to sing.[26] Leading them in song,
Ephrem is likened to an eagle among doves, partridges, and swallows.[27] Like Moses,
he is provided with a speech to the women.[28] A few themes stand out: First, the women
have been saved from the "error of [their] fathers"—idolatry. Second, since, like men,
the women have been baptized, with them they receive new life in the Eucharist, and
together they participate in "a single salvation," consequently they should "sing praise
in a loud voice." Third, the silence imposed on Eve has been lifted thanks to Mary.
Finally, the women should not only sing aloud, they should no longer veil their faces:

> Your silent mouth which your mother Eve closed,
> Is now opened by Mary, your sister, to sing praise.

> The old woman (Eve) tied a cord of silence around your tongues;
> The Son of the virgin loosed your bonds that you may sing out.

> The married one put a muzzle of silence on your mouths;
> But the virgin opened the closed door of your tongues.

> Until now, your sex was brought low because of Eve;
> But from now on, it is restored by Mary to sing Alleluia!

> Because of the wickedness of Eve, your mother, you were under judgment;
> But because of the child of Mary, your sister, you have been set free.

> Uncover your faces to sing praise without shame
> To the One who granted you freedom of speech by his birth."[29]

Jacob supplements this lengthy presentation of Ephrem as a second Moses for women with a description of the anti-heretical role of his female choirs.[30] Like Moses, he is described as a commander leading his forces in battle. At the same time, both men are defenders of learning against falsehood. Ephrem "led women and went forth to do battle" against the forces of Satan, that is to say, against the heretics, who are specifically identified as Marcionites, Manichaeans, Arians, Sabellians, and Bardaisanites.[31] Here a new function of the women's choirs is introduced. In Ephrem's speech the women were exhorted to give praise and thanks to God for rescuing them from idolatry and for granting them salvation. Now they are portrayed as the primary troops in the battle against heresy.

As he nears the climax of his homily, Jacob again recapitulates Ephrem's accomplishments as a teacher and opponent of heresy.[32] Once more martial imagery predominates, and it is again closely linked with women, songs, and the struggle against heresy:

> This man forged the chosen weapon of the faith;
> through him, the straightforward were strengthened.
> This man introduced women to doctrinal disputes;
> with (their) soft tones he was victorious in the battle against all heresies.
> This man's mouth was a bow, and his words were arrows;
> he forged songs like spearheads for the weapon which he fashioned.
> This man hurled wonderful melodies against the evil;
> with his instruction, he eliminated stumbling blocks which had multiplied.[33]

The followers of Marcion and Bardaisan are explicitly mentioned again as representative of the erroneous views he has overcome.[34]

Jacob ends his homily with two vivid portrayals of the saint in his battles against heresy (lines 169–84). First he is seen as an athlete, a gladiator struggling against the onslaught of heresies (169–77). Vibrant images from the arena merge seamlessly with hagiographic and theological themes:

> When he stripped off the evil world with its vices
> so his foot would not become entangled during the struggle for perfection,
> when he was standing like an athlete in the great battle,
> perspiring in the arena from the contest,
> when he was contending, he was dipped in the blood of the Son of God,[35]
> so that the hand of the opponent would slip when it took hold of him (171–173).

Finally, Ephrem is both sheepdog and shepherd guarding his sheep in "enclosures of homilies and hymns," shooting his arrows at the "wild animals," the heresies "encircling him," keeping watch against thieves while he "meditated on sweet melodies," and driving away demons "from the flock which was purchased by the blood of the Son of God" (180–84).

Summary of literary and biblical themes

To summarize, Jacob presents a vivid image of Ephrem as a second Moses, battling on behalf of Divine Truth and leading the people—more specifically, leading the women—in songs celebrating God's triumph, as well as in songs that continue the contest into the present time. He skillfully integrates his views into a mosaic of biblical texts about holy war and songs of triumph and thanksgiving. Jacob's homily is also a spirited defense of the institution of women's choirs. His defense is based on several points, beginning with the assertion that this liturgical role has been traditional for women since Ephrem, whose innovation was itself based on Scripture—i.e., both on imitation of Moses' actions as recounted in Exodus 15, and on the conviction that deliverance through Christ is vastly greater than the deliverance of the Israelites at the Red Sea.

Further, as Jacob portrays them, Moses and Ephrem both taught that women are indeed redeemed equally with men and therefore ought to give praise aloud. Just as the Israelite women were encouraged to give thanks and praise for deliverance from Egypt, Christian women are to give thanks and praise for their deliverance from death and from idolatry. Mary's role as second Eve reinforces the call for women to sing aloud with unveiled faces,[36] just as they participate equally in the sacraments of baptism and Eucharist. Finally, like a commander in battle, Ephrem has enlisted the women to fight with him against heresy by singing his hymns.

Jacob presents Ephrem so strongly as a second Moses that the listener is apt to forget that there is a gap of 350 years between Jesus and Ephrem and that Paul in 1 Cor. 14:34 and 1 Tim. 2:11–15, to which he alluded in the *mêmrâ*, interpreted the Christian message for women differently. By rhetorically collapsing the temporal framework, he has obviated the need to say explicitly that the Pauline prohibition is being rejected. His argument can work only for an audience that already assumes not only that Ephrem is important and that he did institute women's choirs, but also that Mary has ended the "silence of Eve."

We may wonder, then, how much of this picture was painted before Jacob began to compose his *mêmrâ*. We will look, first, at the evidence of women's choirs in early Christian sources, the use of 1 Corinthians and 1 Timothy and its "second Eve" motif to oppose them, and the suspicion of heresy that accompanied them in the eyes of some Greek and Latin writers. Then we will consider the "second Eve" motif in two Syriac writers, Aphrahat and Ephrem, both of whom associate it with women's singing in paradise. Finally, we will consider how all these themes coalesced in Jacob's time.

(2) Women's choirs in the early church in general and the arguments against them in Greek and Latin sources

Relying mainly on allusions in Ignatius of Antioch's letters, Quasten asserted that women's singing had not been an issue in the first two Christian centuries when it was customary for the entire community to sing in unison.[37] Be this as it may, there is very little early evidence of women's choirs either for singing alone or antiphonally. When the subject is broached, the views expressed are mostly negative. The earliest Greek testimony to a female choir is Eusebius' report in chapter 7 of his *Church History* on Paul of Samosata, a third-century bishop of Antioch criticized for his christological views. According to the church historian, Paul discarded traditional hymns to Christ in favor of hymns to himself, sung by women trained to sing "in the middle of the church" on the feast of the Pasch.[38] Since Paul is presented as an arrogant man with heretical views and aberrant practices, the use of women's choirs seems to fall under criticism as well.[39]

Philo, the first-century Alexandrian Jewish writer, wrote enthusiastically in his *On the Contemplative Life* about the antiphonal singing of choirs of men and women, *therapeutae* and *therapeutrides*, members of an ascetic community at Lake Mareotis in Egypt. Portraying the communal meal in deliberate contrast to pagan symposia, Philo emphasized a theme of "sober inebriation."[40] At the end of the meal the vigil of songs begins, first with men and women in two separate choirs, then together in a single choir, all in imitation of the Israelite song of victory led by Moses and Miriam after the crossing of the Red Sea:

> They rise up all together and standing in the middle of the refectory form themselves first into two choirs, one of men and one of women, the leader and precentor chosen for each being the most honoured amongst them and also the most musical. Then they sing hymns to God composed of many measures and set to many melodies, sometimes chanting together, sometimes taking up the harmony antiphonally, hands and feet keeping time in accompaniment, and rapt with enthusiasm reproduce sometimes the lyrics of the procession, sometimes of the halt and of the wheeling and counter-wheeling of a choric dance.
>
> Then when each choir has separately done its own part in the feast, having drunk, as in the Bacchic rites, of the strong wine of God's love, they mix and both together become a single choir, a copy of the choir set up of old beside the Red Sea in honor of the wonders there wrought. For at the command of God the sea became a source of salvation to one party and of perdition to the other . . . This wonderful sight and experience, an act transcending word and thought and hope, so filled with ecstasy both men and women that forming a single choir they sang hymns of thanksgiving to God their Savior, the men led by the prophet Moses and the women by the prophetess Miriam.[41]

Eusebius had firsthand knowledge of Philo's treatise, which he names and quotes several times.[42] In a famous misapprehension, he presents the group described by Philo as if it were a Christian community exemplifying fourth-century ideals: notably of asceticism, hierarchical organization, allegorical exegesis, and hymnody.[43] With respect to the last, he notes they composed "new psalms: 'So that they not only contemplate but make songs and hymns to God in all kinds of metres and melodies, though they perforce arrange them in the more sacred measures.' "[44] Further, he describes their celebration of the "great feast"—which he implies to be the Paschal Vigil—giving particular attention to the manner of their singing:

> [Philo] relates the vigils for the entire night of the great feast, and the exercises during them, and the hymns which we are accustomed to recite, and how while one sings regularly with cadence, the rest listen in silence and join in singing only the refrain of the hymns . . .[45]

But here Eusebius describes a performance by a soloist with a communal refrain. He omits Philo's description of sacred enthusiasm and his description of two choirs—one of men, the other of women—singing antiphonally.

Others were critical of women's participation in congregational song as well as in separate women's choirs. They invoked the Pauline (and deutero-Pauline) injunction against women's speaking in church to oppose women's voices being heard at all in the church. Cyril of Jerusalem (c. 315–386) specified for catechumens awaiting exorcism that men and women be segregated: then the men might read to one another. "The assembly of virgins, however, should be gathered together, quietly reciting psalms or reading, so that their lips move, but the ears of others do not hear—'For I do not permit that a woman speak in the Church' (1 Cor. 14:34). And the married woman should do likewise: she should pray and move her lips, while not allowing her voice to be heard."[46] According to Isidore of Pelusium (d. c. 435), women were permitted to sing psalms in church only to prevent them from gossiping, but since this privilege has been abused, women should be prohibited from singing in church ("and also from loitering in the city") since "the majority of the people . . . misuse the sweetness of melody to arouse passion, thinking that it is no better than the songs of the stage."[47]

Ambrose took a more generous view. Psalmody has so many benefits that the entire congregation should join in—even women:

> The Apostle admonishes women to be silent in church, yet they do well to join in a psalm; this is gratifying for all ages and fitting for both sexes. Old men ignore the stiffness of age to sing [a psalm], and melancholy veterans echo it in the joy of their hearts; young men sing one without the bane of lust, as do adolescents without threat from their insecure age or the temptation of sensual pleasure; even young women sing psalms with no loss of wifely decency, and girls sing a hymn to God with sweet and supple voice while maintaining decorum and suffering no lapse of modesty.[48]

Ambrose does not speak of women's choirs or antiphonal singing, however, since, "It is after all a great bond of unity for the full number of people to join in one chorus. The strings of a cithara differ, but create one harmony."[49]

Perhaps of greatest relevance to Jacob's defense of women's singing is Jerome's complaint in his *Dialogue against the Pelagians*: he attributes to Pelagius an argument that mirrors the line of reasoning that Jacob later pursues in defense of Ephrem's practice:

> . . . in order to win the favor of your Amazons [*Amazonas tuas*], you wrote in another place, with a great display of generosity: 'Women should also have a knowledge of the law'; when the apostle teaches that women should keep silent in Church, and, if they lack knowledge in any matter, they should consult their husbands at home. It is not enough for you to allow your army [*agmini tuo*] of women a knowledge of the Scriptures, unless you can enjoy the pleasure of their voices and their singing [*earum voce et canticis*]. For you add and set down the thesis: 'Women should also sing psalms [*psallere*] to God.' But who does not know that women should sing psalms [*psallendum esse feminis*] in their own cells [*in cubiculis suis*], and apart from the company of men, and the gathering of crowds? Namely, you allow them to sing out what should

be performed by them secretly and without any witnesses, **as though they were law-fully constituted teachers.**[50]

On the other hand, Theodoret provides evidence from a west Syrian context that women's choirs played an important role in combating not only heresy but also idolatry at least until the later fourth century. In the third book of his *Church History* in the midst of tales of the tyranny of the apostate Emperor Julian and the heroic men who dared to defy him, Theodoret includes the story of one heroic "woman named Publia, of high reputation and illustrious for deeds of virtue," who lived in Antioch or its vicinity.[51] She had been married and had a son, John, who was a presbyter in Antioch "and was often elected to the apostolic see but from time to time declined the dignity." It is not clear whether she was widowed or whether she and her husband had agreed to live chastely, but Publia had embraced the life of chastity: "She maintained a company of virgins vowed to virginity for life, and spent her time in praising God who had made and saved her."

When the Emperor Julian happened to pass by, she and her virgins taunted him by singing the psalms loudly: "they struck up all the louder music, chiefly chanting those songs that mock the helplessness of idols, saying in the words of David: 'The idols of the nations are silver and gold, the work of human hands.' And after describing their insensibility, they added, 'Let them that make them and place their trust in them become like them' (Ps. 115:3, 8)."[52] When rebuked by the emperor, she refused to be silent and instead began to lead her choir in Psalm 68, "Let God arise and let his enemies be scattered." For her impudence the "choir mistress" [τοῦ χοροῦ τὴν διδάσκαλον] had her ears boxed and her face slapped. Undaunted, she went home "where she kept up her attack upon him with her spiritual songs [ταῖς πνευματικαῖς . . . μελωδίαις] just as the composer and teacher of the song laid the wicked spirit that vexed Saul."[53] Although Theodoret does not hesitate implicitly to compare Publia to King David, there is no indication that she composed her own songs. Rather it seems she led her virgins in singing biblical psalms redolent of holy war and full of praise for God as Creator and Savior from idolatry.

As we have seen, in his *mêmrâ* on Ephrem, written more than a century after Publia's encounter with the emperor, Jacob laid considerable emphasis upon the same themes. Again, in his homily "On the Fall of the Idols," Jacob stresses this theme and demonstrates incidentally his knowledge of contemporaneous pagan cults.[54] There is ample evidence of the continued importance of paganism in Edessa and its environs into his time and beyond.[55] So it seems likely he would have known of women's choirs such as Publia's and have regarded the women's choirs as still an important force in the Christian opposition to idolatry. But Jacob also provides theological and exegetical defenses for the women's choirs. Where are they rooted? Publia herself, in Theodoret's account, seems to have provided the Old Testament rationale for her choir by invoking Psalms 68 and 115. Jacob makes a similar argument by invoking Psalm 108. Invoking the example of Moses, Jacob resembles Philo, although it is not evident that he knew Philo's work directly. Jacob's mariological defense against the Pauline injunction to silence appears to be an answer to Western critics like Jerome. This line of argument is rooted in Aphrahat and Ephrem, as we shall see in the next section.

(3) Second Eve mariology and the silence of women

The argument put forth by Jacob—a positive Second Eve typology—that the "children of Mary" are freed from the punishment imposed on the "daughters of Eve" does not appear within the canonical New Testament. Further, only one instance of a negative Second Eve typology is explicit, in 1 Timothy 2:11–15:

> Let a woman learn in silence and with all submissiveness. I permit no woman to teach or to have authority over men; she is to keep silent. For Adam was formed first, then Eve; and Adam was not deceived, but the woman was deceived and became a transgressor. Yet woman will be saved through bearing children, if she continues in faith and love and holiness, with modesty.

The deutero-Pauline author took Paul's prohibition (1 Cor. 14:34–35) of women's speaking in church and added a basis not merely in "the Law" but also in Eve's sin as well as in the order of Creation. In the Genesis narrative (Gen. 3:16), Eve's curse did not entail silence, but here the author of 1 Timothy interprets Adam's dominion over Eve as imposing silence upon her.[56] Jacob alluded to one or both of these New Testament *pericopes* when he introduced the theme of women's new role:

> By you even our sisters were strengthened to give praise,
> for women had not been allowed to speak in church. (40)[57]

In those initial lines (40–43) and especially in the later section contrasting Eve and Mary (108–113), he constantly emphasizes that Eve's behavior imposed silence on women, and Mary (who is named only in the later verses) or her son—he carefully alternates the agency—has brought freedom of speech. He seems to intend a refutation of the views expressed in 1 Timothy and perhaps to answer Western criticism of women's choirs as well. To what degree did earlier Syriac writers prepare the ground for him?

"Second Eve" typology plays a significant role in early Syriac Christian literature, especially in Ephrem.[58] Jacob's emphasis on the "silence of Eve" and its reversal by Mary is, however, rarely found. Aphrahat and Ephrem, however, lay the groundwork for this emphasis first by associating sinful women with music making and then by asserting that in paradise the association no longer applies.

Aphrahat makes use of a "second Eve" typology, which he associates negatively with women, music, and believing men's struggles to be faithful to God.[59] In a crucial passage in *Demonstration* 6:6, music and the image of the harp are associated with woman as temptress and insidious weapon against the (male) athletes of God:

> On this account, brothers, we know and have seen that from the beginning women have been a way for the Adversary to gain access to men, and until the end he will [continue to] accomplish this. For [women] are the weapon of Satan, and through them he fights against the [spiritual] athletes. Through them he plays music at all times, for they have been like a harp for him from the first day.[60]

Next he asserts that Eve is responsible for "the curse of the Law" as well as for the curses on both Adam and herself as enumerated in Gen. 3: 16–19; here he omits mention of Adam's dominion over her (Gen. 3:16b):

For because of her the curse of the Law was established, and because of her the promise unto death was made. For with pangs she bears children and delivers them to
death. Because of her the earth was cursed that it should bring forth thorns and
tares.[61]

In referring here to "the curse of the Law," Aphrahat shows his familiarity with Paul's
arguments in Galatians 3 and Romans 5. In Gal. 3:10–14, Paul claimed that the curse
pronounced on those who fail to keep the Law (Deut. 27:26) is undone for those
redeemed by Christ from "the curse of the Law," since they become the heirs of the
promise made to Abraham.[62] In Romans 5, Paul links Adam's sin with death as well as
with the universal need for redemption in Christ. Aphrahat has transposed all this to
Eve. For him, Mary, as mother of Jesus, participates in undoing the "curse" of Eve:

> But now, by the coming of the child of the blessed Mary, the thorns are uprooted, the
> sweat is wiped away, the fig tree is cursed, the dust is made salty, the curse is nailed to
> the cross, the point of the sword is removed from before the tree of life (which is given
> as food to the faithful), and paradise is promised to the blessed and the virgins and
> the holy ones.[63]

At this point Aphrahat launches into a stirring portrayal of the eschatological
banquet full of nuptial images applied especially to the unmarried, both male and
female: The chaste will "rest in the sanctuary of the Most High." Christ, the "Only-
begotten [*Îhîdâyâ* ܝܚܝܕܝܐ] from the bosom ['*ûbâ* ܥܘܒܐ] of His Father shall cause all
the single ones [*ihîdâyê* ܝܚܝܕܝܐ] to rejoice." Notably here he applies Gal. 3:28, "there is
neither slave nor free, neither male nor female," only to the unmarried in paradise.
Finally, turning to the virginal women, "the pure virgins who are betrothed to Christ,"
he asserts that they "are far removed from the curse of the Law, and are redeemed from
the condemnation of the daughters of Eve; for they are not wedded to men so as to
receive the curses and come into the pains. They take no thought of death, because
they do not deliver children to him."[64] Evidently the promise of paradise, undoing the
curses of Eve, is already present in this world for the virginal daughters of the
covenant, since they do not bear children.

Here Aphrahat adds: "And instead of the groans of the daughters of Eve, they utter
the songs of the Bridegroom." Although this might be taken as indicating a singing
role for the daughters of the covenant in the present time, most probably it belongs to
the eschatological future and to his vivid evocation of paradise, when "those that go
to the kingdom shall rejoice and exult and dance and sing praises." For he ends the
section by contrasting the condition of the "daughters of Eve" with the future, resurrected state of the virginal brides of Christ: "The adornment of the daughters of Eve
is wool that wears out and perishes, but the garments of these wear not out. Old age
withers the beauty of the daughters of Eve, but the beauty of these shall be renewed
in the time of the Resurrection."[65]

So we may conclude that Aphrahat certainly sees a place of exceptional glory for
the chaste in paradise. In that future realm virginal women will participate uniquely
in the reversal of the curses visited upon Eve. That future privileged position is anticipated here and now by their freedom from the sufferings attendant upon childbear-

ing. Mary's role in the undoing of the curses upon humankind apparently has no further consequence in the present time for women, whether virginal or not. Neither the "silence of Eve" nor its undoing by Mary is mentioned here or elsewhere by Aphrahat.[66] His negative association of women and music with Satan is counteracted by connecting music and song with the festivities of paradise. Despite his assertion that women will participate in the nuptial celebrations of that future time, however, he gives no clear indication that this has consequences for the present age. It is not clear that the daughters of the covenant have a singing role in the Christian community of his time and place.

Ephrem extensively applies the notion of Mary as "a new Eve."[67] Yet he provides only one clear antecedent for Jacob's distinctive mariological theme: the undoing of the "silence of Eve." In his *Hymns on Paradise* he once alludes to the silence imposed upon Eve and, perhaps, implicitly contrasts it with the role of women as liturgical singers:

> Eve's mouth was sealed in a beneficial silence
> But once again her mouth is a kithara for her Creator.[68]

Like Aphrahat, then, he associates women's singing with paradise. But he gives clearer testimony that the paradisal state is anticipated here and now by the singing of women in the congregation, as we shall see.

(4) Evidence internal to Ephrem's own writings about his musical accomplishments and especially about women's choirs singing his madrâshê

Ephrem's *madrâshê* contain many allusions to singing as well as to musical instruments. Because of his well-known fondness for metaphorical expression, these references cannot be simply equated with liturgical practice in his time; they must be carefully and systematically examined and interpreted. Although a full treatment of this issue is beyond the scope of this discussion, a few samples will suffice to show some of his major themes: 1) music and song represent true—or false—teaching; 2) Paradise is linked with music and song; 3) the young and virginal (both male and female) sing at the festivals of the Church, especially Easter.

According to Ephrem's *Hymns on Virginity* 27–30, the Church has learned from Christ to play on three harps [ܟܢܪ̈ܐ]: Hebrew Scripture, the New Testament and Nature[69]—the three sources of authoritative teaching which correspond to the Three in whose names Christians are baptized.[70] This is an important but clearly metaphorical allusion to a musical instrument. The limitations of the teaching of Moses, the error and excess of Solomon as well as of idolaters and heretics are also represented by playing harps or other musical instruments and singing.[71] In the case of Solomon and some others accused of improper beliefs and practices, Ephrem may intend to include a criticism of the actual practice of music, but his primary target seems to be the idolatry or heresy itself, which is symbolized by bad music just as good teaching is symbolized by good music. It is more difficult to decide how literally to take his views on music in paradise: at the end of time, the righteous dead will be resurrected to "sing glory on their kitharas" while the living "sing glory with their harps" and the angels "blow their horns" but the "evil ones will inherit a shutting of the mouth."[72]

A connection both to paradise and to festive liturgical practice in his time is provided in the second of Ephrem's *Hymns on the Resurrection*, where he likens his compositions to blossoms he has gathered and brought back from paradise to scatter them about for the feast of Easter—a festival of music:[73]

> This joyful festival is entirely made up
>> of tongues and voices:
> innocent young women and men [ܒܬܘ̈ܠܬܐ ܘܥܠ̈ܝܡܐ]
>> sounding like trumpets and horns [ܫܝܦܘܪ̈ܐ ܘܩܪ̈ܢܬܐ]
> while infant girls and boys [ܛܠ̈ܝܬܐ ܘܛܠ̈ܝܐ]
>> resemble harps and lyres [ܟܢܪ̈ܐ ܘܩܝ̈ܬܪܐ];
> their voices intertwine
>> as they reach up together towards heaven.
> giving glory to the Lord of glory.
> Blessed is He for whom the silent have thundered out.[74]

Each group within the congregation makes an appropriate offering. Throughout the hymn the young and the chaste offer their songs.[75] The musical instruments—trumpets, horns, harps and lyres—are all symbolized by human voices, evidently not played in the service. The ordained—bishop, priests and deacons—offer their homilies, ministry and reading, respectively.[76] The wealthy and powerful offer their benefactions, and the ordinary people present their manner of life.[77] Ephrem himself humbly offers his compositions, the flowers of his mind "garlanded in all kinds of wreathes, laid at the door of each ear!"[78] Young women [ܒܬܘ̈ܠܬܐ] are specifically identified with the singing of *madrâshê.*[79]

There is no clear indication here whether these young women (or any of the various groups of youthful and/or virginal singers) sang in separate choirs, as later they would, or, if so, whether Ephrem founded female choirs and initiated the practice of having them sing *madrâshê* or whether he was continuing a custom that was already in place. It is clear that Ephrem composed his hymns for the regular worship of the community, apparently without instrumental accompaniment. Their performance was understood to be an integral part of the worship. This is most noteworthy, as we shall see, in the case of the girls and women. The context attested here is neither the all-female environment of a monastic enclosure nor a special occasion associated with *martyria.*

Further, by the early fifth century the *Canons of Rabbula* assign the singing in worship services of psalms as well as of *madrâshê* to the "daughters of the covenant," traditional groups of ascetic women living in the towns and villages.[80] Manuscripts of Ephrem's *madrâshê* indicate the melody [ܒܪ ܩܠܐ bar qâlâ] to which each hymn is to be sung. Since some of the manuscripts date to the early sixth century (the earliest dated to 517), we can be confident that they were sung at least from that time onward.[81] In some cases Archbishop Gregorios Ibrahim and Dr. George Kiraz have matched the melodies from the manuscripts with melodies in the liturgical book still in use in the Syrian Orthodox tradition, *Beth Gazo.*[82] It is plausible to assume continuity in both the practice of women's singing the *madrâshê* and perhaps also the melodies according to which they were sung within the Syriac environment.

Fourth- and fifth-century Greek and Latin writers on Ephrem's musical accomplishments:

Among the fourth- and fifth-century writers who briefly recount the life and work of Ephrem, only two mention his contributions to music.[83] Jerome, Epiphanius, and Palladius variously praise his deeds or his writings without referring to music, hymns or choirs.[84] On the other hand, both Sozomen and Theodoret portray him as composing his hymns to counteract the compositions of Harmonius, the putative son of Bardaisan.[85]

Sozomen pairs Ephrem with Didymus "the Blind" of Alexandria to make the point that these two men, each in his own way, surpassed conventional ways of learning to go directly to the truth. Didymus, despite blindness since childhood—or even because of it—was able to achieve extraordinary depth and breadth in learning. According to Sozomen, the great saint Antony had praised and consoled him with the words, "It is not a severe thing, nor does it deserve to be grieved over, O Didymus, that you are deprived of the organs of sight which are possessed by rats, mice, and the lowest animals; but it is a great blessing to possess eyes like angels, whereby you can contemplate keenly the Divine Being, and see accurately the true knowledge."[86]

Likewise Ephrem, despite his lack of all instruction, achieved eloquence and erudition sufficient to impress his Greek Christian contemporaries. His musical accomplishments were due not only to his natural abilities but also to his imitation of the songs of Bardaisan's aptly named son, Harmonius. Thanks to his exposure to Greek learning, Harmonius "was the first to subdue his native tongue to meters and musical laws [μέτροις καὶ νόμοις μουσικοῖς]; these verses he delivered to the choirs [χοροῖς παραδοῦναι], and even now the Syrians frequently sing [ψάλλουσιν], not the precise copies by Harmonius, but the same melodies" [οὐ' τοῖς Ἁρμονίου συγγράμμασιν ἀλλὰ τοῖς μέλεσι χρώμενοι].[87] Because Ephrem, "although ignorant of Greek learning" [καίπερ Ἑλληνικῆς παιδείας ἄμοιρος], feared that the heretical opinions of Bardaisan would be imbibed along with these compositions for the lyre [οἷά γε ὑπὸ λύραν ἃ συνεγράψατο] by the "Syrians . . . charmed with the elegance of the diction and the rhythm of the melody" [τῳ κάλλει τῶν ὀνομάτων καὶ τῷ ῥυθμῷ τῆς μελωδίας], he composed "similar poems" [ἑτέρας γραφὰς συναδούσας] in the form of "sacred hymns" [ἐν θείοις ὕμνοῖς] and "praises of good men" [ἐγκωμίοις ἀγαθῶν ἀνδρῶν]. The Syrians have sung [ψάλλουσιν] Ephrem's compositions since that time, he informs his reader, "according to the law of the ode established by Harmonius" [κατὰ τὸν νόμον τῆς Ἁρμονίου ᾠδῆς].[88]

Theodoret gives a shorter but similar account. He, too, stresses Ephrem, was "totally untainted by heathen education," and that he "adopted the music of [Harmonius's] songs, but set them to piety and so gave the hearers at once great delight and a healing medicine." À propos of his writings in general, the historian notes Ephrem "was able to expose the niceties of heathen error, and lay bare the weakness of all heretical artifices." Specifically of the songs, he notes they "are still used to enliven the festivals of our victorious martyrs."[89] Finally, in a letter addressed to monks in Constantinople, he alludes to Ephrem as "the harp of the Spirit."[90]

Thus, prior to the sixth century apart from Ephrem's own writings, the only extant sources on the subject of Ephrem's musical compositions are the brief accounts within these two church histories written in Greek in the first half of the fifth century. Both trace the Syriac writer's melodies to a Greek root via Harmonius, and both assert that he wrote to counteract the heretical teachings of Bardaisan. Theodoret links Ephrem's hymns to the feasts of the martyrs and perhaps also to a broader anti-heretical and anti-pagan use. Neither of the historians mentions a special role for women's choirs.

On the first point, the role of Harmonius, their testimony has been amply refuted.[91] Although an early source attests that Bardaisan had a son, his name is not mentioned; the compositions Sozomen and Theodoret attributed to him belong to his father. Sozomen has been accused of inventing this aptly named son to promote the view that this distinctly Syriac contribution to early Christian culture was instead rooted in Greek culture. Theodoret uncritically incorporated this misinformation into his own account.

Without discounting Sozomen's Greek chauvinism, it is worth noting that both he and especially Theodoret appear to stress Ephrem's lack of education as a way of protecting him from the charge of uncritical use of pagan customs. Likewise, while the emphasis on the anti-heretical dimension of Ephrem's work is present in both authors, it is more prominent in Theodoret's testimony. His concern seems to be less to establish cultural priority than to defend the custom of singing hymns by showing its usefulness against heresy and for the promotion of piety. Finally, his enthusiastic assertion that Ephrem's hymns were used at the feasts of martyrs—a notion completely without corroboration—appears to be an attempt to anchor a pious custom from his own context upon the authority of the Syriac hymnodist. In short, both fifth-century Greek ecclesiastical historians, but especially Theodoret, seem to be on the defensive regarding Christian hymnody. Despite their apparent need to justify this accomplishment, they portray Ephrem positively as hymnodist, but they neither mention women's choirs nor provide any other information about who sang the hymns.

(5) Historical context of Jacob's mêmrâ

What prompted Jacob to compose this *mêmrâ*? It is plausible that it was written for Ephrem's feast,[92] but this does not inform us why he chose this emphasis for his praise. Since the work is a vigorous defense of women's choirs, it seems likely someone had challenged their propriety. There are a few probable sources for such a challenge: first, from the West; second, from within the Syriac-speaking church in reaction against Origenistic currents; third, from the Antiochene dyophysite theological factions in the Syriac-speaking church. I propose that these three factors coalesced to prompt Jacob's defense.

We have already reviewed the evidence of opposition to women's choirs in Greek and Latin sources. A second possible source of opposition to women's choirs may have been a reaction to Origenism within the Syriac Christian environment. Stephen bar

Sudaili, an Origenist and a native of the region of Edessa, attempted to promote his doctrines there in the early decades of the sixth century. Both Jacob of Serug and Philoxenus of Mabbug opposed Stephen's efforts. Writing to two presbyters of the Edessene Church, Philoxenus urged that they "be zealous that [Stephen's writings] not be given to anyone and especially to those nuns [*dayryâthâ*] who dwell in the church building [ܪ̈ܐܝܬܐ ܟܢܘܫܬܐ ܒܥܕܬܐ ܕܥܡܪܝܢ] lest they be led astray by the simplicity and weakness natural to women."[93] His anxiety about the theological views of the "nuns living in the church building at Edessa" may indicate that Stephen directed his appeals especially to women, or that he had some special success among women. The liturgical role of the nuns living in the church buildings at Edessa might cause further anxiety about their theological views. If so, Philoxenus or others may have thought elimination of the women's choirs would be essential to controlling the threat of Stephen's Origenism. If so, then Jacob's homily would be a rejection of such a proposal in the name of Syriac Christian tradition as well as the usefulness of women's choirs to combat heresy and idolatry. He may have reasoned that depriving the women of their traditional liturgical role might have served only to aggravate the situation and to accelerate their alienation from orthodoxy.

Finally, the christological controversies that so bitterly divided Eastern Christians for centuries contained among their theological and exegetical doctrines differing social implications for women. I propose that Syrian Orthodox Miaphysite Christians like Jacob had a special stake in retaining the allegiance of women. A combination of mariological doctrine with a spirituality of Christ's unique presence in virgins had provided a powerful self-understanding for Pulcheria the Virgin Empress in her conflict with Nestorius.[94] Ephrem's *Hymns on Virginity* have strong resonance with Pulcheria's view and may have constituted part of the theological background for it.[95]

In the sixth century Empress Theodora strongly espoused the Miaphysite cause while her husband, the Emperor Justinian, leaned more to the Chalcedonian Christology. The geo-political aspects of the ambivalent policy that resulted from this strained partnership have been studied; its advantages and disadvantages for retaining the entirety of Justinian's empire have been outlined.[96] Whereas two of the earliest accounts, those of Procopius and of Evagrius Scholasticus, both Chalcedonian in their sympathies, portrayed this imperial partnership as calculated and conniving, an entirely different picture emerges in the contemporaneous account of the Miaphysite John of Ephesus, where Theodora's former life as actress and prostitute is simply and briefly mentioned *en route* to a detailed account of her piety, self-discipline, and devoted concern and tireless advocacy for the Miaphysite Christians and their church.[97] Given her combined political and ecclesiological concerns as well as her extraordinary political gifts, it is reasonable to pose the question whether Theodora, like Pulcheria, found an affirmation of female power in the Alexandrian christological emphasis with its accompanying mariological dimension. Although Pulcheria's virginal ideology would not fit Theodora, the exaltation of Mary as *Theotokos* may still have served as a model of female imperial power. In any case, it is plausible Theodora looked favorably not merely on her own power, but also on the leadership of women in other contexts—such as in the church for which she labored and negotiated so tirelessly. Thus it is plausible the christological controversies in their sixth-century phase included disputes over women's ecclesial leadership.

Other aspects of the role of gender in these controversies can only be sketched here: 1) the *imago dei* in the competing theological and exegetical traditions of Antioch and Alexandria, and 2) the ecclesiastical offices held by women as attested by canonical documents in various contexts (either Greek vs. Syriac, or West vs. East Syrian). First, the presence of the *imago dei* in woman is problematic for the Antiochene exegetical tradition.[98] Both John Chrysostom and Theodore of Mopsuestia discuss the question of women's leadership with respect to traditions about Eve and the Pauline (and deutero-Pauline) injunctions about women's silence and affirm that the prohibition holds.[99] Their concern is not specified as women's singing, and it may instead focus on women's ordination to an office higher than the diaconate.[100]

This leads to the second question regarding offices held by women, especially during the fourth to sixth centuries—the time frame of concern in this paper. Women in the diaconate have received most attention in the scholarly literature; the significance of this office for women in the early church in general and in the Syriac and Greek traditions is clear.[101] The role of the "daughters of the covenant" (ascetic women in the Syriac tradition) became interwoven with the office of deaconess during the time in question.[102] Among the duties designated sometimes for deaconesses, more often for "daughters of the covenant," in fifth- and sixth-century canonical and hagiographic sources is the singing of psalms and *madrâshê.*[103] One source attesting this practice is the collection of canons of Marutha of Maipherkat, an East Syrian document which ante-dates the christological controversies; another East Syrian document is the collection from the Synod of Mar George in 676.[104] The association of deaconess with chanting continued into the modern period in a rite of ordination that survives in several manuscripts.[105]

But of greatest interest here is the clustering of sources that are, like Jacob's *mêmrâ,* attributed to sixth-century West Syrian (Syrian Orthodox, or Miaphysite) writers: John of Ephesus and Rabbula of Edessa both confirm the importance in their churches of choirs composed of women trained in Scripture and in singing.[106] Finally, the Testament of our Lord, a church order that may have originated in and definitely was used in the same sixth-century West Syrian context, assigned a prominent public role to women.[107] The "widows [*armalâthâ*] who sit in front" [ܐܪܡܠܬܐ ܗܢܝܢ ܕܝܬܒܢ] perhaps also identified as presbyters [ܩܫܝܫܬܐ qashîshâthâ],[108] sit on the bêmâ [ܒܐܡܐ, a raised platform in the middle of the church] with male clergy, are sometimes listed after the presbyters and deacons and before the lesser orders of men, are ordained with a prayer parallel to the male presbyters and deacons, perhaps implying the laying on of hands [χειροτονία, Syriac kîrûtûnîya ܟܝܪܘܛܘܢܝܐ], and are responsible for a variety of prayers and chants in the public liturgy.[109]

Jacob died in 521, during the reign of the Emperor Justin I and six years prior to Justinian's accession to full imperial power. It might then be assumed Theodora had not yet emerged as imperial patroness of the Syrian Orthodox/Miaphysite cause within Jacob's lifetime, and thus he cannot have had her image before him in espousing the cause of the singing women of Syriac liturgical tradition. However, John of

Ephesus dates Theodora's first intervention on behalf of the persecuted anti-Chalcedonians as early as 519. At that time, she intervened successfully on behalf of Bishop Mare of Amida to change his place of exile from Petra to Egypt.[110] Thus, it is narrowly possible Jacob took up his pen in his last years with Theodora in mind, and it is even possible, if unlikely, that Jacob's homily would have "crossed the desk" of the empress! At least it is plausible she was involved in some way in the coalescence of woman-friendly themes in Miaphysite tradition: Mariology, clearer affirmation of the presence of the *imago dei* in women, and a greater public liturgical role for some women.

These same considerations are likely to have led Jacob vigorously to support the continued role of Syrian Christian women as liturgical singers. Despite the discontinuity of Syriac tradition on this point with established Western Christian attitudes, despite the anti-Origenist anxieties of his comrade at arms, Philoxenus, Jacob's Alexandrian christological and mariological tradition led him in the same direction as his Syriac liturgical tradition: to defend unequivocally the right of Christian women to sing aloud with unveiled faces in the public liturgical assembly.

Endnotes

[1]See Kies den Biesen, *Bibliography of Ephrem the Syrian* (Giove in Umbria, 2002), esp. 30–38, 110–12, for lists of the collections of Ephrem's hymns in Beck's editions and for modern translations.

[2]See James McKinnon, *Music in Early Christian Literature* [=McKinnon, Music] (New York: Cambridge University Press, 1987), 92–95.

[3]First published by Paul Bedjan, ed., *Acta Martyrum et Sanctorum Syriace* (Leipzig, 1892; rep. Hildesheim: Olms, 1968), III, 665–678. Of the 12 mss. identified by A. Vööbus [in *Handschriftliche (Überlieferung der Mêmrê Dichtung von Jaqob von Serug*, 2 vols., Corpus Scriptorum Christianorum Orientalium [= CSCO], 344–345 [1973])], 6 were selected for the critical edition with English translation by Joseph P. Amar, *A Metrical Homily on Holy Mar Ephrem by Mar Jacob of Serug* [= Amar, Homily], Patrologia Orientalis [= PO] 47 (1995), 1–76; on his selection of mss., cf. esp. 11–13. I will generally follow his text and translation, including his numbering of the lines, but occasionally I will prefer the readings of other mss. or supply a different translation; these exceptions will be noted.

[4]No one has questioned the attribution to Jacob of Serug. On Jacob and his corpus, see Tanios Bou Mansour, *La Théologie de Jacques de Saroug* (Kaslik: Université Saint-Esprit, 1993); K. Alwan, "Bibliographie générale raisonnée de Jacques de Saroug," *Parole de l'Orient* 13 (1986): 313–83; additional bibliography in Jacob of Serug, *On the Mother of God*, trans. Mary Hansbury, intro. Sebastian Brock (Crestwood, NY: St. Vladimir's Press, 1998), 101–102.

[5]Amar has suggested a date prior to the last decade of the fifth century on the grounds that there is no mention of the unrest in Edessa of 494–506, as described by Joshua the Stylite [William Wright, ed. *The Chronicle of Joshua the Stylite*, Cambridge: Cambridge University Press, 1882, Ch. 59–60; discussed by Amar, Homily, 16, 18, who replicates the argument of Micheline Albert concerning the dating of Jacob's homilies against the Jews; see M. Albert, ed. and trans., Jacques de Saroug, *Homilies contre les juifs*, PO 38 (1976): 22–23], but if this is a relevant criterion for the dating of this hymn, the period from 506 until Jacob's death in 521 still deserves consideration. Further study of the content and purpose of the work in order to discern its historical setting may contribute to a more secure dating.

[6]Eric Werner, *The Sacred Bridge: The Interdependence of Liturgy and Music in Synagogue and Church during the First Millennium*, (New York: Columbia University Press, 1959), vol. 1, 218; Joseph P. Amar, *The Syriac "Vita" Tradition of Ephrem the Syrian* [= Amar, Vita], Catholic University of America dissertation, 1988, UMI 89–19389, 43–44; Sebastian Brock, intro., trans., Saint Ephrem, *Hymns on Paradise*, (Crestwood, NY: St. Vladimir's Press, 1990) 22–25; McVey, "Jacob of Serug on Ephrem and the Singing of Women" *The Syrian Antiochian Perspective* I (1992): 36–41; Amar, Homily, 20–21. An important step toward confirming

the role of women's choirs using canonical sources has been made by Susan Ashbrook Harvey, "Women's Service in Ancient Syriac Christianity" (= Harvey, Women's Service) in *Kanon: Jahrbuch der Gesellschaft für das Recht der Ostkirchen* 16 (2000): *Mutter, Nonne, Diakonin,* ed. Eva Synek, 226–41, esp. 236–37; we will return to this work later in the present article. See also S.A. Harvey, "Spoken words, voiced silence: Biblical Women in Syriac Tradition" *Journal of Early Christian Studies* [=JECS] 9 (2001): 105–131, esp. 126–129. I am grateful to Susan Harvey for her encouragement to finish the present article, an earlier version of which I had shared with her, see ibid., n. 85.

[7]In addition to noting the presence of both biblical and Greek rhetorical features, Amar has observed the scarcity of biographic data, emphasis on Ephrem's role as teacher of orthodox doctrine, pride in the Syrian nation, and the promotion of Syrian women [Amar, Homily, 18–22]. Further on the probable use of Greek rhetorical conventions in this and other Syriac hagiographic *mêmrê,* see Kathleen E. McVey, *The Mêmrâ on the Life of Severus of Antioch Composed by George Bishop of the Arab Tribes: A Critical Edition of the Syriac Text, English Translation and Literary and Historical Commentary* (Harvard diss., 1977), 471–565, esp. 531–35.

[8]Amar, Homily, 32–57 lines 37–127.

[9]As he had done in the introduction (Amar, Homily, 24–29, lines 1–20) with expressions of his own inadequacy to his lofty subject, here in lines 37–45 (Amar, Homily, 32–35).

[10]Psalm 108:1–9, passim, following the numbering of *Peshitta* and NRSV. See also Psalm 60:5–12, and Psalm 57:7–11. Psalm 108 consists entirely of a conflation of Psalms 57:7–11 and 60:5–12. Whereas Psalm 57 is "a prayer for deliverance from personal enemies," Psalms 60 and 108 invoke divine deliverance and victory over the nations according to *The New Oxford Annotated Bible with the Apocrypha,* ed. Herbert G. May and Bruce M. Metzger (New York, 1977), 698–701, 742.

[11]Amar, Homily, 32–35, lines 37–39, with slight modifications, notably reading "helmet" rather than "strengthener of my head," retaining the clear allusion to warfare as in most modern English, and the personification of Teaching.

[12]1 Cor. 14:34. The wording of the *Peshitta* is similar to the *mêmrâ.* 1 Tim. 2:12 is also close. The manuscript tradition of Jacob's *mêmrâ* is, however, not unanimous in this reading. It may be that a later editor has added this New Testament allusion.

[13]Amar, Homily, 34–35, lines 40–44, translation slightly revised.

[14]1 Cor. 14:34–35. See also 1 Pet. 3:1, and 1 Tim. 2:11–15, which will be discussed below.

[15]Amar, Homily, 34–35, line 45.

[16]Ibid., 36–37, line 48.

[17]Ibid., lines 46–48.

[18]Ibid., 36–39, lines 51–60, translation revised.

[19]Ibid., 38–43, lines 61–73.

[20]Ibid., 42–45, lines 74–78.

[21]Ibid., 44–45, lines 79–85.

[22]Ibid., 44–45, lines 83–84, my translation following mss. designated by Amar ACE; on the mss., see note 3 above.

[23]Fokkelien van Dijk-Hemmes, I. "Traces of Women's Texts in the Hebrew Bible" in Athalia Brenner and Fokkelien van Dijk-Hemmes, *On Gendering Texts: Female and Male Voices in the Hebrew Bible* (Leiden: Brill, 1993), esp. "The Song of Miriam," 38–42.

[24]Ibid., esp. 29–37, where Dijk-Hemmes bases her argument on the parallels adduced by Goitein between the biblical texts and modern Yemenite Jews, on the one hand, and pre-Islamic Arab women's poetry, on the other. For discussion of archaeological evidence from the Biblical period, see Carol L. Meyers, "Of Drums and Damsels: Women's Performance in Ancient Israel," *The Biblical Archaeologist* 54 (1991): 16–27.

[25]Amar, Homily, 44–53, lines 86–114.

[26]Ibid., 44–49, lines 86–97.

[27]Ibid., 48–49, lines 98–101.

[28]Ibid., 48–53, lines 102–114.

[29]Ibid., 50–53, lines 108–113 translation revised.

[30]Ibid., 52–57, lines 115–25.

[31]Ibid., 52–55, lines 115–22.

[32]Ibid., 62–67, lines 149–162.

[33]Ibid., 62–65, lines 151–54.

[34]Ibid., 64–67, lines 160–61.

[35]Rev. 5:9.

[36]The further question of the veiling of women, although interesting and important, is too complex to be addressed here.

[37]J. Quasten, "The Liturgical Singing of Women in Christian Antiquity," *Catholic Historical Review* 27 (1941), 149–65. Idem., *Music and Worship in Pagan and Christian Antiquity* (= Quasten, Music), trans. Boniface Ramsey (Washington, D.C.: National Association of Pastoral Musicians, 1983), 75–87 (English translation of *Musik und Gesang in den Kulten der heidnischen Antike und christlichen Frühzeit*, 2 ed. Munster, Aschendorff, 1973). These are the only systematic treatments of women's singing in the early church; the sources are revisited by McKinnon (McKinnon, Music, cited in n. 2 above), selections #121, #154, #160, #233, #276, #334, #201 but without an overall discussion of the evidence on women's singing. We will look at each of these briefly here.

[38]Eusebius, *Church History* [= Eusebius, HE] 7.30. 10–11 [*Eusebius Werke* 2.1–2.2: *Die Kirchengeschichte*, ed. E. Schwartz, Theodor Mommsen, F. Winkelmann, GCS (Berlin: Akademie Verlag, 1999), 2.2, 710]; English translation: Eusebius, *The Ecclesiastical History*, trans. Kirsopp Lake, Loeb Classical Library (=Loeb), 2 vols. (Cambridge: Harvard University Press, 1975), 2, 218–19.

[39]Eusebius had included Bardaisan in his *Church History* (Eusebius, HE 4.30; Schwartz, 2.1, 392; Lake, 1, 398–99), and he used the *Dialogue on Fate* in his *Preparation of the Gospel* 6.10 [*Eusebius Werke* 8.1 *Praeparatio Evangelica* 1–10, ed. Karl Mras, GCS (Berlin: Akademie Verlag, 1954) 335–44], but he never mentioned Harmonius or any other connection of Bardaisan with singing or music. For discussion see H. J. W. Drijvers, *Bardaisan of Edessa* (Assen: Van Ġorcum, 1966) esp. 63–68. Apparently Eusebius was also unaware of Ephrem's existence. This is not surprising, of course, since Eusebius died in 339—relatively early in Ephrem's life.

[40]Hans Lewy, *Sobria ebrietas: Untersuchungen zur Geschichte der Antiken Mystik* (Giessen: Topelmann, 1929).

[41]Philo, *On the Contemplative Life* (= Philo, Cont.) §83–89, trans. and intro. F. H. Colson and G. H. Whitaker, Loeb 363 (=Loeb Philo 9), (Cambridge: Harvard University Press, 1941), 104–69, esp. 164–69. For a new translation with notes on Eusebius' understanding of this community and its possible relation to the Essenes and Qumran, see Philo of Alexandria, *The contemplative life, The giants, and Selections*, trans. and intro. David Winston, preface by John Dillon (New York: Paulist Press, 1981), 41–57, 315–21. There is also a brief allusion to the "two choirs, one of men and one of women" led by "Moses and his sister" in Philo's *Life of Moses* §180, in Loeb Philo, vol. 6, 368–69. In his *Life of Moses* 1.32, Gregory of Nyssa mentions the song of victory (τροπαριον) but does not mention the two choirs here or later in the treatise à propos of the spiritual meaning of Crossing the Red Sea (cf. Gregory, *Life of Moses* 2.122–130); Grégoire de Nysse, *La Vie de Moïse*, intro., ed. and trans. Jean Daniélou, SC 1 *ter*, 3 ed. (Paris: Editions du Cerf, 1968), 72–73, 180–87; Gregory of Nyssa, *The Life of Moses*, trans., intro. and notes by A. J. Malherbe and E. Ferguson, (New York: Paulist, 1978), 39, 83–85.

[42]The name of the treatise is in Eusebius, HE 2.17.3 (Schwartz, 1, 142; Lake, 1, 146–47); quotations from Eusebius, HE 2.17.6–24 (Schwartz, 1, 144–152; Lake, 1, 146–57).

[43]Eusebius, HE 2.17 (Schwartz, 1, 142–52; Lake, 1, 146–57). On Eusebius's misunderstanding and its consequences, see F. C. Conybeare, ed., Philo of Alexandria, *About the Contemplative Life* (Oxford: Clarendon, 1895; rep. New York: Garland, 1987), v–x.

[44]Eusebius, HE 2.17.13 (Schwartz, 1,148; Lake, 1, 150–51).

[45]Eusebius, HE 2.17.22 (Schwartz, 1, 152; Lake, 1, 154–55).

[46]McKinnon, Music #154, 75–76.

[47]Ibid., # 121, 61.

[48]Ibid., # 276, 126–27.

[49]Ibid., # 276, 127.

[50]*Contra Pelagianos* 1, 25 in *Sancti Eusebii Hieronymi Opera Omnia*, ed. Vallarsi, in J.P. Migne, *Patrologia Latina* (= PL) 23, 517–630, esp. 23, 542; Jerome, *Dogmatic and polemical works*, trans. John N. Hritzu, Fathers of the Church 53 (Washington, D.C.: Catholic University of America Press, 1965), 269–70, but cf. Quasten, Music, 13, for the last sentence as translated here. The Latin text reads: *Verum tu donas quod non*

licet; ut quod verecunde facere debeant, et absque ullo arbitro, magistri auctoritate proclament. Construing the last three words differently, Hritzu translates: "But you give them permission to do what is unlawful, and, *thus, they cite the authority of their master in defense of an act which should be done with modesty and not in view of spectators,*" (emphasis added in text and both translations).

[51]Theodoret, *Kirchengeschichte* 3.18–19, ed. Léon Parmentier (Berlin: Akademie Verlag, 1998), GCS N.F. 5 (= Theodoret, HE), 197–199; English trans. (under HE 3.14) from *The Ecclesiastical History, Dialogues and Letters,* trans. B. Jackson, A Select Library of Nicene and Post-Nicene Fathers of the Christian Church (= NPNF) ser. 2 (Grand Rapids: Eerdmans, 1983), 3, 33–159, esp. 102–103 (modified slightly).

[52]Ibid.

[53]1 Samuel 16:14–23.

[54]P. Martin, "Discours de Jacques de Saroug sur la chute des idoles," *Zeitschrift der deutschen morgenländischen Gesellschaft* [= ZDMG] 29 (1875), 107–47. H. J. W. Drijvers, *Cults and Beliefs at Edessa,* (Leiden: Brill, 1980) 37, n. 71.

[55]J. B. Segal, *Edessa, The Blessed City* (Oxford: Clarendon Press, 1970) 105ff.; H. Drijvers, "The Persistence of Pagan Cults and Practices in Christian Syria," *East of Byzantium: Syria and Armenia in the Formative Period,* eds. N. Garsoian, T. Mathews and R. Thomson, (Washington, D.C.: Dumbarton Oaks, 1982), 35–44.

[56]Luke Timothy Johnson, *The First and Second Letters to Timothy: A New Translation with Introduction and Commentary,* The Anchor Bible, vol. 35a (New York: Doubleday, 2001), esp. 198–211.

[57]See nn. 12, 14 above.

[58]Most important for this mariological theme are: E. Beck, "Die Mariologie der echten Schriften Ephräms," *Oriens Christianus* 40 (1956): 22–39; R. Murray, "Mary, the Second Eve in the Early Syriac Fathers," *Eastern Churches Review* III.4 (1971): 372–84; Robert Murray, "The Lance which Re-opened Paradise, a Mysterious Reading in the early Syriac Fathers," in *Orientalia Cristiana Periodica* 39 (1973): 224–34; P. Yousif, "Marie et les derniers temps chez saint Ephrem de Nisibe," *Études Mariales* 42 (1985): 29–55; Sebastian Brock, *Bride of Light,* Moran 'Etho 6 (Kottayam: SEERI, 1994). Further bibliography in Kies den Biesen, Bibliography (cited in n. 1 above), esp. 34, 100.

[59]Most recently on Aphrahat's Mariology, see Adam Lehto, "Women in Aphrahat: Some Observations" (= Lehto, Women) *Hugoye: Journal of Syriac Studies* 4.2 (2001) http://syrcom.cua.edu/Hugoye/Vol4No2/HV4N2Lehto.html, esp. 3–10.

[60]Lehto's translation, Lehto, Women, 5.

[61]Aphrahat, *Selected Demonstrations* (= Aphrahat, Dem.), trans. John Gwynn, NPNF ser. 2, v. 13, (Grand Rapids: Eerdmans, 1957), 345–412, esp. 367a. For the Syriac text, see *Aphraatis Sapientis Persae Demonstrationes,* ed. and Latin trans. J. Parisot, Patrologia Syriaca 1 (Paris: Firmin-Didot, 1894), Patrologia Syriaca 2 (Paris: Firmin-Didot, 1894), 1–497.

[62]Through Paul's use in Galatians, it is clear that "the curse of the Law" alludes to Deuteronomy 27, not to Genesis 3:14–19, *pace* Lehto, Women, 5.

[63]Aphrahat, Dem. 6.6, following Lehto's modification of Gwynn, 367a; Lehto, Women, 7.

[64]Aphrahat, Dem. 6.6, following Gwynn, 367b.

[65]Aphrahat, Dem. 6.6, following Gwynn, 368a.

[66]Nor, as Lehto notes, does Aphrahat ever cite 1 Tim. 2:11–15; Lehto, Women, 6.

[67]See note 58 above for Ephrem's Mariology.

[68]St. Ephrem the Syrian, *Hymns on Paradise,* intro. and trans. by Sebastian Brock (Crestwood, N.Y.: St. Vladimir's Seminary Press, 1990) 6.8, p. 111. For the Syriac text: E. Beck, ed. trans., *Des Heiligen Ephraem des Syrers Hymnen de Paradiso und Contra Julianum,* CSCO 174 (Louvain: CSCO, 1957), 21.

[69]Ephrem, *Hymns on Virginity* (= Virg.) 27–30; esp. 27.4–5; 28.1; 29.1–2, 4; 30.1, *Ephrem the Syrian: Hymns,* trans. and intro. Kathleen E. McVey, preface by John Meyendorff (= McVey, Ephrem) (New York: Paulist Press, 1989), 383–84, 386, 390–91, 394; part quoted in English also in McKinnon, Music # 204. For the Syriac text: E. Beck, ed., *Des heiligen Ephraem des Syrers Hymnen de Virginitate,* CSCO 223 (Louvain: CSCO, 1962), 99–113.

[70]Ephrem, Virg. 27; esp. 27.4, English trans. McVey, Ephrem, 383.

[71]Ephrem, Virg. 27.1–3; 29.2, 6–7, 12–13, English trans. McVey, Ephrem, 382, 391–93. See also *Hymns against Heresies* 2.7, E. Beck, ed. and German trans., *Des heiligen Ephraem des Syrers Hymnen contra Haereses,* CSCO 169–70 (Louvain: CSCO, 1957), quoted in English by McKinnon, Music #202, 94.

[72]Ephrem, Virg. 27.6, English trans. McVey, Ephrem, 384, interpreting 1 Thess. 16–17.

[73]Ephrem, *Hymns on the Resurrection* (= Res.) 2.1, S. Brock, intro. and trans., *The Harp of the Spirit: Eighteen Poems of Saint Ephrem*, 2 ed. (= Brock, Harp) (San Bernardino, Calif.: Borgo Press, 1984), 73–76; for the Syriac text, see E. Beck, ed. and trans., *Des Heiligen Ephraem des Syrers Paschahymnen*, CSCO 248 (Louvain: CSCO, 1964), 82; excerpted in McKinnon, Music #201, 93–94.

[74]Ephrem, Res. 2.2; (Beck 82–83; English trans. Brock, Harp, 73).

[75]The very young—children—in Res. 2.7.2 and 2.7.8 [ܛ̈ܠܝܐ] and 2.7.10 [ܛܠܝܐ] and 2.8.2 [ܛ̈ܠܝܐ]; and in Ephrem, Res. 2.9.5 and Res. 2.9.7: unmarried young men [ܓܕܘ̈ܕܐ] and women [ܒ̈ܬܘܠܬܐ] (against the emphasis of Brock's translation "strong young men" here; Beck, 84, Brock, Harp, 75); and in Res. 2.4.8 chaste men and women [ܟܢ̈ܫܐ ܢܟ̈ܦܬܐ] (Beck 83, against the emphasis of Brock's translation in Brock, Harp, 74: "unmarried girls and boys").

[76]Ephrem, Res. 2.9.1–4; Beck, 84; English trans. Brock, Harp, 75.

[77]Ephrem, Res. 2.9.8–9; Beck, 84; English trans. Brock, Harp, 75.

[78]Ephrem, Res. 2.5.8–9; Beck, 83; English trans. Brock, Harp, 74.

[79]Ephrem, Res. 2.9.7; Beck, 84; English trans. Brock, Harp, 75.

[80]On the "daughters of the covenant," their duties, and their relationship to deaconesses, see Harvey, Women's Service (cited in n. 6 above).

[81]On the manuscripts and melodies for the Nativity Hymns, for example, see Ephraem, *Hymnen de Nativitate (Epiphania)*, ed. E. Beck, CSCO 186 (Louvain: CSCO, 1959), viii ff. and xx ff.

[82]Gregorios Y. Ibrahim and George A. Kiraz, "Ephrem's *Madroshe* and the Syrian Orthodox *Beth Gazo*: A loose, but fascinating, affinity" in *Hugoye: Journal of Syriac Studies* 2.1 (1999) http://syrcom.cua.edu/Hugoye/Vol2No1/HV2N1IbrahimKiraz.html. The article includes audio samples of the chants as well as bibliography.

[83]For a survey of the sources and the secondary literature pertinent to Ephrem's life, see Amar, Vita, 9–61.

[84]Epiphanius, *Panarion* 52.22.7; ed. K. Holl, GCS (Leipzig: Hinrichs: 1915) 2, 284. Jerome, *de viris inlustribus* 115 ; ed. E.C. Richardson, Texte und Untersuchungen 14.1 (Leipzig, 1896), 51. Palladius, *historia lausiaca* 40; ed. C. Butler, Texts and Studies 6 (Cambridge: Cambridge University Press, 1904) 2, 126–27; the Syriac versions, ed. and trans. R. Draguet, *Les Formes Syriaques de la Matière de L'Histoire Lausiaque* (Louvain: CSCO, 1978), Syriac text : CSCO 398, 286–89; French trans. CSCO 399, 190–92.

[85]Sozomenus, *Kirchengeschichte* (= Sozomen, HE 3.16), ed. J. Bidez, 2 ed. G. Hansen, GCS (Berlin: Akademie Verlag, 1960) 127–31; English trans., C.D. Hartranft, *The Ecclesiastical History of Sozomen*, NPNF ser. 2 (Grand Rapids: Eerdmans, 1983) 2, 295–97. Theodoret, HE 4.26, cf. also Theodoret, HE 2.30.11–14 (Parmentier 169–70; English trans. Jackson, as if Theodoret, HE 2.26, NPNF, 92).

[86]Sozomen, HE 3.15 (Bidez 126; English trans. Hartranft, 295).

[87]Sozomen, HE 3.16 (Bidez 128; English trans. Hartranft, 296).

[88]Sozomen, HE 3.16 (Bidez 129; English trans. Hartranft, 296).

[89]Theodoret, HE 4.29.1–3 (Parmentier 269); English trans. Jackson as if Theodoret, HE 4.26, NPNF 129.

[90]Theodoret, "Letter 145: To the Monks of Constantinople" in *The Ecclesiastical History, Dialogues and Letters*, trans. B. Jackson, NPNF ser. 2 (Grand Rapids: Eerdmans, 1983), 3, 312–316, esp. 315.

[91]Drijvers, Bardaisan, 180–83. Further, Sebastian P. Brock, "Syriac and Greek Hymnography: Problems of Origin," 77–81.

[92]Amar, Homily, 15.

[93]A. L. Frothingham, *Stephen bar Sudaili, the Syrian mystic, and the Book of Hierotheos* (Leiden: Brill, 1886), 44f. Further on Stephen, cf. F. S. Marsh, ed., trans., *The Book which is called the Book of the Holy Hierotheos with Extracts from the Proleomena and Commentary of Theodosius of Antioch and from the book "Book of Excerpts" and other works of Gregory Bar Hebraeus* (London: Williams and Norgate, 1927).

[94]Kenneth G. Holum, *Theodosian Empresses: Women and Imperial Dominion in Late Antiquity* (Berkeley: University of California Press, 1982), esp. 79–174.

[95]Kathleen McVey, "Ephrem the Syrian's theology of divine indwelling and Aelia Pulcheria Augusta" Studia Patristica 35, *Papers presented at the Thirteenth International Conference on Patristic Studies held in Oxford 1999*, (Leuven: Peeters, 2001), 458–65.

[96]See, for example, Robert Browning, *Justinian and Theodora*, rev. ed. (New York: Thames and Hudson, 1987), 142–53, *et passim*; W. H. C. Frend, *The Rise of the Monophysite Movement: Chapters in the History*

of the Church in the Fifth and Sixth Centuries (Cambridge: Cambridge University Press, 1972), 255–95.

[97]For this enlightening new perspective on Theodora's portrayal, as well as for updated bibliography discussing the traditional materials such as Procopius's *Anecdota*, see Susan A. Harvey, "Theodora the 'Believing Queen': A Study in Syriac Historiographical Tradition" (= Harvey, Theodora) in *Hugoye* 4.2 (2001) http://syrcom.cua.edu/Hugoye/Vol4No2/HV4N2Harvey.html.

[98]Although the two essential scholarly treatments assess the views of the major figures (Diodore, Theodore, Nestorius , John Chrysostom, and Theodoret) differently, it is clear this was a contentious matter for these early exegetes: Nonna Verna Harrison, "Women, Human Identity, and the Image of God: Antiochene Interpretations," JECS 9 (2001): 205–49; Frederick McLeod, *The Image of God in the Antiochene Tradition* (Washington, D.C.: Catholic University of America Press, 1999), esp. 191–231.

[99]McLeod, Image, esp. 211–20.

[100]See McLeod's remarks on Cyrus of Edessa, ibid., 219–20.

[101]*Ordained Women in the Early Church: A Documentary History*, ed. and trans. Kevin Madigan and Carolyn Osiek (Baltimore: Johns Hopkins University Press, 2005); for the Syriac traditions, see Sebastian Brock, "Deaconesses in the Syriac Tradition" (= Brock, Deaconesses) in *Woman in Prism and Focus: Her Profile in Major World Religions and in Christian Traditions*, ed. by Prasanna Vazheeparampil (Rome: Mar Thoma Yogam, 1996), 205–18.

[102]Harvey, Women's Service (cited in n. 6 above), esp. 230–38.

[103]Ibid., 8–12.

[104]Ibid., 9.

[105]Brock, Deaconesses, 211–17.

[106]Harvey, Women's Service, 233–37, where she links these with Jacob's *mêmrâ* and its descendent, the Syriac *vita* of Ephrem, but without emphasis on the shared Miaphysite Christology.

[107]For the Syriac text with Latin translation, see *Testamentum Domini nostri Jesu Christi*, ed. and trans. I.E. Rahmani (Mainz: Kirchheim, 1899; repr. Hildesheim: Olms, 1968) (= *Test. Dom.*). For a concise account of the history of scholarship, versions, questions of date and place of origin, see *The Testamentum Domini: A Text for Students*, with intro., transl. and notes by Grant Sperry-White (Bramcote, Nottingham: Grove Books Ltd., 1991). As to its use in West Syrian tradition: Severus of Antioch was acquainted with it, Jacob of Edessa probably was its translator from Greek to Syriac in AD 687, and a version of it is included in the *Synodicon* of the West Syrian Church (see A. Vööbus, ed. and trans., *The Synodicon in the West Syrian Tradition*, CSCO 367–68 [Louvain: CSCO, 1975], esp. 2–4).

[108]Test. Dom. 1.35 and 1.43 (Rahmani 86:1) and 102.18.

[109]Test. Dom. 1.40–43 (Rahmani 94–105); also see Sperry-White, 31–45; Madigan and Osiek, 150–61; Harvey, Women's Ministry, 228–29.

[110]John of Ephesus, *Lives of the Eastern Saints*, ed. and trans. E. W. Brooks, PO 17, 19 (1923, 1925); esp. Ch. 13 (PO 17:189); see the discussion in Harvey, "Theodora," esp. 9–10.

15

We "being many are one body": The Conciliarity of the Church as Exemplified in Lay Women

Elizabeth Theokritoff

It is frequently and truly said that the essential nature of the Church is easier to illustrate or describe than to define;[1] so there is some justification for approaching the subject by presenting a few selections from a cloud of witnesses. But first, I should say something about the aspect of the Church's nature that I will be trying to convey.

I use the term "conciliarity" to translate *sobornost*—a notion that has been articulated primarily within the Russian tradition, but is by no means confined to it. Much could be said about the meaning and implications of this rich concept, sometimes glossed as "communality in freedom." My concern here, however, is with the way I have seen it lived out, and I would summarize this as an awareness that *we are the Church*. The Church is not an institution, an authority, a hierarchy set *over against* us; and today, it probably also needs to be added that it is not an object of our "consumer choice." Rather, it is the unity in which we live, *by virtue of which we have life in Christ*. This not at all the same as saying that we collectively determine the character of the Church, as if it were a sort of ideal democracy. We are not the source, but the receptacle; we are born from above, and as a result of that birth we, together, form the temple of the Holy Spirit. We all have the responsibility to witness to its truth and defend it when it is threatened, from whatever source. This is what the oft-quoted Encyclical of the Orthodox Patriarchs (1848) means when it says "the defender of religion is the whole body of the people." This does not apply only to doctrinal truth; it may apply equally to the true word of spiritual insight that our brother or sister needs to hear. The Lord may speak this word through a bishop or priest, an abbot or abbess; he may also speak it through any other member of his body.

I will be taking my examples mainly from history. But I have chosen people whose lives, whose churchmanship, strikes me as strangely familiar: people who are obvious spiritual forebears of those I myself have known, and who have taught me by example what it means to be a member of Christ's body.

Why lay women? Certainly, one could find men too who exemplify the same qualities of churchmanship. But it is in discussions about the place of women in the Church that one becomes most aware of a clash of ecclesiologies. Most Orthodox women with any ecumenical experience have probably at some point faced questions such as: How can you be wholeheartedly committed to a Church that is never likely to ordain you as priest? Much of the answer is likely to lie in the fact that being a full, and fully responsible, member of the Church has nothing to do with ordination. This does not, of course, dispose of the question of whether women can be priests. But it does strike at the root of the disturbingly narrow and clerical understanding of the Church that causes that question to loom so large. I hope that the very diversity of the people discussed here will help us keep in mind the breadth of the reality that we refer to when we speak of "the Church."

Missionaries, mentors, and spiritual mothers

Since we are instructed to concentrate on the formative years of our tradition, I will begin with the story of St. Thecla, disciple and co-worker of St. Paul.[2] I am fully aware that the historicity of this life is questionable. But what is not in question is the inspiration that Thecla's story has provided for generations of Orthodox women through the centuries: we might want to discover why.

Thecla is the embodiment of the principle that in Christ there is neither male nor female. Having heard Paul's preaching through her open window, she seeks him out and sits at his feet to learn from him. Paul defers baptizing her, afraid that a beautiful and unprotected young girl would not be able to withstand the temptations which are sure to assail her (*AThe* 6:13–15). Being unbaptized does not save her from persecution, however; but after emerging victorious from several encounters with the wild beasts, she finally baptizes herself in a pool (*AThe* 9:6–9). She might therefore be seen as somewhat outside the structures of the Church, but then, one might say the same of Paul himself. Thecla's story deliberately highlights the parallels. Consider the way she announces her baptism to Paul: "He who assists you in preaching assisted me to baptize" (*AThe* 10:2). She herself goes on to fulfill the role of a missionary preacher, as well as a confessor of the faith, an intercessor for the sick, and a spiritual mother to virgins who were converted by her and came to share her anchoritic life (*AThe* 10:14–17).

So Thecla stands as the prototype of martyr, monastic and missionary preacher. But perhaps more than that, she provides an example of how the Lord may perform mighty works through any member of his body. In that sense, we may see a worthy successor to Thecla in the early fourth-century saint Nino, "Equal to the Apostles and Enlightener of Georgia," in Orthodox tradition. According to the earliest version of her life, Nino was taken to Georgia as a captive; she was able to use those unpromising circumstances to convert the royal family, and through them the entire kingdom.[3] Again like Thecla, she reminds us that performing baptismal initiation into the Church is fundamentally a charism given to every baptized Christian; it seems that she baptized the Georgian king even after clergy had arrived.[4]

Of those for whom Thecla was an inspiration and heavenly patron, one of the best known is St. Macrina (ca. 327–379).[5] Macrina was the older sister and mentor of two of the Church's greatest theologians, St. Basil the Great and St. Gregory of Nyssa; Gregory calls her his "teacher." We are well aware of the contribution of these church fathers, whose legacy is still very much with us; less often do we pause to wonder how much of that contribution might have been lost to the Church without their sister's guidance and support.

Just before Macrina was born, her mother had a dream in which a resplendent Being addressed the unborn child as "Thecla." So Macrina grew up regarding that as her secret name, and it was certainly indicative of her character and inclinations. When her fiancé died, the young teenager decided firmly that she would live a life of virginity. She helped her widowed mother run the household and estates and bring up the eight younger siblings, and once the children were grown up, she turned the family home into a monastery. Monasticism in Asia Minor during that period was in its formative stages and quite unstructured. The first to compose a monastic rule would be her brother Basil; and the strong emphasis on service to the poor and needy which marks his Rule, as well as his episcopal ministry, was very likely influenced by his sister's domestic monastery, which never turned away a beggar[6] and fed throngs from miles around during famines.[7] When Macrina embarked on her monastic life, however, her eldest brother was still a rather bumptious young student in Athens, destined for a glittering career in the law courts. But when he completed his studies and came home to Cappadocia, Macrina decided to take him in hand. It seems that she very rapidly succeeded in changing his aspirations and values quite radically. Instead of pursuing fame and adulation, he dedicated himself to the ascetic life. And as it turned out, his skills in rhetoric and argumentation did not go to waste either; rather, they were put to use in the service of the Church, as he "expounded doctrine, explained the nature of the created world and improved human morals," to paraphrase the festal hymn dedicated to his memory.

Helping others to find their vocation, to achieve their full potential in the service of Christ, is a vital but sometimes neglected way in which Church members contribute to the building up of the whole. This may be said also of encouraging and supporting those who bear the burden of ordained ministry in the Church. Gregory of Nyssa, a much more diffident and retiring man than his brother Basil, laments to his sister the difficulties of his life as a prominent bishop: first exiled by an Arian emperor, then embroiled in all sorts of disputes and unpleasantness in the Church itself. Gently but firmly, Macrina reproaches him for not appreciating the grace and blessings given to him; he is the man to whom the churches look to give them support and help them set their affairs in order. And she concludes: "Is it not the prayers of your parents that have raised you to these heights when you yourself have little or no predisposition for such things?"[8]

There are two important points in Macrina's wise response here. First, the affirmation of his ministry: You are doing God's work, and by his grace you really can make a difference in the life of the Church; and second, her reminder that the hierarch, no less than the rest of us, is ultimately carried by *the Church as a whole*, living and departed. Gregory is what he is by the prayers of his parents—and, though she is too modest to mention it, no doubt Macrina's as well.

It should not be assumed that Macrina's case is altogether exceptional just because the bishops whose lives she touched so remarkably were her brothers. Hearing how she interacts with them, I am reminded constantly of words in the consecration address of a bishop well known to me for many years: "What you see is what you get; but what you get is also what you have given me.... A parish certainly sets its mark upon its priest."[9]

Upholding the Church: Practical service and spiritual guidance

Even in late antiquity, we should not assume that a woman's influence is confined to the "domestic Church" of her family circle (not that the domestic sphere is of negligible importance either). If we want a fourth-century example of the sort of indomitable grandmother who seems to carry the Church on her shoulders in times of crisis, we need look no further than St. Melania the Elder (ca. 350).[10] Melania was a lady from the highest echelons of Roman society, whose influence, however, rested on something more than social position. Widowed at twenty-two, she decided to dedicate herself to a life of celibacy, and like many of her contemporaries who felt a similar vocation, she betook herself to Egypt in order to sit at the feet of some of the great monastic Fathers. But when an Arian bishop took over the throne of Alexandria, a substantial number of monks and clergy were exiled to Palestine; so Melania followed them, provided for them out of her personal fortune, and even on occasion served them with her own hands.[11] The local governor thought he saw an opportunity to blackmail her and had her arrested, apparently unaware that she was a free Roman citizen. Melania hastened to disabuse him, informing her of the identity of her father and her late husband, and adding for good measure, "with the dull-witted, one must show the pride of a hawk." Not surprisingly, the magistrate offered an abject apology and allowed her to resume her ministrations. Melania was a force to be reckoned with when civil authorities threatened the welfare of the Church.

Melania's life was not only one of practical service, though she did found, and fund, numerous philanthropic institutions. The integrity of the faith and the unity of the Church were also central concerns for her. The monastery that she founded in Jerusalem, with the help of Jerome's sometime friend Rufinus, gave free hospitality to visiting monks and clergy; but we learn that the two of them were also instrumental in healing a schism involving 400 monks, as well as converting heretics who denied the divinity of the Holy Spirit.[12]

It seems that Melania also possessed the gift of discernment, the grace of speaking to others the word that they need to hear. She has her place as a spiritual mother in what Kallistos Ware calls the "apostolic succession of saints and spirit-bearers."[13] Bishop Kallistos goes on to underline that this succession and that of the episcopate together "are essential for the true functioning of the body of Christ, and *it is through their interaction that the life of the Church on earth is accomplished*" [my emphasis].

Both Macrina and Melania provide examples of such interaction: if Macrina can be credited with giving the Church St. Basil the Great, then we could say that Melania gave Evagrius to the Church.[14] This great ascetic writer spent an extended stay at her monastery as a deeply troubled young deacon, making himself sick with anguish over whether to pursue or abandon his monastic vocation; and it was her timely guidance and her prayers that enabled him to resolve this inner conflict.

Melania, as an abbess, was a laywoman in a particularly prominent position. But it needs to be emphasized that there are no formal prerequisites for the role of spiritual guide and intercessor. I have in mind a very powerful example from Russia in the 1930s. Matrionushka was born without limbs and blind from the age of two, and she is known from the account of a doctor who later became a bishop.[15] When he was threatened with an extension of his stay in prison camp, a fellow believer advised him to seek the help of a holy woman from her home town: "Cry out three times, 'Matrionushka, help me! . . . .'" he was told. "She will hear you and help you." So on being freed shortly afterwards, the doctor goes to visit her in the little house where she spends her days lying in a box on the table. She recognizes him instantly, even though they had never met. The two talked for a long time; he found in her untold strength and comfort for the road that lay ahead of him, and confessed himself "staggered" at her wisdom, discernment and spiritual stature. As they parted, she said to him: "When you stand before the altar of God, remember the servant of God Matrona." Ordination had never entered his mind at that time; but when the prospect did arise, there can be little doubt that he remembered the holy woman's words. In a backhanded acknowledgement of her importance for the suffering Church, the authorities later dragged this outwardly helpless woman off to prison, where she died.

Concern for unity in truth

I want to return to the concern for the unity of the Church and integrity of its faith that was also such a marked feature of Melania the Elder's life. Her granddaughter and namesake,[16] who followed closely is her footsteps, followed her also in this respect. An avid reader of Scripture and whatever other theological writings she could lay hands on,[17] bilingual in Latin and Greek, the younger St. Melania must have been as well equipped as anyone to give an account of her faith; and she seems to have lost no opportunity to do so. By her time, it was the Nestorian heresy rather than the Arian that threatened the Church, but again, it was competing with orthodox faith for imperial support. We learn that Melania had lengthy discussions with the ladies of the imperial household, winning over those who had fallen for Nestorius' teaching and strengthening those who were wavering.[18] So great was her zeal for orthodox faith that she once refused to receive Holy Communion from her chaplain because he had commemorated in the Liturgy a woman reputed to have had heretical sympathies. We are not likely to find such rigor edifying. But that should not blind us to the degree of commitment and "ownership" that it reveals. Here is a practical illustration of the principle that the whole body of the Church is the protector of the faith: the integrity of the Church is too important a matter to be left only to the clergy, even where liturgical matters are involved. I would suggest that precisely the same ecclesial consciousness was being played out, at the opposite end of the ecumenical spectrum, some years ago in the Anglican/Orthodox Fellowship of St. Alban and St. Sergius, when a small group led by founder-member Militza Zernov insisted that Orthodox Liturgies at the Fellowship Conference should be interrupted just before Communion by the reading of Fr. Sergei Bulgakov's prayer of repentance for Christian disunity.

If we are talking about lay responsibility for maintaining the unity-in-truth of the Church, it is clear that such a responsibility rested to a unique degree upon the shoulders of emperors/empresses of the Christian Roman Empire. It should be noted very clearly that the emperor did not dictate the faith of the Church; but he (or, in several cases, she) inevitably exerted a major influence on the process of formulating and proclaiming that faith.

Most Christians in the West today probably feel uncomfortable with the whole idea of a ruler's involvement in Church life. But three points should be made:

1) It is almost inevitable that when there are dissensions or factions among believers, decisions made by civil authorities will have some effect on the outcome.

2) The question of interest here is not: *Should* a ruler have an influence on church life?, but rather: How does a anyone whose decisions have an impact on the unity and welfare of the Church make responsible use of that influence?

3) In Byzantium, we are not talking about rulers of a secularized state influencing from the outside the life of a religious community to which they do not belong; we are talking about church members whose civic position gives them a particularly important role in the life of a body to which they do belong.

It is a noteworthy fact that three out of seven Ecumenical Councils, plus the Council that actually succeeded in restoring the veneration of icons (Constantinople, 843), were actually or effectively convened by empresses. The first of these remarkable women, St. Pulcheria,[19] is a good example of a civil ruler for whom churchmanship definitely came first. Her active involvement in the Councils of Ephesus and Chalcedon was consistent with the whole tenor of her life. Orphaned at a young age, she organized her sisters into a sort of domestic monastery, vowing herself (and them) to virginity when she was 14. This had the added advantage of keeping ambitious would-be suitors at bay; but the simplicity of her life, and the extensive philanthropic work that went with it, indicate that Pulcheria's dedication to celibacy was not a mere political ploy. On the other hand, she clearly believed that she could fulfill her vocation better in the palace as Augusta than in a monastery.[20] She was probably right. She was evidently gifted with more theological acumen that her brother, the emperor Theodosius II, who contrived to be persuaded first by Nestorius and then, a few years later, by Eutyches. It was to her that first St. Cyril of Alexandria[21] and later Pope St. Leo of Rome wrote, in quite technical language, explaining the doctrinal issues at stake in the Nestorian and Monophysite controversies respectively.[22]

Pulcheria's support for, and encouragement of, the Council of Ephesus was undoubtedly linked to her own personal devotion to the Mother of God. That Council marks the victory of veneration for the Virgin, which was probably seen by many, Pulcheria included, as the basis for women's dignity in the Church. There is a telling (though possibly apocryphal) story of an encounter between the empress and Nestorius. One Easter, as she was going to receive Communion in the sanctuary, as her custom was, the bishop barred her way. "Have I not given birth to God?" says Pulcheria; to which Nestorius replies, "You have given birth to the devil!"[23] We do not know what was going on in Pulcheria's mind, but the language is less that of a princess pushing her privileges and more that of a churchwoman claiming her rightful dignity as exemplified by the Mother of God—her freedom to accept whatever calling God has given her.

The calling, in Pulcheria's case, was the defense of Orthodoxy. Her brother, the emperor, died while there was still unfinished business with the Eutychian heresy. Since it would have been thought irregular for Pulcheria to continue ruling alone, she took a consort—which raised some eyebrows, even though he promised to respect her vows of virginity. It may well be that she risked appearing to compromise herself in this way specifically in order to see the Council of Chalcedon through to a successful conclusion.[24]

But there was also another woman who played a key role in the story of Chalcedon. Pulcheria had chosen the site so that the Council would be under the patronage of the local saint, the virgin-martyr Euphemia (whose relics were a major focus of veneration there, and now lie in great honor in the Patriarchal Church in Constantinople). The roles played by the saints in the Church is a major subject on its own, which we cannot cover here; but the case of Euphemia is worth mentioning, as a reminder that we cannot make rigid divisions between the living and the departed when considering the life of the Church. There is a story that she miraculously indicated which of the proposed definitions was correct,[25] but this appears only in much later versions of her *Life*, and its authenticity is suspect. There the matter might rest, were it not for some much more recent evidence of her particular concern with resolving conflicts in the Church. The well-known Athonite elder Fr. Paisios (+1994) had been having difficulties with a bishop in Thessaloniki, when there was a knock on the door of his cell late one night: there on his doorstep was St. Euphemia. Finally she managed to satisfy him that she was not some demonic hallucination; they talked all night, and in the course of the conversion she was able to show him how to resolve his problems with the bishop.[26]

Resisting iconoclasm: The body of the Church defends its faith

Of all the doctrinal struggles to shake the Eastern churches, the iconoclast controversy affords the clearest example of the whole body of the people taking responsibility for defending the faith of the Church. It is a matter of debate how far iconoclasm was part of a deliberate ideological campaign to make the earthly emperor the prime locus of power.[27] But the struggle undoubtedly did reflect a clash of priorities: the iconoclast emperors saw the Church as a department of state to serve the interests of the empire, while the Church consciousness rejected the idea that the teaching of the Church, and the worship expressive of that teaching, can be tailored to political expediencies.[28] It can also be said that some strands in iconoclasm, at least, were concerned to truncate the Church by driving a wedge between the floor and the walls, so to speak—the living and the departed.[29]

On both fronts, the Church as a whole fought back. It has been observed that reference to "the Church" as protagonist, as the offerer of praise and petition, is particularly marked in hymnography dating from this period, such as the Kanon to the Mother of God by another Thecla, the nun and hymnographer.[30] If we wonder why the "grassroots" element was so strong in the resistance to iconoclasm, two reasons suggest themselves. First, there were of course hierarchs who opposed iconoclasm—

until they were removed. In any attempt on the part of the state to gain control over the Church, dealing with the hierarchy is the easy part. It is typical that the most intractable resistance comes from the mass of the people, which is much harder to replace or otherwise neutralize. And second, such resistance is most likely when, as here, the threat is directed against practical expressions of the Church's faith. Even people quite unsophisticated in articulating their faith can recognize when it is under threat, and they will defend it with their very bodies. Tradition attributes just such direct action to a group of nuns and secular women mobilized by the nun Theodosia to prevent the destruction of the famous icon of Christ over the Halki Gate. Arriving too late to head off the official sent to do the deed, the women shook the ladder, with the result that he fell to his death. The women were arrested and summarily executed.[31] There are doubts about the historicity of this particular incident,[32] but the existence of the story suggests strongly that such instances of direct action, often at great personal cost, did happen, as they still do. A Greek youth group visiting Russian Karelia in 1994 were introduced to a woman approaching her 100th birthday, the Eldress Varvara, who had spent twenty-five years living in a cemetery chapel to prevent its demolition, during which time she had of course been supported and provided for by an entire network of other Church members.[33]

The defeat of iconoclasm, however, required more than the dogged resistance of the laity; it required regime change. This came in the form of two empresses who outlived their iconoclast husbands. The Emperor (as she was styled) Eirene used her position to convene the Seventh Ecumenical Council and to neutralize, albeit temporarily, the power of the heavily iconoclast army.[34] She may have acted principally at the behest of the formerly iconoclast patriarch, who now announced that he had seen the error of his ways and was retiring to a monastery.[35] If so, that surely signifies a willingness to listen and accept guidance—qualities no less vital to the wellbeing of the Church than immovably obduracy in defence of truth. Her renewed encouragement of monasticism in the capital equally signals a readiness to allow the Church its freedom, however uncomfortable that might be for the civil rulers.[36]

Eirene's reign was followed by some sixty years of renewed iconoclasm; but they were years in which the ladies of the imperial house maintained the Orthodox tradition at the highest level, despite their iconoclast husbands, fathers, or sons. The historian Judith Herrin remarks that "there seems to be no equivalent example [in history] of three generations of women placing themselves at the head of what became a clearly identified movement, and succeeding against all the odds."[37] She does not attempt to explore why Byzantium should be uniquely distinguished for its empresses, but I would suggest that the reason is not unrelated to our subject.

In the 830s, the empress Theodora, wife of iconoclast emperor Theophilos, was quietly bringing her children up to venerate icons, aided and abetted by her stepmother-in-law.[38] When her husband died and she became regent, she overcame the conflicting pull of loyalty to his memory and moved to convene the Council at which the specter of iconoclasm was finally laid to rest. Theodora lacked the theological sophistication of a Pulcheria. But she represented the "silent (or silenced) majority" of church people who recognized loyalty to their faith as a higher calling than obedience to the emperor; and unlike commoners who shared her faith, she was in a position to remove the constraints upon the Church. On the other hand, she was also in a position to insist firmly on a degree of compromise and accommodation (not with iconoclast belief, but with its former protagonists) that was quite unpalatable to some of the most resolute champions of Orthodoxy[39] but probably did much to ensure that this resolution of the conflict actually endured. The freedom and peace thus granted to the Church of Constantinople laid the foundations, among other things, for the missionary work that was to change the face of Europe.[40]

Fools, elders and hierarchs: The power of humility

We have discussed several people who played important roles in championing and even defining the faith of the Church, making prudent use of their power and position in order to do so. However, as we all know, *defining* true faith in a way that is not misleading is only half the battle; true faith "on paper" is worth little if it is not lived out with integrity. It should not, however, be thought that only the defining is an ecclesial matter, whereas the "living out" is an individual matter. When it comes to integrity of Christian living, we also have a responsibility to edify each other, and here powerlessness and lack of position may sometimes be the best qualifications. I am thinking particularly of those who follow the strange and rare vocation of fools for Christ—people of such self-emptying that they are able to serve as God's instrument for humbling others, without damage to their own spiritual lives.

It is symptomatic that the earliest holy fool known to us does not even have a name,[41] though tradition later identifies her as Isidora. We are told simply that she lived in a large monastery near Tabennisi in Egypt; she was despised and abused by the other sisters and spent her time working in the kitchen, with a dishcloth tied round her head. And thus she might have ended her days, had not the holy anchorite Pitiroum been told by an angel to go to that monastery to meet someone whose spiritual stature surpassed his own, for "her heart never departs from God." All the sisters are duly summoned to meet him, but he is puzzled; someone must be missing. Finally they bring in the community's skivvy; the elder falls at her feet and begs for her blessing. A few days later the blessed fool, disturbed by the veneration that she is now receiving, slips away and is never seen again.

This story is quite reminiscent of the encounter between Zosimas and Mary of Egypt.[42] Both Pitiroum and Zosimas believed that they had attained great heights—they had something to give to the rest of the Church community. I think we miss the point of the stories if we are not prepared to accept that they were probably right. It is not only stumbling beginners in the spiritual way, but, no less, those who are far advanced, that need to learn from other, quite unexpected parts of Christ's body "how many and varied are the ways to salvation."[43] And conversely, those who are still imperfect, though some lack of humility, may nevertheless have much to teach the rest of us.

Even hierarchs may need on occasion to be corrected, and even in the way they minister to their flock. The divine grace that "completes that which is wanting" (prayer at ordination) may do so through all sorts of intermediaries. Again, the holy fool is an apt instrument. St. Seraphim of Sarov's beloved community of Diveyevo was watched over by two such people. The difficulties endured by this monastery in the years following the saint's death came to a head when the bishop arrived to depose the acting superior chosen by the sisters and install a quite unsuitable abbess; one of the holy fools abused him, much to his consternation, while the other slapped him in the face. The bishop did not change his mind, although the matter was soon taken out of his hands. But his refusal to allow either woman to be disciplined reflects a deep-seated conviction that "the voice of God does not always make itself heard through the hierarchy."[44]

It should not, of course, be inferred that the principle way of edifying one another is to rebuke other people; hence the need to reiterate that it is out of their utter humility that "fools" may on occasion usefully adopt such a course. The greatest contribution anyone can make to the building up of the Church is to acquire the mind of Christ. Without such a mind, the body will never function properly, and someone has to take the first step. Indeed, most of the Beatitudes could be summed up by saying: "blessed are those with whom the power games end." We find a remarkable example of such initiative in an elderly nun living in Russia in Soviet times, who had no alternative but to attend a church where she knew the priest to be an unbeliever. She would even go to confession to this priest; she considered this important, "as an example of humility and of the inadmissibility of splits in the Church."[45] *That* is leadership in the Church!

Mutual prayer: The lifeblood of the Church

So far, we have mentioned only briefly and in passing the primary and most important way in which all members participate fully in the Church—prayer. "Mutual prayer is the [life-]blood of the Church, and the glorification of God is her breath," writes Khomiakov.[46] This linkage is very important: there is total, seamless continuity between "private" prayer, and the worship offered by the gathered Church. In part perhaps because of the terrible pressures on the structures of the Church during the persecutions of the twentieth century, there seems to be a renewed awareness in our own times of the significance for the Church of the extra-liturgical prayer of all its members. One aspect of this is the development of the intercessory dimension of the "Jesus Prayer": "the old prayer in a new form," as it was characterized by a woman who learned this use of the prayer from nuns with whom she was imprisoned.[47] This intercession actually extends to the supremely churchly—we might actually say, sacramental—work of sanctifying and "de-polluting" the entire creation. One of the most striking brief expositions of the Jesus Prayer comes from Nadezhda Gorodetzky, an old friend and close associate of Fr. Lev Gillet. Introducing Western Christians to the Prayer in the dark days of the Second World War, she writes:

> We can apply this Name [of Jesus] to people, books, flowers, to all things we meet, see or think. The Name of Jesus may become a mystical key to the world, an instrument of the hidden offering of everything and everyone, setting the divine seal on the world. One might perhaps speak here of the priesthood of all believers. In union with our High Priest, we implore the Spirit: Make my prayer into a sacrament.[48]

It is surely significant that she refers to the *priesthood of all believers*—that quality conferred on all by virtue of their membership of the Church.

The conscientious exercise of such a universal priesthood is vital not only for the Church's work of offering up and sanctifying the world but also for the well being of the institution of the Church. It would be absurd to try to quantify the part played by the prayer of church members—living and departed—in the survival and eventual resurgence of churches under hostile regimes; but no believing Christian is likely to doubt that it was highly significant. Many of those heroes and heroines of prayer will be known only to God. Those known to humans as well include the three holy women of Korca in Albania.[49] Two of them (to the best of my knowledge) are still living. In the years when all religious observance was outlawed—traces of dyed eggshells near one's house after Easter could mean a lengthy spell in prison—these women kept in touch with the handful of priests who continued to serve secretly. After hearing a priest talk about praying ceaselessly, they decided to do precisely that. During Lent, and on various other occasions, they would divide the twenty-four hours into two-hour shifts. During each shift, one would be praying; one doing chores, sleeping, and so forth; and one guarding the door. Many people sought their intercessions. They lived to see the seemingly impossible: the restoration of freedom to the Church. Difficulties for the Church did not end with the fall of communism, however. The restoration of the Church required a synod of bishops; but there were no priests left in Albania who would be eligible for the office (Orthodox bishops are required to be celibate), and the government would not accept a complement of foreign hierarchs. The Archbishop called on all the people to pray for a resolution of this impasse. In response, the women's group in Korca embarked on one of their forty-day vigils; at the end of this period, the deadlock was broken when the government offered a compromise.[50]

Here we have an extraordinary parable in real life of the interdependence that characterizes the life of the Church in its deepest essence. The Church cannot function without a hierarchy: that is something obvious from the outside. Much less evident, however, is the fact that the hierarchy cannot function without the prayers and self-offering of the whole body—among the first, in this case, two elderly housewives.

Final thoughts on being the Church

It is time now to try to draw some threads together, and to describe some of the aspects of conciliarity that I have tried to illustrate.

1) First and foremost, *no one is saved alone.*[51] Even those who might seem to be the most isolated, the most tenuously related to Church structures, have a vital importance for the entire community, and in one way or another *depend on* the entire community. No one even walks the path of salvation alone, because the Way is also the Head of the body.

2) Pastoral care in the broadest sense, bearing one another's burdens, works in every direction. It is not simply that the hierarchy and clergy have a responsibility for the rest of us. Each of us has some responsibility for the spiritual well-being of the brothers and sisters around us, and also for that of the hierarchs. It is by our commu-

nal prayers, and our support in various ways, that they are enabled to fulfill their cru-cial role in the Church. That support may range from the highly sophisticated to very basic, practical acts of service; its nature depends more on circumstances than on our own ideas of what we have to offer. Besides the Pauline image of the hand, the foot and so on, we should also think in terms of being the body's stem cells—ready to adapt to whatever its needs may be.

3) The Spirit whose temple we together form is the *Spirit of truth*. The bishops have a unique responsibility for proclaiming the true faith; but the truth they proclaim dwells in the entire body. Being prepared to bear witness to our faith, in one way or another, is everyone's responsibility. It is everyone's responsibility to guard vigilantly against distortions of the Church's faith or attempts to water it down. Of course, this does not mean that every, or any, individual decides for him/herself what constitutes distortion. But it does mean that *concern* for the truth is never something that can be left solely to "experts."

4) Last, but by no means least, the conciliarity of the Church is inseparable from the oneness of the Church. In our plurality and diversity we are one body, one organ-ism; we are not merely diverse individuals who get on well enough together and agree to differ in a civil manner. This translates into a shared responsibility to maintain existing unity—to do whatever is in our power to heal and resolve conflicts, disagree-ments, and factions within the communion of the Church. And, of course, to avoid the various sorts of scandal which can drive people away from the Church. Breaking the unity of the Church is always an act of mutilation, however humanly justified it might seem under particular circumstances.

In consequence, a sense of the oneness of the Church also involves shared respon-sibility in respect of existing disunities. The conciliar consciousness of the Church cannot remain indifferent to the scandal of divisions between Christians. Nor can it rest content with an amiable coexistence that relegates unity of faith to a matter of aca-demic minutiae. A cooperation that stops short of oneness will always be seen as inad-equate. The prayer, and the task, of the whole body of the Church is "the good estate of the holy Churches of God and the union of all" (Litany in the Orthodox Liturgy).

Endnotes

[1]Cf. Georges Florovsky, "The Church: Her Nature and Task," reprinted in *Bible, Church, Tradition: An Eastern Orthodox View* (Belmont, MA: Notable and Academic Books, 1987), 58.

[2]The Acts of Paul and Thecla; William Hone (ed.), *The Lost Books of the Bible* (Avenel, NJ: Gramercy, reprint of 1906 edition), 99–111; hereinafter *AThe*.

[3]Extract from the *Historia Ecclesiastica* of Tyrannius Rufinus, Bk. I, ch. 10, tr. D.M. Lang, *Lives and Leg-ends of the Georgian Saints* (Oxford: Mowbrays, 1956, 1976), 15–19; see also extract from the Georgian *Life*, ibid., 19–39.

[4]Lang, p. 32. Even though the earlier *Life* has no reference to her baptizing, it has been plausibly argued that such a striking detail is more likely to reflect early tradition than later embroidery; see Paul Crego, "St Nino and the Role of Women in the Evangelization of the Georgians," *St. Nina Quarterly* 3.1 (Winter 1999): 3.

[5]See Gregory of Nyssa, *Life of St. Macrina*, PG 46: 959–1000; trans. in Joan Petersen, ed. and trans., *Handmaids of the Lord: Holy Women of Late Antiquity and the Early Middle Ages* (Cistercian Studies 143; Kalamazoo: Cistercian, 1996), 51–86; henceforth cited as Petersen followed by page number.

[6]Ibid., 68.

[7]Ibid., 61.

[8]Ibid., 68–69.

[9]Consecration address delivered by Bishop-elect Basil [of Sergievo] at his nomination at Vespers on Saturday, March 6, 1993; *Cathedral Newsletter* (London) no. 259, March 1993.

[10]See Palladius of Heliopolis, *Lausiac History*, 46; trans. in Petersen, *Handmaids*, 299–307. The chapters are numbered according to the 1904 edition of C. Butler. A Greek text appears in PG 34: 995–1250, but with the chapters in a completely different order.

[11]Giving basic, practical help and support to churchmen who are targets of persecution because of their prominence is not to be underestimated as a means whereby Church members can use their differing circumstances to benefit each other. Paladius refers to other such cases, including that of a young girl who hid St. Athanasius the Great for two years (*Lausiac History*, 63).

[12]Petersen, 303.

[13] Bishop Kallistos Ware, "The Spiritual Guide in Orthodox Christianity' " *The Inner Kingdom*, Collected Works, Vol. I (Crestwood, NY: St. Vladimir's Seminary Press, 2000), 131.

[14]See *Lausiac History*, 38.

[15]Bishop Stefan (Nikitin), "Matrionushka," *Sourozh* 15 (February 1984): 19–22 (trans. from *Nadezhda* 7 [1982]: 241–245). Author's note: "Matrionushka" is a diminutive form of "Matrona."

[16]On Melania the Younger see Palladius, *Lausiac History*, 61, trans. in Petersen, *Handmaids* 308–10; *Life* by Gerontius, trans. Petersen, *Handmaids* 311–361 (based on D. Gorce, ed., *Vie de sainte Melanie, Sources Chrétiennes* 90, Paris, 1962).

[17]Petersen, 327.

[18]Ibid., 346, 345.

[19]See Kenneth G. Holum, *Theodosian Empresses* (Berkeley and Los Angeles: University of California Press, 1981), 82–216.

[20]With the connivance of Archbishop Proclus, she resisted her sister-in-law's attempts to have her tonsured a deaconess (Holum, 192).

[21]"Letter to the Empresses," *Acta Conciliorum Oecumenicorum* I.5, 26–61.

[22]Holum, 203.

[23]Ibid., 152–153.

[24]As suggested by Holum, 216. As to her key role in the Council, it is significant that on two occasions, the assembled bishops reversed protocol by acclaiming first the empress and then the emperor (Holum, 215).

[25]In the course of the council, the texts of two rival definitions were placed on the saint's relics overnight: in the morning, the dyophysite definition was in her head and the monophysite definition under her feet (Synaxarion notice, 11 July).

[26]Kyriacos C. Markides, *The Mountain of Silence* (New York: Doubleday, 2002), 84–85.

[27]The various theories to explain the outbreak of iconoclasm are summarized in Alice-Mary Talbot, ed., *Byzantine Defenders of Images* (Washington, D.C.: Dumbarton Oaks, 1998), xii–xiii.

[28]Hence the iconoclasts' fierce and often brutal opposition to monasticism, which has traditionally been obstinately resistant to serving secular agendas of whatever sort. It is significant that Theodore of Stoudion, the leading monastic opponent of iconoclasm, formulates an understanding of monasticism as a "special ministry *of the Church*" (my italics), an example to the rest of the body (see Alexander Schmemann, *The Historical Road of Eastern Orthodoxy* (Crestwood, NY: St. Vladimir's Seminary Press, 1977), 212–213.

[29]It is not coincidental that one of the Empress Eirene's first acts on restoring the icons was to replace the relics of St. Euphemia, which had been thrown into the sea by order of Constantine V. See Charles Diehl, *Byzantine Empresses* (London: Elek Books, 1963), 76; Judith Herrin, *Women in Purple: Rulers of Medieval Byzantium* (Princeton and Oxford: Princeton University Press, 2001), 98.

[30]Eva Catafygiotu Topping, "Thekla the Nun: In Praise of Woman," in *Holy Mothers of Orthodoxy* (Minneapolis: Light and Life Publishing, 1987), 15–16, 27, n. 39.

[31]N. Constas, trans., Synaxarion notice of St. Theodosia of Constantinople [18 July], in Talbot, *Defenders*, 5–7.

[32]Constas, in Talbot, *Defenders*, 1–2.

[33]Archim. Nektarios Antonopoulos, *Rosoi Neomartyres kai Omologetes 1917–1922* [Russian New Martyrs and Confessors, 1917–1922] (Athens: Akritas, 2000), 70–71.

[34]See Diehl, *Byzantine Empresses*, 65–93; Steven Runciman, "The Empress Irene the Athenian," in Derek Barker, ed., *Medieval Women* (Oxford: Basil Blackwell, 1978); Herrin, *Women in Purple*, 72–152.

[35]Ibid., 83.

[36]Herrin, after arguing that Eirene's efforts to restore the icons owed more to the patriarch's *volte-face* than to her own long-standing convictions, reaches the puzzling conclusion that the empress' policy "appears to be in line with the general subordination of theological matters to political needs in Byzantium during the eighth century" (ibid., 85)

[37]Ibid., 3.

[38]On Theodora, see Diehl, *Byzantine Empresses*, 94–113; Herrin, *Women in Purple*, 202ff. On the dowager empress Euphrosyne, see Herrin, 153ff.

[39]Cf. Diehl, 102–104 (a rather cynical account). We see the empress promising to "rule with a firm hand" when confronted by Symeon the Stylite of Lesbos, who refused to accept the compensation set aside for exiled confessors and to intercede for her departed husband; D. Domingo-Forasté, trans., "Life of Sts. David, Symeon and George of Lesbos," ch. 27, in Talbot, *Defenders*, 213–215.

[40]Cf. Diehl, 105; Dimitri Obolensky, *The Byzantine Commonwealth: Eastern Europe 500–1453* (London: Sphere Books, 1974), 101ff. On initial missionary contacts with the Bulgarians, see Herrin, 218.

[41]See *Lausiac History*, 34: "The woman who pretended to be a fool."

[42]*Life of St. Mary of Egypt* chs. II, IX–X, in Benedicta Ward, S.L.G., *Harlots of the Desert* (Kalamazoo: Cistercian, 1987), 37–38, 42–43. Mary, a former prostitute, lived in total isolation in the desert for seventeen years; she was discovered by "chance" by Zosimas, a monk of great spiritual attainments who had been wondering whether anyone on earth could edify him further. When they met, each begged the other's blessing.

[43]Ibid., 38.

[44]Valentine Zander, *St. Seraphim of Sarov* (London: SPCK, 1975), 130–131.

[45]Sergei Fudel, *Light in the Darkness* (Crestwood, NY: St. Vladimir's Seminary Press, 1989), 98.

[46]Alexy Khomiakov, *The Church Is One* (London: Fellowship of St. Alban and St. Sergius, 1968), §§ 9, 41; cf. § 38ff.

[47]C. Babington-Smith, *Iulia de Beausobre: A Russian Christian in the West* (London: Darton, Longman and Todd, 1983), 38–39; the "Jesus Prayer" centers on the name of Jesus and usually takes the form: "Lord, Jesus Christ, be merciful to me [a sinner]."

[48]N. Gorodetzky, "The Prayer of Jesus," *Blackfriars* xxiii, no. 263 (1942): 76. This article is quoted at some length in Gillet's much better known *The Jesus Prayer*, by A Monk of the Eastern Church (rev. edition; Crestwood, NY: St. Vladimir's' Seminary Press 1987), 88–90.

[49]Luke Veronis, "Personal Reflections on Life in the Missionary Field," *Again Magazine* 22.1 (Jan.–Mar. 2000): 17–18; private communications from Fr. Luke Veronis and Dr. Peter Gilbert, both formerly of the Resurrection of Christ Academy, Durres.

[50]There is also another woman whose sacrifice is crucial to this story: The compromise offered by the government required that two bishops should be Albanians, and this could be achieved only if Fr. Kosma, an elderly priest who had served all through the persecutions, would separate from his wife so as to be consecrated bishop. After much prayer, Fr. Kosma and his wife agreed to this for the good of the Church.

[51]Cf. Khomiakov, §§ 9, 38.

PART 5

Ecclesiology:
Word and Silence

16

Orthodox Ecclesiology from the Perspective of Preaching

J. Sergius Halvorsen

What does ecclesiology have to do with preaching?

"Preaching" and "ecclesiology" are two words that are not often found in the same sentence, let alone as the subject of a chapter in a book. "Preaching," on the one hand, describes a very concrete activity: it is applied pastoral theology that always involves real people, living in families and communities, dealing with real-life challenges. On the other hand, "ecclesiology" is one of the more slippery words in theological discourse, and it often comes with the connotation of being somewhat abstract, vague, and perhaps even a bit boring. However, as the title of the chapter implies, the task at hand is to approach the subject of Orthodox ecclesiology homiletically; or in other words investigate how Orthodox ecclesiology is established and shaped by preaching in a concrete and pastorally relevant way.

While the modern connotations of "ecclesiology" may be abstract and philosophical, the Greek roots of the word are not. If the Church (*ekklesia*) is the community that is "called out" by God's Word, then it is through preaching that God continues to call his people out of the world of sin and death. It is through the bold, persuasive, kerygmatic preaching of the gospel of Jesus Christ that people are initially called to follow Jesus Christ, and called into the Church, and it is also through preaching that the Christian community is strengthened and fortified to fulfill the evangelical mandate that Christ gives his disciples. St. John Chrysostom (347–407), a likely source for an Orthodox Christian perspective on preaching and whose preaching is the primary focus of this chapter, accords the highest honor to the power of the spoken word in his discussion of priestly ministry.

St. John compares the spiritual work of caring for the body of Christ to the physical effort that athletes devote to their training. However, according to St. John the pastor's task is even more difficult, since he is not contending with flesh and blood but against the unseen powers of evil. Moreover, the body of Christ is even more prone to disease and vulnerable to attack than our flesh, and it can become infected more quickly and takes longer to be cured. The physician treating ailments of the flesh has a myriad of tools and treatment options at his disposal, which can be used to diagnose and treat injuries and illnesses: medical instruments, drugs, surgery, rehabilitation therapy, dietary modification, a change of climate for the patient, or even something as simple as a good night's sleep. However, the pastor has only one resource with which to affect the cure of the human soul.

> When all is said and done, there is only one means and only one method of treatment available, and that is teaching by word of mouth. That is the best instrument, the best diet, and the best climate. It takes the place of medicine, cautery and surgery. When we need to cauterize or cut, we must use this. Without it all else is useless. By it we rouse the soul's lethargy or reduce its inflammation, we remove excrescences and supply defects, and, in short, do everything which contributes to its health.[1]

Building up the body of Christ, "training it up to perfect health and incredible beauty"[2] and strengthening it to fulfill God's commission, is the fundamental task of the preacher, and thus the ultimate purpose for preaching. St. John Chrysostom refers to preaching as that which provides a rich spiritual banquet to feed the faithful.[3] Through preaching, a meaningful understanding of the Church, and most importantly, a meaningful understanding of one's place within the Church is cultivated in the mind of the faithful. Orthodox ecclesiology, from the perspective of preaching, seeks to answer the questions What does it mean for me to be a member of the Church? What does Christ command and empower me to do as a member of his body?

As has been said by many, Christians preach because Christ preached, and because he commanded his disciples to do so as well. If one boils down Christ's preaching to its most direct form, then the message to the Church and of the Church is: "Repent, for the kingdom of heaven is at hand."[4] However, being the Church is not a static but an essentially dynamic and evangelical reality, as evident in Christ's commission to the disciples:

> Go therefore and make disciples of all nations, baptizing them in the name of the Father and of the Son and of the Holy Spirit, teaching them to observe all that I have commanded you; and lo, I am with you always, to the close of the age."[5]

The so-called "Great Commission" is in fact a wonderful summary of an Orthodox ecclesiology from the perspective of preaching. Christians, whom Christ sends (*apostello*) into the world, call the people to repent from their sins and join a new community of adherents to the teaching of Jesus, who are sacramentally united to God—Father, Son and Holy Spirit—through baptism. This is not an abstract business. The sins from which people must repent are real and concrete, and the grace and hope which God promises and gives to those who follow him, are also real and concrete. Therefore, since preaching is the act of calling the people out of the world into the kingdom of God, ecclesiology, from the perspective of preaching, involves not only defining what the Church *is* and what one *should* do, but also what the Church is *not* and what one *should not* do. Moreover, the goal of preaching is to persuade the hearer to take concrete action in his or her life and follow Christ: therefore static definitions of the fallen world and the Church are not sufficient. Effective preaching inspires one to leave the former and enter the latter.

The rhetorical component of preaching, the act of persuading the faithful to follow Christ, to "lay aside all earthly cares that we may receive the King of all,"[6] is that which sets preaching apart from more "objective" or scientific forms of discourse. This is not to say that scientific discourse is not interested in persuasion, since there is a vested interest in proving the veracity of certain ideas over other competing ideas. However, preaching is far less circumspect in its rhetorical intent. Like political discourse, preaching is an open and direct attempt to persuade people to take concrete action. If a lecture on a cutting-edge theory on the thermodynamics of combustion is scientific discourse, then preaching is like being awakened in the middle of the night by a firefighter who tells you that your high-rise hotel is on fire. Therefore, to address Orthodox ecclesiology from the perspective of preaching requires an examination of the action that the preacher is asking the hearer to take: how preaching calls people out of the fallen world and into the kingdom of God.

Orthodox preaching: St. John Chrysostom

"Orthodox Christian" preaching comprises an extremely large body of work, the majority of which has never been written down. For close to two thousand years, across several continents and in more than a dozen languages, Orthodox Christian preachers have used the spoken word to shape and guide the Church. Acknowledging that numerous trends and practices exist within the Orthodox Christian tradition of preaching, and acknowledging that an attempt to summarize them would be entirely impractical in this investigation, I have chosen to focus primarily on the *Baptismal Instructions*[7] by St. John Chrysostom, because they offer two distinct advantages in this examination of Orthodox ecclesiology from the perspective of preaching.

The first advantage is that the man on whom the Church has bestowed the title "Golden Mouth" is arguably one of the most successful preachers that ever lived. For twelve years (386–397) he was the dominant preacher in Antioch, and from 398 to 404 he had an illustrious though stormy tenure as the Archbishop of Constantinople.[8] Over nine hundred of his sermons are extant,[9] the majority of which come from the period in which he served the church in Antioch. After St. John died on a forced march to exile on 14 September 407, St. John's supporters labored for thirty years officially to rehabilitate his memory, and in 438 his relics were ceremoniously returned to Constantinople, where he was interred in the Church of the Holy Apostles, the traditional burial place of bishops and emperors.[10] It is interesting to note that St. John's rehabilitation and canonization were not directly tied to the resolution of any particular theological controversy or schism,[11] and even today, he is not regarded for novel theological articulation. Rather, his renown, both during his life and following his death, has always been for his preeminence as a preacher and pastor of the Church.

The second advantage to using the *Baptismal Instructions* of St. John Chrysostom in this investigation is that these sermons focus entirely on issues related to becoming a Christian: the transition from unbeliever, to catechumen, to Christian. As such the *Instructions* define both the process of entering the Church as well as defining the Church into which the neophytes are being grafted. One could object that sermons on baptismal instructions are not a helpful place to look for a preacher's view on ecclesiology, because they are only addressed to newcomers and a more mature ecclesiology could be found in sermons addressed to a different audience. While Orthodox ecclesiology can undoubtedly be found in other sermons, preaching that directly addresses the sacramental transition from "non-believer" to "Christian" serves as a benchmark for Orthodox ecclesiology. Furthermore, for St. John, the Church is a community of "newly baptized" who continually retain the freshness of their conversion; it does not wear off:

> For the rest of my discourse I wish to direct my words to the newly baptized. By newly baptized I mean not only those who have just been judged worthy of the gift of the Spirit, but also those who received it a year or more ago. For if they should be willing, they too will be able to enjoy this title [newly baptized] continuously. For this newness does not know old age nor is it subject to disease. It is not overcome by despondency, nor is it eclipsed by time. It yields to nothing, it is conquered by nothing except sin alone. Sin is for it the weight of years.[12]

St. John is using the term "new" not in the sense of an interval of time, but rather in the sense of something being pure and untainted (e.g. "Fresh as the new fallen snow"). In this sense, one may have been baptized ten years ago, and still be "newly baptized." Indeed, it is the hope that throughout one's entire life, he or she would always be "newly baptized" since the only reason that one would no longer enjoy the newness of baptism would be because he or she had fallen into sin.

This timeless definition of the "newly baptized" is an ideal introduction to an Orthodox ecclesiology from the perspective of preaching.[13] A new member of the Church steps into a timeless reality, or rather, a reality in which time is transformed, and transfigured. Unlike the fallen world where new things quickly become old (new house, new clothes, new job), the Church offers the possibility of a life in which nothing grows stale, in which one's relationship with God never grows cold. The Church is a dynamic reality—the inauguration of the new heaven and the new earth, the new Jerusalem where tears are wiped away, death is no more, crying and pain have passed away, and the Lord says, "Behold I make all things new."[14]

> Vessels and pails measure the water drawn from natural springs; the water from the spiritual fountains is measured by our understanding, our fervent desire, and the sobriety with which we approach them. He who comes with these dispositions straightway carries away blessings beyond number, since the grace of God, working invisibly, lightens the burden of his conscience, brings him abundant assurance, and prepares him henceforth to put off from the shore of the earth and to weigh anchor for heaven. For it is possible for a man who is still in the embrace of his body to have nothing in common with the earth, but to set before his eyes all the joys of heaven and to contemplate them unceasingly.[15]

This is the Orthodox ecclesiology that St. John Chrysostom presents in his sermons to the "newly baptized," both in the temporal and spiritual sense. However, as nice and glorious as it all sounds, there is one problem—*sin*.

The problem of sin

When Orthodox Christians start talking about the kingdom of God, and about the holy mysteries, and about *theosis* and *synergia* and divine energies, and the One Holy Catholic and Apostolic Church, there are some who may say to themselves, "Dear Lord, here we go again!" This is not to say that there is anything questionable or inappropriate about such teachings, for indeed these are some of the pillars of the Orthodox Christian tradition. However, when speaking of such things, it is all too easy to overlook the problem of sin and fall into a thinly veiled kind of triumphalism. In an academic context, triumphalism is considered "bad form," at the very least. But, when preachers ignore the problem of sin and preach triumphalism, there are grave spiritual consequences.

Because everyone likes to think highly of himself or herself, the smallest hint of triumphalism in preaching can easily tempt the hearers to believe that they have "arrived" at spiritual perfection merely by the virtue of their presence in church on Sunday morning, and therefore they are entitled to take all manner of liberty concerning their personal life and ethical behavior. Preaching that ignores sin promotes a false ecclesiology of triumphalism of the worst kind that leads people down the first terrible steps towards *jihad*. Lurking in the heart of every person is a demon of triumphalism so cunning and so clever that even when a community receives the very best preaching possible, there is still a danger that people will consider themselves above reproach, and without need of spiritual and moral correction.

One of the earliest recorded instances of a response to this kind of triumphalistic distortion of the Christian faith is St. Paul's admonition to the church in Corinth. First, through an ironic complement, he chastises them for assuming that they have more authority than the apostles,[16] and then he directly addresses their lapses in sexual morality, conflict resolution among the brethren, and community life as manifested in shabby eucharistic piety.[17] According to St. Paul, members of the Corinthian community made some tragic miscalculations regarding the Church into which they had been baptized. He takes great pains to explain that initiation into the body of Christ[18] by baptism does *not* mean that "anything goes," and even in cases where the gospel does allow for certain freedom (in this case regarding what one eats), ultimately the welfare of one's neighbor is the highest priority.[19] For St. Paul, baptism is a free gift of salvation in Jesus Christ, *not* a free ticket to the excesses of life.

St. John Chrysostom repeatedly conveys the same idea throughout the *Instructions*. He alludes to this when he speaks about the Christian as the perpetual "neophyte," defining youthfulness as a spiritual virtue and age as the result of sin.

> It is possible, then, for one who is an old man according to the age of his body to be a young man and a neophyte because of the bloom of grace. It is also possible for one who is young in years to be old and bent under the multitude of sins. For wherever sin finds an entrance, it produces many a stain and many a wrinkle.[20]

In other words, just because one is baptized, it does not mean that sin is a thing of the past.

> Imitate [St. Paul], I beg you, and you will be able to be called newly baptized not only for two, three, ten or twenty days, but you will be able to deserve this greeting after ten, twenty, or thirty years have passed and, to tell you the truth, through your whole life. If we shall be eager to make brighter by good deeds the light within us—I mean the grace of the Spirit—so that it is never quenched, we shall enjoy the title of newly baptized for all time. But just as the sober and vigilant man whose conduct is worthy can continue to be a neophyte, so is it possible after a single day for a man to relax his vigilance and become unworthy of that title.[21]

Remarkably, in the *Instructions* St. John makes direct reference to newly baptized people who, during Bright Week,[22] have already foregone attendance of the divine services in favor of spectacles.

> Again there are chariot races and satanic spectacles in the hippodrome, and our congregation is shrinking. It is on this account and because I feared and anticipated the negligence which comes from ease and security that I exhorted you and encouraged you in your love not to squander the wealth you had won by fasting, nor to inflict on yourselves the outrage which comes from Satan's spectacles. As it seems, no profit came to you from this exhortation. See how some who heard my previous instruction have today rushed away. They gave up the chance to hear this spiritual discourse and have run off to the hippodrome. They have cast altogether out of their minds the memory of the holy season of Lent, the feast of salvation on the day of the Resurrection, their awesome and ineffable communion in the divine mysteries and my series of instructions.[23]

What a remarkable turn of events! Some of the people who had just a few days before been baptized and chrismated, who had put on Christ, who had been made members of the One Holy Catholic and Apostolic Church and received Christ's precious Body and Blood, have now opted to attend "Satan's spectacles" instead of the liturgical services. What does this say of baptism? Moreover, what does this say of the Church? What does it mean to be a member of the body of Christ, if, so shortly after receiving profound sacramental grace, one can traipse off to the hippodrome, ostensibly in search of another Constantinopolitan thrill after having experienced what the Christians had to offer? In another sermon, St. John refers to a different manifestation of the same basic problem. In this instance, a number of people in his congregation have begun speaking against him and siding with a rival preacher in Constantinople who was not in communion with St. John.[24]

> [W]hen they have attained maturity in this church, some never attend church again or do so only once a year (and then, at random and when they feel like it); others, while they attend more frequently, do so in a random and frivolous fashion too, talking and making witty comments about nothing. Others again make a good show of being zealous, yet they're the very ones who are the agents of this disaster. If, then, it's for these reasons that you're zealous, it would be better for you too to be ranked with those who don't care.[25]

St. John's unabashed confrontation of the problem of members of the community turning away from the teachings of Christ, and turning away from the community itself, throws cold water on the smoldering coals of triumphalism. Even those who were received into the Christian faith through the "awe inspiring rite of initiation" after having been catechized by St. John Chrysostom himself, could just walk away in search of "better things" elsewhere.

Faithful or unfaithful

On a philosophical level, concrete pastoral dilemmas like those addressed by St. John Chrysostom, can lead to a discussion of ecclesiology that defines the Church in eschatological terms of the "already-and-not-yet." In order to speak of the Church in terms of the "already-and-not-yet" means that one needs to imagine that he or she is looking at the Church as an impartial observer. "Over here with the Holy Trinity, Mary the Theotokos and the saints—the Church Vigilant—we have the 'already.' But, over here, among bishops and priests and deacons, and laypeople who are living and struggling right now—the Church Militant—we find the 'not yet.'" Once this dual reality has been set up, the next step is often to refer to "the tension between already and not yet." On a philosophical level, this model is helpful inasmuch as it describes the internal tug-of-war that exists within any Christian who takes his life of faith seriously. "I do not do the good I want, but the evil I do not want is what I do."[26] However, from the perspective of preaching, the "already-and-not-yet" model is very weak rhetoric.

In preaching, you can't really get people to see from two perspectives simultaneously,[27] and therein lies the real downfall of the "already/not yet" paradigm. If a preacher uses imagery that requires someone to look at the problem as an impartial observer, somewhere "out there" where he or she can look down on the Holy Trinity and the saints, then the preacher is actually asking the hearers, albeit momentarily, to dissociate themselves from the dynamic of salvation.[28] However, when one puts oneself back into the drama, there is an existential conundrum. "If I am 'already,' how can I be 'not-yet'?" Within the Orthodox Christian context, it would be very easy for a preacher to use "mystery" as a way out of this existential dilemma, "How can you be already-and-not-yet? Oh, it is a 'mystery.'" The recourse to "mystery" can be a powerful and effective theological strategy, particularly when dealing with subjects that are, by definition, beyond the bounds of total human comprehension (for example, the divine nature, the hypostatic union, the Lord's Supper).[29] However, even though explaining the "already-and-not-yet" paradigm as a mystery is not theologically incorrect, it makes weak rhetoric even weaker.

Psychologically, people are inherently uncomfortable with tension of any kind, and they will do just about anything to find a resolution. There may be some who find the so-called "mystery" of the "tension between already-and-not-yet" to be helpful, and their particular response to the "tension" may lead them to a more committed, virtuous Christian life. However, the vast majority of people, seeking to resolve the tension that has been created, will be lead to one of the following three outcomes: 1) If the person is prone to depression, he or she might lament that they are wretched, and that because they seem to be forever stuck in the "not-yet," this may be, "One more piece of evidence for why God doesn't really love me"; 2) It is possible that the person will ignore the whole issue entirely as being too complex and "theological"; or 3) They will surreptitiously put themselves in the "already" camp and then they will thank God that they are not like those poor folks who "out there" in the "not-yet."[30] Once again triumphalism rears its ugly head.

Since the goal of preaching is to inspire the hearer to live in obedience to the gospel of Jesus Christ, the "already-not-yet" imagery is not at all helpful for an understanding of Orthodox Christian ecclesiology from the perspective of preaching, and it is notable that St. John Chrysostom does not use this kind of imagery in the *Instructions*. Instead, he uses imagery that defines the Church as a community of persons who have received great favor and great responsibility from God through Christ's perfect self-sacrifice on the cross. Having received this great gift, having received this Great Commission, the question is not about being "already" or "not yet." Rather, the question is, "Am I going to be faithful to the commands of the One who delivered me from bondage to sin and death by his precious Body and Blood?" The fact that some of the newly baptized leave the Church is definitely a pastoral crisis for St. John, one which he addresses head on, but it is not a theological or ecclesiological crisis. These persons received a Great Commission, a great gift from the Author of Life, and because "He does not force his mastership,"[31] everyone who freely becomes a member of the Church is just as free to leave. It is not a question of ecclesiology; it is a question of faithfulness.

Thus, the imagery that St. John uses is never passive, never static. The gift of salvation cannot be comfortably stashed in the bank. Rather, inherent to salvation is divine *leitourgia*, the work of God, a mission that God gives a person to do on God's behalf. Orthodox Christian ecclesiology from the perspective of preaching, and particularly the preaching of St. John Chrysostom, defines the Church as those persons who have been freed from slavery to the devil in order to be slaves of Christ (*doulos christou*)[32] who have been given power, grace, and strength to do the bidding of God.

Imagery of the Church

One of the most powerful images that St. John uses, and one he uses most frequently, is that of a newly enlisted soldier. He speaks of a "marvelous," "most unusual,"[33] "spiritual enlistment"[34] of the "new soldiers of Christ, both men and women—for the army of Christ knows no distinction of sex."[35] The military image of newly enlisted warriors of Christ is tremendously powerful since it conveys both a sense of great honor and immanent action. Unlike an earthly army in which only free men are able to enlist, Christ accepts those who heretofore have been under bondage to Satan.[36] Thus, to become a Christian, to receive the grace of holy baptism, is to be commissioned by God to fight on his behalf, even though one may be far less than an ideal candidate. St. John's military rhetoric is designed to function just like that of a military commander who seeks to inspire his troops and convince them that even though the odds may not appear to be on their side, in fact they already possess an advantage over the enemy.

> Like valiant and vigilant soldiers of the Spirit, shine up your spiritual weapons each day so that the enemy may see the glitter of your arms, retreat far off, and never even consider making a stand from close at hand. When he sees not only that your armor shines but that you are prepared to defend yourselves on every side, when he sees that the treasure house of your understanding has been carefully secured, he will cover his face and go away, knowing that it will profit him nothing even if he tries ten thousand attacks.[37]

Throughout his sermons on baptismal instructions St. John goes to great lengths to convey the idea that a Christian is one who has been set apart. To become a member of Christ's Holy Church is to enter a new reality, albeit, one from which each member may freely walk away at any time. In his preaching, St. John never even hints at the much later notion regarding "parts of a sacrament," such as an "outward and sensible sign" or an "inward and spiritual grace."[38] Rather, he acknowledges that baptism works a very real and profound change in ones' relationship to Christ, and on this change in relationship every other change is dependent.

> Let us, then, no longer stay gaping after the good things of this life, such as luxurious foods and expensive clothing. For you have the greatest of garments, you have a spiritual banquet, you have the glory which comes from on high; Christ has become all things for you: table, clothing, house, head and root. For all you who have been baptized into Christ have put on Christ.[39]

Just like the aforementioned military imagery, St. John presents this imagery of the new relationship one has with Christ through baptism as a means of bolstering his initial exhortation to no longer to lust after the "good things of this life." This change that God works in one's life through baptism and chrismation is a change in relationship to God; it is a "quantum leap" from estrangement to divine intimacy, which is always a catalyst for concrete action.

Throughout the *Instructions* St. John uses a variety of images to establish this idea of "a new relationship," and in every instance, the change in relationship is always directly linked with concrete moral and ascetical action.

> We have been enrolled as citizens of another state, the heavenly Jerusalem. Therefore, let us show forth works worthy of that state, so that by these works, through which we practice virtue and invite others to glorify the Master, we may win an abundance of favor from above.[40]

As with the above examples, whether St. John is using imagery of marriage,[41] or bearers of the imperial insignia,[42] or those who now see the world with spiritual eyes and perceive value not on the world's terms, but on God's terms,[43] the goal is always the same: to convey to the hearer the idea that God has bestowed a great honor upon one completely undeserving such a gift. And, most importantly, with this honor comes a tremendous responsibility to embrace the spiritual life, to engage in the ascetical struggle against impurity and evil, and in all things to be obedient to the commands of Jesus Christ.

St. John not only speaks of the gifts that God bestows upon the individual Christian, but he also shows how divine gifts are to be regarded in light of the Christian community. He directly addresses this in his discussion of the baptismal rite, which includes a renunciation of Satan.[44]

> [A]ll these gifts are given to all of you in common, so that the rich man may not look down on the poor man, nor the poor man consider that he has any less than the rich man; for in Christ Jesus there is neither male nor female, there is no Scythian, no barbarian, no Jew, no Greek; not only is there no difference of age or nature, but even every difference of honor is canceled out; there is one esteem for all, one gift, one brotherhood binding us together, the same grace—so then, when you have all been led into [the church], then must you all together bend your knee and not stand erect; you must stretch your hands to heaven and thank God for this gift.[45]

Anytime there is a gathering of people, of any sort, people will instinctively try to figure out where they stand in the social hierarchy. "Am I richer or poorer, older or younger, stronger or weaker, more beautiful or ugly than the people around me?" And, certainly, this kind of thing can easily happen among Christians, all of whom are eager to see themselves as "more valuable," or "better" than their neighbor. However, St. John is very careful to show that each Christian person has been given such a tremendous gift and in the eyes of God has been raised up to a level of dignity infinitely higher than any worldly honor, that all value distinctions between persons, which may have existed prior to baptism, are reduced to nothing in comparison.

> Tell me, if the emperor happened to take ten individuals and dress them all in purple and sit them on the imperial throne and give all of them the same honor, which of the ten would dare disdain the other, on the grounds that they were richer or held greater prestige? None.[46]

St. John defines the Church as a community of equals, commissioned by God to carry out his will on earth.

However, it is very important to note that as St. John blasts the social hierarchy of the fallen world that so often dictates how people treat one another, he does not reject the hierarchical nature of the Church regarding ecclesiastical order and ministry. Arguing against a rival community for whom "ordination has disappeared and perished" he ironically proposes that if they are indeed members of the one true Church, then everyone should come forward, and serve as priests. Furthermore, he concludes that if anyone can serve as a priest, then it was in vain that this altar was built, and it was in vain that the fullness of the Church exists, and it was in vain that the number of priests exists. He concludes his argument with a bit of incendiary rhetoric.

> Let's take these things and destroy them. 'Heaven forbid!' someone says. You do the things that you do and you exclaim: 'Heaven forbid!'? How can you say: 'Heaven forbid!' while these very things are happening? I speak and I give testimony, not with a view to my own position, but with a view to your salvation.[47]

The ecclesiology presented in the *Instructions* stresses the absolute sovereignty of God, and it dismisses any and all of the worldly distinctions that divide and separate people from one another: fame, class, wealth, race, and gender. However, there are particular ministries within the Church that can only be performed by those individuals who have the talent and ability to carry them out.[48] In this sense, there is a hierarchy within the community of recipients of God's great gift of salvation in Christ—the Church—but this hierarchy exists solely for the edification and strengthening of the faithful. For example, he makes a clear distinction between catechumens and their teachers, but the distinction is one of ministerial function, not social stature or intrinsic value.

> [T]he catechumen is a sheep without a seal; he is a deserted inn and a hostel without a door, which lies open to all without distinction; he is a lair for robbers, a refuge for wild beasts, a dwelling place for demons. And yet, our Master decreed that through His loving-kindness this deserted, doorless inn, this robbers' refuge, should become a royal palace. On this account He sent us, your teachers, and those exorcists to prepare the inn beforehand. And by our instruction, we who teach you are making strong and secure the walls of the inn, which were weak and unsound.[49]

The ecclesiastical hierarchy that St. John presents is rooted in teaching authority. However, it is interesting to note that in the twelve sermons that comprise the *Instructions* there are only three direct references to heresies.[50] In the introduction to his translation of the *Instructions* Paul Harkins comments on the literary characteristics that have been used to authenticate St. John Chrysostom's work, two of which are "the predominance of moral considerations over speculative theology," and the "primacy of pastoral preoccupations."[51] Therefore, even though one does not find technical, philosophical discussions of theology in St. John's preaching, this does not necessarily mean that the "correction of false doctrine" is not one of his primary goals. Rather, what this absence of technical theological argument suggests is that for St. John the moral and ethical assumptions of the faithful are the primary locus of "correct doctrine." In other words, it is of primary importance for members of the Church to understand, to affirm, and to be persuaded to live a life in obedience to the teachings of Jesus Christ. Any sort of philosophical, theological discussion is only important inasmuch as it has direct bearing upon the shared ascetical life of the community commissioned to fulfill God's commandments and witness to the truth of the gospel. The way this plays out will be addressed in the following discussion of the role of the spoken word in the Church.

The Church as an army of preachers

Although St. John does not address the spoken word in the *Instructions* in the same technical kind of way that he addresses it in his treatise *On the Priesthood*, he nevertheless advocates the primacy of the spoken word in the lives of all the faithful, just as he advocates the primacy of the spoken word in the priestly ministry. This can be seen in the way he treats the matter of swearing oaths. Of all the concrete pastoral admonitions that St. John delivers in the *Instructions*, the one that he returns to again and again is his proscription against swearing oaths. At one point, he begins to explain why

"we are called the faithful, whereas the uninitiated are called catechumens," but then
he interrupts himself and launches into a tirade against the swearing of oaths.

> But what is happening to me? My anxiety over your swearing has come upon me
> again and has charged me with sloth and draws my discourse back to that topic.
> Therefore, let us put off until the next instruction the discussion of the names of
> faithful and catechumens and turn ourselves now to my advice and counsel on the
> matter of swearing. Swearing is a dreadful and harmful thing; it is a destructive drug,
> a bane and a danger, a hidden wound, a sore unseen, an obscure ulcer spreading its
> poison in the soul; it is an arrow of Satan, a flaming javelin, a two edged sword, a
> sharp-honed scimitar, an unpardonable sin, and indefensible transgression, a deep
> gulf, a precipitous crag, a strong trap, a taut-stretched net, a fetter that cannot be bro-
> ken, a noose from which no one escapes.[52]

Why is this so important? The simplest explanation is that the Christian is called to a
life of purity, and as Christ taught, it is not what goes into a man that defiles him, but
what comes out of human beings (words) that defile them.[53] For St. John, certainly
any kind of obscene language or coarse jesting would be inappropriate for the Christian, but an even greater concern would be the swearing of oaths using the name of
God as surety for ones business transaction.[54] A likely explanation for this stern prohibition is that in any sort of business negotiation, particularly those that would have
occurred in the marketplace in fourth-century Antioch and Constantinople, both
parties make claims that stretch the truth. To use a bit of anachronistic language, we
can easily imagine a seller saying, "I swear that I had to pay $150 for this wholesale, and
I am giving you the best deal you'll find anywhere." or conversely, we can hear the
buyer claiming, "I swear that I can only afford to pay $100 for this, and not a penny
more." If someone invokes the name of the deity in such a transaction, to make the
oath even more powerful, one is in fact making God subservient to one's potentially
shady business transactions; one is co-opting the divine name into a rhetoric of com-
mercial deception. Through the misuse of words in the swearing of oaths, the person
sinfully implies that Jesus Christ is just another pagan idol to be used for advantage in
everyday commerce. This belittling of Christ through the abuse of language, is,
according to St. John, a deadly serious sin.

> It is very serious because it does not seem to be serious, and I am afraid of it because
> nobody is afraid of it. Disease is incurable precisely when it does not seem to be a dis-
> ease. Merely to speak is not a crime; so swearing does not seem to be a crime, and
> people feel quite free to venture on this lawless path.[55]

St. John's repeated and at times seemingly overblown attacks against the swearing of
oaths, while dealing very much with concrete, pastoral concerns, are in fact a powerful example of how he is correcting false doctrine through his own spoken word. He
practices what he preaches. Furthermore, in the context of arguing against the swearing of oaths, St. John argues that the very first step towards authentic Christian piety
is the ability to control what one says.[56]

> [S]how yourselves good fighters from the very outset; make yours a brilliant luster by making the beauty of this [baptismal] garment more shining and brilliant in every way. Let no idle or random word escape your lips. Let us consider first whether what we say can be of any benefit and if it can provide edification for those who hear it; then let us say what we have to say with great fear, just as if someone were standing by and writing down our words. Let us remember what our Lord said. "I tell you, that of every idle word men speak, they shall give account on the Day of Judgment."[57]

It is through the spoken word that the Christian shows himself to be a good fighter, and conversely it is through the spoken word that the neophyte can most easily foul the luster of his robe of baptismal forgiveness and grace. The Christian life begins in the rite of initiation through words that are spoken, and statements of faith made by the candidate, or as St. John says it, "the tongue is the pen with which we write our contracts with God,"[58] and it is through the spoken word that the faithful have the opportunity to glorify God in prayer, and proclaim his truth to a hungry world.

> The tongue stands in the middle ready for either use; you are its master. So also does a sword lie in the middle; if you use it against the enemy, it becomes an instrument for your safety; if you use it to wound yourself, it is not the steel but your own transgression of the law which causes your death. Let us think of the tongue in the same way, as a sword lying in the middle. Sharpen it to accuse yourself of your own sins, but do not use it to wound your brother.[59]

Beginning with the words that come forth from their lips, St. John calls the faithful to their vocation as faithful warriors of Christ. He does so by directly and unflinchingly attacking sin and the false doctrine that leads people to disobey the commandments of Christ. However, like any army that is going to be successful in battle, there must be inspiration, a desire to fight and give up one's very life in the service of the Master. Thus, the final element of Orthodox ecclesiology from the perspective of preaching is inspiration.

Once the community has been called to repent, and shown the errors of the false teaching that led them into sin in the first place, they must be inspired to take action, to take up the Cross and follow Christ, to love their enemy, to bless those who curse, and to lay down their life for another. St. John accomplishes this task masterfully by showing the newly baptized how God has given them power and grace to live as Christians.

> Blessed be God, who alone does wonderful things,[60] who does all things and transforms them. Before yesterday you were captives, but now you are free and citizens of the Church; lately you lived in the shame of your sins, but now you live in freedom and justice. You are not only free, but also holy; not only holy, but also just; not only just, but also sons; not only sons, but also heirs; not only heirs, but also brothers of Christ; not only brothers of Christ, but also joint heirs; not only joint heirs, but also members; not only members, but also the temple; not only the temple, but also instruments of the Spirit.[61]

For St. John, the Church is the community of believers who have been changed in order to be victorious over the devil, sin, and death in Christ.

> [W]hen the devil sees so vast a change, and sees that those who heretofore were sub-
> ject to his tyranny have been exalted to such a height and judged worthy of such love
> by the Master, he will depart in confusion and will not dare to look them in the face.
> He cannot endure the brilliance which flashes forth from their faces, but his eyes are
> so blinded by the rays of light which their eyes send forth that he turns his back and
> flees.[62]

To be a Christian, to be a member of the Church, is to have one's nature completely refashioned. St. John uses the contrasting image of cleaning and smelting to explain the difference. If a very, very dirty, tarnished vessel is cleaned, faint hints of the past filth will remain as stains on the metal. However, baptism is not a cleaning, but a melting down and complete refashioning of human nature.

> God takes this nature of ours . . . and smelts it anew. He plunges it into the waters as
> into the smelting furnace and lets the grace of the Spirit fall on it instead of the flames.
> Then He brings us forth from the furnace, renewed like newly-molded vessels, to rival
> the rays of the sun with our brightness. He has broken the old man to pieces but has
> produced a new man who shines brighter than the old.[63]

St. John is extremely consistent in the rhetorical strategy he uses to inspire the Church to action. Rarely does he use prolepsis, speaking from the perspective of a time that is yet to come, and inspiring the faithful from the perspective of a reality that is yet to come.[64] In the *Instructions* St. John occasionally speaks of the favor that the faithful will receive from God for their virtue and faithfulness, but far more often he speaks about the very real change that Christ has worked in their lives today, the spiritual grace that has been given, and the power to defeat sin and the devil. In the *Instructions* St. John is far more concerned about demonstrating the transforming presence of God today, in the lives of the hearers, than he is about speaking of glories that are yet to come. The true glory of Christ, in the Johannine sense, is when he perfectly accomplishes the Father's will through his voluntary death on the cross. The true glory of the Church is when its members rise up to the call of God to transform the world through voluntary, Christ-like self-sacrifice of their own, on behalf of the neighbor, for the glory of God. St. John's hearers are given little opportunity to ponder any glory other than that of the Crucified Messiah.

> I exhort you, let us not become too careless. You came forth from Egypt. Never again
> seek Egypt nor the evils of Egypt. Never think of the mud and the brickmaking. The
> things of the present life are mud and brickmaking, since gold itself, before it is con-
> verted into gold, is nothing more than earth. . . . In their day the Jews were unable to
> see the face of Moses transfigured, although he was their fellow slave and kinsman.
> But you have seen the face of Christ in His Glory.[65]

The Church is the community of people who have been changed and empowered to act on God's behalf. They still have free will; they are able, at any moment, to abandon their commission, reject the love of their adoptive heavenly father, and soil the garment of baptismal purity. There are certainly no guarantees that every one who has been baptized will live according to the gracious gift of new life that has been given.

But nevertheless, they have been changed through baptism and chrismation, and having received the gift of sonship, the gift of adoption in Christ, they must now fulfill Christ's Great Commission by relying on the power of God in faith and in love. It is not a commission that is fulfilled by individuals "doing their own thing" but rather by a family, a community called out from the world: the *ekklesia*, the Church working in unity with God, Father, Son and Holy Spirit, and in unity with one another. In short, the Church is people united in Christ, fulfilling the Gospel commandments.

> Unity of faith exists when we are all one, when we all similarly recognize that we're bound together. If that's why you've received a spiritual gift, so that you might build up others, see that you don't destroy yourself, through envying another. God has honored you and positioned you so that you might prepare another. Indeed, it was towards this end that the apostle existed, and it was towards this end that the prophet prophesied and persuaded, and the evangelist preached the gospel and that the shepherd and the teacher existed. They were all bound up in one task. Don't talk to me about the disparity among the spiritual gifts, but that they all had one task. Unity exists at the moment when we all believe alike.[66]

Endnotes

[1]St. John Chrysostom, *Six Books on the Priesthood,* iv.3; trans., Graham Neville (Crestwood, NY: St. Vladimir's Seminary Press, 1984), 115.

[2]*Six Books on the Priesthood,* iv.2, 114.

[3]*St. John Chrysostom: Baptismal Instructions,* trans. Paul W. Harkins, in *Ancient Christian Writers,* ed., S. J. Johannes Quasten & Walter J. Burghardt, vol. 31 (New York: Paulist Press, 1963), 119. Stav. 8.1. Vol. 31 is a collection of twelve sermons some of which are addressed to catechumens preparing for baptism, and some to the newly baptized neophytes. The translations referred to here are from three sources: (1) from the Stavronikita (henceforth cited as "Stav.), an eleventh-century parchment codex containing twenty-four John Chrysostom homilies; (2) from the "Series of Montfaucon," (henceforth cited as Montf.), which includes two John Chrysostom homilies; and (3) the "Papadopoulos-Kerameus Series" (henceforth cited as PK) of manuscripts, which can be found in *Varia graeca sacra* (St. Petersburg 1909), 154–183. *Ancient Christian Writers* is henceforth cited as ACW followed by page number(s).

[4]Matt. 3:2, 4:17.

[5]Matt. 28:19–20.

[6]"Let us who mystically represent the Cherubim and who sing the thrice-holy hymn to the life creating Trinity, now lay aside all earthly cares that we may receive the King of all who comes invisibly upborne by the angelic host. Alleluia. Alleluia. Alleluia": the Cherubic Hymn sung during the Great Entrance during the Divine Liturgy of the Orthodox Church.

[7]See footnote 3.

[8]Wendy Mayer and Pauline Allen, *John Chrysostom* (London: Routledge, 2000), 9–10; henceforth cited as Mayer and Allen, followed by the page number(s).

[9]Mayer and Allen, 7.

[10]J. N. D. Kelly *Golden Mouth: The Story of John Chrysostom Ascetic, Preacher, Bishop* (Ithaca, NY: Cornell University Press, 1995) 289–90. The circumstances surrounding the life of St. John Chrysostom are themselves an interesting commentary on ecclesiology inasmuch as the man who is revered as one of the greatest saints of the Church died in exile, having been "officially" condemned and deposed by the same church that would later canonize him.

[11]His direct involvement with the controversy surrounding the exiled Egyptian monks, the Tall Brothers, contributed to the growing tension between Alexandria and Constantinople.

[12]Stav. 6.21, ACW, 141.

[13]It is important to acknowledge a related discussion pertaining to so-called "baptismal ecclesiology" and "eucharistic ecclesiology." Admittedly, by focusing only on baptismal instructions, this investigation is necessarily going to present more of a "baptismal ecclesiology." While beyond the scope of this paper, it would be very interesting to perform a much larger survey of St. John Chrysostom's sermons to see how he uses baptismal and eucharistic imagery. However, it is interesting to note that in the *Instructions* St. John only makes a few passing references to the Eucharist, and then only as part of a larger argument for the purity of one's words (Montf. 2.15, ACW, 177) and as part of imagery in which the devils are terrified by the blood "smeared on the mouths" of the faithful (Stav. 3.15, ACW, 61).

[14]Rev. 21:1–5.

[15]Stav. 7.11, ACW, 108.

[16]1 Cor. 4:8.

[17]1 Cor. 5, 6 & 11:17–33 respectively.

[18]1 Cor. 10:16, 12:27.

[19]1 Cor. 8:13 (regarding food offered to idols) ". . . if food is a cause of my brothers falling, I will never eat meat, lest I cause my brother to fall."

[20]Stav. 6.22, ACW, 102.

[21]Stav. 5.20, ACW, 89.

[22]The week following Pascha during which those who had just been baptized during the paschal vigil would receive lessons and exhortations to be faithful to their new Christian life.

[23]Stav. 6.1 ACW, 80.

[24]Mayer and Allen, 59–60. While impossible to ascertain his precise identity, the rival preacher may have been Severian of Gabala, or the Novatian, Sisinnius.

[25]"On Ephesians," Homily 11:89 A; Mayer and Allen, 71–72.

[26]Rom. 7:19.

[27]For a discussion of perspective and "point of view" in preaching, see David Buttrick *Homiletic: Moves and Structures* (Philadelphia: Fortress Press, 1987), 55–68.

[28]In fact, it can be argued that philosophically, this places the hearer in a blasphemous perspective: one in this he considers himself equal to, or greater than God.

[29]From an Orthodox Christian perspective, "mystery" is particularly helpful when responding to some of the theological articulations that are firmly rooted in medieval scholasticism like transubstantiation or purgatory.

[30]See Luke 18:10–14.

[31]Montf. 2.49, ACW, 188

[32]Rom 1:1.

[33]Stav. 1.1, ACW, 23.

[34]Stav. 1.8, ACW, 25.

[35]Stav. 1.40, ACW, 39.

[36]Montf. 2.30, ACW, 182.

[37]Stav. 5.27, ACW, 91–92.

[38]John Wesley grapples with this particular definition in his sermon, "The New Birth," in *John Wesley's Sermons: An Anthology*, edited by Albert C. Outler and Richard P. Heitzenrater (Nashville: Abingdon Press, 1991), 342–43.

[39]Montf. 2.13–14, ACW, 176–77; Gal. 3:27. Immediately following this bold claim, St. John takes his hearer on a glorious tour through the biblical sources for these images that he uses to describe the new relationship that one shares with Christ through baptism.

[40]Stav. 4.29, ACW, 77.

[41]Stav. 6.24, ACW, 102; PK 3.6–10, ACW, 162–64.

[42]Stav. 4.17–19, ACW, 72–73.

[43]Stav. 7.12–22, ACW, 108–113; Stav. 8.8, 8.14, ACW, 122–23, 125; PK 3.11, ACW, 164.

[44]In its present form, the Orthodox Christian baptismal rite includes a threefold renunciation of Satan in which the priest, the candidate, and baptismal sponsors face "West" (away from the altar) and the priest asks, "Do you renounce Satan, and all his works and his angels and all his pride?" to which the candidate replies, "I do renounce him." The threefold renunciation is followed by the command by the priest, "Then blow and spit upon him."

[45]PK 3.21, ACW, 167.

[46]80E–F, Mayer and Allen, 61.

[47]87B–C, Mayer and Allen, 69.

[48]Regarding priestly ministry, St. John states that only very few men are even qualified to consider such a weighty responsibility. *On the Priesthood*, ii.2, 54.

[49]PK 2.16; ACW, 155.

[50]Stav. 1.22, ACW, 31: contra Arians and Sabellius; PK 2.12, ACW, 152–153: contra Docetism.

[51]ACW, 14.

[52]PK 2.18, ACW, 155–56.

[53]Mark 7:20.

[54]This understanding of the function of oaths in St. John's time was the result of discussions I had with Fr. Paul Tarazi, and Timothy Clark.

[55]PK 1.38, ACW, 143.

[56]PK 1.37, ACW, 143; Montf. 2.37, ACW, 184.

[57]Matt. 12:36–7; Stav. 4.23, ACW, 75.

[58]Stav. 3.20, ACW, 63.

[59]PK 1.34, ACW, 142.

[60]Ps. 71:18.

[61]Stav. 3.5, ACW, 57.

[62]Stav 4.5, ACW, 68.

[63]PK 1.22, ACW, 139

[64]A wonderful example of prolepsis is King Richard V's "St. Crispin Day Speech" in the eponymous play by Shakespeare. One also sees prolepsis in the anaphora of St. John Chrysostom, where God is thanked for having, "endowed us with Thy Kingdom which is to come."

[65]Stav. 3.23,5, ACW, 64.

[66]83E–84A, Mayer and Allen, 65.

17

The "Sounds of Silence" in the Gathered Community: T.S. Eliot and the Church

Maxine Walker

> If the lost word is lost, if the spent word is spent
> If the unheard, unspoken
> Word is unspoken, unheard;
> Still is the unspoken word, the Word unheard,
> The Word without a word, the Word within
> The world and for the world;
> And the light shone in darkness and
> Against the Word the unstilled world still whirled
> About the centre of the silent Word.
>
> (T. S. Eliot, "Ash Wednesday" V 65)[1]

Kallistos Ware says about Symeon the New Theologian that often the poets are the best theologians of all. "It would be good for the Church if we paid them greater heed." The Bishop of Diokleia calls St. Symeon a theologian-poet in the long line extending from St. Ephrem the Syrian, through Dante, St. John of the Cross, Milton and Blake, up to T. S. Eliot in our "own" twentieth century.[2] Taking up the bishop's notion, what might T.S. Eliot have to say to the Church if we paid him greater heed?

Throughout the various stages of Thomas Stearns Eliot's notable career as poet, editor, essayist, dramatist, literary critic, and Nobel Prize winner, the quest for unity and coherence in an ideologically divided world captivated his intellect and imagination. T. S. Eliot's early poems are well known as major representatives of the ills of modernism, i.e., the alienation of persons from tradition and community, the loss of the transcendent world, an intellectualism separated from feeling, the inaccessibility of meaning and the paralysis to solve political and cultural problems. In early critical work, such as his essay on "Tradition and the Individual Talent,"[3] Eliot was working toward a position of attacking the absence of moral and religious criteria in literature and critiquing those who sought to substitute art for religion. During his Harvard student days, he was highly influenced by Irving Babbitt who argued that the legacy of Rousseau and the Romantics created a climate of emotional anarchy and narrow self-expression. What was needed to confound the multiple polarities that attracted the intellectual elite of the period, including the lure of humanism that countered conventional scientific naturalism, was a "whole"—much like tradition that confirms individual talent.[4]

Eliot's conversion to the Church of England in 1927 fortified this quest for an infinite center.[5] He had rejected the Unitarian beliefs of his youth as a "toothless form of religion." The mystery of the Ineffable haunted and hounded him as did the quest for divine patterns that would cohere and unify thought and experience.[6] The essential elements of the faith for Eliot were the continuation of tradition in the Anglo-Catholic movement within the Church of England, the emphasis upon the apostolic mission of the Church, the importance of sacramental worship with its historical and ritualistic continuity. Of such matters, many Christians affirm, but this affirmation was imaginative and intellectually shaped by the poet who defined and critiqued poetry from the 1920s to the 1960s. Eliot biographer, Peter Ackroyd, says of Eliot's Christian observances that there was something from a deeper source that required a kind of "uncertainty," something stranger and more abiding than his poetic genius could offer:

> . . . [W]ithin Eliot's own work, the structure of orthodox faith and the language of devotion are broken apart in order to make room for something *much stranger and more tenuous*, like the sound of someone crying in an empty church.[7]

In the context of this fourth Orthodox and Wesleyan Consultation theme, T. S. Eliot's *Four Quartets*, especially the fourth poem, "Little Gidding," has much to say to our respective traditions about that which is "strange and more tenuous" in the "gathered community." That is to say, how will the gathered community speak that which cannot be spoken? What is the unifying center? How is Tradition now?

Little Gidding, *as an historical place*, is a very small community not far from George Herbert's parish church, both near Cambridge, England. Pilgrims over the years have come to visit and pray at this spot that housed a seventeenth-century Anglican community. Nicholas Ferrar, an ordained Anglican deacon, founded little Gidding in 1625. However, he refused to take higher orders and returned from London to Little Gidding to devote himself to a simple life of prayer and good works.

King Charles visited the community after his final defeat at Naseby, and the victorious Cromwell forces later desecrated the site. "Little Gidding," *as the poem*, is the remembrance of the profound inner religious life of that small community that saw so much political and religious conflict. Eliot came to see this religious community as an intersection of time and place, in which the intersection of history and now happen in "the timeless moment."

How do we get to this time and place? Consider the oft-quoted passage about making a pilgrimage and entering a sacred, consecrated site:

> If *you*[8] came this way,
> Taking any route, starting from anywhere,
> At any time or at any season,
> It would always be the same: *you* would have to put off
> Sense and notion. *You* are not here to verify
> Instruct yourself, or inform curiosity
> Or carry report. *You* are here to kneel

Where prayer has been valid. And prayer is more
Than an order of words, the conscious occupation
Of the praying mind, or the sound of the voice praying.
And what the dead had no speech for, when living,
They can tell *you*, being dead: the communication
Of the dead is tongued with fire beyond the language of
The living.
             Here, the intersection of the timeless moment
             Is England and nowhere. Never and always.
                    ("Little Gidding" I 139)

The "Silent" who gather

Upon first reading, silencing all that "you" are accustomed to doing characterizes the gathering of the faithful. The quality of this silence commands "you" to listen to the dead, and silence speaks the mystery of saintly witnesses surrounding those in prayer.

However, in conjunction with the repetition of the notion of "silence" is the repetition of the pronoun, "you." Who is this subject of direct address in this poem? Is the identification of "you" in Eliot's poem in any way helpful in understanding the "we" of the familiar eucharistic declaration, "We celebrate the memorial of our redemption...." The "we," of course, at the opening proclamation of the Eucharist are those who are baptized, but are "we" also the "you" in some way similar to Eliot's usage?

The importance of these pronouns for the "gathered community" is precise identification: who are the gathered? John Xiros Cooper, Eliot scholar at the University of British Columbia, argues that Eliot in the *Four Quartets* wrote to the intellectual "mandarins" whose social theories were exploded by the moral ruins of World War II.[9] T. S. Eliot, academic, poet, literary critic, dramatist was a part of a group that Cooper calls the "North Atlantic mandarinate."[10] "Eliot's work in the 1930s speaks directly to a demoralized mandarinate shaken by the economic wreckage of the Great Depression, by the impotence of the 'democracies' in resisting totalitarianism, by the indifference of the powerful to the plight of the masses and to the humiliation, finally, of the events at Munich in the autumn of 1938...."[11]

What Eliot believed about the broken "mandarins" of the late 1930s and 1940s was that secular humanist intellectuals could not/cannot be brought easily from worldly renunciation to affirmation of the divine. Eliot's way was to begin with the "irresistible path of art, the safe haven of inwardness of art."[12]

> As long as [the mandarins'] fundamental beliefs or truth itself or art were essentially autonomous and complete in themselves, then society did not *really*[sic] matter, except as a source of danger. Learning how to live with this contradiction, learning how to be *in* [sic] society, but *not of it* [sic] has been one of the historic "achievements" of High Modernism.[13]

Unlike Bohemians of another generation, modern mandarins were not encouraged to forsake society but to cultivate an inner freedom with a kind of cultural elitism.

Who then are "we"? "We" are the academic and professional who view culture with an informed wariness and in various churches see the encroachment of culture into the gathering of the faithful. Those of us in the academy within our own Wesleyan tradition, as well as others in the Church catholic, have withdrawn to our own kind of scholarly, yea even singular, understanding of Church.

Whereas Eliot's early modern mandarinate retreated into the autonomy of art, the vestiges of the modern churches, of various denominational and non-denominational stripes, have retreated too frequently into an individual private expression. Assurance is often the label for a privileged spiritual experience made public and affirmed by incorporated cultural features in churches, in the name of evangelism and church growth. The seeker/user-friendly church with a kind of family values experience of a private amazing encounter with God extends the pragmatic methods that gave rise to this phenomenon in the first place. Dogma, sacraments, creeds, saints were (and are) in many contemporary churches less important than a functional church, a culturally relevant church.[14]

Curiously enough, as the children of baby boomers grew up, many in the quest for the spiritually awesome experience in church grew into a hunger for a more ancient, more orthodox version of the Faith—a hunger for the spiritual disciplines of prayer, Bible study, and the sacraments rather than the self-esteem psychobabble, entertainment, and cultural encroachments unfortunately endemic in much of the free church tradition and, often with comic results, in mainline churches. As Eliot notes in the one of the *Four Quartets*, "Dry Salvages," "we had the experience but missed the meaning" (II 133).

Nazarene theologian Dean Blevins points out that "Congregational life, particularly worship, [can] serve as an arena where religious 'actors' fulfill their personal drama in a private transaction between God and self, often in almost exclusive anonymity."[15] On the other hand, Eliot observed about Anglo-Catholicism that a rite might be established without a life-giving remembrance of meaning attached to it. The series of acts themselves may be the only rational justification required by those who perform them. The *rite qua rite* may be the significant thing.[16]

If Wesley were to enter the conversation at this point, might he say, "even in this his [God's] wonderful wisdom appears, directing their mistakes to his own glory . . . ?"[17] And so poet T. S. Eliot, as fellow Anglican, fares forward:

> You say I am repeating
> Something I have said before. I shall say it again.
> Shall I say it again? In order to arrive there,
> To arrive where you are, to get from where you are not,
>   You must go by a way wherein there is no ecstasy.
> In order to arrive at what you do not know
>   You must go by the way of dispossession.
> In order to arrive at what you are not
>   You must go through the way in which you are not.[18]
>
>   ("East Coker" III 127)

Eliot found the paradoxical "answer" to fare forward in the nature of speech, the Word itself, the "gift of the Incarnation." For the mandarins, he needed to take them up the ladder of art to the divine mysteries; for the church modern, Eliot takes us from the "darkness of God" to the "disturbance of spring." The way is paradox, the Incarnation.

The sound and silence of paradox

From his earliest poetic triumph in the "Wasteland" (*Criterion* 1922), Eliot's paradoxes and metaphors of time and space confronted modern man cut off from the springs of imagination and belief and showed him to be a stranger on the landscape:

> What are the roots that clutch, what branches grow
> Out of this stony rubbish? Son of man,
> You cannot say, or guess, for you know only
> A heap of broken images, where the sun beats,
> And the dead tree gives no shelter, the cricket no relief.
> And the dry stone no sound of water.
>> (*The Wasteland* I "The Burial of the Dead" 38)

Nearly twenty years later, in the composition of *Four Quartets*, Eliot's paradoxes and metaphors become patterns of the dead *speaking*. The religious community of the historical "Little Gidding" was defined by the actions of Nicholas Ferrar and the events of the English Civil War, and now is part of history for us.[19] History tells us something precisely because it is silent. "Living history" (such as reconstructions of historical moments, e.g., Plimoth Plantation) is synchronic and inaccessible to us without the interpretation of the present. So it is with the saints in the Christian tradition; the diachronic construction of story makes history intelligible.

In every church, we stand in a graveyard, a place where lifetimes were part of the "pattern," the pattern of a lifetime of moments. In every church service, we are standing in a place where the silent dead speak. They speak of the intense moment when Divine Love bisects the temporal. "Love is most nearly itself / when here and now cease to matter" ("East Coker" V 129). The significance of this paradox is that with its wisdom that moves deeper than knowledge, we can "feel" winds move the vast waters to a place that is unfamiliar, still, and still moving. Now time can be redeemed. The Incarnation and Christ's presence in the Eucharist is the turning point of the world, the true axis for all paradoxes.

> At the still point of the turning world. Neither flesh nor fleshless;
> Neither from nor towards; at the still point, there the dance is,
> But neither arrest nor movement. And do not call it fixity,
> Where past and future are gathered.
>> ("Burnt Norton" II 119)

The movement of the liturgy must lead through the conceptual limits of discourse to paradox—the contradictory world of experience in time and the mystery of the eternal and unknowable.

The mandarins cannot find the way to redeem time because aesthetic artifacts are objects that belong to time—words and music move only in time. They cannot achieve the stillness of the timeless Center. So it is with privatized religious experience that seeks to know the timeless in time. This kind of emotional expressive religious experience is desire, and thus movement. *Experience qua experience* only imposes old patterns. Adam, the ruined millionaire, has the fever that can only be restored with a freezing fire. The Church must be his dying nurse led by the Wounded Surgeon.

At first, the poet's grasp of the world whether past or present seems hopeless, i.e., speaking is a "raid on the inarticulate, a general mess of the imprecision of feeling" ("East Coker" V 174–181). Sometimes there are the sounds of shrieking voices in "Burnt Norton," or "crying shadows," "loud laments." They are the voices of temptation against the stillness of the Incarnate Word.

> The Word in the desert
> Is most attacked by voices of temptation
> The crying shadow in the funeral dance.
> The loud lament of the disconsolate chimera.
>
> ("Burnt Norton" V 122)

The Word has been "lost" as most persons live according to their private individual experience; they mistake the circle for the Center. Much restless, much lamenting, much grief, much desire reign in the turning world as the poem moves to the stillness of the timeless point at its Center.

The poet is echoing that moment of kneeling, of confession, of profound prayer before any absolution. In the poetry, absolution is Love entering time and dawning awareness of how unfathomable is the stillness and timelessness of Love's essence.[20] ". . . [t]he only significant moments are those of holy dying, so that the whole of an individual's life can be condensed and refined to just those moments in which the destructive fire is consciously known and accepted as the fire of Love. The whole of history is then condensed to those few significant moments (which are essentially all one and the same moment)."[21]

One Eliot scholar puts it this way, "without God, time is unreal, a meaningless, endless succession of before and after in which 'being' is impossible. Without God, time is truly 'unredeemable.'"[22] The Incarnation is a moment in time, and time is given meaning through that moment.

In the sacraments, in the Eucharist, sequential time and the timeless moment intersect again. Hear the sequential moments in time in the narrative spoken in the Eucharist: "On the night he was handed over to suffering and death. . . . After supper, he took the cup. . . . and when he had given thanks, he gave it to them. . . . whenever you drink it . . ." (Book of Common Prayer, Holy Eucharist II).

It is only in sequential time that we know our limitations and in which we can experience Love, a moment of vision and joy. It is the world of experience that will affirm the Light beyond the senses.

The way to the Light comes in a specific time and place. In "Little Gidding," the poem opens on an afternoon scene of a late November afternoon as darkness descends, and the shafts of weak light hit frozen water. The metaphor from this striking scene leads to Eliot's paradox, "In my beginning is my end" ("East Coker" I): the world of experience, even the world of private experience, is not to be abandoned for it affirms the light beyond sense. Liturgical studies Professor James White agrees that the sign-acts and sign-value of the Eucharist begin with the " 'handling' of the bread and wine. A private sacrament is a contradiction."[23] The paradox is that the bread is Bread; it is death and life. Eliot would insist on more than the minimalist approach to the sacraments:

> The dripping blood our only drink.
> The bloody flesh our only food:
> In spite of which we like to think
> That we are sound, substantial flesh and blood—
> Again, in spite of that, we call this Friday good.
>
> ("East Coker" IV 128)

"Little Gidding" the poem closes on St. Lucy's day, a day approaching the shortest day of the year. The paradox of "winter lightning" is Pentecostal fire in the dark, darker, darkest time of the year. This the descent of the Holy Ghost at the baptism of Christ, in the tongues of flame which inspired the disciples so that they began to speak with other tongues as the Spirit gave them utterance at the birth of the Church, as the Holy Spirit is invoked in the *epiclesis*.

So as the poem "Little Gidding" historically concludes in 1942, strife and sin and death are conquered with the words of Julian of Norwich, "All Shall be Well." Julian of Norwich is dead and here and now, because paradox uncovers the deeper communion of all things. Spiritual sense is wholly dominant while the natural sense remains— the mystery of the sacraments.[24]

Words silent before the Word

As noted, Eliot uses paradox as a ladder from natural sense to spiritual understanding,[25] and throughout his poetry the first world is of natural experience with the language of sense experience. But sense-experience language frustrates the sense of thought, i.e., the philosophical mind seeking definitions of clarity and understanding of the nature of things. Transformation through paradox is needed so that words in the world are perceived as the divine Word in action:[26]

> Love is the unfamiliar Name
> Behind the hands that wove
> The intolerable shirt of flame
> Which human power cannot remove.
> We only live, only suspire
> Consumed by either fire or fire.
>
> ("Little Gidding" IV 144)

Hence in the world of human communication by speech, poetry is its most perfect counterpart; the revelation and illumination and transfiguration of life through the word.[27] And the saints are those who have purified and perfected the dialect of the tribe, who speak the language of the Incarnation in timeless moments.

> But to apprehend
> The point of intersection of the timeless
> With time, is an occupation for the saint—
> No occupation either, but something given
> And taken, in a lifetime's death in love,
> Ardour and selflessness and self-surrender.
>
> ("Dry Salvages" V 136)

The dialect of the tribe is ours to speak as well. Ethicist Stanley Hauerwas points out, "The words we use matter. Loss of eloquence in worship is a moral loss.[28] It matters that the Word is followed by Table, if we are to be rightly formed as Christians. It matters what kind of music shapes our response to the psalms, since what the psalm declares is not separable from how we as the Church sing that declaration."[29] Truthful habits of speech and gesture in worship of the Trinity are the hallmarks of the one holy, catholic, and apostolic Church. The rite and the experience are one. "I have tasted / The savour of putrid flesh in the spoon" (Chorus *Murder in the Cathedral*).

Tradition is now

But what about the many "contemporary churches" [a contradictory term at best], even in the Wesleyan tradition, who focus almost exclusively on God-in-the-present? "Most people can find some kind of refuge in tradition, but if that has also been foreclosed, as it had for the folk cultures of the new masses in Eliot's time, the simple formulas and programmatic optimisms of the propagandists and publicists will probably have to do."[30] Long before his conversion, Eliot was concerned about the significance of an historical sense that would give meaning to individual work. Most notably in "Tradition and the Individual Talent," Eliot explores what makes something "traditional":[31]

> ... the historical sense involves a perception, not only of the pastness of the past, put of its presence ... This historical sense, which is a sense of the timeless as well as of the temporal and of the timeless and of the temporal together, is what makes a writer "traditional." (*Selected Essays* 41)

Saints affirm this understanding. It is given to the saint "to apprehend the point of intersection of the timeless / With time ...." It is given to the saint to employ the divine narrative in time. In "Little Gidding" a stranger, a kind of spiritual master, appears:

> I caught the sudden look of some dead master
> Whom I had known, forgotten, half recalled
> Both one and many; ...
> Both intimate and unidentifiable.
>
> ("Little Gidding" II 140)

"Faces and places" return in new patterns. As Allchin notes, "saints of different times and places come together in unexpected, unlooked for ways,"[32] and saints experience/experienced the intersection of *chronos* and *kairos.*

Saints are not just moral exemplars whose lives are to be emulated. The Church also participates in their lives via the hearing and retelling of their stories, through the creative working of the Holy Spirit. Iconic catechesis must be interpreted for 1940s mandarins and twenty-first-century gathered communities.

Eliot concludes that we die with the dying, but we are also born with the dead. They return and bring us with them. In this way, "history becomes a buried pattern of prayerful moments."[33]

"We are [indeed] born with the dead." In our Wesleyan heritage we begin with "John Wesley who is a spiritual Father in God and is a saint in modern Protestantism."[34] "Communion in the life of God reveals unexpected 'family' likenesses across the centuries and shows the continuity of Presence at every moment."[35]

Throughout this presentation I have noted that the work of T. S. Eliot may be a site for thinking about silence that can both snuff out and sustain "inner catholicity" [a phrase from Thomas Merton]. What seems evident from Eliot's poetry is that the paradox is a rhetorical trope that shows us the essential character and nature of the Incarnation and the descent of the Dove. In God's gifts of Eucharist, the *rite*, we *experience* the union of all times and places with eternity, and we cannot respond with words but with prayer. The Eucharist gathers the Church in all the contexts where it has previously occurred and will occur and asks that we neither stop nor move in the stillness between the waves until all contraries become one.

> We shall not cease from exploration
> And the end of all our exploring
> Will be to arrive where we started
> And know the place for the first time.
> Through the unknown, remembered gate
> When the last of earth left to discover
> Is that which was the beginning;
> . . .
>
> heard, half-heard, in the stillness
> Between two waves of the sea.
> Quick now, here, now, always—
> A condition of complete simplicity
> (Costing not less than everything)
> And all shall be well and
> All manner of thing shall be well
> When the tongues of flame are in-folded
> Into the crowned knot of fire
> And the fire and rose are one.
>
> ("Little Gidding" V 145)

Endnotes

[1] All quotes from T. S. Eliot's poetry are from T.S. Eliot, *The Complete Poems and Plays 1909–1950* (New York: Harcourt, Brace & World, Inc., copyright by T.S. Eliot 1958, 1962; 1971 renewed by Esme Valerie Eliot). Dates of publication and historical settings for *Four Quartets:*

A. "East Coker," (1940) Somerset, England, ancestral home of the Eliot family

B. "Burnt Norton," (1941) Gloucestershire, England, a manor house and garden which derives its name from its original site of a house that burned down in the seventeenth century

C. "The Dry Salvages," (1941) Ledge of rock off Cape Ann, Gloucester Harbor, MA

D. "Little Gidding," (1942) Cambridgeshire England, site of seventeenth-century, small Anglican religious community led by Nicholas Ferrar

Four Quartets was published as a complete sequence in 1944.

[2] As an undergraduate Eliot read William James's *Varieties of Religious Experience* and took careful notes. These notes were supplemented by his studies of saints' lives and writings, devotional manuals and textbooks on meditation and contemplation, especially the work of St. John of the Cross. (Cleo McNelly Kearns, "Religion, literature, and society in the work of T. S. Eliot," in *The Cambridge Companion to T. S. Eliot*, ed. David A. Moody (Cambridge: Cambridge Univ. Press, 1994), 84. Eliot also read Evelyn Underhill's *Mysticism* (1911), and actually "felt more at home with the religious tone of Underhill's *Mysticism*." In particular, Eliot took note of her three great classes of symbols which mystics used in describing their experiences: three "deep cravings of the self, three great expressions of man's restlessness, which only mystic truth can fully satisfy." (Miller, t.s. eliot, 179–180).

[3] T. S. Eliot, "Tradition and the Individual Talent," *The Sacred Wood: Essays on Poetry and Criticism* (London: Methune, 1920).

[4] Peter Ackroyd, *T. S. Eliot* (London: Abacus, 1985) 50.

[5] T. S. Eliot's understanding of "finite centers" was highly influenced by F. H. Bradley's *Appearance and Reality*. Eliot throughout his life described himself as a "Bradleyan."

Biographer Ackroyd says, "[Eliot] felt an immediate affinity with Bradley's own skepticism about the uses of conceptual intelligence in either recognizing or defining 'reality.' For Bradley 'Reality is One,' a seamless and coherent whole which is 'non-relational.' " (Ackroyd, 49).

Eliot's Harvard thesis "Experience and the Objects of Knowledge in the Philosophy of F. H. Bradley" draws out Bradley's implications that "lived truths are 'partial and fragmentary' and the experiences of the Bradleyan 'finite centres' are 'mad and strange' but, paradoxically, they are all that can be known to be real' . . . . The purpose is to reach beyond the miasma of private experience and construct a world, or rather an interpretation of the world, 'as comprehensive and coherent as possible" (Ackroyd, 69–70).

[6] Eliot's confirmation and baptism not only strengthened his views about "cultural barbarism" and his questions about whether civilization had validity apart from apart from Christianity, but also his new faith increased his oppositional stance to the prevailing political ideologies of his time. This resistance was evident in notable essays based on the idea that Christian principles are the best defense against fascism and Marxism, e.g., "Idea of a Christian Society" (1939) and "Notes Towards the Definition of Culture" (1948). Also notable for Christian perspectives that alarmed many of his intellectual colleagues and critics: his 1934 lecture series at the University of Virginia, "After Strange Gods" and "For Lancelot Andrewes," 1927.

[7] Ackroyd, 163.

[8] This author's italics.

[9] John Xiros Cooper, *T. S. Eliot and the Ideology of Four Quartets* (Cambridge: Cambridge University Press, 1995) 122.

[10] Cooper, 32.

[11] Cooper, 33–34.

[12] Cooper, 135.

[13] Cooper, 123.

[14] Stanley Hauerwas in a celebratory essay for Don Saliers says: "The heart of Saliers' work has been to try to remind his Church, the Methodist Church, that faithful and truthful worship of the crucified God is evangelism. That he has done so has not won him universal claim among Methodists. That he insists that worship be done 'right' is seen by some as a threat to Church growth." ("Worship, Evangelism, Ethics: On Eliminating the 'And' " in *Liturgy and the Moral Self: Humanity at the Full Stretch Before God. Essays in Honor*

of Don E. Saliers, eds. Bryon E. Anderson and Bruce T. Morrell (Collegeville, MN: A Pueblo Book, 1998), 103.

[15]Dean G. Blevins, "'The Holy Church, Holy People': A Wesleyan Exploration in Congregational Holiness and Personal Testament," *Wesleyan Theological Journal* 39:2 (Fall 2004): 54–73.

[16]Ackroyd, 164.

[17]John Wesley, Sermon 74, "Of the Church," in Sermons III, ed. Albert C. Outler, vol. 3(1986) of *The Bicentennial Edition of the Works of John Wesley* (Nashville: Abingdon Press, 1976), 46–47.

[18]Remember the faith that took men from home "At the call of a wandering preacher" (Chorus from "The Rock" VIII).

In "Tradition and the Individual Talent" as well in its companion piece, "The Function of Criticism," Eliot saw that "literature" was not just a collection of writings of individuals but a system of relations in which individual works have significance. "These systems were interdependent, and all were increasingly under threat, not only from wars, unregulated market forces and the 'crudities of industrialism' . . . . In general [Eliot] insisted all writers must recognize something outside themselves to which they owed 'allegiance' and 'devotion,' something in the light of which sacrifices of idiosyncrasy, personality, and ideology might with justification be made." (Kearns, 78).

[19]Julia Maniedes Reibetanz, *A Reading of Eliot's Four Quartets* (Ann Arbor: MI: UMI Research Press, 1970, 1983), from *Studies in Modern Literature,* Walton Litz, General Series editor. 17:A.

[20]David A. Moody, *The Cambridge Companion to T. S. Eliot* (Cambridge: Cambridge University Press, 1994).

[21]Moody, 154.

[22]Reibetanz, 53.

[23]James F. White, *Sacraments as God's Self Giving* (Nashville: Abingdon Press, 1983, 2001), 31.

[24]Poet John Donne talks about the mystery of the being and becoming this way:

> As West and East
> In all flatt Maps (and I am one) are one,
> So death doth touch the resurrection.

(Quoted in George Williamson, *A Reader's Guide to T.S. Eliot. Second Edition with Epilogue entitled T. S. Eliot, 1888–1965.* [New York: Octagon Books 1953, 1966], 235).

[25]Moody, 149.

[26]Moody, 147.

[27]Elizabeth Drew, *T. S. Eliot: The Design of His Poetry* (New York: Charles Scribner's, 1949), 203.

[28]S. Hauerwas, "Worship, Evangelism, Ethics," 98.

[29]Hauerwas, 99.

[30]Cooper, 130.

[31]"The opportunity to take up and differ from a preceding position in matters cultural and even cosmic made, in Eliot's view, for a living as opposed to a dead tradition" (Kearns, *Cambridge Companion,* 79). On the maternal memory of the Church, Pope John Paul II says, " . . . Tradition as the task assumed by the Church of transmitting . . . the mystery of Christ and the entirety of his teaching preserved in her memory . . . is a task in which the Church is constantly sustained by the Holy Spirit" (*Memory and Identity: Conversations at the Dawn of a Millennium.*149).

[32]A.M. Allchin, *The Living Presence of the Past: The Dynamic Christian Tradition* (New York: The Seabury Press, 1980), 93.

[33]Moody, 151.

[34]William J. Abraham, "The End of Wesleyan Theology," *Wesleyan Theological Journal* 40.1 (Spring 2005): 25.

[35]Allchin, 93.